ALL THINGS ARE FULL OF GODS

All Things Are Full of Gods

The Mysteries of Mind and Life

David Bentley Hart

Yale
UNIVERSITY PRESS

New Haven and London

Yale University Press books may be purchased in quantity for educational, business, or promotional use. For information, please email sales.press@yale.edu (U.S. office) or sales@yaleup.co.uk (U.K. office).

Set in Janson type by Westchester Publishing Services, Danbury, CT.
Printed in the United States of America.

Library of Congress Control Number: 2024933456
ISBN 978-0-300-25472-3 (hardcover: alk. paper)

A catalogue record for this book is available from the British Library.

This paper meets the requirements of ANSI/NISO Z39.48-1992 (Permanence of Paper).

10 9 8 7 6 5 4 3 2 1

In memory of Dr. Thomas L. Benson,
to whom I owe more than I ever
found the opportunity to tell him

तत् त्वम् असि

That thou art.

—*Chāndogya Upaniṣad*

πάντα πλήρη θεῶν εἰσίν.

All things are full of gods.

—Thales of Miletus

λέγει Ἰησοῦς· εἰ ἐγένετο ἡ σὰρξ ἕνεκεν τοῦ πνεύματος, θαῦμα ἐστιν· εἰ δὲ τὸ πνεῦμα ἕνεκεν τοῦ σώματος, θαῦμά ἐστι τῶν θαυμάτων· ἀλλὰ θαυμάζω ἐπὶ τούτῳ ὅτι ὁ τοσοῦτος πλοῦτος ἐνοικεῖ ταύτην τὴν πτωχείαν.

Jesus says: If the flesh came into being on account of the spirit, it is a marvel; and if the spirit on account of the body, it is a marvel among marvels. Yet what I marvel at is this: that such great wealth dwells within this poverty.

—The Gospel of Thomas

Natur ist . . . der sichtbare Geist, Geist die unsichtbare Natur.

Nature is . . . visible spirit, spirit invisible nature.

—F. W. J. Schelling, *Ideen zu einer Philosophie der Natur*

Contents

Acknowledgments

THIS PROJECT OUGHT to have come to fruition sooner than it did, but its maturation suffered many unanticipated delays—not least among them the general shutdown of society at large (and academic facilities in particular) during the COVID pandemic. It began as early as 2015, when I took up a single-year fellowship at the Notre Dame Institute for Advanced Study, funded by the John Templeton Foundation. My association with the institute then unexpectedly extended over a period of three years, in varying forms. It was during that time that most of what appears in these pages took shape, albeit originally in a very different shape and modality; and, in the normal run of things, I would have completed the book soon thereafter, and would not have taxed the patience of my editors at Yale for as long as I have.

I especially want to thank the four redoubtable souls without whom NDIAS would not have operated so very smoothly and so delightfully in those days: Brad Gregory, Don Stelluto, Carolyn Sherman, and Grant Osborne. I should also thank all my many colleagues there during my tenure, many of whom at one time or another—generally in the context of lunchtime seminars but sometimes over a coffee or in a corridor—offered observations on my work that made me aware of many questions I might otherwise have failed to address, or even to consider. Above all, I owe a particular debt of gratitude to all of those who participated in the large colloquium on my project that NDIAS organized in March 2016, again with the support of the Templeton Foundation: John Betz, Stephen R. L. Clark, Celia Deane-Drummond, William Desmond, Robert

Gimello, Paul Griffiths, Michael Hanby, Bradley Malkovsky, Jennifer Newsome Martin, Gerald McKenny, John Milbank, Anna Bonta Moreland, Cyril O'Regan, Gretchen Reydams-Schils, D. C. Schindler, Janet Soskice, and Luke Wright.

Once again, as has been the case several times before, I owe many thanks to my principal editor at Yale University Press, Jennifer Banks; and on this occasion I owe her a special debt of gratitude for finding a title for this book when I was hopelessly groping about for one.

I have no doubt that I should thank a great many other persons as well, and wish that I were as acutely conscious of who they are as I should be. The most I can do here, however, is send my gratitude out on the waters in the hope that somehow it may be carried to them upon the tides.

Introduction

On a Divine Colloquy

THIS IS A LONG BOOK, relatively speaking, but it could easily have been far longer. In fact, at one time it was. I have tested the patience of my editors intolerably by making them wait while this volume has passed through several metamorphoses—dilating, contracting, twisting, turning, and at last arriving at its present, somewhat unexpected shape. Perhaps this is appropriate, given the protean nature of the problem it addresses and the elusiveness of any good solutions. It has become an accepted fashion in books concerning the philosophy of mind that they should be both enormous and largely inconclusive, marked by an extravagance of exposition and a dearth of elucidation. One now standard pattern is that of a large and compendious tome, comprehensively reciting all the difficulties and ambiguities that routinely frustrate our efforts to understand the mystery of mental life, culminating in what almost invariably turns out to be more a rephrasing of the enigma than a resolution. No one in particular is to blame for this. Given that the majority of the large volumes in philosophy of mind that have appeared in recent decades have been written from a materialist or physicalist—or, at any rate, "methodologically naturalist"—perspective, which simply cannot provide a logically coherent account of mental life, it is only to be expected that a wealth of details should as often as not be offered as compensation for a scarcity of substance. When one has devoted many years to what turns out to be a hopeless expedition in search of a destination one will never reach (or even glimpse), one can at least try to rescue something from the ordeal by providing a colorful itinerary of that otherwise thwarted journey. The landscapes traversed are often fascinating and exotic in their own right, and travel literature is an honorable genre. Still, where one ends up is largely determined by where one chooses to start out.

When I began this book, I was somewhat burdened by the sense that I was obliged to answer those other volumes point for point, precisely and indefatigably. And so, as its composition proceeded—interrupted midway by the pandemic quarantine that settled over the world in 2020 and persisted for roughly a year and a half—it naturally began to assume the dimensions of yet another ponderous inventory of every variation ever worked on every bad idea in the field. Before I knew what I was doing, I was engaged in building a Tower of Babel, though one whose vertical aspirations were repeatedly being delayed by lateral additions of new wings and annexes to its base, the whole edifice scaffolded by an ever more intricate critical apparatus. Then I came to my senses. I may one day revive that version of my project in some form, if I am seized by a mood of giddy titanism or should feel the piercing need to compile an archive of "important documentation" for the curious; perhaps a series of short monographs on discrete aspects of the topic would work; or I may mercifully consign all of it to oblivion, where a great many gigantic academic texts should end up. For now, however, I have decided to confine myself to an exposition of my central argument, without performing the usual ritual of endless prelude. That still involves considerable expository work, but also allows for much of it to be done with attention only to the problem's general topography, so to speak. As I say, almost all of the solutions regularly proposed to the question of the origin and nature of mind are not really solutions at all, but rather mere reformulations of the question itself, restating it in ways that momentarily—but only momentarily—look like answers; and most of those proposals can be dismissed in principle without the need for a survey of every particular variant of their explanatory failures. If one realizes, for instance, that the "supervenience" theory of mental activity is essentially a recapitulation of the paradox it addresses, mistaken for a kind of clarification, then there is no need to lay out at length every individual iteration of its futility. If one discovers that reflective self-consciousness cannot be adequately explained by reference to some "higher order" faculty or action of the brain, it does not matter in the end whether one prefers to call this faculty or action a "perception" or a "thought." If one recognizes that all versions of "functionalism" depend upon a logical fallacy and, in any event, provide no cogent explanations of mental experience, it is best to deal with the issue economically and then to move on to more serious matters. Many of the more finely granular inquiries in Anglophone philosophy of mind do not really interest me, I should also admit, mostly because I am convinced they are intrinsically uninteresting. Many involve obviously inadjudicable claims and propose distinctions that are not so much logical or empirical as semantic. I honor those who labor in those fields, I suppose, but I do not believe the harvest will ever come.

If any of this sounds dismissive, that is certainly not my intention. Writing on these matters over a span of several years has given me a fine appreciation of how intractable their central mysteries are. Neither is any of this to say that there are not a great many interesting books and articles out there on the problem of mind of a very technical nature, which anyone truly interested in this matter might profitably consult. It *is* to say, however, that in many respects the nature of that problem is not nearly as difficult to understand as we often like to imagine it is, and that the reason it seems to be so is that we tend to approach it already needlessly burdened by a number of peculiarly modern presuppositions—to most of which the actual phenomena of conscious, intentional, rational mental activity should actually discourage us from clinging. But, of course, we are usually creatures of our times. What we take to be the rational position on any topic is as often as not simply one of our historical moment's prevailing prejudices; and our historical moment just happens to be late modernity. As a result we see the world very differently from the way it was seen by most of humanity throughout most of recorded time. The problem of mind as we struggle with it today is not really an ancient concern of philosophy; it is a specifically contemporary issue. That does not diminish its gravity or complexity, but it is as well to place things in proper perspective. Before the advent and eventual triumph of the mechanical philosophy in early modernity, and then the gradual but more or less total triumph of a materialist metaphysics of nature (even among those who believe in a realm beyond the merely physical), most developed philosophies, East and West alike, presumed that mind or something mindlike, transcendent or immanent or both, was the more original truth of things, pervading, sustaining, and giving existence to all that is. In such a vision of reality, material bodies and physical order and corporeal life seemed in many ways far more mysterious than either spirit or mental agency ever did.

Whether or not this was the correct way of seeing things, what is most important to recognize here is that the contrary prejudice typical of our time—that matter governed by purely mechanistic and nonmental laws is the foundation of all reality, mind included—is neither more rational nor more empirically plausible. In fact, the argument of this book will be that it is far and away the most implausible position on offer. Still, materialism is the presupposition that has shaped and continues to guide these debates, and it exercises so powerful a sway over the minds of many philosophers and scientists today that they continue to adhere to it even when evidence and reason alike would seem to urge its abandonment. In many cases, the entire project of the philosophy of mind today is simply an elaborate effort to arrive at that prejudice as though it were a rationally entailed conclusion, no matter what contortions of reasoning this might require. Of course, as Cicero remarked as long ago as 44 B.C.E. in his *On Divination*, "It is impossible to say anything so absurd that it has not been said by some philosopher" (*nihil tam absurde dici potest quod non dicatur ab aliquo philosophorum*), and in no philosophical field today is the truth of this maxim more plenteously confirmed than in philosophy of mind. No claim, however exorbitant or even seemingly perverse, is so extreme that some philosopher with a commitment to an entirely "physicalist" or "naturalist" or "materialist" account of mind has not proposed it—even the claim that all the mental phenomena that most of us take to be indubitable, like consciousness or intentionality or ratiocination, are in fact nonexistent. It would be difficult to exaggerate how fanatical this devotion to an essentially mechanistic materialism can prove at times. Otherwise seemingly sane and intelligent persons regularly advance arguments that, but for their deep and fervent faith in a materialist picture of nature, they would undoubtedly recognize as absurd and circular. Some are even willing to grant that the evident phenomena of conscious mental life are irreconcilable with a physicalist metaphysics; but, rather than conclude from this that physicalism should be rejected for having failed the test of the empirical evidence, they conclude that the evidence must be rejected for having failed the test of their metaphysics. This is the chief danger in any ideology: the power of determining our vision of the world before we have ever turned our eyes toward it. As a rule, in philosophy and the sciences, when a theory fails to explain a phenomenon, it is the theory that must be eliminated; only in modern philosophy of mind is it routinely the case that the phenomenon is eliminated in favor of the theory. This speaks of a problem far worse than mere intellectual indolence; it is the effect of a tragic captivity of reason to an arid dogmatism.[1]

The case I want to advance in what follows is that in fact mind cannot be reduced to purely material causes; but I wish to do so in a way quite different from the one that most Anglophone philosophy of mind presumes such an argument should take. As a rule, modern analytic philosophers who address the question of mind do so from within a hermetically sealed Cartesian model of the "mind-body problem." As a result, they tend to assume that there are only two options available: either a thoroughgoing materialism (which regards mental realities as wholly reducible to or emergent from mindless and mechanical physical causes) *or* a radical dualism (which regards the mental and the material as two irreconcilably different realities that somehow act in concert in certain physical beings). Even many philosophers who attempt to move beyond this opposition—certain proponents of a metaphysically naturalist version of "panpsychism," for instance, or of "neutral monism"—tend to do so by trying to correct or amplify rather than wholly abandon the mechanical picture of nature. Occasionally, one or another dissident will modestly note that there is at least a third possibility, "idealism," but by this they generally mean only something like the early George Berkeley's view that all phenomenal reality is nothing other than a collection of mental impressions, inhering in no material substrate, sustained in being and coherent order solely by the will of God, and devoid of any independent causal (that is, mechanical) powers; in this view of things, we are really disembodied souls—or, at any rate, souls whose "bodies" are immaterial—who merely share by God's grace in the divine dream of a concrete world. (The later Berkeley, the one almost no one recalls, is more sophisticated.) But that sort of idealism these days is very much a boutique philosophical accessory. As a rule, we are told that we are obliged to decide between two different mechanistic pictures: either a materialist picture of a cosmic machine generating mental agency as a mere mechanical function or a Cartesian picture that posits, in addition to mechanical nature, something else as well, a parallel level of causality in the form of a resident alien called the "soul"—or, as Gilbert Ryle put it, a "ghost in the machine."

I reject all these models of mind and body, or of mind and matter. I reject first and foremost the mechanistic view of matter, which is to say the view that nature is the product of a purely mechanical causality, or at any rate operates solely by such a causality. For just this reason, I also reject the view of mind as merely a *res cogitans*—an intrinsically bodiless and unextended "thinking something"—in purely *extrinsic* association with a mechanical material order. I reject too every theory of the emergence of mind from a non-mental reality, as well as any theory of the mental as a kind of physical "property" always already inherent in a material realm that in other respects functions mechanically. My position is definitely a kind of "idealism," but of a far more ancient and classical sort than the merely eidetic theory of the early Berkeley. It is also, I suppose, a kind of "panpsychism," though not of a variety compatible with a "naturalist" view of things. And it is also a kind of "vitalism," though by this I do not mean a theory of life as some indefinable quintessence infused from without into an otherwise mechanical nature; rather, I mean that life is itself the pervasive "organic" logic of the material order from the first, not emerging from that order but instead creating, governing, forming, and quickening it from within. I believe, moreover, not only that mind and life are both irreducible; I believe that they are one and the same irreducibility. And, in fact, I would add language to that combination as well, as yet another aspect of one and the same irreducible phenomenon, ultimately inexplicable in mechanistic terms. It is also my conviction that a truly scrupulous phenomenology of mental agency discloses an absolute engagement of the mind in an infinite act of knowing that is nothing less than the source and end of all three of these realities, and indeed of all things; or, to say this more simply, all acts of the mind are participations in the mind of God.[2]

Another way of describing my project in this book is as an attempt to affirm the principal four *Mahāvākyas* or "Great Sayings" of Upaniṣadic tradition. These are: *Prajñānam brahma:* "Consciousness is *Brahman* [Godhead]" or "*Brahman* is mind"; *Tat tvam asi:* "That [the divine presence in all things] is what you are"; *Aham brahm-āsmi:* "I am Godhead" or, perhaps, "This 'I' is divine"; and, above all, *Ayam Ātmā Brahma:* "this *Ātman* [spirit, highest self] is *Brahman*."[3] I could just as well say, however, that what follows is a defense of an essentially "Neoplatonic" understanding of the mind in relation to being. Or, then again, I might also say that what I hope to demonstrate is that "in the beginning was the Logos."[4] However one phrases it, mine is ultimately an unapologetically metaphysical approach to the thornier problems of mind and life and language, for the simple reason that every purely physical approach necessarily contradicts itself. I might as well acknowledge also that I am convinced that one of the most pressing imperatives for philosophy of mind is to free it from its analytic captivity, which is to say, from the Anglophone tradition's mythology of propositional transparency. The latter may attest to an honorable desire for precision, but so very often it depends upon a host of essentially arbitrary assumptions. Analytic method is all too prone to mistake oversimplification for clarification, banality for exactitude, and imaginative narrowness for intellectual rigor; moreover, its typical *modus operandi* is as often as not an unhappy combination of speculative timidity and methodological overconfidence.[5] I do not know whether all of this is just an accident of philosophical history, and therefore corrigible within analytic tradition itself; I know only that Anglophone philosophy has produced at once the most copious and most frequently fruitless literature on the so-called mind-body problem. As often as not, this has been a result of too great a trust in "analysis" as such, in the precise sense of the word: a "dissolution" of mental phenomena into ever more partial and fragmentary aspects. This has usually meant artificially isolating some facet of mentality—consciousness, intentionality, purposive behavior, sense perception, and so forth—and then treating it as a genuinely discrete faculty that can be explained by reduction to some purely instrumental operation, all the while ignoring or eliminating or treating as nugatory its very "mentality" as such: that is, its involvement in the other features of actual conscious, subjective, unified, intentional, rational mental agency, in all their manifest structural inseparability from one another. The result of this is a misleadingly composite picture of what in actuality is a profound unity. Moreover, all of this tends to be done in accord with a tacit or explicit Darwinian calculus of survivability and functionality, which dictates attempting to explain mental agency in terms of something entirely other than itself. The question of evolutionary benefit is no doubt an inherently interesting one, but simply to presume that mind can be understood adequately in much the same way that we understand the development of the opposable thumb is more a distraction than anything else; it generates many false questions, many needless dilemmas, and a host of obscurities that are probably only figments of a defective mode of inquiry, but it casts very little light on the abiding enigma of subjective interiority or rational intentionality in a world ostensibly composed from unthinking material forces.

Now, admittedly, there are quite a few Anglophone philosophers who have struggled nobly against these tendencies, and so I must assume that the problem lies not with the tradition as a whole, but only with certain prejudices that have found a happy shelter in its methods, or that have conscripted those methods into an ideological project. Still, I think that philosophy of mind in the Anglophone world needs to be substantially qualified by the application of methods and perspectives from outside the analytic stream: continental tradition, both classical and modern, and both metaphysical and phenomenological; classical Indian philosophy, which arguably began addressing many of the subtlest problems of consciousness centuries before any school of Western philosophy did; and any other approaches that might help make Anglophone philosophy of mind better at treating mental acts in their indivisible totality rather than as a collection of disconnected capacities. Just as modern "systems biology" attempts to break free from an "atomic" genetic logic defectively imitative of the methods of physics, so as ideally to investigate life in the only form in which it actually exists—as organic systems rather than mere accumulations of brute physical forces—philosophy of mind should liberate itself from the nonsensical notion that mental agency can be understood mechanically, as a combination of extrinsically allied parts and discrete functions. Whatever the mind may be, it is not a machine; it is an act that, like any act, can be understood only in its intrinsic unity.

A word about the form of the text that follows: As I said, this book was at first destined to be far longer than it is, when I still conceived of it as a comprehensive treatise, engorged with a surfeit of ponderous expository detail. But in fact I have written a book on the model of a Platonic dialogue. My reasons for this are many, but chief among them is simply that I have become convinced that this is still the best form in which to present philosophical ideas. For one thing, it spares both author and reader certain of those formal stylistic requirements—laboriously modulated transitions between different phases of an argument, for instance, or tedious prolegomenal passages introducing new topics—that even an essayist with the lightest of touches is typically obliged to observe. For another, it discourages obfuscations (such as needless passages of formal logical notation, which often serve no purpose other than to translate ideas easily stated in normal language into a pseudo-mathematical idiom, principally in order to endow the obvious with the mystique of the intimidatingly recondite). And, for yet another, it ideally imposes a needed degree of intellectual honesty upon the author's arguments precisely at those junctures where the temptation might be strong to ignore a fissure or frailty in his or her reasoning and to move swiftly onward; once one grants the characters on the page the right to interrogate a premise or to object to an inadequately demonstrated conclusion, it often proves surprisingly difficult to make them hold their tongues thereafter. This can be extremely useful, because a truly interesting philosophical argument is usually as much about asking the right questions as about supplying plausible answers; and it is my conviction that, in this field of philosophy in particular, the correct questions need to be recovered from four centuries and more of forgetfulness.

Then, too, there is one other advantage to the form that I suppose I should mention. One of the early readers of the manuscript for this book remarked in his written comments that he thought it reasonable to assume that the character of Psyche speaks for me. This is true, but not only of her. Psyche speaks for my convictions regarding the structure of life and mind, Hermes speaks for my view of the mysteries and nature of language, and Eros speaks for my beliefs regarding the ultimate end of rational desire and mental intention, and all of that is rather obvious; but Hephaistos also speaks for me, or at any rate for my doubts and hesitations, my impatience with an attitude of absolute certitude where some degree of uncertainty seems not only inevitable but virtuous, and perhaps even for my frustration at not being any better able than anyone else is to prove my convictions on these issues to be absolutely correct, to the world at large or even to myself. I do not know if, like Whitman, I can claim to contain multitudes, but I like to think my mind is at least open enough to accommodate a quartet. I am of the *party* of Psyche, Hermes, and Eros, it is true; but Hephaistos is *part* of me.

And one last note, while we are at it: In many ways, this book is a companion to my earlier *The Experience of God: Being, Consciousness, Bliss*;[6] much of it is something of an enlargement on that book's fourth chapter in particular. One does not have to have read that volume to make sense of this one; but having done so might make the larger context and reasoning of my argument in what follows all the clearer.

Characters and Setting of the Dialogue

NOTE

The story of Psyche and Eros may or may not originally have been an item of Hellenistic (or earlier) folklore, but the only version of it we possess is a late antique romance from the second century of the Common Era, appearing in Apuleius's novel *Metamorphoses* (also known as *The Golden Ass*). It tells of how a young human woman of astonishing beauty and innocence becomes the bride of the god of love. Eros appears in the text under his Roman name as Cupid, but Psyche retains the Greek form of her name rather than suffering its conversion into its Latin equivalent, Anima. In either form, however, her name can mean at once both "life" and "mind" (and, perhaps, "self"), and is usually translated as "soul." Apuleius's narrative is an extraordinarily lovely fable, and at its end—after many adventures, trials, and poignant peripeties—Psyche is translated to the celestial court and given ambrosia to drink by the hand of Zeus (or, rather, Jupiter) himself, which transforms her into one of the immortals.

DRAMATIS PERSONAE

PSYCHE: Goddess of the soul and of life, a late arrival among the Olympian deities but also a figure who—having been born among human beings and only thereafter raised to the station of a goddess—stands on both sides of the division between divine and mortal, celestial and terrestrial, supernal and mundane. Among her many other names is JIVA.

EROS: Psyche's husband, the god of love, passionate love in particular, also associated with fertility and the power of life. He bears a bow whose arrows wound the heart with insatiable romantic yearning, and he has great wings the hue of moonlight that can carry him in an instant to any quarter of heaven or earth. He is also known as KAMA or KAMADEVA.

HERMES: The messenger of the gods, the divine intermediary between heaven and earth, as swift as thought when on the wing. He is the great divine scribe, the god of the written and the spoken word, and so is at once an oracular god and the god of interpretation. He is also a deity of boundaries and meeting-places, who as the divine psychopomp guides the souls of the dead from this world into the next; and he is a guardian of flocks and herds and those who tend them. Another of his names is PUSHAN.

HEPHAISTOS: The god of craftsmen, blacksmiths, metallurgy, and manufacture, tutelary divinity of the hammer, the tongs, and the blazing forge, among whose most prodigious feats of invention is the fabrication of seemingly living automata to serve him in his labors. His talent in the making of all things elaborate and splendid is boundless. He is the deity of all technical virtuosity, ingenuity, and skill. He is also called VISHVAKARMA.

THE SCENE OF THE ACTION

Having largely retreated from the human world for want of worshippers, the Graeco-Roman gods now pass most of their days in what they call the *Metakosmia* (*Intermundia* in Latin)—the "spaces between the worlds"—a *plurale tantum* term they have borrowed from the philosopher Epicurus. It is a realm situated in the empty places outside mortal nature. Here they have created beautiful and radiant habitations for themselves, palaces of intricately wrought porphyry and gold (or the ethereal equivalents thereof) and every other rare and precious material, enclosing gardens and sparkling fountains, surrounded by a paradise of emerald woodlands, floriferous meadows, fruit-laden orchards, fragrant breezes, rolling hills, flowing rivers, and sounding seas. Theirs are lives of uninterrupted bliss, devoted to the pleasures of leisure, food and drink, love, poetry, music, and all the other arts, as well as (of course) philosophy. In the last of these pursuits, they are especially partial to discussions of the nature of existence, of the mystery of mind, and of whether there is a transcendent God from whom they and all other things come, as well as what the nature of such a God must be.[1] Unlike the gods of Epicurus, however, they are not indifferent to our world or ignorant of what happens here. They keep abreast of human affairs, if only for old times' sake, and take a special interest in our arts, philosophies, and sciences.

The dialogue takes place at the estate of Eros and Psyche, in one of its many gardens. Everything is in blossom. In that place, everything always is.

DAY ONE
Mind, Life, and Pictures of Reality

I

The Irreducible

Eros, Hermes, and Hephaistos are reclining, each upon a separate garden bench fashioned from ethereal "marble"; having for the moment desisted from the casual conversation in which they have been engaged for the last hour or so, they are listening to the breeze stirring the leaves about them and to the birds singing overhead. Enter Psyche. In her hand is a refulgently red rose blossom at which she is gazing with unusual intensity. Finding an unoccupied bench, she seats herself and turns to Eros.

Psyche: Do you see this flower, my love?

Eros: Of course, my soul, very clearly.

Psyche: I plucked it just now from the rose tree at the center of our courtyard.

Eros: So I guessed.

Psyche: [*Addressing all three:*] And yet I didn't do so impulsively. I was detained for some time by my own indecision. I happened to note this one blossom among all the others, and was drawn to its singular perfection and beauty, but I deliberated for some time before breaking it from its branch. On the one hand, I found its loveliness too delicious to resist; on the other, I wasn't entirely sure that I cared to remove it from its natural place, where it shone out to such exquisite effect amid that inordinate, gorgeous pattern of blossoms and leaves.

Eros: Evidently you made your choice in the end.

Hephaistos: I can't honestly say that this is the most enthralling tale you've ever told.

PSYCHE: Indeed. It's very ordinary. And yet—and this was what was occupying my thoughts just now when I came upon the three of you here—I find myself fascinated by the conclusions one might draw from it.

HERMES: Such as that you take your time to make up your mind?

PSYCHE: No. Or, rather, yes, that's true, and that's significant in itself. For, in taking my time, I was considering a course of action prospectively, weighing one desire and one rationale against another until I arrived at a decision. Then, in keeping with the purpose I'd elected, I acted and, having acted, I began to reflect on what I'd done, out of a further desire to understand the implications of my actions. And all of this required a certain period of time because I wasn't merely storing information in my mind in a disordered aggregate, but instead was arranging my reflections in a particular intelligible order according to a grammar of logical continuities, reasoning upon my actions, employing concepts that I had to communicate to myself by way of signs—words, that is, indicating ideas in relation to one another—the whole process guided by my longing to understand as much as I could.

HEPHAISTOS: Again, my dear Psyche, as enchanting a *raconteuse* as you usually are, I can't pretend to find any of this nearly as absorbing as you evidently do.

PSYCHE: And yet you ought to. For what I concluded from this admittedly humble episode is that mental acts are irreducible to material causes; that consciousness, intentionality, and mental unity aren't physical phenomena or emergent products of material forces, but instead belong to a reality more basic than the physical order; that the mechanical view of nature that has prevailed in Western culture for roughly four centuries is incoherent and inadequate to all the available empirical evidence; that in fact the foundation of all reality is spiritual rather than material, and that the material order, to the degree that it exists at all (on which we may reserve judgment), originates in the spiritual; that all rational activity, from the merest recognition of an object of perception, thought, or will to the most involved process of ratiocination, is possible only because of the mind's constant, transcendental preoccupation with an infinite horizon of intelligibility that, for want of a better word, we should call God; and that the existence of all things is possible only as the result of an infinite act of intelligence that, once again, we should call God.

HEPHAISTOS: [*Sighing:*] Ah, that again.

PSYCHE: Yes, *that* again. My further conclusions, dear Phaesty, are that the brain doesn't produce the mind, even if the mind operates within the world *through* or *as* the brain; that none of the sciences as they exist at present—no neuroscience, however advanced, no form of biochemistry, and not even the most revolutionary forms of modern physics—will ever produce a coherent causal narrative of the relation between the physical and the mental; that no machine ever has been, or ever will be, conscious, capable of thought, or possessed of functions even remotely analogous to the operations of the mind; that the hope for a day when men and women will be able to download their conscious minds into computers is destined to be bitterly disappointed; and that, once again—simply to reiterate the point—there's an infinite, metaphysically simple God in whom all things live, move, and exist.

HEPHAISTOS: [*With a sardonic lilt in his voice:*] My goodness me. [*Slowly sitting up upon his bench:*] Assuming that you're not trifling with us, I can say only that your conclusions are rather, ah . . . *extravagant*, given the evidence you've offered.

EROS: [*Also sitting up:*] They seem eminently reasonable to me.

HEPHAISTOS: [*Smirking:*] As truly *shocking* as I find that, I suspect you're guided more by love than by reason.

HERMES: To the contrary, my friend. I agree with both of them.

PSYCHE: Oh, yes, that reminds me. Another of my conclusions is that love and reason are inseparable aspects of mental life, and that both alike are always already present in all of organic life. Yet another is that life itself is more than the quantitative effect of material forces; it is instead a kind of intentional intelligence pervading all things.

HEPHAISTOS: I see. The mind of God again, no doubt. [*With a laugh:*] Curiouser and curiouser. Well, I know that I'm in a distinct minority here, but I trust you'll all pardon me if I remain true to my materialist convictions and continue to reject talk of God as anything more than a fantastical rhetorical resort to an explanatory cipher. And I hope you'll also not think less of me if, despite the staggering evidence of a rose blossom plucked after deliberation from a tree, I continue to believe that the most rational and logically parsimonious explanation for the existence of all things—including mental phenomena—is that they're the physical results of wholly material causes, operating in strict obedience to purely physical laws of causation.

EROS: I don't always believe you're quite as insensible to the mysteriousness of life and mind as you affect to be.

HEPHAISTOS: I assure you, there's no affectation involved. I certainly see no need to explain life as the force of the divine mind in all things, or some spark of divine fire animating material organisms. We have no need of that hypothesis, to coin a phrase, or of any other form of "vitalism." Organic life is the fortuitous product of unguided chemical interactions. Each species is the product of a phylogeny stretching back through time to a sea of rudimentary and barely active chemical elements, and any given individual organism is merely a kind of machine, a functioning combination of intrinsically purposeless parts, all constructed from an ensemble of largely inert chemical ingredients.

HERMES: [*At last joining the others in an upright posture:*] Do you truly believe that?

HEPHAISTOS: Indeed I do. In fact, I'd go so far as to say that the demarcation we habitually draw between organic life and simple chemical reactions is more a convention of semantics than anything else, or at the very least no more than a relative judgment made along a continuum; ultimately, there's no essential distinction between the simple volatility of elementary chemistry and the vitality of organisms, no point of inflection—not even that of organic matter's accidental acquisition of the properties of homeostasis and replication—at which the one is miraculously transformed into the other.

EROS: None whatsoever?

HEPHAISTOS: None. Even the distinction between life and death, to be pitilessly honest, is really just a convention, a mere division between differing kinds of chemical processes; what we arbitrarily single out as meriting the name "life" is merely a functional arrangement of elements that in themselves aren't alive. The whole evolutionary history of living things is that of the gradual, relentless concrescence of ever more layers of complexity upon a simple chemical basis. Any given organism is an item of chemical technology, albeit one that evolved by way of natural selection and modular accumulations rather than by being designed by an intending intelligence; hence, life can always be reduced to its chemical components again without leaving behind any mystical residue or supernatural *tertium quid* that we might call the "life force" or the divine spark or anything of that sort. Similarly, we gods—like our parents the titans and their parents Ouranos and Gea, as well as whatever other celestial and supercelestial beings there may be—arose originally from, and can be analytically reduced again to, the aethers and their natural fluctuations and native energies. So too, mind is merely a mechanical function or emergent property of the neural machinery by which organisms interact with their environments. Or rather, perhaps, mind is simply identical to that neural machinery and its interactions. Don't scowl like that, Eros. This isn't to deny the marvel and beauty of either life or mind; it's merely to deny that any but a natural explanation is required to account for them.

Eros: Do you deny that you yourself are a *living* being, then, rather than a machine?

Hephaistos: Why make that distinction? Of course I'm a living being, but I reject the notion that my "life" is anything other than an accumulation and integration of countless, minute, essentially lifeless, essentially mechanical parts. I deny that life is anything but the complex operation of innumerable little machines organized into a larger machine, just as I deny that mind is anything other than the cumulative integrated result of numberless, minute, essentially mindless ingredients and processes—an axon here, a flicker of electricity there, a neurological filter for discriminating between lateral and vertical intensities, a cerebral module that's developed a capacity for retaining mnemonic traces—and so on. I, like every living and conscious thing, am a mereological illusion . . . or an apparition . . . a composite totality that seems whole and entire in itself, though really I'm just the emergent result of a vast collection of discrete parts and forces and tiny molecular mechanisms acting, if not in perfect concert, at least in close synchrony so long as . . . well, so long as their physiological *momentum* keeps them flowing together in a common structure.

HERMES: All of that raises questions regarding the meanings of quite a few words—"natural," for instance, or "cause," or "emergent" . . .

HEPHAISTOS: Perhaps. But you don't deny, do you, that life evolves from simpler into more complex forms?

HERMES: Of course not. We know it does. Our grandparents watched it happening on the earth and in the seas over vast ages. At least, the grandparents of three of us did. [*To Psyche:*] I realize you arrived among us a little later. [*To Hephaistos again:*] What I most certainly do deny, however, is that biological evolution was a purely mechanical process, or that the Neo-Darwinian model of evolution is exhaustively explanatory—or even largely explanatory. At most, it's only a partial, local, restricted truth within the embrace of a far larger, more vastly encompassing truth about the origin of life.

HEPHAISTOS: It may or may not be; but, even if it's insufficient, whatever theory may come to supplement it will still be situated within the realm of natural forces and causes.

PSYCHE: Again, what's "natural"?

HEPHAISTOS: I tend to take it to mean "physical."

PSYCHE: That we can debate. But I must commend you, Phaesty, for having so quickly recognized that the issue of the origin and structure of mind is inseparable from that of the origin and structure of life. That's very astute of you indeed, because inevitably both issues center upon one and the same question: whether, that is, a purely mechanistic understanding of nature—or its many descendants or sequels or variants, such as philosophical naturalism or physicalism—can be made to account for the very things that had to be subtracted from the picture of nature in early modernity in order to produce the mechanical philosophy to begin with. That is, can mechanism explain what mechanism originally abstained from trying to explain on principle? For certain reasons, incidentally, I would add language to the list of intrinsically irreducible realities.

HEPHAISTOS: Add as many items as you please, but my response will remain unchanged. Any complex phenomenon may *seem* to resist reduction to simpler, more elementary causes; but, as a rule, that proves nothing, since what *seems* to be the case is often nothing more than the current *status quaestionis*, which will be revised in time by deeper scientific investigation. When you say no scientific method or discipline could possibly provide a causal narrative of mind—as you so often *have* said—what you mean is that there's no way of bridging the divide between third-person data about physical events and first-person conscious experience. And I assume that's because the former consists in purely objective inventories of material objects and electrochemical episodes, united by physical connections, while the latter is composed of subjective phenomenal awareness and private thoughts, connected by consecutive rational associations and subsisting in private intuitions and private interpretations.

PSYCHE: Very good. You put it very succinctly. That's indeed my view. Simply said, a strictly quantitative method can't illuminate a strictly qualitative phenomenon like consciousness, and a strictly third-person method can't illuminate a strictly first-person experience. And so, my dear friend, to imagine that the absolute difference between objective physical states and subjective mental states can be overcome in terms of physical causality is a category error, if only because modern scientific method is applicable only to the former while offering no avenue of access to the latter. The sciences don't even have a means of asking the correct questions here. For another thing, no matter how many correlations we isolate between neurological states and mental events, it's a fairly venerable axiom that correlation isn't causation. Granting all due respect to the cognitive sciences, and to all their inventories of the correspondences between mental and brain states, none of that will ever yield the explanation we seek. We're talking about merely apparent *quantitative* associations between totally *qualitatively* dissimilar phenomena. The nature of the relation is so obscure that we can't even presume to know which side, if either, might enjoy causal priority; we have no better reason for speaking of the mind as what the brain does than for speaking of the brain as an instrument the mind employs. All that the sciences of our day can do with regard to this issue is remind us—as if we needed reminding—that minds and bodies aren't functionally severable in our normal experience.

HEPHAISTOS: It's always perilous to presume to know what the sciences of the future may or may not achieve.

PSYCHE: Not when it's a matter of logic. As you say, consciousness, uniquely, is first-person in its phenomenal structure, all the way down. In fact, it's the very phenomenon of the "first person" as such, the sole act whereby someone is anyone at all, with a private inner life, and it's wholly inaccessible to any scrutiny from outside. Of course, we can observe behaviors in others that resemble our own and that we know in our own cases to be associated with consciousness, but that doesn't provide us any immediate intuition of the subjectivity behind them when we observe them in others. Even the most exhaustive surveillance of all those electrical events in the neurons of the brain that we can reasonably assume to be the physical concomitants of mental states can never admit us into the singular, continuous, wholly interior reality of another's personal experience—that inward, conscious self that's pure perspective as such, never to be captured as an object within the field of some other perspective.

HEPHAISTOS: Goodness gracious me.

PSYCHE: Mock if you like, my dear, but I'm only acknowledging modern scientific method's understanding of itself. That method absolutely insists that a verifiable scientific description must be a rigorously third-person narrative of structural and causal connections and consequences. It's precisely the first-person perspective that must ideally be subdued within—and even banished from—our view of any phenomenon if observation, experiment, and theory are to yield a properly "scientific" account of that phenomenon; any remainder of the purely subjective, however meager, constitutes only an area of unintelligibility. This rule is fair enough, perhaps—*perhaps*—when we're talking about, say, cell-division as viewed through a microscope; but it becomes an insurmountable obstacle when applied to the phenomenon of subjectivity. Now the object of investigation is the very thing that our prevailing method, on principle, refuses from the first to take into consideration. So yes, we can say with utter certainty that consciousness can't be described solely in terms of, say, sensory stimulus and neurological response, simply because neither stimulus nor response is in itself a mental phenomenon; neither one, considered as a purely physical reality, entails conceptual content, intentional meaning, volition, desire, beliefs, or personal awareness. So the notion that there's a purely physical basis for subjective experience remains at best a conjecture regarding a kind of connection for which there's no analogy anywhere else in nature. An electrical pulse as such is not a thought or a private impression; or at least, if it is, we have no language for describing—no conceptual grammar for understanding—that arcane identity.

Once again, my dear friend, yes: we can in fact confidently assume that no purely empirical explanation of the relation of physical to mental events will ever be found. We'll never devise any causal model adequate to explain the relation between the two, or even isolate any aspect of that relation as an object of scientific scrutiny. The problem has nothing to do with the limitations of our current scientific techniques or knowledge; it's entirely one of logic. No matter how sophisticated the cognitive sciences may become, mere quantitative advances in physical data will never be able to span the qualitative abyss between the objective and subjective dimensions of reality.

HEPHAISTOS: Abyss? Really?

PSYCHE: It *is* an abyss. We need only consider the real features of mental life—the intricate interweaving of recognition, judgment, desire, will, deliberation, evaluation, and internal language that I described in regard to the rose I plucked from my tree, for instance—to see that they're irreconcilable with any mechanical picture of things. It's the very reality of correlations between objective brain events and subjective mental states that forms the central mystery confronting us; so even the most exhaustive catalogue possible of all the neurological concomitants of mental actions would still amount only to a series of reiterations of that mystery. If what we are seeking is a causal model in purely physicalist terms of the convertibility between the physical and the mental, then all that our repeated expeditions into the jungles of neurology can achieve is to show us we've been looking in the wrong place. Frankly, to my mind the notion that first-person experience could be reduced to third-person functions is utterly devoid of rational content. It's like claiming that one's height is reducible to one's charisma.

HEPHAISTOS: [*Smiling and then sighing:*] So you say. But that may itself be merely a matter of our current state of knowledge. What if that absolute qualitative distinction between the third- and first-person perspectives is itself only apparent rather than real? And what if this seemingly singular, purely subjective reality of consciousness and thought you speak of with such certainty *could* be disassembled into an immense collection of very tiny, purely objective parts? What if intrinsic consciousness is a kind of holographic illusion, so to speak, generated by a plurality of partial representations, all of which can be dissolved again back into the purely extrinsic relations of unconscious things? Or, if that should prove impossible, what if instead there are occult properties invested in matter at its most elementary levels—and by "occult" I mean merely "hidden from view"—that are already what you might call "subjective" in nature? What if the seemingly absolute qualitative abyss you describe between subjective and objective phenomena is actually a distinction between two sides of a single physical continuum that we simply haven't as yet properly descried and described?

PSYCHE: My goodness, so many what-ifs. They'll take some time to answer, though I'm perfectly willing to try to do so. Mind you, how unified consciousness could be an illusion, when illusion itself would seem to require a unified consciousness in which to appear, we can discuss in time. Again, though, I have to emphasize that the problem here isn't a matter merely of how much information we possess, or of how much empirical data we've failed as yet to discover; it's that the logical constraints that govern the sciences absolutely prohibit them from any meaningful empirical or theoretical investigation of the mind's inner states. So on this score we really can't accept promissory notes for scientific discoveries in some unspecified future that will chase all our perplexities away, since plain logic tells us that they're worthless. I know that your preferred term for the working premises of modern science is "methodological naturalism"; well, it's precisely such naturalism that's incapable of explaining mental acts, no matter how developed its methods may become in time. If, of course, at some future date we should abandon the third-person rigorism of modern science altogether, and find a way of speaking of consciousness and subjective interiority in a language that also yields a satisfactory physical description of reality, it will be only because we've so radically revised our every concept of the physical that we're no longer talking about what the sciences today recognize as their proper field of study. I think that unlikely. Whatever the case, Phaesty dear, I cordially encourage you to try skipping over that qualitative abyss if you doubt it's there. I assure you, you'll fall in.

HEPHAISTOS: Do you? Well, even if I were to plummet down into its depths, it wouldn't necessarily mean that I'm wrong in principle. It might mean merely that I lack the necessary dialectical tools. I'm not a philosopher, after all; I'm merely a god, and a god of limited agility at that. [*Looking at Eros and Hermes in turn:*] I'm just a poor, lame, lumbering blacksmith slouching my ungainly way among gods as fleet as thought itself.

HERMES: Oh, now, let's not be coy. False humility doesn't suit you.

PSYCHE: Quite so. And, anyway, I wouldn't place the burden of persuasion entirely on your shoulders, Phaesty, broad and brawny though they are. I admit that we can't conclude just from the qualitative difference between objectivity and subjectivity that there aren't, as you say, *occult* propensities in matter that might explain the reality of mental phenomena. I have other reasons for thinking it logically impossible that mental states are merely physical in nature. My view, to be clear, is not only that you can't in practice produce an account of how the third-person objective facts of electrochemistry are causally connected to mental events, though in fact you can't; rather, it's also that it's logically impossible for physical events—understood mechanistically, at least—to produce mental events by way of purely material causes. I grant, though, that the conclusions I've drawn from my confessedly not very thrilling adventure at the rose tree require some exposition. So, let me propose the following: I'll lay out my arguments against the physicalist reductionism you favor. I encourage you to raise what objections you like; but, if I should prove reasonably successful in convincing you of the solvency of my arguments, you must then allow me to attempt to convince you also that an honest phenomenology of ordinary mental acts demonstrates that it's at least reasonable—and more reasonable than any alternative—to conclude that mind is the ground of reality and that, moreover, infinite mind—the mind of God—is the source and end and encompassing element of every finite mind.

HEPHAISTOS: That sounds like a very time-consuming exercise.

PSYCHE: Happily, being gods, we have literally all the time in the universe at our disposal. [*Turning to Hermes:*] What do you say?

HERMES: I'm entirely agreeable to the suggestion.

PSYCHE: [*To Eros:*] And you, my love?

EROS: I adore you.

PSYCHE: We'll take that as a yes. [*Turning back to Hephaistos:*] So, what say you?

HEPHAISTOS: [*After a moment of silence:*] Very well, then. The floor—or, rather, the greensward—is yours.

II

Physicalism, Dualism, Form

PSYCHE: [*Setting aside her rose:*] Don't misunderstand me, Phaesty dear, I'm not saying that I don't appreciate how difficult these issues are. Just because I had a flash of what I take to be insight, I don't deceive myself that what strikes me as obvious must be obvious to others. Still, it amazes me how little amazed we often are by consciousness and life and . . .

HEPHAISTOS: Surely that's for the best. Otherwise we'd be walking around in a constant daze, astonished and preoccupied by absolutely everything.

PSYCHE: Well, yes, precisely so. And I suppose that's why our habits of thought tend to draw a veil before those mysteries. But that's also my point: everything that exists for us does so wholly *within* consciousness, and that's in part why consciousness isn't some discrete phenomenon among other phenomena that we can isolate and examine; it's the very ground and possibility of any phenomenon—phenomenality as such—the mind's openness both to itself and to the whole of reality. It's the element in which everything subsists for us, the medium in which our minds and our world meet. Even when we try to reflect impartially on subjective mental states, our reflections are themselves just so many more subjective mental states. We have no world other than the one that comes to us in private awareness, and there's no method, scientific or otherwise, that allows us to get around this fact.

Hephaistos: [*Shrugging:*] In one sense, that's undeniable. I mean, so long as you're you and I'm I, there's a private dimension of mental acts that can't be shared directly between us. But what does that amount to, in the end? You also can't digest my breakfast for me, nor can I perform such a service for you. Every act is specific to an agent, but that doesn't detract from its general and essential attributes. The accidental features of a mental act that make it particular to you or to me don't mean that what's common to the nature of our mental actions can't be illumined by a rigorously inductive, rigorously impersonal science. At least, you've no reason to assume so until you've exhausted every imaginable empirical and theoretical approach.

Psyche: The privacy of mental states is a very different sort of thing from the specificity of physiological functions. I'm saying that mind resists that sort of scientific scrutiny not because it's merely *particular* to me or to you, but because the very nature of that particularity—or, rather, of that privacy—is a phenomenon intrinsically unavailable to scientific method. An impersonal, third-person, inductive investigation of any normal object of scrutiny is always possible, no doubt; but an impersonal account of a thoroughly personal dimension of reality, or a third-person account of a first-person experience, is not. When you digest your breakfast, the correspondence between the physiological processes and the physical reality of metabolism is more or less one-to-one, all occurring on a single physical plane. When you're aware of the feeling of digesting your breakfast, from the opposite side of the event, so to speak, the correspondence between the processes of metabolism and your private consciousness is one between two intrinsically different kinds of reality—intrinsically different descriptions—occurring on two distinct planes. Your analogy doesn't hold, my friend.

Moreover, perhaps it's true that the surest path to certain kinds of scientific knowledge is the construction of strictly third-person accounts of things; but we mustn't forget that there really is no such thing as a third-person *perspective*. All perspective is, by definition, first-person. The third-person vantage is a methodological fiction without any objective existence. It's a mere distillate of an accumulation of first-person reports;

and then, of course, even those supposedly impersonal reports must still be translated through the privacy of our own minds. You may tell me about an experience you've had, and a thousand of your friends may report the same experience; but you're all still offering me only subjective reports, and I know those reports only as a subjective experience of my own, regarding which I must pass a personal judgment, based on my own sense of what constitutes a credible claim. The myth of pure "objective" verification encourages us to imagine that the proper authority of the first-person vantage can be alienated from itself and situated instead in some fabulous, unbiased place of observation located nowhere, or everywhere, or wherever we want, but somehow outside of subjectivity. But a myth is all it is. *That* "third person" is a mirage, like the spectral companion that wanderers in wild places sometimes hallucinate walking alongside them. In the end, there's only the first-person vantage; and whatever can't be eliminated from that vantage without eliminating the vantage itself must be regarded as an indubitable fact—a primary datum, the ground of knowledge upon which all other claims about reality are founded.

HEPHAISTOS: I've already lost track of the point you're making.

PSYCHE: Forgive me. Sometimes I rush ahead of myself. All I mean to say is that standard scientific method isn't going to help us in understanding something at once alien to the very premises of that method and yet also fundamental to its credibility. More fundamental than that, to be honest. In every instant, we're confronted not merely by the mystery of subjectivity, but also by the reality that subjectivity is what we and our world most essentially are. Just consider what it is to be conscious. We know both ourselves and the reality we inhabit in a single unified act of awareness, one that allows us to contemplate ourselves and the world simultaneously, and also to assume each moment into a continuous activity that unites past and present—and, for that matter, future—in a single experience. Then too, nearly every moment of experience also involves conscious and intentional acts of recognition, evaluation, judgment, and will. In a single movement of the mind—or certainly in what seems to be a single present moment of awareness—we perceive reality as both one and incalculably diverse, at one and the same time grasping the world as a profound unity and as a collection of countless particular things, while also arranging those things in our thoughts according to an enormously complex hierarchy of general and abstract concepts, and relating them to one another in the *now* of perception. Hence the mind is always at work synthesizing the physical with the non-physical—the empirical with the abstract or general or transcendental. This also involves ordering our experience in a continuous temporal sequence that necessarily incorporates both memory and expectation in our awareness of the present. The mind can do this, moreover, while also pursuing entirely different reflections along private avenues of thought. And that doesn't begin to exhaust the unifying powers of the conscious mind. Even as it receives and, in a sense, composes the world, it's able also to imagine alternative possibilities, to recognize not only what the world is but also what it might be; and, in fact, that constant interaction of our minds with alternative possibilities, which of their nature can't act physically upon us, is an integral dimension of our perceptions of what's really present before us. The mind is open to the possible and even to the seemingly impossible, and this is all part of how it grasps and interprets the real. Then too, at the same time, it's aware *of itself* as being aware; its own act of consciousness is also self-consciousness, and any intentional act of the mind—that is, any directing of mental attention toward a specific object or end—is also an intentional act of the mind toward itself, known to itself as acting toward that end. And in all of this there's also such a rich palette of shadings and nuances of sensibility, such subtle distinctions of affect and mood, such an ineffable web of associations, such varying intensities of perception. . . .

Hephaistos: Yes, yes. You needn't rhapsodize so. I freely stipulate that the mind's native powers are quite majestic. They're as nothing else in nature. Hurrah, says I. That still doesn't preclude their having a material provenance.

Psyche: Of course not. But I hope nevertheless to convince you that the impotence of the sciences to explain any of this isn't just an epistemic limitation, but rather a sign of something essential to the nature of mind as such. Those native powers aren't just astonishing; they're impossible in purely materialist terms. It's not simply the case that we lack the right instrumentation or haven't yet devised the best possible experiments. Of course, it's tempting to imagine that all the mysteries of mental existence *must* be explicable entirely in terms, say, of interactions between neurology and the physical environment, and that mind must rest, both evolutionarily and organically, upon a simple basis of physiological stimulus and response, and that stimulus and response must in their turn be founded wholly upon biochemistry, and biochemistry wholly upon elementary physics. But electrochemical events and nerve cells are *not* simply the same thing as, say, ideas, beliefs, reasoning, awareness, and so forth. And only modern habits of thought make anyone imagine that this is a distinction that one should in principle be able to conjure away. According to the mechanical view of reality, which has reigned over the modern imagination for roughly four centuries, matter is mindless mass and causality is mindless force, and physical reality is entirely determined by mindless impulses and momentums rather than by rationales or purposes. Well, I make bold to assert that, as long as our thinking is confined within that barren paradigm, the presence of mind within this supposedly mindless material order will remain an enigma without solution.

It's certainly one that could never be dispelled in the narrow, early modern terms that still prevail in most analytic philosophy of mind. I mean to say, how often do we see it asserted that there are only two ways of accounting for mental realities? *Either* we must adopt a materialism that takes mind to be identical to, emergent from, or an epiphenomenon of brute, unguided physical events *or* we must adopt a "substance dualism" that tells us that in conscious beings two utterly disparate realities—the machine of the body and its ghostly tenant the soul—are somehow miraculously joined so as to operate in tandem. Occasionally, a third possibility called "idealism" is admitted into the picture, according to which all seemingly physical phenomena are really only appearances existing within disembodied minds, but this usually tends to be adduced as little more than a *reductio ad absurdum* (whether that's fair or not). All three of these approaches, however greatly they may seem to differ from one another, share one crucial "mechanistic" assumption in common: to wit, that matter as such, insofar as such a thing might or might not really exist, must by definition be the intrinsically dead, entirely unconscious, non-intentional, and purposeless matter of the mechanical philosophy. The materialist model tells us that mind and life are late results of accidental convergences and divergences of mindless mechanical force, and in their depths are always still really governed by that force. The dualist model tells us that mind and life inhabit material reality as anomalous residents of a world of dead and insensate mass. And the idealist model tells us that mind and life preclude the reality of matter altogether as anything but "a spume that plays upon a ghostly paradigm of things" because, if it really existed, it would be nothing but a dead mechanism incapable of union with mental reality.

Eros: I do love Yeats.

Psyche: Well, I reject the underlying premise that matter is something essentially dead and unthinking. As false as it is to mistake mind for the physical result of mindless forces, just so false is it to mistake life for a mechanical organization of intrinsically dead elements.

Hephaistos: Let's say I were to agree with you, provisionally at least. It seems to me that all you're doing is reverting to a point I already made in passing: that matter may possess some intrinsic properties as yet unknown to us that explain the emergence of "life" and "mind." We needn't mystify those properties, however, with the language of vitalism or of dualism, as if life were some abstruse additional force introduced into organisms, or as if mind were some substance in addition to matter; rather, we need only revise our understanding of matter's inherent powers.

Psyche: You misunderstand me. I'm not talking about some adventitious supplement to matter called the "life force" or what have you. But I also deny that it's sufficient to speak of some basic material "property" from which life and mind might spontaneously arise. I don't believe that life can be educed from lifeless ingredients or mind from mindless parts; but, then again, I also doubt the existence of anything truly lifeless or mindless. Life and mind are structural realities, hierarchical orderings of complex relations, and as such don't simply *emerge* from lower causes—at least, not from interactions of a purely mechanistic and material kind. I believe it far more plausible to assume that all of existing nature, matter included, is already fully mindlike—and hence directed toward life and consciousness—in its very essence. Mind and life—and language too—are possible only by way of a kind of "downward" causation that informs their "upward" evolution in particular beings.

HEPHAISTOS: You're talking about what Aristotelians call formal causality, aren't you? A pretty picture, but not a compellingly logical one.

PSYCHE: Don't be impatient. And don't disdain my pretty picture before I've added shading and pigments. I simply don't think the question of the place of mind within nature can be answered except by reconsidering the place of nature within mind. Part of the intellectual patrimony of early modernity—bequeathed to the world in varying ways by such worthies as Galileo, Bacon, Descartes, and Newton—was a vision of nature divided by an impermeable partition between its objective and subjective aspects. We were asked to presume a universe of lifeless, mindless matter, and only then to ask how life and mind had made their habitation there—in it but not of it, so to speak. We were also expected to grant that the realm of the really real is the world that Galileo told us was the only one properly available to the sciences: the world of bare mass, force, momentum, and measurable quantities. And then we were asked to believe also that all the phenomenal qualities that seem inherent in reality—color, sound, fragrance, taste, even our conditioned feelings of temporal duration—are mere superimpositions on that reality made by our apparatus of perception. The world of experience is, so we were told, a captivating masquerade, a pageant by which the physical communicates itself to our minds under the dissembling guises of the phenomenal; and so the true order of things is certified in its truthfulness precisely by its absolute phenomenal indigence. Galileo's only aim, of course, was to delineate what mathematics, which is the language of the sciences as he conceived them, is able to describe; but in time his understanding of the specifically physical became modern culture's general metaphysics. That's an inversion of any sane ontology. It's a choice—and only a choice—to view the mathematical, quantitative description of physical events as reality in itself rather than as a very tenuous abstraction, while treating the formal and phenomenal aspects of experience as accidental and largely illusory effects of perception. Seen in that light, the mind is already banished to the exterior of the physical order—as is, paradoxically, every actual *experience* of that order. So too, life has come to be seen as an epiphenomenon, a name for transitory coalescences of briefly persisting form on the surface of a sea of blindly deterministic material forces.

Hephaistos: I don't disagree. But what reason do you have for rejecting such a picture, other than personal revulsion?

Psyche: Many reasons, but chiefly its arbitrariness. Why not see the laws of life as primary rather than as the accidental effects of lifeless causes? Why not, too, regard reality as what arises in the interplay of mind and world? Of what world do we have any evidence other than the one that exists within our perceptions? Why speak as if a mathematical and quantitative distillate, artificially extracted from the phenomenal and qualitative richness of experience, is reality as such? What is this excruciatingly attenuated world of pure mathematical relations except the fading ghost or dying echo of the world of phenomena, of whose regularities it's merely an abstract calculus? And yet that calculus would have nothing to measure if the phenomena that exist in the nuptial union between mind and being weren't already there. Physics so conceived simply isn't a complete description of reality. It can't be.[1]

I realize that modern persons, gods no less than mortals, are accustomed to thinking that there are two vying pictures of the world—as Wilfrid Sellars calls them, the "manifest image" and the "scientific image"—and that only the latter—the physical realm underlying phenomena, the quantifiable rather than the qualitative—is to be accorded the status of objective reality; they take it for granted that the perceived world is an apparition only, because supposedly physical reality is entirely unlike mind, and consciousness can have no direct relation to a world with which it's irreconcilable. Thus the phenomenal world must be a mere representation, fabricated by the neurological apparatus of bodies and brains, a translation of the intractable reality of the physical into the manipulable fiction of the perceived. But why?

What if, instead, the real were thought of precisely as a realm of *form*, in which the world and the mind both participate according to their distinctive modes, in different but complementary ways? What if the phenomenal order reveals the true deep principles that hold all things together, while the abstract mathematical order merely represents certain incidental features and minimal conditions of its empirical structure? What if the theoretical schism between experience and world alienates us from the way in which the true world reveals itself to us, and in which the world fulfills itself by becoming mind, and in which the mind fulfills itself by becoming the world—always, of course, through each being open, in its distinctive way, to the real causality of form, which gives shape to both? For more than a century, after all, physics has been exposing the mathematical subtext of phenomena—that impalpable, invisible, noumenal realm of mass and velocity and trajectory and exchanges of energy—as itself a mirage of reason: pure measurement rather than the measurement of discrete objects, an action sustained from "below" not by a solid invariable substrate of materiality but by superposed potentialities, without locality, contextuality, separability. . . . The world of quantum mechanics isn't mechanical at all. Over against that, surely it's the phenomenal and eidetic realm—at once received and composed by mind—that might be thought the real nature of things. Maybe reality in itself is the single event of formal causality, of formation "from above," an event which has at once both a material and a mental side, neither of which exists apart from the other. Maybe the marriage of mind and world in the perception of the red of this red, red rose lying beside me is how the world exists: as *manifestation*, made actual through the mindlike structure of nature and the natural structure of mind. Maybe nothing fully exists except as made manifest in thought, just as mentality exists only in being the site of the world's manifestation of itself.

Hephaistos: That's a great many maybes, to paraphrase you.

Psyche: [*With a gentle laugh:*] If it helps, I'll add that, precisely because I reject materialism, I reject also the sort of vitalism we were just talking about—the kind, that is, that perished in the nineteenth century, if it ever really existed—the notion that there's some mysterious *vis essentialis*, some invisible biological galvanism or catalyst or quintessence, in addition to the material elements in living organisms . . . a superadded, quasi-physical ingredient quickening an otherwise lifeless mechanism. This is still too dualistic a concept. When I speak of the principle of life, I mean . . . well, to use a handy word, *psychē*. I mean a principle at once of vitality and of mentality, as well as of the entelechy intrinsic within living things, which isn't some physical quantum in addition to the material order, but is instead the structural and formal and teleological rational principle pervading and arranging and even granting coherent existence to the whole cosmos.

HEPHAISTOS: So we really are back in the realm of Aristotelian causes—the formal and the final, at least—and also maybe back in the realm of a World-Soul, or at least of primitive animisms. [*Taking a deep breath:*] All of this is so very pre-scientific.

PSYCHE: [*With a sigh:*] Is it? You're so certain you know what we don't yet know. But I confess you may have a point. I do believe that life and mind are a single reality—that where there's one there's the other—and for that reason I regard the seventeenth-century mechanistic metaphysics of matter as far and away the least rational among serious proposals. I think it better to embrace panpsychisms, vitalisms, even animisms than to fall prey to the mechanistic delusion. The forms of belief that see nature as thronged with vital intelligence—with dryads and hamadryads, nereids and nymphs, *kami* and *tama*, elves and fairies—or that see all living things as surcharged with *mana* or *tanka* or spirit . . . or *thought*, belong to a far more rational, far more accurate and empirical picture of the living world than does the sterile mechanism of modern prejudice, which can't explain anything. Thales was right, you know: all things are full of gods.

HEPHAISTOS: Well, of course, I'm aware of the existence of dryads and such—and of gods, needless to say—but I would still regard them—*us*—as physically reducible or emergent beings.

PSYCHE: They may have arisen from physical causes, but not solely by virtue of physical causality. They and their native haunts—the forests and seas, the grottoes and caverns, the mountains and valleys, the rivers and cataracts—arose even more originally from something very like mind. Or, perhaps I should say, their natures *descend* from something like mind, and matter rises up to meet that descending power and to be informed by it. I believe that the material history of all things is itself the product of a spiritual history: form descending into matter, matter ascending into form, producing . . . life . . . producing everything.

HEPHAISTOS: Yes, but we're going in circles now. Tell me, though, why do you keep mentioning language as a mysterious third aspect of this irreducible reality? There you lose me.

HERMES: I believe I can answer that.

HEPHAISTOS: I'm all ears.

HERMES: Don't you see? It follows almost inevitably from what our dear Psyche has already said. If all of nature is pervaded by mind, and if life itself is a mindlike reality, then the whole of being is in a sense a kind of intelligible structure of meaning and purpose and communication. I'm sure Psyche intends to address the issue of mental intentionality . . .

PSYCHE: I do indeed.

HERMES: Very good. Intentionality is that aspect of mental life that involves meanings, rationales, purposes; it involves communication and interpretation and the use of signs and symbolic thinking. Don't you see? The mind, in acting intentionally toward the world, is engaging in a kind of semeiotic and linguistic communion with all things. And language in itself is nothing but intentionality, through and through; apart from intentionality, there are merely sounds shed upon the air or traces impressed upon paper, but no words, no meanings, no language. And, that being so, perhaps nature itself—as intrinsically mindlike in its structure—might be conceived of as an intricate structure of signs and meanings, and as an intentional *act.* It stands to reason, at least, that if life and mind are one, then life is also a kind of rational semantics and syntax.

HEPHAISTOS: But in what sense is language an *irreducible* reality?

Hermes: In the same sense as mind and life are: if one attempts to account for the existence of language in terms entirely of its physical evolution or physical structure, decomposing it down to its most fundamental material causes—let's say, oh, small inarticulate noises, phonemes, vague gestures with one's hands, meaningful facial expressions, marks and images scratched on cave walls—one won't be able to reconstruct the history of its emergence from those causes without invoking higher causes, such as symbolic reasoning, purposes, abstract concepts, signs and symbols, and so on. The moment there's so much as the first glimmer of language there's already a whole structure of symbolic meaning in place. No anthropologist, no matter how diligent, has ever discovered some intermediary form of communication, located somewhere in between meaningless lingual vociferations and fully meaningful words; no philologist, no matter how clever, has ever been able to fabricate a plausible pre-linguistic system of signification, or even a primitive form of language lacking the essential features of fully developed tongues. It's impossible. No physicalist narrative of the co-evolution of linguistic faculties, no matter how excruciatingly gradual, can account for this radical interdependency of symbolic thought, syntax, semantics, and intention. The evolution of language can't simply have been an ascent from "below"—from primitive chance utterances and gestures into a syntactical and semantical system. The system must in some sense have been there from the beginning in principle, prompting those animal noises and gesticulations from "above" to rise upward into itself—into intelligible language—and impressing itself upon those sounds and gestures as an organizing form.

Hephaistos: [*After a moment's silence:*] Formal causality again. This is all very contestable, needless to say, and I find it rather distastefully contrary to the hard-won rational perspective of the modern age. So, let me boil this down. For you two—or you three, I presume—mind and life and language are all prior realities . . . or rather one multifarious reality that exists primarily as a "higher" causality informing "lower" levels of causality, and this reality exists in "lower" causes—material things, that is—only so far as that "higher" causality shapes and guides them.

And this higher reality is some kind of formal—or maybe today we'd say informational—structure beyond the physical . . . a sort of ideal order existing as . . . as thought. Fair enough?

PSYCHE: Very fair.

HEPHAISTOS: Very well, then, you have my undivided attention. But I think we've had enough prologue for now. It's time we began to impose some precision on the language we're using.

PSYCHE: I couldn't agree more.

III

Fallacies of Method

PSYCHE: Let me start with certain fallacies that I hope we can avoid.

HEPHAISTOS: [*With a suspicious tilt of the head:*] All right.

PSYCHE: As I say, I take it as axiomatic that the quantitative by itself can't explain the qualitative. At least, Galileo's division between the measurable and the perceptible worlds is one of the founding gestures of modern scientific culture, and I'm willing to grant and abide by the epistemological limits this imposes on us. A method entirely designed to address the realm of the "nomological"—of impersonal causal law—can't illuminate the realm of the "pathological"—of personal feeling and subjective agency. The difference—the abyss—separating these realms is, well . . . *qualitatively* absolute, and no increase in third-person knowledge can close that abyss.[2]

HEPHAISTOS: Again, unless it's not an abyss, because the supposedly purely qualitative turns out to be an "occult" dimension of the quantitative.

PSYCHE: I promise, we'll get to that. But I believe I can in fact demonstrate that it truly is an abyss, and that the irreconcilability of the phenomena of mind with the mechanistic picture of nature is effectively infinite. And, to that end, I want to admonish against falling prey to what I call the *pleonastic fallacy:* that is, the error of thinking that an infinite qualitative distance can be crossed, or even simply diminished, by a sufficient number of finite quantitative steps. The distinction between objective physical events and subjective phenomenal episodes is, I submit, just such an infinite, untraversable distance. No accumulation of mindless physical proficiencies by themselves would ever be enough to add up to even the most elementary of mental powers.

HEPHAISTOS: I can as yet neither accept nor reject the latter claim; but, in principle, I can accept your admonition. [*Raising his hand:*] I hereby pledge that I'll strive to avoid all ontological or explanatory pleonasms. I shall not, I promise, seek to conquer the infinite by way of the incremental. [*Lowering his hand again:*] All right?

PSYCHE: Well, then, I'm more than halfway to winning this debate.

HEPHAISTOS: That I doubt.

PSYCHE: [*With a wry smile:*] Another error to be avoided is what I call the *fallacy of terminal dualism*—by which I mean the mistake of thinking any dualistic account of the relation of mind to matter could constitute an adequate explanation rather than a mere deferral of the problem to another level of mystery.

HEPHAISTOS: Yes, so you've said: no Cartesian ghost in a machine for you. At least we're in agreement there. Something tells me, though, that yours aren't the customary reasons for rejecting dualism: the interaction problem, the causal closure of the physical, the conservation of energy . . . ?

PSYCHE: Oh, certainly not. Perish the thought. I have none of those reservations. For one thing, I regard the so-called interaction problem as silly. Anyone who argues that it would be impossible for a physical mechanical object like a body to interact with an incorporeal noetic substance like the Cartesian soul—presumably because a disembodied intellect can't press buttons or pull levers—is talking nonsense. That's simply to assume that the only real kind of causation is of the mechanical, push-and-pull variety, and such an assumption merely "petitions the principle," as it were. Obviously, even if we're dualists, we're not obliged to conceive of the interaction between soul and body as a kind of *physical* alliance between two disparate substances, interacting in the way two mechanical objects would. The entire hypothesis of a dualism of substances—a dualism, that is, not just numerical, but truly qualitative—implicitly suggests that there are radically differing kinds of causality. And it's preposterous to think that the "incorporeality" of the soul should be thought of as some sort of privation, as if the soul really were just a ghost—just a shadow or wisp of ectoplasm—merely lacking powers that bodies possess, rather than an agency with capacities of a different order, transcending the physical. And it's just as absurd to regard a living body—with its capacities for growth, regeneration, reproduction, homeostasis, and responsiveness to mental intentions, as well as its endlessly diverse coordinated powers, including the power of acquiring new powers—as a mere machine, with a specific range of limited operations. I'm no Cartesian, but I doubt even the Cartesian view is so patently ridiculous as that.[3]

As for the alleged "causal closure of the physical," that's simply an inane prejudice—or, rather, a vacuous tautology—not a rational or scientific principle. It's a bracingly austere dogma, I suppose, that physical actions can have only physical causes, and that nothing mental—such as beliefs, volitions, desires, trains of thought, processes of reasoning, what have you—can influence the flow of physical eventuality. You may think you pluck a rose from a rose tree because you desire to do so; but no, says this morbid fideism, your desires had no role in the act at all; indeed, those desires are themselves only physical results of prior physical causes, or else they're illusions—or both, I suppose. But what doctrinaire gibberish that is. Again, there's no reason for accepting the premise that all causality is mechanical, and so certainly none for conceding the impossibility of real mental causation. Physics isn't a science of predetermination, after all, but just a set of limit-conditions. It might tell us that mental causes can't violate certain minimal principles of causal possibility—a man can't choose to do something forbidden by gravity, but he can choose to do a great many things within the boundaries of the law of gravity. Anyway, we're all fully aware that, at higher levels of organization, there are all sorts of effective non-physical causes.

Hephaistos: Such as?

Psyche: Meaning, for instance.

Hephaistos: Meaning?

Psyche: Of course. If you ask me to hand you a flower and I do so, it was the meaning of your words—which isn't a physical item present in them, but a hermeneutical perspective on them that exists only in our minds—that created the causal link between your wishes and my actions.

Hephaistos: All right, fair enough. But what of the conservation of energy? Even if mental causation differs in kind from mechanical causes, it would surely have to be something in addition to the sum total of physical matter and energy—some additional *force.*

Psyche: Oh, that's just the same error redoubled. No, Phaesty my dear, even if I were concerned about such matters, I wouldn't presume that mental causation needs to add to or subtract from the physical totality of the universe, material or energetic. Again, it's just a mechanistic prejudice that there are no forms of causality other than exchanges of energy between quanta of mass in motion. If, say, there's such a thing as free will—and I believe there is—it operates according to rationales and purposes, final causes rather than mere efficient forces, directing actions toward one course rather than another. But that doesn't mean any additional *physical* impulse has been superadded to reality; and, even if I took such concerns to heart, it's a perfectly logically coherent possibility that physical causes can be directed along different paths within a distribution of possibilities by a kind of causality that *isn't* a physical force, without thereby compromising the total balance of matter and energy in the material order. Why can't mental intention simply provide the flow of energy one terminus rather than another? Why is that a problem? Not that I care, since the scientific principle itself is too general and vague when it comes even to physical causality, and certainly doesn't amount to a rule of absolute physical determinism. So why should we assume that thought or choice functions in the way a mechanical interaction does, by way of physical rather than rational consequence? Goodness, for all we know free will acts like what some quantum theorists call "decoherence": not an addition, but rather a subtraction—a *loss* of information, so to speak—by which a general range of possibility is diminished down to a single local actuality, and the indeterminacy of a potential physical state is resolved into a simpler actual physical state.

HEPHAISTOS: You don't really think that.

PSYCHE: No, but I don't feel the need for any physical theory at all, since I don't believe that all causality is physical. I'm just humoring you. To the degree that a principle like causal closure has any application, it's merely a useful approximation, rather like Newtonian physics in the quantum age—sufficient at the practical level, deficient at the theoretical. To me, it's perfectly reasonable to think mental causation can impress itself like a formal cause on an ensemble of physical forces without itself being yet a further such force, or another physical quantity or impetus. All these classic objections to dualism start from a dogmatic materialism and so—*quelle surprise!*—that's also where they end up.

I might add, to introduce yet a further objection that you haven't mentioned, I'm also not impressed by the argument that mental functions are clearly bound to the brain: that a concussion can render one unconscious, for example, or that a brain trauma can affect one's cognitive abilities, all of which a dualist should surely find perplexing. But that's just the interaction problem inverted. Not even Descartes imagined that the soul can be part of a psychophysical composite without being limited in its operations by the actions, passions, and capacities of the body; he thought of body and soul in union as composing a kind of tertiary substance. Unsatisfactory in my view, but not quite as idiotic as the caricatures suggest.

No, Phaesty, my rejection of dualism as a *final* answer to the problem of mind and body comes from different considerations altogether.

HEPHAISTOS: All right. What are they?

PSYCHE: For one thing, I object in principle to all dualistic answers to any question. Every duality within a single reality must be resoluble to a more basic unity, a more original shared principle, or it remains a mystery. Simply to juxtapose two disparate substances and then declare that, just by being associated with one another, they've been reconciled is to trade in paradox. If body and mind are distinct and yet interact, then there's some ground of commonality that they share, more basic and encompassing than the difference between them.

Now, admittedly, we know that in the early modern period there were dualists who believed that body and soul don't interact at all, but instead merely cooperate—or operate in coordination, to be more precise. Malebranche, for example, proposed a theory of "occasionalism," which says that, despite all appearances, soul and body don't directly influence one another at all, but are instead miraculously synchronized with one another in parallel streams of causality by the will of God. One mental event leads to another, one corporeal event to another, yet neither level of operation really affects the other; they appear to do so only because of the persistent, pervasive harmonizing activity of divine providence.[4] There's something convenient in a claim that unimpeachably unfalsifiable; but, since I don't believe souls are ghosts or bodies machines, I can't say it appeals to me—certainly not enough to make me want to abandon the commonsense view of things. So I have to believe that, to whatever degree body and soul differ from one another, they're also always already reconciled to one another at a deeper level where they operate as a single agency. Anyway, the "will of God" isn't a real answer to anything, since "will" is neither a logical nor an ontological principle. After all, not even God could reconcile intrinsically irreconcilable substances, any more than God could create a square circle. Omnipotence extends as far as the very ends of all that's possible; but it doesn't extend to the logically impossible. If the world of God's creation contains both mind and matter as fully distinct realities—which, again, I don't really grant—then it seems strange to suggest that they're mutually inimical principles; how could they both proceed from the one divine nature, then? More to the point, I find the notion hideous. If I consist in two separate causal streams that can never really interact, then I, as an embodied soul or an ensouled body, do not actually exist; and I have the impertinence to believe that I do. When I pluck a rose, it's my hand that does the work; when a thought passes through my mind, it's that thought itself that causes certain regions of my brain to flicker and flare. I'm not a fiction composed from two separate histories, only apparently combined with one another as a kind of divine stage effect. At least, I hope I'm not. Body and soul act in concert, not just in harmony. Indeed, I believe, body simply is soul made concretely manifest.

No, in the end, a dualism can never be more than a provisional answer to any question; for two qualitatively different *relata* to be reconciled, there must be some broader, simpler, more encompassing unity in which they participate, some more basic ontological ground, a shared medium underlying both and repugnant to neither. Any two material objects, for instance, however they may differ in configuration or consistency, can enter into some kind of relation with one another precisely because both participate in the more fundamental unifying reality of materiality; they're not antithetical or alien to one another *in essence;* and the term of their union is neither accidental nor extrinsic to what they are. So, too, the relation between mind and matter, if they're really distinct from one another, has to be traceable to some metaphysical or logical medium that comprises them both in itself and provides the basis of their congruity. Only at that level can one hope for any sort of answer to the "problem of mind." All *final* answers are in some way monistic, or they aren't final. The many must become the one, the dual must become the single, the complex must become the simple if reason is to reach the answers it seeks. Actually, that's a rule that will prove extremely important later.

Hephaistos: I'm still not clear: do you or do you not accept some kind of dualism of body and soul?

Psyche: Some kind, perhaps, *conditionally;* or some kind of distinction conceptually, at least. But not an ultimate duality, no. Chiefly I believe that "soul" is simply the rational life principle that expresses itself in the whole organism, body and mind alike. The ancient view, that is, as opposed to the modern. I don't deny that there's a kind of dual relationship between mind and matter, but I think it's only a provisional or contingent structural reality . . . a kind of synthetic dynamism intrinsic to finite existence. At some deeper level they're one. And in any organism, the living, thinking, *animate* reality is that organism itself, as a single totality, in both physiology and psychology. Whatever provisional distinctions we admit, therefore, I'm interested in the more original, more fundamental unity that underlies their relation—the primordial reality in which body and mind alike arise as an integrated expression. I suppose I could accept something like the early Berkeley's idealism of disembodied minds, at least up to a point, as being an improvement on Descartes or Malebranche, simply because it dissolves that galling duality altogether. For Berkeley, physical causes are merely apparent; in reality, they're just coherent juxtapositions of phenomena in a purely mental "space" that have the appearance of physically causal sequences. God superimposes the impression of heat upon the impression of leaping flames; fire doesn't *cause* heat, but is simply associated with it by a kind of divine narrative convention. The difficulty for me is that I believe in matter too, as a real expression of that primordial reality I mentioned, and believe in real physical relations too. How dreary, after all, to eliminate one dimension of the real in favor of another, whether mind in favor of matter or matter in favor of mind, when one should instead be eliminating the intellectual error of supposing a conflict or ultimate irreconcilability between them. After all, while I'm sympathetic to relativizing any hard-and-fast division between logical and physical causality—as I'll explain in time—I can't very well start by demanding that the materialist accept the self-evident reality of mental phenomena while myself attempting to circumvent the self-evident reality of the physical order.

In the end, it seems clear to me that all our quandaries begin with the mechanical philosophy; for, if physical causality is devoid of mental properties, mind can be only a ghost or an illusion, and plainly it's neither. This is why I still prefer certain more ancient views of things. After all, neither Platonists, nor Aristotelians, nor Stoics, nor any of the Jewish or Christian or Muslim or other metaphysicians of late antiquity or the Middle Ages, could have conceived of the body or the cosmos as a machine; they saw matter as being always already informed by indwelling rational causes, and thus open to—and in fact directed toward and filled with—mind. Nor did they conceive of spirit as being immaterial in a purely privative sense, in the way that a vacuum isn't aerial. If anything, they thought of spirit as being more substantial, more actual than matter, a higher reality in which matter had to participate in order to be anything at all.

HEPHAISTOS: So, lest we get caught on this hook indefinitely, just tell me: what's your preferred model of the relation?

PSYCHE: I'd say it's this: whatever the nature of matter may be, the primal reality of all things is mind. To the degree that matter exists in its own proper nature, it does so as a product of mind, subsisting as a set of rational relations within a larger . . . a larger *equation*, as it were. This I believe because I don't think mind can be a physically reducible or emergent reality arising from truly mindless matter, nor do I think matter could possibly constitute the simpler, more comprehensive ground of unity between the corporeal and the mental. Matter without mind can't become mind, but mind can become all things. Mind *in itself* must be that simpler, more basic, unifying ground, and matter must be an expression of mind—infinite mind, in fact. My position is idealism, in short, not of the sort the early Berkeley espoused, but of that classical variety that sees the material realm not as a mere mirage, but rather as a real but dependent emanation of the noetic—the higher mental—realm. It's also, perhaps, Aristotelian, in that I insist that mind and life are one reality ultimately: that the same principle of rational relations that creates the integrated and self-replicating reality of an organism is also the principle of its consciousness and mental agency. And that principle is . . . well, in Greek, *psychē* . . . "soul," "life." . . .

HEPHAISTOS: Now we're lapsing into metaphysics, for which I confess I have small appetite. Just tell me, are we talking about "mind" in some grand unified sense—the mind of God—or are we talking about individual minds, such as yours and mine?

PSYCHE: Both. We're talking about infinite mind as the ground and end of all things, and about individual minds and bodies as finite contractions or irisations or crystallizations or radiations of that more original reality. What I'm hoping is that I can convince you that an examination of the latter points toward the reality of the former. This can't be proved in an absolute way, but I think it can be shown to be the most rational option on offer for making sense of reality. But we aren't there as yet. I'm glad you asked, however, because it reminds me that I also wanted to warn against the *psychologistic fallacy*. One of the especially evil aspects of Cartesianism, of course, is that it understands mind, soul, affectivity, reason, psychological personality, and all the other forms of mental existence as all one and the same thing, all belonging to a little mysterious monad that's also the individual psychological self of any given person, only extrinsically associated with a body. Thus, where any aspect of this curious entity could be seen as lacking, the whole could be presumed absent. To the physicalist critic, this psychologistic holism, for want of a better term, is that little homunculus's most convenient attribute; it's rather easy to find evidence against the existence of an indivisible psychological subject within us, responsible for every facet of our cognitive and intentional and perceptual lives; a skeptic need only demonstrate one instance of mental life that eludes the control of the psychological self to call the soul in its entirety into question.

HEPHAISTOS: So, when you speak of the soul—the *psychē*, that is—how would you like me to take it?

PSYCHE: In the full range of its classical acceptations. Even the Platonists, for instance, though they took a fairly grim view of the material order, and though many modern philosophers clumsily conflate their views with Cartesian dualism, didn't see the soul as just some small indivisible entity that was at once the psychological self, the subject of phenomenal experience, and the intellect, all extrinsically allied to a corporeal automaton. For them, the soul was the body's life, spiritual and organic at once, an organizing principle of spiritual and physical unity and harmony, comprising the appetites and passions no less than rational intellect, while the body was a material reflection of a rational and ideal order. For them, matter might have seemed at times a disagreeable sort of thing, but it wasn't the inert, opaque matter of mechanistic thought; rather, it was a real if imperfect mirror of eternal splendors and verities, open to the light of spirit. Then, for Aristotelian tradition, the human soul was the "form" that gave life and order to the body and mind, the very essence and nature of the whole rational and animal organism, the vital power animating, pervading, and shaping human beings into living, developing unities. And so on. Throughout the ancient and mediaeval world, the soul was the source and immanent entelechy of corporeal life, encompassing everything living: animal functions and abstract intellect, sensation and reason, emotion and ratiocination, flesh and spirit, natural aptitude and supernatural longing. Think, say, of Neoplatonism's vision of the human soul as at once grounding and grounded in and informing nature, communicating at large in the one ubiquitous soul of all things, rising up at its heights beyond this world to the divine mind from which all things flow, and even touching upon the absolute divine oneness in which and by which all things are. That's certainly not the little psychological homunculus of Cartesian thought. Rather, it's a reality at once particular and universal, both "mine" and transcendent of "me" in my psychological finitude, within me and beyond me, constituting me in myself but also placing me in communion with all life and spirit in the universe.

And, of course, there are some fairly ghastly implications in the Cartesian view. Recall that it denied reason to animals, and as a result denied all the other attributes of mental life to them as well, including the capacity for conscious experiences such as pain, and claimed that animals are just carnal machines, which only *seem* to have feelings. No one in antiquity or the Middle Ages could have embraced so foul a notion. In the ancient view, all that lives is soul, and all that is soul is aware. I won't discuss the atrocities to which the Cartesian doctrine sometimes led. All I'll say is that the impoverishment of the concept of soul to some isolated incorporeal thing that's at once the individual self as well as all the self's mental properties, propensities, memories, and actions is absurd for any number of reasons.

Hephaistos: I agree, of course, though for very different reasons.

Psyche: Very different indeed, I'd think. One of mine, for instance, is that I think it's evident that consciousness isn't simply a psychological phenomenon. The little "empirical ego" in each of us subsists within a wider, deeper mental reality, and is sustained by what—again, to misappropriate the language of Kant—one might call the "transcendental ego." There's an "I think" in each of us more basic than the ego, more basic than psychological identity. This remains constant and immutable—and uniformly the same from one person to another—even as our personal psychological selves grow and change and fade away. It's the unmoving ground of the mutable self, the pure subjectivity underlying psychological distinctions. I mean, an amnesiac whose entire past has vanished irrecoverably still has suffered no disruption of that pure vanishing point of personal perspective; the basic activity of his or her mind in taking in the world, quite apart from any psychological impressions, is exactly the same as it was prior to his or her loss of memory. He or she may not necessarily retain the same mental acuity as before, let alone the same contents of conscious thought; but the fundamental *act* of consciousness remains just as it was when he or she was in full possession of a continuous psychological identity.

HEPHAISTOS: All right, I understand. We're discussing the soul, not simply the self. To your mind, the latter exists by virtue of the former, but the former is more than the latter.

PSYCHE: Precisely.

HEPHAISTOS: Well, so what? Even a physicalist like me can agree with that, albeit on wholly different premises and with a preference for some term other than "soul." I think of those deeper, more impersonal, more imperturbably constant aspects of the mind as physiological rather than transcendental, and to me their persistence even in a violently disordered mind is a good argument that what we call mind is really just the composite effect of various separable brain-functions.

PSYCHE: How curious, since to me it seems to prove just the opposite. Oh, well . . . we'll get to the issue in time.

HEPHAISTOS: Not if your index of dangerous fallacies goes on interminably.

PSYCHE: All right, a few more, but quickly. There's the *mereological* or *decompositional fallacy:* the notion that it's enough to reduce a phenomenon to its constituent physical parts in order to explain what it is and how it came to exist. A tempting notion, but unless, after dissolving a phenomenon into its physical ingredients, one can reconstruct that phenomenon from those ingredients according to wholly physical principles, without invoking any higher causes of organization whatsoever, one has achieved only a certain quantification of the phenomenon's material structure; one has explained nothing.

Related to this is the *genetic fallacy:* the mistake of thinking that to have described a thing's material history and physical origin, phylogenic or ontogenic, is to have explained that thing exhaustively. So too there's the *cui bono fallacy:* the notion that, if one can simply identify "what good" or "what use" a natural power or faculty might serve, one has adequately accounted for it; but it's not enough to claim that, say, consciousness evolved because it was evolutionarily advantageous unless one can also give a plausible account of *how* it could have arisen from mindless matter in the first place. And then there's what I call the *Narcissean*—or maybe *Narcissistic*—*fallacy.*

HEPHAISTOS: That one sounds vaguely interesting, at least.

PSYCHE: I don't know about that. It might also just be called the *fallacy of displacement.* It's merely the error we make when we project our own mental agency onto some inanimate medium or device we're employing, as though it were the source of that agency, rather as Narcissus mistook his own reflection for another person—but that's a fallacy peculiarly applicable to computational theories of the mind, which we'll address in due time.

HEPHAISTOS: I look forward to that discussion with particular keenness, I have to say. I think computers in particular pose a formidable problem for your view of things.

PSYCHE: We'll see.

IV

Terms

Hermes: If I may interject here, it might be wise to define a few of our terms a bit more exactly before moving on. We've spoken fairly freely of "mind," of "consciousness," of "intentionality," but whether we all understand the same things by those words isn't clear.

Psyche: Quite true. Yes. Well, by "consciousness" I mean subjective experience, immediate awareness, existing in an entirely private and incommunicable way. One can also call it "phenomenal" or "qualitative" consciousness, because it's the experience of how things appear or seem or feel, the private awareness of a single *quale* or of several *qualia*, to use the preferred technical term—the "what it's like," that is, of seeing the color blue, or of tasting a glass of wine, or of feeling a draft of wind come in through a window. It applies, though, not only to sensory experience, even though a great deal of philosophy of mind often proceeds as if it does. It includes all forms of subjective experience, including one's awareness of one's own emotional states, of one's intuitions, of the atmosphere of one's moods or convictions, of what it feels like to believe something or to imagine something . . . even one's awareness of one's awareness.

Hermes: So I thought.

Psyche: Mind you, this is complicated by the reality that some philosophers like to distinguish between consciousness and awareness, or consciousness and cognizance, postulating that there may be such a thing as unconscious experience. Maybe we're aware of things of which our conscious intellect is not immediately apprised: a subliminal perception or suggestion, perhaps, or something just at the periphery of our attention that the conscious mind doesn't quite register. The *field* of one's awareness or cognizance may be wider and more constant than the specific focus of mental attention, and consciousness may exist only by degrees, according to the contractions or intensifications of that attention. Some philosophers even speak of "access consciousness,"[5] a kind of mental state one possesses that has no phenomenal content but that becomes actively conscious in relation to other mental states, such as when one is, say, reasoning something out, or constructing a discourse. I find all of that only marginally interesting, however, and rather beside the point. When I use the word, therefore, I mean all forms of subjective, immediate, private knowledge, in whatever degree or intensity it happens to exist.

As for "intentionality," that's simply the technical term for what the mind does when it's directed toward something under a particular aspect. That is, it's the "aboutness" of mental activity, the directedness of the mind toward meaning, identification, recognition, purpose, or some other end; it's the mind's ability and will to interpret, to understand what it perceives as *this* or *that*, or as meaning this thing or that thing. A man walking his dog sees *that* moving object at a distance as a squirrel he'd rather his dog not catch the scent of; a driver sees *this* red and white octagon as an instruction to stop her car and look both ways before proceeding; I speak *these* words as intending a certain intelligible content for you to interpret; I see a certain statue not simply as a shape without name or reference, but precisely as an image of, say, Artemis drawing her bow; or, alternatively, if I don't recognize what the figure represents, I interpret it simply as an object obstructing my vision; and so forth.

When I speak of "thought," I mean merely the flow of reason or impressions or memories or anything else in the mind, connected in mental sequences, one thought yielding to another, one thought giving rise to another. By "cognition," I mean merely the process of knowing or recognizing something. By "subjective unity" or "unity of consciousness," I mean the ability of the mind to receive the world in a unified and integrated field of experience, as something simultaneous and continuous, from the unique perspective of an individual self. By "mind," I mean all these acts and powers, as well as others that don't occur to me just now.

I'll add only that, even if I tend to speak of these various aspects of the mind in separation from one another, I don't in fact believe they're ever really entirely separate and distinct realities in themselves. For instance, I don't believe there's real consciousness without some kind of intentionality, or vice-versa, and I don't believe that either can be separated in practice from the profound unity of subjective mental life, or from sequences of thought, and so forth. When I spoke about degrees of attentiveness a moment ago, for instance, I was implicitly taking note of the dependency of consciousness upon intentionality. That is, the more we mentally attend to something—direct our minds at it, that is, under some particular aspect, such as "object" or "sign" or "meaning"—the more conscious we are of it; and, conversely, the more we're conscious of something, the more it commands our attention. At the same time, the aspect under which we're conscious of that thing is dependent on how we think about it, and how we reflect upon it; and such reflection is an intentional exercise; and so on and so forth. There are complexities within complexities, distinctions within distinctions, but no real separations here into independent faculties or functions. I mention this only because a very great deal of current philosophy of mind consists in isolating one or another aspect of mental activity—usually consciousness—and attempting either to explain it or to explain it away, without acknowledging how inextricably interwoven it is with all those other aspects, and then to try to redescribe those remaining aspects as just so many physical functions. Many Anglophone philosophers blunderingly segregate intentionality from consciousness, for instance, as if the former were merely a matter of mental propositions—"that tree is an elm," "she's interested in me," that sort of thing—and as if consciousness were nothing but sheer sense-impression, self-evident without any directedness of the mind. It's a divide-and-conquer approach; it's also sheer fantasy. Mental acts are not just the coordinated operations of separable faculties.

HEPHAISTOS: As you shall no doubt argue at length anon. So then, what now?

PSYCHE: A little intellectual history, I think.

V

The Rise of Mechanism

Psyche: So much of our understanding of nature is shaped by how we choose to interrogate it. Understanding is so often the ward of method, and every method begins from certain presuppositions about what we should ask and how we should ask it, and those presuppositions in turn determine what answers we can elicit, or can even recognize as meaningful. We're also all too often unaware that our method is bound to a metaphysics that we simply unwittingly presume, or presume with only partial awareness. In fact, our metaphysics is often nothing other than our method, mistaken for the very truth it's supposed to help us seek. At least, that's very much the story of a great deal of modern science and philosophy.

I'm not, let me hasten to say, an absolutely doctrinaire Aristotelian. But, as you've noted, dear Phaesty, I do have a habit of speaking an Aristotelian patois when the topic is causality. I find it convenient to do so, but I'm also trying to point toward a wider truth. We're all old enough, we immortals, to remember a time when the vision of nature fostered by the dominant schools of Western philosophy was one of a very particular kind of integral order. There was no hard-and-fast division between what we would now regard as physical and metaphysical explanations, principally because either would have seemed incomplete in isolation from the other. The fourfold system of causality that we associate with Aristotelian tradition, for instance, which was the standard vision of cosmic order in the pre-modern Western and Islamic worlds, depicted the cosmos as an interweaving of logical relations, some coming from "above," as it were, some from "below," but all also from "within"—which is the detail of the story too often forgotten. Of the classical tetrad of causes—the material, the efficient, the formal, and the final—it's often said that modern science retained only the first two; in fact, it retained none, and this was because modern intellectual culture had already come to misunderstand these causes as *forces* standing in extrinsic relation to one another. The old model was not—as we often forget—a scientific account of things in anything like the modern sense; nor today would it actually constitute a rival to the sciences as we know them. But we tend to remember the scheme only in broad outline, while rarely recalling what it was a scheme *for*.

HEPHAISTOS: Oh, it's not all that mysterious, as I recall.

HERMES: All right. How would you characterize it then?

HEPHAISTOS: Well, more or less as the sort of process I engage in whenever I return to my workshop. If I wish to make a vessel of gold, the molten ore is my "material" cause, the idea I have of the vessel I'm making and of all the attributes proper to such an object are its "formal" cause, the implements and exertions by which I fashion it are the "efficient" causes, and the end for which it's intended—say, a vessel for drinking wine or holding flowers or filling a niche in a temple—is its "final" cause. The final cause guides the whole process and so prompts specific kinds of efficient causes into action, which in turn impress the formal cause upon the material cause. Simple enough.

PSYCHE: Simple enough, but also too simple in itself. Admittedly, it's common to think in terms of the manufacture of an artifact when trying to describe the fourfold scheme, but that can also obscure the deeper logic of the concept.

HEPHAISTOS: Or make its deficiencies obvious. What else is that scheme except the logic of manufacture illegitimately transposed from its proper, limited sphere and forced upon our picture of nature, as if everything—from a blade of grass to a whale to the heavens themselves—were a kind of teleologically guided invention? Surely modern science couldn't have been born so long as that picture of intrinsic purposes and predetermined forms held sway over the human imagination.

Psyche: But you're reversing the order of logic here. Surely you know that this fourfold structure of causality was seen as holding true at every level of concrete existence. It was never merely the logic of artificial compositions illicitly extended to natural kinds. For instance, you spoke of molten gold as the material cause of the vessel you were crafting; but, at a lower level, gold itself might be accounted the form, as imposed on a collection of molecular or atomic constituents; and, at the lowest and most ubiquitous level of all physical things, there's "prime matter," the universal substrate underlying all substances, which is nothing in itself except a kind of pure potency. Well, that's just the logic of causal hierarchy—of "top-down causality," as it's sometimes called.

Hephaistos: Which is precisely the problem, because it mistakes emergent realities—natural systems that arise from a material basis and that then, having emerged, exercise an influence of their own—for primordial realities that don't emerge from matter, but that instead give matter—or, rather, "prime matter"—actuality from "above." But what's "prime matter"? What is this substrate in things that isn't actually anything at all, but only purely potential, with no actuality of its own apart from the formal causes that give it substance and shape?

Psyche: As you yourself just said, it's simply a principle of possibility as such, the capacity for becoming, which remains unchanging throughout all the changes that the things of the cosmos go through. It's what makes it possible for a seed to become a tree . . . or gold to become a vessel . . . while also remaining one continuous process.

Hephaistos: But that's precisely my point: see how the metaphor of the workshop has been inverted, allowing for the illegitimate imputation of a kind of designing logic to nature's processes. Even the mere potential for something to be anything at all has been mistaken for something analogous to some infinitely ductile material element ready to be wrought into a product of magical manufacture.

Psyche: I would say the opposite: that a simple logic of predication—which is what the fourfold scheme of causality really is—has traditionally informed our understanding of the rational structure underlying all things, including objects of human manufacture, and has revealed such manufacture to be only a special instance of that more general order of rational relations by which anything that exists *can* exist. The lowest level—prime matter—isn't some sort of ductile element. It's not a thing in itself. It's just a name for the possibility of both stability and change within certain limits. It's simply a logical predicate that names a kind of continuity underlying—and thereby permitting—real change.

HEPHAISTOS: A logic of . . . *predication?*

PSYCHE: Yes. Really, that's all that's at stake. It's rather unfortunate, actually, that we use one word, "causality," to characterize both the premodern scheme for describing nature's rational order and the modern scheme for describing its mechanical functions. Try, though, for a moment to cast your mind back to ancient days and to think of the fourfold classification not as a primitive version of modern physics, but rather as a sophisticated way of isolating and defining any given object or event. If I ask you to explain to me what something is and what it does—what its substance and its operations are—I'm asking you at once what kind of thing it is, and what it consists of, and how it came to be, and what the full range of its potentials is. In short, I'm asking for its material, formal, efficient, and final *definitions.* If, for example, I had never seen a tree before and were to ask you to explain one to me fully, you might first tell me about its vegetal constitution—the organic nature of the materials composing it—as well as about the nature of trees in general and about the kind of tree it is in particular; and then you might tell me how it grew from a seed, and then what its ultimate state should be if all its potentials had been rendered actual—assuming it proceeds without hindrance to that state; and then you might even add an explanation of how it fits into the environment as a whole. In short, you'd be describing its entire natural structure to me, not telling me a tale about how it had been put together by some extrinsic agency from disparate parts, like one of those automata of yours. You'd be describing the web of intrinsic rational relations by which it's identifiable as the thing it is. This, I submit, is the true meaning of the old Aristotelian scheme, which we lose sight of when we insist on describing it always in terms of human making. It concerns a still deeper logic of explanation, which may not be sufficient in itself as a model of the sciences, but which nonetheless, at a more fundamental level, is what makes the sciences possible. We can't dispense with these dimensions of understanding—these definitions—and still have anything for science to be about. They constitute a basic logic that must be presumed if asking questions about things is to be an intelligible practice. To abandon them would be to leave nothing behind except perhaps Kant's imperceptible, unthinkable "noumenon" or "thing-in-itself," which the mind can never reach or even conceive of (and which, incidentally, is a nonsensical concept).[6]

HEPHAISTOS: But surely the ancient scheme is also a theory of actual causation: that is, a theory of how things come to be.

PSYCHE: Of course. That's essential to any logical description of an object. The entire universe, on this view, exists because "matter," in the sense of pure potentiality, is always being made actual through the imposition of forms, accomplished by the working of effective forces defined by the ends toward which they're moving. But that way of seeing things isn't a rival account of reality over against the processes of physical causation investigated by today's sciences; rather, it's a picture of what underlies those processes, the basic rational integrity of reality that assures us that causes are not just arbitrary relations—that my kiss on my beloved's cheek will not result in the beloved turning into a pig rather than merely blushing with pleasure. I mean, the rational consistency of causation—the complex, ordered reality of a cosmos rather than a diffuse chaos of energetic collisions—is nothing to take for granted.

Now, I admit that the presupposition informing the older vision was that reality and our knowledge of it have one and the same shape—that the world out there already has a nature like that of something thought through, according to a specific intentionality, under the aspects of mental forms—and hence the, so to speak, *repetition* of the world in our perceptions and thoughts actually reflects its intrinsic nature. So yes: this web of "causes" is at once a system of predication and also a general ontology—a picture of the structure of existence itself, as well as of the structure of mind, and the structure of the interaction of the two. The world consists in an intricate reticulation of rational relations, and the mind in mirroring those relations really knows the world. Only then do the sciences conduct us more deeply into the mysteries of the realities we already know, by enriching our explanatory palette. But the sciences don't render our primordial knowledge of the real illusory.

HEPHAISTOS: Don't they? Alternatively, one could argue that all of this is precisely why the older scheme was an impediment to the development of early modern science: it rendered natural philosophers unable to distinguish between the world as a reality in itself and the world as a representation of our thoughts. The two had to be severed from one another before the real work of discovery could begin.

PSYCHE: Is that what happened, though? Is that the whole reason for which early modern science rejected what it took to be the Aristotelian view of things?

HEPHAISTOS: Naturally. It was in order to make room for unprejudiced empirical and theoretical investigation of the physical world. Final and formal causes, even if they're real, can't be examined directly, and they're far too likely to be called upon to provide easy explanations where we have no evidence. So it was necessary to eschew them altogether, to approach nature as a collection of mechanisms that could be examined without any presuppositions regarding some mystically indwelling teleology or some invisible informing power from "above." Scientists learned to start from the barest facts, not from the ends and purposes we imagine we see imprinted on nature, and to proceed by small, cumulative steps, experimentally, inductively. And the success of this philosophy is beyond contestation. The scrupulous refusal of all metaphysical conjectures about "higher" causes required scientists to exercise the most precise attentiveness possible to the facts, and to dedicate themselves to observation, experiment, and classification. And see what prodigies it has led to.

PSYCHE: I grant all this. But, then, did the new perspective really sever reality from representation, or did it merely offer a substitute representation—one that was useful in some ways and pernicious in others? What you're saying, after all, is that the extraordinary fruitfulness of modern scientific method was achieved in large part by a severe *narrowing* of investigative focus. Far from rescuing the real from our commonsense representations of the world, as you suggest, it subordinated reality to another, *entirely* metaphorical representation, and by this artifice succeeded in isolating certain organic and physical functions from their normal contexts. It advanced by way of an elective abstinence from attempts to know reality as such and by a concentration on mathematical descriptions of purely physical events. It was achieved precisely by piously refraining from speculations regarding vast ranges of experience and knowledge. Very well. So the first principle of the new organon was a negative one: the exclusion of any consideration of formal and final causes, as well as of any distinct principle of "life," in favor of an ideally inductive method purged of metaphysical assumptions, and of a conception of natural systems as mere machine processes, and of an understanding of all real causality as an exchange of energy through antecedent forces working upon material mass. Everything physical became, in a sense, reducible to the mechanics of local motion; in time, especially as the centuries wore on, even complex organic order came to be understood as the emergent result of physical forces moving through time from past to future as if through Newtonian space, producing consequences that were all mathematically calculable, with all discrete physical causes ultimately reducible to the most basic level of material existence.

Initially, of course, this program hadn't yet been complicated by the problems we're discussing. In the first pale dawn of modern method, most thinkers were content to draw brackets around physical nature, and to allow for the existence of realities—mind, soul, disembodied spirits, God—that they saw as essentially extrinsic to the purely mechanical order those realities animated, inhabited, or created. They didn't treat matter as the universal principle of all existing things. But they did replace the classical concept of God as infinite being and rationality, in which all things exist, with the God of deism, the craftsman who had constructed the machine from without. And they replaced the classical concept of the soul—the rational life-principle informing and shaping and vivifying living things—with that Cartesian ghost haunting the dead matter of the machine of the body: a disembodied "thinking thing" magically animating a corpse. For a time, the new dualism flourished, content to segregate the physical from the mental and to grant each its own domain, but of course such ontological liberality proved unsustainable. Reason abhors a dualism. No scientist worth his or her salt can rest satisfied with some realm of forbidden mystery, either within nature or adjacent to it. For the truly inquiring scientific intellect, any ultimate ground of explanation must be one that unites all dimensions of being in a simpler, more conceptually parsimonious principle. Thus, inevitably, what began as method soon metastasized into a metaphysics, almost by inadvertence. For a truly scientific view of reality, it came to be believed, everything—even mind—must be reducible to one and the same mechanics of motion. Those methodological brackets that had been so helpfully drawn around the physical order now became the very shape of reality itself.

This created an irresoluble dilemma, though. It had been the very principles and characteristics of mind that had been excluded from the scientific picture of nature in order to make the new method possible. Form and finality are paradigms, ideal structures, purposes, expressions of intentionality; they are of their nature intrinsically mindlike relations. Hence they had to be banished from our picture of nature: reduced to subjective impressions, illicit projections. Hence, too, the need for that gray mathematical abstraction that Galileo identified as science's proper realm of study, but that so many came to think of as reality in itself. At one time, the belief that there was a coincidence between the structure of mind and the structure of nature had provided the mediating principle between them: form. As we've already effectively said, it was assumed that the human intellect can truly know the external world for two related reasons: firstly, because the form inhabiting an object of knowledge and the form appearing in the mind are one and the same form, expressed in two different modes; and, secondly, because the object of knowledge and the mind itself both together belong to one and the same source of intelligibility and being underlying all things, so that the knowing and the known are, at their ground, always already one. According to the new model, however, what real communion could exist between mind and matter?

Matter is supposedly nothing more than mass and force, and all material actions are supposedly nothing more than exchanges of energy accomplished by thoughtless movement, immediate contact, direct force, and direct resistance. The universe came to be seen as, in essence, mindless technology, a composite of intrinsically unrelated parts, in which unified subjectivity, intentional directedness, incommunicable privacy of perspective, the capacity for abstract concepts, and all the other mysterious powers of mind have no proper place. There's no room in such an order for mind as it truly exists. A proper reduction of mind to matter, in this vision of things, could only be the mind's elimination.

HEPHAISTOS: All to the good. No proper inductive method begins already assured of the results of its investigation. Neither can we explain a phenomenon just by attaching it to some purpose. You complain of tautologies; but what could be more vacuous than to say that the explanation of a tree is that it exists for the purpose of being a tree?

PSYCHE: Conversely, how do you interpret the processes that produce a tree if you're not first aware that it's a tree you're investigating? A tree, apprehended as an organic hierarchy of parts and causes, with a specific ontogeny and phenotype, is the phenomenal reality whose manifest teleology instructs the scientist in what he or she is measuring. It's not as if, absent that phenomenon, we could simply immerse ourselves in the welter of atomic—or even molecular or cellular—events and then inductively construct the object of our investigations. And, really, how trite of you, Phaesty. Anyone who begins with the assumption that nature is a purely mechanistic order has done precisely what you say the sciences should strive to avoid doing: start, that is, from an assurance of what the results of one's investigations must look like.

I tend to think that early modern method misunderstood itself. Even just as a working fiction, the mechanical model was never of more than limited usefulness. Pure induction is a fantasy—a desirable one maybe, but unattainable at the last. An investigator of nature can't reconstruct reality *ab ovo*, just arranging and rearranging catalogues of bare particulars until he or she somehow sifts out individual objects and begins to discern integrated systems. Even the most rigorously empirical science must begin the work of analysis, at even the most elementary of levels, by attempting to interpret each datum in light of some presumed end. Even evolutionary theory asks *why* one particular mechanism evolved rather than another, and can provide a theoretical answer only by reference to the final result of the evolutionary line under scrutiny. Even if form and purpose have been *conceptually* demoted in rank to posterior effects, produced by the unguided interactions of material forces and "selected" by purely material conditions, in practice the scientist must frequently proceed *as if* forms and ends were causes. Evolutionary biologists explain an evolutionary adaptation partly by "reverse engineering" it from whatever purposes it serves in the present, and by trying to imagine what other purposes its earlier forms might have served in the past. The best way of understanding an organism is often to treat it as an intentional system, with innate purposes, even if modern metaphysical dogmas oblige the researcher to turn around and proclaim that such purposes and guiding paradigms are only apparently real—useful fictions of method and nothing more.

HEPHAISTOS: Well, yes. As Kant pointed out, we're destined by our natural faculties of perception and representation to perceive natural phenomena in teleological terms.

PSYCHE: But how does one then know that it's only a perception? If the method yields sound results, maybe that's because the method is in keeping with reality. Why presume the mechanical perspective is correct and the teleological perspective false even in cases where it's the latter rather than the former that produces intelligible explanations?

HEPHAISTOS: Some presuppositions are just basic.

PSYCHE: And some seem basic because they're just indurated dogmas, and by presuming those dogmas a scientist isn't merely suspending judgment. Rather, he or she is determining in advance what he or she will choose to regard as real or as only apparent, no matter what he or she observes.

I would note too that, before "higher causes" like form and finality could be excised from the grammar of the sciences, they first had to be radically misconstrued. By the late sixteenth century, the residual Aristotelian terminology still found in the sciences had long since been evacuated of its original meaning. When, say, Francis Bacon took leave of final causality, it wasn't really the final causality of distant previous epochs he was abandoning, but something already altered and compromised by mechanistic habits of thought. Form and finality had already come to be conceived of as physical forces or influences extrinsic to one another, and to the efficient causes they evoked, and to the material substrate to which they gave shape and substance. Efficiency too was already thought of not as a rationally guided movement toward an end, prompting certain potentials to become actual for that purpose, but chiefly as pure force and instrumentality, while prime matter was no longer understood essentially as pure potentiality, but rather as some sort of universal physical stuff possessing boundless plasticity. The elements of nature weren't imagined, as they had been in the classical and mediaeval synthesis, as having an intrinsic disposition toward order or vital integrity; they were seen simply as inert ingredients upon which formal determinations were adventitiously impressed, under the external guidance of final causes that operated merely as factitious designs. And so, seen thus, form and finality soon came to seem not only superfluous suppositions, but little more than features of an inferior and obsolete mechanical model.

But, of course, one can't really reject something one doesn't understand. The old concept of an *aitia* or *causa* simply didn't mean what moderns mean when they speak of a "cause." As I've already suggested, it's more correct to think of *aitiai* or *causae*, in the ancient or mediaeval sense, as "explanations," "rationales," "logical descriptions," or (still better) "rational relations"—not a defective physics, but that grammar of predication I spoke of earlier, describing the inherent logical structure of anything that exists insofar as it exists, and reflecting a world in which things and events are at once discretely identifiable and yet also part of the larger dynamic continuum of the whole. It was a simple logical picture of a reality in which both stability and change can be recognized and described. And these relations were intrinsic, indiscerptibly integral, and distinct dimensions of a single causal logic, not separate forces arranged in only accidental alliance. A final cause was most properly an inherent natural end, not just an externally imposed design, even if sometimes design was required to produce certain objects; it was at once a thing's intrinsic fullness and its participation in the totality of nature. As I say, it's a shame that we use the word "cause" univocally here, given that an "aetiological" or "causal" relation in this ancient sense is less like a physical interaction or exchange of energy than it is like a mathematical equation, or like the syntax of a coherent sentence, or perhaps like the coordination between memory and expectation in our awareness of the present. Admittedly, as I've said, this is a picture of reality that comes from ages in which it was assumed that the structure of the world was analogous to the structure of rational thought. But, then again, wasn't that an eminently sensible assumption, given that there appears to be a more than illusory or accidental reciprocal openness between mind and world, and given that the mind appears genuinely able to penetrate the physical order by way of purely noetic practices like mathematics and logic?

Hephaistos: Eminently sensible assumptions can also be eminently false.

Psyche: True, but here the question is whether the sensible assumption is also the one that makes better sense of the data. If nature abounds in phenomena that the mechanistic paradigm can't accommodate, like consciousness—which is to say phenomenality as such, the entire "appearing" of the world to any mind at all—why on earth or in the heavens or here in the Intermundia should anyone conclude that this paradigm captures the entirety of reality, or that the older mindlike paradigm of nature is an illegitimate supposition, or just some version of the pathetic fallacy imposing personal characteristics on impersonal forces? I repeat, even if the attenuated causal language of mechanism served a sound purpose in shaping the sciences, it did so not by expanding—but by severely contracting—the realm of its competencies. And that certainly leaves human thinkers no better off with regard to the questions we're discussing here than their ancestors were. In fact, the modern position is by far the more perplexing. At least those more ancient theorists enjoyed a perspective in which the mind was seen not as some astounding and imponderable anomaly within nature that had to be forcibly reconciled with an austerely impoverished model of physical reality, but rather as the most perfect and concentrated expression of nature's inmost principles. For modern theorists, the situation is very different. Inasmuch as induction fails to provide them with a clear physicalist narrative for intentionality or consciousness, all they can do is live by a blind unreasoning faith in mechanism and choose to believe that some future science will disclose laws sufficient to account for the physical emergence of these phenomena, despite how very contradictory the idea seems to be at present. Or else they must decide, like those philosophers who call themselves "mysterians," simply to assume the physicalist picture of things while accepting that they'll never understand exactly how mind fits into it.[7] Modern "naturalists" are no less dogmatic than their ancestors; they merely have far fewer clear reasons for the dogmas they embrace. The older, premodern physical logic was coherent, even if it was putatively speculative; the newer, modern logic is incoherent, even though it's allegedly empirical. When mechanistic method became a metaphysics, and the tinted filter through which it viewed nature was mistaken for an unveiling of nature's true colorations, all explanations became tales of emergence, even in cases of realities—life, consciousness, language, and even existence itself—where such tales seemed difficult to distinguish from stories of magic.

HEPHAISTOS: It seems to me that we're simply talking about different frames of reference. All right, the older causal logic was a predicative logic and the newer is a physical calculus. It remains the fact that it's the latter that allows for the modern sciences.

PSYCHE: Indeed, but it also remains the fact, for just that reason, that the modern sciences, requiring the very restricted method they do, mustn't be mistaken for a universal model of truth. In the older metaphysics, one kind of causality didn't exclude another; all forms of causality were integrally complementary and interdependent. Well, why think otherwise, especially when there are phenomena that become more explicable in light of those various kinds of causality? Nothing in the modern sciences obliges us to think of form or finality as logically superfluous concepts or to believe in a physical nature that's really thoroughly mechanical. Standard evolutionary theory tells us that the semblance of purpose in nature is the accidental result of ages of phylogenic attrition and selection; an older vision of things might tell us instead that the process of attrition and selection is the actualization of a certain purposiveness in the structure of things, a certain tendency toward the fullest realization and expression of potentialities inherent within nature and its laws. Logically, neither claim can be proved over against the other purely from the observable physical evidence, and in fact neither actually excludes the other; either might be a licit perspective on the whole of things as interpreted from one vantage or its opposite. The issue then becomes which perspective can accommodate all the phenomena better, including the various phenomena of mental agency.

The mystery lies in the existence of the totality: why this ordered universe, with all its laws, exists at all. After all, the sciences shed no light upon the origin of the lawfulness that informs material nature, even though they must presume that lawfulness as the necessary prior condition of all physical theories. It's possible to distinguish material aetiology from formal teleology in purely analytic terms, but empirically they remain indistinguishable; we can observe only the lawful and rational continuity of natural processes and forces—material and formal, energetic and logical—and certainly have no grounds for imagining that such lawfulness and rational consistency are just givens, without any intrinsic purposefulness to hold it all together. You say the more complex coherence of systems and processes and organisms is emergent. It seems clear to me that reality has the coherence it does because it's invested with a coherence directly analogous to the mind's rational agency—form, finality, rational continuity . . .

Hephaistos: I'm not disdainful of your views. I merely repeat that there are perils in unexamined assumptions.

Psyche: I agree. And I'm not disdainful of your cautions. I merely claim that there are unexamined assumptions in the dominant modern picture of reality that are, if anything, more ideological and less reasonable—and so even more perilous—than those of earlier ages. At least, some of those older conceptions seem to make room for the presence of mental phenomena within the material order without paradox.

Actually, I'm not even sure that the modern picture yields a cogent notion of causation, let alone mentality. Once the whole concept of cause had been reduced from an integral system of rationales to single instances of local physical efficiency, causality became a mere brute fact—something of a logical black box. As is so very much a part of the peculiar genius of the modern sciences, description flourishes precisely because explanation has been left to wither. Hume certainly understood this. Once the supposedly spectral causal agencies of the old system had been chased away, he found causality itself now to be imponderable, logically nothing more than an arbitrary sequence of regular phenomenal juxtapositions. It presumed no abiding substrate of continuity—no prime matter—and no formal or final laws of intrinsic order. It had lost the rational necessity of an equation or syntactically coherent predicative sentence. The earlier understanding of causal relations faded into the obscurity of an occult principle whose only discernible logic is "it happens."[8] So now we're presented with the experience of a mind "in here" in each of us, which seems to function by a series of rational connections, and a mechanical world "out there," which seems to function by accidental concatenations of unthinking material forces; and we're asked to adopt a unified theory that collapses the former into the latter, however implausible that seems.

By contrast, there was at least a *logic* of change in the Aristotelian model—the integral logic of potentiality and actuality. It was a basic principle that, in any finite causal relation, change occurs in the effect, not in the cause itself. But, of course, in the realm of the finite, agent and patient functions are impossible to confine each to a single pole of any causal relationship. When two finite substances are involved in a causal relation, that is, each undergoes some change, because each is limited and lacking in some property the other can supply, and so each functions as both a cause and an effect in that relation. Each actualizes some potential latent in the other. Ice melts upon a burning coal but also cools the coal; and neither can affect the other without also being affected in turn. Each—to use a term slowly gaining more credence in the philosophy of science—has a disposition to a state that the other has a faculty for making active. But, of course, "disposition" here is just another word for "potential." Causality in that way of seeing things isn't just the extrinsic application of efficient force, merely randomly inducing a reaction, but an equation reached by addition and subtraction, so to speak: an intricate harmony of intrinsic dispositions and extrinsic occasions, one event awakening and being awakened by another.

HEPHAISTOS: Yes, yes. Very fancy rhetoric, but very obscure reasoning. And naturally you see all of that as, once again, analogous to mental functioning, one thought awakening and being awakened by another—as though physical causality were already a kind of thinking—from which you then deduce some original ground of mentality in all things. All right, so you're offering a picture that renders mind more explicable by first rendering matter mental. But reasoning by metaphor isn't reasoning.

EROS: See, you're hardly the lumbering simpleton you claim to be. And yet it's you, old friend, who are reasoning by metaphor—the metaphor of the machine.

HEPHAISTOS: He speaks.

EROS: When inspired to do so, yes.

VI

The Organic, the Mechanistic, and the Erotic

EROS: Maybe you think it extravagant and unwarranted of my dear Psyche to draw an analogy between the integrity of natural processes and that of reasoning. So you'll surely think me even more profligate in proposing an analogy between those processes and the ecstasy of love.

HEPHAISTOS: Can I possibly dissuade you from doing so?

EROS: No. Let's say that organic nature really is in a sense an integral relation of rational causes, at once physical and formal, drawn into a unity by an intrinsic purpose—an "antecedent finality," to use a recondite philosophical phrase. Let's say nature truly is shaped and animated by something that's at once life and mind—*psychē*, that is. As such, the movement of life toward its final cause is at least analogous to intentionality, to desire . . . to love.

HEPHAISTOS: Oh, please, let's not wander into those meadows just now. You know I suffer from an acute allergy to their native floras.

EROS: Well, I'll refrain for now from going further along that path, if only out of respect for your personal history. But I'll have more to say later. I'll say here only that I think even you'd have to grant that there's a distinction between extrinsic and intrinsic purpose—between teleology as external planning and teleology as internal drive. Perhaps the power of nature lacks the sort of full conscious intentionality of, say, a divine or human mind—though perhaps it doesn't—but even so, we have to distinguish between the real autonomous and intentional agency of organic life and the wholly dependent purposiveness of a lifeless mechanism.[9]

HEPHAISTOS: Do we? What if those seemingly intrinsic intentions have simply been imposed on organic life by extrinsic forces, such as aspects of the environment? Then they're simply mechanical functions that appear to be essentially intentional.

EROS: And how can they receive the impression of those forces, and adapt to them, unless they're already intentionally oriented to interpret their environment and then adjust—even at the cellular level? Let me ask you something. You're a master of artificial "organisms." Have you ever found a way to make your automata capable of adapting to unforeseen circumstances, or of acquiring abilities in excess of those you mechanically equipped them with? Of changing their minds, or of giving up on a task they deem pointless or impossible to fulfill? Do you observe in any of them a drive toward growth, change, adaptation . . . or just homeostasis? Or are they always and only functioning assemblages of essentially unrelated parts, limited to the operations you've fashioned them to perform? If called on to perform a task beyond their powers, they nevertheless never relent, except by wearing down. If they break down entirely, you simply put them back together so that they start functioning again as before. Could you do the same with a living organism once its genuinely living integrity as an organism has been "disassembled," so to speak?

HEPHAISTOS: Your argument is that organic life has many capacities my inventions don't? Well, yes, I concede as much without reservation. But why do you also seem to think life's power of acquiring new powers something unique or inherent?

EROS: Evolution tells us that it is—and that life achieves those new abilities in part by the supreme expression of love, replication, but also (we now know) by all sorts of coordinated intentional acts of natural genetic self-engineering.[10] Even in the case of individual organisms it seems plausible to think that life is called to ends that transcend its limited physical situation, and that prompt it to "reason" its way past impediments that would simply defeat a mindless mechanism. To deny teleology *tout court* is to assert that each given tree, say, is the product of an accidental sequences of causal events, extrinsic to one another;

but in fact there's a coherent intentional structure that's simply what a tree is, and all the causal events composing a tree are held together by this rational order of formation, purpose, material ground, and efficient force. Every natural potentiality within the tree is always being realized by some actuality in the tree, within the, so to speak, complete "equation" that the tree is—the complete idea or form or range of intrinsic possibilities. Moreover, there's an intrinsic drive in the tree toward that completion, and an adaptive ingenuity right within its very cells that allows it to pursue that end, come what may.

HEPHAISTOS: Well, of course. Again, I gladly concede that, by comparison to me and what poor ingenuity I possess, evolution is by far *il miglior fabbro.* I can't invest any of my creations with algorithms for adapting to unforeseen circumstances comparable to what ages of phylogenic development can achieve. But let's not indulge in fantasy here. In the case of evolution, we're talking not about final causes imposing new formal powers on a material substrate, but about simple natural selection—chance mutation within a predictable stochastic range of mutability, fortuitously selected for survival and replication by external circumstances. We're not discussing a dynamism by which higher causes guide lower causes, but one by which lower causes generate the illusion of higher causes. Don't mystify the process.

EROS: I think you'll find that that sort of Neo-Darwinian gradualism has been exposed as false. Life is much more active and intentional than that. At least, seventy-odd years of experimental evidence says so. But, even if the Neo-Darwinian picture of chance mutation and fortuitous selection were the whole story of evolution, and no new synthesis were needed—to repeat a point we've already made—there would be no reason to assume that both levels of causality weren't real, and good reasons for presuming that both must be. It's not as if one can observe the *absence* of finality and form; as governing constraints on efficient and material reality, they might of course *seem* to emerge from that reality. But that doesn't mean that, logically, they aren't in fact necessary dimensions of the causal whole. That same efficient and material reality is always arranged in concrete patterns with integrity in themselves and with the power of taking part in the larger patterns of reality as a whole, and this just as surely *seems* to be because of a governing logical order pervading all things. None of these "causes" or "rationales" exists independently of the others; what we're talking about isn't a collection of separated causal forces working upon one another from outside one another, but rather a single causal structure that, precisely as a structure, brings about the reality of phenomenal nature. The question this raises, in regard to the more mechanical picture of reality, is whether the structure of life—ontogenic and phylogenic, organismic and evolutionary alike—really can emerge in such a way that the "higher" is always only the residue of the "lower." And can mind emerge from truly mechanistic material causes? Is emergence of that sort even logically conceivable?

PSYCHE: My love.

EROS: Yes, my soul?

PSYCHE: I'm impressed.

EROS: I'm not just a pretty face, my soul.

PSYCHE: [*With a hint of fond salacity in her voice:*] Oh, how well I know that. But can we agree to address the question of organic life's structure later? I fear we may be entering upon too large a question for the little time that remains before our dinner.

EROS: Perhaps that's for the best.

HEPHAISTOS: Well, wait a moment, let's not curtail the natural course of the argument before I'm satisfied that I know where we stand. I'm still not entirely sure whether we've made any advance on our topic at all. Are you simply arguing for a vaguely Aristotelian science in the hope that it will prove a little more amenable to the phenomenon of mind as you conceive it? Because, as far as I can see, you still haven't shown me how this antique system of predication, as you describe it, closes the qualitative abyss you insist exists between the first-person interiority of mind and the third-person exteriority of nature. You've merely shown me that you can describe nature in a way that looks more analogous to mental acts than does my preferred mechanical imagery.

PSYCHE: I think we've done more than that, but I also grant that we're only at the beginning. And, no, I'm not arguing for any kind of science as such, and am quite happy to laud the advances achieved by the modern sciences as a result of the new methods developed in the early modern period. But I lament—indeed, abominate—the misprision of that method for a metaphysics of the real as such. For me, it's enough for now to argue that certain of the distinctive marks of mind that the mechanical philosophy banished from our picture of nature are perhaps there nonetheless and that, while the modern sciences have prescinded or abstracted from mental features in pursuit of a set of limited aims, they've never yet demonstrated their dispensability in our understanding of reality. It suffices for now to show that mind needn't be seen as an anomalous resident within an essentially mechanical reality or as an illusion dissembling a host of purely mechanistic functions. As for the interiority of mental life, well, perhaps that is itself the ground of the supposedly third-person order of physical nature. After all, it remains very difficult to say how mind can inhabit a world whose deepest reality is that of a mindless machine; but there are countless ways of coherently imagining how a world whose deepest reality is that of an integral phenomenal and rational structure should inhabit mind. Maybe, then, we'll find reasons to conclude that it's only by inhabiting mind that the world exists at all.

For today, however, let me simply observe how odd it is that a basically mechanistic physicalism as a philosophy or metaphysics seems to have survived the end of physics as a mechanical science. Isn't it really the case that the ardent materialist of today is still living in an antiquated world-picture, in a way that an Aristotelian or Platonist or what have you isn't? Even very intelligent and well-informed naturalist philosophers and scientists seem, when pressed upon such matters, to live conceptually inside a Baroque cosmos, a clockwork universe of gears and springs and weights and pendulums, local mass and local motion and bare extrinsic relations of impetus and blunt force. And yet the physical order they *actually* inhabit is one in which space and time bend and dilate and contract, and quantum-scale objects are at once particles and waves, and the substrate of all things seems to consist in a realm of ghostly superpositions and fantastic entanglements, and an unobserved particle can pass through two slits simultaneously while also passing through each but not the other while yet also passing through neither, and an electron can leap from one orbit of an atomic nucleus to another without crossing any interval in between, and two entangled particles are simultaneously determined in coordination, no matter how far apart they may be, and it may well be the case that it's really the act of observation—or even the consciousness in the act of observation—that induces the apparent collapse of the potentiality wave into a local actuality. Or not. Whatever the case, so much of reality begins to look like a dream in which the connections are often fluid and negotiable. A universe without absolute locality, without separability—and the demonstration of Bell's Inequalities surely leaves us in just such a universe—is hardly a mechanism.

It does occur to me, however, that so much that's paradoxical in the standard model of quantum mechanics wouldn't have seemed the least problematic in antiquity.

HEPHAISTOS: [*Raising one eyebrow and frowning sardonically:*] Let me guess: because quantum events might be without sufficient physical causes, in the mechanical sense at least, while still having sufficient *reasons*, in an Aristotelian sense.

PSYCHE: Well, yes, even if you seem to be scoffing at the suggestion. Doesn't it seem to you that part of the enigma of the quantum realm lies as much in how we think about causality and actuality as in anything else? Modern tendencies of thought make us see problems where we might otherwise not. I'm not saying that the questions aren't real, but only that it's a matter of how you ask them, and with what presuppositions, whether they appear difficult to answer. One modern tendency is to think of potentiality only in statistical terms, as a mode of logic but not of ontology; thus it never occurs to many modern scientists that potentiality might be a real mode of existence, waiting to become actuality. They simply seem to think that reality leaps out of nowhere, in obedience to laws of mathematical probability. Another is to think—even when quantum theory should have disabused us of the prejudice—that all real causality must be somehow mechanical, a transfer of energy operating within the physical constraints of spacetime. It was very different for, say, the ancient

Aristotelian or Neoplatonist, for whom it wouldn't have seemed at all paradoxical to find, for example, that there's an instantaneous correlation of determination between two entangled entities when one of them is observed, because he or she would be thinking in terms of many kinds of causality, including the, so to speak, *vertical* causality of formation, working upon a real realm of potential. It wouldn't have struck him or her as some sort of *spukhafte Fernwirkung*, contrary to all logic.[11] Formal causation isn't a horizontal relation between two physical things, or a physical transfer of energy that has to cross space, but is instead a rational specification that's transcendent of time and space, an immediate translation of potency into actuality—which is an event both logical and ontological—and so would be simultaneous for any quantum entanglement as a whole. It would have seemed perfectly obvious that the shared wave function of the two entities would instantly collapse from the indeterminacy of the possible into the specificity of the actual, even if the whole universe should occupy the interval between them; the form determining them would be something from outside the extension of space and time. Nor would a good late antique Neoplatonist have recoiled from the thought that the instant of formal determination and the instant of conscious observation might be one and the same event. Mind and nature, for him or her, would not have been strictly separate orders. And, of course, it shouldn't be inconceivable to us now that consciousness operates at an oblique angle, so to speak, to the texture of spacetime—whatever that very ambiguous mathematical reality might happen to be—or that mind acts like a formal cause impressing itself instantaneously on the "fabric" of spacetime in a way that would have no temporal, "horizontal" physical history. Since form's a principle that seamlessly unites the ontic and the epistemic—that is, one and the same form actualizes both matter's and mind's potencies—it's not all that mystifying that observation might be the real occasion of the collapse of the possible into the actual.

Hephaistos: Ah, I see. You're thinking of the quantum realm as something like prime matter. Yes, well, it would be . . . *amusing* to discover that Aristotle was our first quantum theorist. If, that is, the standard Copenhagen interpretation of quantum mechanics is presumed.

Psyche: That's not necessary. Even if we presume an Everettian multiverse, still the collapse of probability into actuality—or several actualities—might be occasioned by consciousness . . . and by formal causality specifying each iteration of the collapse. Anyway, I'm thinking of the quantum realm not so much as prime matter as perhaps the first level of actuality, the threshold between nothing and something—the level of reality where prime matter bears the first impress of higher form.

Hephaistos: Even so, I get the idea: prime matter is simply possibility for you . . . logical and metaphysical, while all formal causes come from above, one level supervening upon another. Each supervenient level is the formal cause of the immediately subvenient; each subvenient level is the material cause of the immediately supervenient. Pure possibility is first given form as, oh, quantum foam, and then that's given form as local particulate matter, and then that's given form as this or that macroscopic object, and so on, right up the chain of being to . . . what? God's ideas? That highest formal causality comes from the mind of God, yes? Not just top-down causality in terms of higher physical levels such as systems, but causality truly from above, descending from the highest ideal dimension of cosmic mind . . . or whatever? It's not that I don't see the appeal in the idea, but you can't just reintroduce non-physical causes into modern science . . .

Psyche: I've no desire to do that, in part because the sciences already presume plenty of non-physical agencies. But we can discuss that later. Let the sciences go their way uninhibited; I ask only that they not continue to mistake method for truth as such. I do, though, want to reintroduce those non-physical causalities, provisionally at least, into our metaphysics . . . or into the logical grammar by which we think of reality. At least, I want to allow for them as theoretical objects. I don't even care to investigate all the logical ramifications of such a model. I'm merely trying to free our minds from the prejudice that a rational reconstruction of reality always properly takes the form of the reduction of phenomena to their most basic material ingredients, and to whatever physical forces might apply exclusively to those ingredients. That's the narrative of absolute mechanical causality and composition from below . . . the narrative that the reality we know simply arises from lower realities, giving itself form as the accidental result of mindless force . . . which I think meaningless. And with it comes the myth of phenomenal reality as only the emergent representation of a qualityless realm of pure extension and force, and of mind as nothing but the faculty that accomplishes that dissimulation, and of the world in which we live and move and exist as a congress of sensory ghosts . . . phantom impressions veiling the quantitative "really real" behind their qualitative ectoplasm. But perhaps nothing simply *emerges.* Maybe phenomena are *formed.* Maybe the quantum realm is nothing but the first responsive level of potency as a real mode of being, a kind of boundary reality between nothing and something. I mean to say, maybe in the quantum realm—as in that of prime matter in the old systems—the principle of non-contradiction doesn't have to hold, because as yet nothing has been *informed* as this or that. And maybe then the realm of the phenomenal—the realm of the finite and the determinate—is where the principle of non-contradiction necessarily *does* obtain, and so there every superposition of possibilities must yield to a collapse into singularity in order to become anything actual.

HEPHAISTOS: [*With a small laugh:*] It still seems to me that you're reinforcing my point about why such thinking is an impediment to the impartial scientific picture of nature.

PSYCHE: Unless, of course, it happens to be true, in which case the myths of mechanistic matter and pure induction are impediments to the true rational picture of reality. And please don't tell me you think the modern preference for a pure physical reductionism a matter of impartiality.

HEPHAISTOS: [*With a sigh:*] I'm not that naïve. I still assume your ultimate goal is to get us to the mind of God. If I understand you, formal causes are like ideas in a mind, and final causes are like mental purposes and intentions; and thus the rational structure holding the whole universe in being is like a great mental event—the Old One's great thought—of which each finite mind is just a natural expression. . . . Yes?

PSYCHE: Well, in a word, yes.

HEPHAISTOS: And yet, it doesn't really get you there in the end. Theoretical cosmology has evolved since the Middle Ages, you know. Let's say you're right, if only in a metaphorical way. Let's say that in some sense it's right to think of nature as having the rational consistency of a complete equation or of a syntactically impeccable sentence—or a paragraph or a book. That too may be the result of a kind of natural selection. What if, as some think, universes are generated out of fluctuations in a timeless quantum landscape? What if universes arise in countless, even infinite variety, and among them are some that are wholly internally coherent spacetime continua, holding together with the complete consistency of equations, and having ends and beginnings perfectly consonant with one another in the way that two halves of an apple are consonant with one another? So, within those universes there seem to be forms and purposes, so to speak, and something like natural intentionality or final causes, or the semblances thereof. Seen from within their temporal and spatial architecture, the causal coherence joining beginnings and ends looks like teleology because, in a wholly fortuitous sense, it is—in the way that you might say 4 is the "teleology" of 2 + 2. But that's not really a case of purpose; it's just a case of what we see as origin and end being already implicit in one another structurally; only from within that structure, experienced as temporal distention, does it seem like a matter of purposes, even though it's really only a concrete pattern of constrained physical relationships. *Sub specie aeternitatis*, however, it's just a completed sum. Well, then, perhaps those are the physical orders that are able to survive without at once collapsing again into the quantum foam, and that are thus selected for survival. And in such universes mind might appear, as a natural *physical* part of the order of relations holding the totality together.

HERMES: Oh, come now, aren't you grasping at . . . well, at universes, I suppose? What an insanely extravagant hypothesis.

HEPHAISTOS: More extravagant than "the mind of God"?

HERMES: Definitely.

HEPHAISTOS: I beg to differ. Presumably, after all, if there were a God, all those many realities would be present in his mind, and so his mind would be a still vaster reality. Really, an infinite multiverse, by comparison to *that* exorbitant hypothesis, is a rather minimalist and parsimonious supposition.

HERMES: Yet again, the atheist is rescued from embarrassment at the last moment by the miraculous intervention of a *multiversum ex machina*. Anyway, that's a silly comparison.

PSYCHE: Now, now, let's not be dismissive. True, Phaesty is trying to leap over the essential problem again, and it may seem rather perverse to suggest that mind might be just a physical fact about one of those internally consistent universes that perhaps just happen to spring out of the quantum foam. I still insist that that's impossible. Still, Phaesty's right: I haven't as yet given sufficient reason to assume some sort of universal mentality underlying the local instances of mindlike order in nature. It seems to me that the best way to answer his proposal, then, is to demonstrate—as has been my desire all along—that there's no possible universe at all in which mind is a natural consequence of mechanical physical causes: to show that, in fact, mind is by its nature unable to inhabit an entirely physical frame of reality, and must always already be in some sense "supernatural" in its origin, orientation, and content. Or, at least, "extra-natural." And then perhaps we can show that mind can exist *only* by virtue of the supernatural element to which it belongs.

HEPHAISTOS: Ah, the tawny beast emerges from its lair.

PSYCHE: Then, before it devours us, let me draw our little colloquy to a close for now with one final observation. Understand, when I talk about the "mind of God," I'm not engaging in any kind of "Intelligent Design" argument, of the typical sort. I think that that's just another version of the mechanistic picture of nature, albeit with a divine artisan added to the picture, a supreme mechanic to put the machine together. Life isn't mechanism, nor does any living thing exist as a mere external artifact of the divine intellect. I'm talking about the existence of all things within the divine. I mean precisely what I say when I liken the order of nature to the structure of mind—in fact, to the structure of consecutive thought: I mean that nature, in its essence, literally *is* thought. The rational relations, as we've called them, that constitute the full substance and life-history of that tree we were discussing earlier hold together in an order of rational entailments precisely because the tree's physical existence is an expression of a unified act of rational intellect. The tree—its growth from a seed to its fully formed adulthood—is an unbroken sequence of rational sequelae, as it were. The fully grown tree is a rational result, in the way that the conclusion of a syllogism is the result of the premises leading to it. The tree is something wholly ideal, not in the sense of a mental impression of the kind Berkeley described, but instead in the sense of the concrete event of a coherent sequence of thoughts. That's why we in turn can perceive and understand the tree rationally—because there's no occult "thing-in-itself" alien to mental perception and language there, no Kantian enigma behind a merely apparent teleology imposed on the tree by our categories.

HEPHAISTOS: [*Sighing deeply and shaking his head:*] You know I've no patience for mysticism, so let me try to abbreviate your disquisition. You reject as impossible the mechanistic presuppositions that all things have their origin and subsistence in essentially lifeless matter and that mind is reducible to a purely material, totally mindless reality; and you propose instead that, if mind is real, it can be only because all things have their origin and subsistence in living mind; hence, ultimately, it is matter that must be reducible to an originally mental reality.

PSYCHE: Precisely. I'd go so far as to say that material reality is merely a kind of phase, so to speak, of mind . . . a concrete state or crystallization . . . the way ice is a phase and state and crystallization of water.

HEPHAISTOS: Of course. What's this other than the trivial trick of turning the picture upside down in its frame? Rather than saying our minds produce a rational representation of the physical process, we now say the physical process is itself the representation—or, I suppose, the *expression*—of a prior act of rational thought. Rather than saying that mind is the strange, fortuitous product of physical reality, we now say that physical reality is the contents of mind made concrete—whatever "concrete" here means. How can I refute that? How can we tell the horse from the cart? All right, the Red King has dreamt it all.

PSYCHE: Indeed he has.

HEPHAISTOS: Then, I imagine, what we're doing when we see and think about the tree is . . . what, exactly?

PSYCHE: Why, just that: really seeing and thinking about the tree. The phenomenon is the thing itself, rather than some dissimulating veil of sensibility drawn before a featureless mathematical world of pure quantity; the "thing in itself" is always already thought, made concrete and communicating itself as molecules and cells, roots, branches, and leaves . . . and perhaps rose blossoms. [*Rising and taking up the rose from the bench:*] But let's leave all of that for another day. So much of what we've said in haste today will have to be unfolded at a much more deliberate pace in days to come. For now, my divine darlings, it's time we betook ourselves to the pleasures of the table—of ambrosia and nectar and every delicacy this paradise of ours affords us—as well as the supreme pleasure of pleasant conversation . . . on topics far lighter than these.

[*Exeunt omnes.*]

DAY TWO

Mind and Matter

I

Qualitative Consciousness

The last flush of dawn has departed from the sky. The dew sparkles like diamonds among the blades of glass. The garden is awash in cool morning breezes. The flowers are almost incandescent in their beds and on their vines. Enter PSYCHE, EROS, HERMES, *and* HEPHAISTOS, *all at a rather languid pace, as if perhaps not wholly recovered from the revels of the previous night.* PSYCHE *and* EROS *seat themselves side-by-side on a single bench,* HERMES *takes another for himself, and* HEPHAISTOS *stretches out supine on yet another, his ankles crossed, his hands clasped behind his head, his eyes turned upward to the sky.*

HEPHAISTOS: [*With a yawn:*] I suppose you'll want to resume our conversation of yesterday directly.

PSYCHE: If you've no objection, yes.

HEPHAISTOS: I'm content. So long as you don't mind my posture. It was a long night—delightful, of course, but long.

PSYCHE: Not in the least. Seeing you in that position pleasantly evokes the image of a patient on a psychoanalyst's couch.

HEPHAISTOS: [*Smiling wryly:*] And you do see me as in need of therapy, don't you?

PSYCHE: I do, I admit, tend to see the modern mechanistic view of things as a kind of psychological disorder—a psychosis perhaps, or a neurosis at the very least. I intend no moral judgment; only a diagnosis. It seems clear to me that the history of modernity's governing metaphysics is the tale of a tragic estrangement from reality, occasioned by a self-induced trauma—a self-imposed psychic dissonance.

Hephaistos: And what, dear Psyche, is the nature of this "dissonance"? I confess, I'm wholly insensible to it, as I am to any trauma I may have suffered.

Hermes: Of course. That's the nature of psychosis.

Psyche: I think we established yesterday what I'm talking about. The modern world created a new concept of matter, one into which the seemingly self-evident phenomena of mind could not be fitted; and then, when this new conceptual model graduated from the servile station of mere heuristic method to the absolute authority of a total picture of all reality—well, inevitably the effort to make sense of those phenomena in terms of that model became a task that was simultaneously necessary and impossible. Hence the psychosis. All attempts at conjuring that dissonance away have ended in failure, to the point that the only robustly surviving naturalist models of mental reality are also the most poignantly deranged: eliminativism, functionalism, physicalist versions of panpsychism . . .

Hephaistos: Ah, now wait a moment . . .

Psyche: I promise I'll define my terms.

Hephaistos: That's not the source of my objection.

Psyche: But I simply have to observe that both this alienation from nature and this impossible task were largely unknown in the pre-modern world, except perhaps in a few cases of unhealthy temperament. The ancient intuition, at least for the most part, started from the undeniable fact of mind—its consciousness and intentionality and intrinsic unity and so forth—and only from there moved toward a picture of the material order compatible with that indubitable reality. Which was quite sensible, really, given that we have no knowledge of the material order except as an object of the mind's consciousness, intentionality, unity, and so forth.

Hephaistos: I see. Then again, what seems indubitable is often the very opposite of the truth, isn't it? Gods and human beings at one time imagined that the sun was a fiery planet circling a stationary earth, precisely because that was how it appeared to their senses, and so to their common sense.

Hermes: Well, now, if you consider the matter, if one isn't thinking in terms of gravity wells, and if one is aware of the infinity of space, then in a sense every point is the still center of the universe, and the sun does in fact orbit the earth, in a Tychonian fashion of course, with the other planets still circling the sun . . .[1]

Hephaistos: Oh, please, have pity on my throbbing head. Pedantic equivocations aren't serious arguments.

Psyche: Now, now, my dears, let's not quarrel. In fact, you both make interesting points—though yours, Phaesty, is interesting chiefly by virtue of its errancy.

Hephaistos: Ah, well, we live to serve.

Psyche: Hermes is referring to a matter of perspective, and that's significant because, indeed, what seems to be the case is often only a matter of the perspective from which one views things. Thus, in terms of gravitation as an object of mathematical description, the heliocentric cosmos is a fact. In terms, however, merely of geometrical relations of center and circumference, the universe is . . . well, "pancentric." It's no truer in those terms to say the earth orbits the sun than that the sun—indeed, the entire universe—orbits the earth. As always, Nicholas of Cusa was right.[2] The issue is, again, what question you're asking. But—and here's where you come in, Phaesty—there's no way in which our commonsense understanding of the mind can be analogous to geocentrism, because that commonsense understanding isn't a matter of one or another perspective *upon* some imponderable quiddity outside ourselves, but is rather a matter of perspective *as such*. It's not a question of how mental experience "seems." The mind can't merely *seem* to be what mind seems to be, because the very reality of "seeming" as such is the reality of mental experience, which is what the mechanistic philosophy can't accommodate. This first-person awareness is a primary datum, the ground of all knowledge, and it simply defies physicalist logic.

Hephaistos: Or so it *seems*, dear Psyche. We've been over this already. What I require are arguments. Explain to me, carefully, precisely what aspects of mental existence you believe can be neither reduced to physical causes nor reconciled to a physicalist philosophy.

PSYCHE: Very well, I shall.

HEPHAISTOS: But please start with the most obvious. Until I've fully recovered from last night, I'd rather not leap into the metaphysical deep end.

PSYCHE: I'll be gentle, I promise. Anyway, we've already touched on the most obvious problem of all, or at least the one most conspicuous in the literature: *qualitative experience.* The problem of all problems here is, of course, first-person subjectivity as such; and, for some reason, in Anglophone philosophy of mind at least, this is usually construed as simply the issue of *qualia*—sheer phenomenal impressions, the "feel" or the "what it's like" of being the subject of experience. It's even come to be called the "hard problem" of philosophy of mind, though in fact it's really only one hard problem among many.[3] And, as a rule, *qualia* are understood chiefly in terms of *sensuous* experience: color, taste, sound, palpation, fragrance, a shock of pain, a quiver of pleasure, and so forth. I find that somewhat inadequate, but the important point here is that every individual *quale* as such appears to be irreducible to anything but itself. It's entirely "interior," as it were, entirely the possession of one subject, utterly and inalienably private, and in every discernible or conceivable aspect radically different from any third-person event—even those events with which it seems to be correlated, such as electrical impulses in the cerebrum. *Qualia* are what are often called "intrinsic properties." But this world of inner sensibility needn't be confined merely to the sensuous. There are also subjective qualities attached to an emotional state, to an apprehension, to a memory, to a frame of mind, to a sudden realization, even to the experience of thinking about something. An incalculable range of purely private experience inflects and illumines every feature of our subjective world, and gives us the world not just as a collection of objective properties "out there," but also as an immediate presence within our very awareness of ourselves. This is crucial, really. Apart from these *qualia*, it's likely we'd have no personal identities at all, no sense of self, no sense of others, let alone any awareness of the world.

HEPHAISTOS: Very well. But need we make a mystery of what seems like a simple feature of organic functions. Surely there are sensations for the very simple reason that they're part of a system of stimulus and response, which evolved as the most efficient means for negotiating physical reality. Surely it's enough to say that *qualia* have a role in the integrated physiology of organisms, preventing them from, oh, trying to take a nap in a camp fire or venturing to kiss a crocodile, and encouraging them to eat and procreate. So *qualia* aren't really just private or intrinsic properties, are they? They're parts of a system of interaction between an organism and its environment, and part of an elaborately calibrated operation of converting so-called inputs into so-called outputs.

PSYCHE: Perhaps, but that hardly addresses the problem. We're talking about the subjective awareness of sensations, not simply sensations themselves; we're talking about that incommunicable "what it's like" of any sensation for the one experiencing it. Suppose your capacity for sensations is nothing but a mode of stimulus and response; suppose also that even those more elusive and rarefied *qualia* I spoke of—say, the ineffable feeling of wistfulness induced by accidentally hearing an old familiar tune, or an inner sense of having a conviction about something, and so on—have some kind of function, even one that confers evolutionary benefit. *Quid sequitur?* What follows from that? Proposing a utilitarian explanation for something does nothing to demonstrate that the phenomenon in question is possible in purely physical or mechanistic terms; and experiences of *qualia* would seem to be anything but. And, if they're not explicable in the sort of mechanistic causal terms you'd accept, it scarcely matters whether they have some ostensible functional usefulness.

Anyway, who's to say that *qualia*, specifically as *qualia*, contribute any functional value at all? Surely stimulus and response can be programmed, so to speak, into a neurological network without the need for personal affectivity. Function alone isn't explanatory here. If the system is predisposed to react to certain stimuli in certain ways, the additional element of a private, non-objective sense of "what it's like" to be aware of that stimulus adds nothing indispensably causal to the function. It doesn't even add to the information those stimuli convey, since *qualia* are in a sense an experiential tautology: as they're supposedly properties entirely of subjective consciousness, present not in things but only in our affective inner worlds, prior to subjective consciousness they wouldn't exist to begin with, and wouldn't need to be registered as part of the environment. They'd convey no real information about the world. So those phenomenal impressions—those forms of feeling—aren't real aspects of any physical stimulant in the environment; they're wholly superfluous to the process. Moreover, as this is so, subjective awareness wouldn't be a feature of our organic architecture that would be visible, so to speak, to natural selection. It seems clear that qualitative consciousness is something ontologically distinct from—even redundant to—the mechanical system of functional relations that you're talking about, and stands outside anything evolution would be able to select for survival. It might even be an impediment to the optimal operation of such a system. After all, a capacity for the *feeling* of fear may seem like an aid to evolutionary success, but the actual feeling of fear as often paralyzes the will as galvanizes it. How much more economical a system that eliminated the affective dimension of stimulation altogether.

Then, too, what about all those *qualia* that seem to have no functional purpose? How did they evolve, and why? Am I supposed to believe that the ineffable sense of buoyant melancholy I feel on listening to Schubert's *Winterreise* or my sense of satisfaction at having imagined a clever quip—or my frustration at having imagined it belatedly, as a bit of *l'esprit d'escalier*—has some kind of meaningful function in a purely practical sense? How vast a range of actual experience must be ignored in order to make a purely functionalist account of subjective sensibility sound reasonable? Even then, the deepest problem with this approach to the question is that it doesn't actually address the real enigma of consciousness as such.

HEPHAISTOS: Your dismissal of functionalism is altogether too cavalier. I have something to say on the matter.

PSYCHE: I'm sure you have, and I'm sure you'll say it. But let's complete our initial inventory of problems.

HEPHAISTOS: We've deferred so many questions already that soon we'll have to begin deferring our deferrals. [*Turning about and sitting upright on his bench:*] Very well, how is it that consciousness in itself defies such explanations?

Psyche: It doesn't need to defy them. They never touch upon it to begin with. In such schemes, consciousness remains an unmentioned mystery, the unspeakable open secret right at the heart of mental life. Remember my admonitions regarding the *cui bono* fallacy. Let's allow the conjecture that subjective qualitative awareness is functional—is utile—even indispensably so. We're still left with an aetiological abyss between the reputedly mindless, wholly mechanistic, intrinsically third-person material order supposedly underlying all things and the entirely inner, first-person world of mental existence that supposedly emerged from it. *Qualia* remain qualitatively distinct from the impersonal *quanta* that allegedly compose the physical order, but physicalist naturalism asks us to suppose that there's some transitional point—evolutionary in the case of the species, physiological in the case of the individual organism—where a state of pure exteriority, pure quantitative existence, all at once acquires interiority, a subjective qualitative experience of itself and the world around it. And it would definitely have had to be all at once. Consciousness isn't a composite state; it's either there or it's not. True, it may deepen by degrees, gradually, as a species or an individual becomes more complex; but, if consciousness emerged from mechanism, at some point there was nothing but ubiquitous objectivity and then, an instant later, there was local subjectivity, however dim or feeble. Somewhere the threshold was crossed. But how? Because it's not really a threshold, is it? It's that aforementioned abyss again. So how did all that mindless quantity suddenly add up to perceiving mind? How, in this instance alone, did the essential aimlessness of matter achieve so intense and intricate a concentration of its many random forces that it was abruptly and fantastically inverted into the very opposite of everything modern orthodoxy tells us matter is? Remember my cautions against the pleonastic fallacy: no matter how many purely objective quantitative steps the supposedly mechanistic material order may have taken in the direction of mind, none of them seems as if it could have constituted that sudden qualitative transition from pure exteriority into an unprecedented inwardness.

Qualia certainly, at least, seem to exist in excess of the physical processes with which they're associated: as subjective experiences, they don't inhere in the objects of experience themselves, but only in our act of perceiving those objects, and they seem to differ from one another far more radically than any one neuronal event differs from any other. As we've said, they can't clearly be causally explained in relation to the electrochemical impulses in the brain's synapses; but neither can they be causally explained in relation to the physical realities they presumably reflect, because those realities as objectively measured lack the purely relative values of qualitative experience—too hot, too cold, just right, as Goldilocks might measure these things—but have only absolute objective measurements of the sort a thermometer registers. Quite apart from the issue of whether the perceptible qualities of things have some real existence in the world of forms—whether the red of the rose blossom that initiated this discussion is more than a *purely* subjective impression—we're confronted with the "what it's like" of experiencing that red as red, which is a deeper, more mysterious, more irreducible reality. Whether red is real "out there," as an objective phenomenon, or only subjectively "in here"—whether our minds are participating in the same universal "form of red" that the rose also participates in, or whether instead the red is merely how our brains represent something that itself has no color—scarcely matters at this point. In either case, what's significant is that there's an "I" to whom that red appears, and upon whom it makes an affective and private impression. Wherever that red exists, it's neither in the molecules and physical processes composing the rose nor in the synapses and electrochemical activity of the brain. It exists elsewhere, in an altogether separate dimension, an experiential and formal space where world and mind meet in an event of subjective, immediate knowledge of an objective . . . well, essence. Where is that "elsewhere"? A machine equipped to record all the data of a rose's appearance, calibrated to report its "redness" to us, doesn't actually in any sense receive the phenomenal impression of red, even if its equipment is so adjusted as to identify what we would see as a red image; there's no experience, no "what it's like," in that computational process, no unified "I" on the inside of that accumulation of data, translating objective quantities into subjective qualities—or, to put it in more ancient metaphysical terms, no "I" experiencing the otherwise hidden qualities that reveal the form indwelling the rose, or that disclose the rose as a rose rather than as just an ensemble of atomic, molecular, and chemical events. . . .

HEPHAISTOS: And, to your mind, that's the great mystery of *qualia?*

PSYCHE: Well, surely you'd grant that no credible modern scientific model exists that can tell us how the electrochemistry of the brain, which is mechanically uniform and physical, can generate the endlessly varied and incommunicable experience of a particular person's inner phenomenal world. Obviously the event is inflected through the apparatus of perception; no one should deny that. The encounter between a certain kind of object and our neurology produces particular kinds of data; the rose's redness, understood as a chromatic translation of properties of light and matter through optic nerves and brains, has a physical side. But it's the other side where the mystery lies: entirely in the subjectivity that's the site of those impressions, giving them their irreducibly subjective character—not just the data received and processed by the brain, but the mental impression *here*, the experience of the data as *mine*, as having a quality *for me*, and as being *like this.* That private feeling of red—that phenomenal "thusness," so to speak—is not the physical event of either the rose itself or my sensory physiology; indeed, it seems superfluous to the physical transaction altogether.

HEPHAISTOS: I don't deny that it's mysterious. And perhaps you're right that to attribute a function to this or that *quale* isn't yet to explain the mechanism of qualitative awareness in itself, or how it's possible; but don't pretend it's clear that what we call *qualia* are in themselves simply devoid of function. Perhaps they're the necessary palette of mental representation, necessary pigments, so to speak, by which our neurology produces a picture of a particular kind of stimulus, as part of the larger system of stimulus and response—input and output, to use those rebarbative terms again. I honestly don't know what to make of your archaic talk of seeing the *form* of the rose, or some transcendental formal cause—roseness, redness, what have you—informing both an object in the world and the mind's perception of that object. As far as I'm concerned, the world that appears to us is the product of a neural translation of diffuse information into a usefully simplified representation; it's that representation—not the rose itself—to which I have mental access, or which itself *is* my mental access to reality, and which allows me to navigate what would otherwise be a trackless ocean of contending sense data. The world we experience is a set of symbolic algorithms, a representational distillate of the world beyond us, a kind of user-interface, to use the jargon of computation. Those *qualia* aren't intrinsic realities, but simply neural transpositions of objective realities out there—filters through which information enters a practically useful state. We aren't seeing red in the rose so much as we're seeing the rose "redly," as a convenient way of registering it and reacting to it, if necessary.

HERMES: "User-interface"? What a grotesque phrase. What exactly does it mean?

HEPHAISTOS: I'm sorry if the *patois* of the technical class abrades your patrician sensibilities. It means simply that, when a system is too complex in itself to be mastered all at once by an operator, it's useful to condense its functions into small, easily manipulated springs or buttons or . . . well, computer icons are the best example. Just as the coding and functions of software are far too arcane and complex for the ordinary user of a computer, and so the operational conventions of a handful of icons—such as, say, the picture of a file-folder to mean "save document"—allow a user to employ a vast system of algorithms that would otherwise be useless to him or her, so too the vast complexity of all the discrete and related activities of the brain is far beyond anyone's powers of comprehension and control, but evolutionary forces have created cognitive fables, as it were, to make it all manageable for us. Our agency as the organisms we are is full of unconscious systems and subsystems that far exceed our capacity for direct understanding and operation, but the simple fictions we employ to tell ourselves what we're doing make it possible for us to function. Evolution has equipped us with a fairytale that cunningly provides us with a script for pulling levers and releasing springs we're not even aware exist.

HERMES: Ah. How very up-to-date you are for a superannuated god. It's still a vulgar locution.

HEPHAISTOS: I yield to your more refined capacity for aristocratic daintiness.

PSYCHE: Now, now, my dears, pull in your claws. Phaesty, that's all well and fine, of course, but it still doesn't explain how it could happen in the first place that a world of mindless matter could produce that particular . . . "interface." But let's set that aside for the nonce. As for reducing *qualia* to purely representational states, I suspect there are qualitative experiences that have no particular representational content. I mean, if we're just talking about sensuous perceptions, that tells us nothing about, say, my awareness of being in a good or bad mood, or of feeling contentment on hearing a sparrow chirp. And there are *qualia* that far exceed any merely informational function. The bliss induced by a particularly great work of art, for instance, or a beautifully turned sentence: that nimbus of affectivity that hangs about many an ordinary experience and that seems inseparable from consciousness as such. You'll have a hard time convincing me that that's some sort of simple "user-interface"—which, I agree, is an unpleasant phrase.

Maybe, though, that's not really very important here either. I reject the very premise that a person's subjective sense of "what it's like" can be demonstrated to add any utility to the brain's operations. As you know, certain philosophers have proposed the thought-experiment of imagining philosophical "zombies"—that is, beings in some other possible universe, physically indistinguishable from the sentient beings that inhabit this universe, capable of all the same outward functions and all the same processes of stimulus and response, but devoid of any affective or phenomenal awareness. What functions could they not perform that conscious entities can?[4]

HEPHAISTOS: Just conceiving of something doesn't make it really possible. Maybe the sort of complex systems of stimulus and response found in developed organisms must always generate a kind of seemingly "subjective" awareness, as a necessary simplifying mechanism of control and organization.

PSYCHE: Which changes nothing. The issue isn't whether such zombies could really exist. It's whether there's anything *logically* inconsistent in such a notion. That's enough to indicate that, when we speak of functional systems of stimulus and response, we aren't talking about the same thing as subjective consciousness; and that difference suffices to indicate that no physical description of the world we inhabit necessarily entails the existence of consciousness. To put it a little absurdly, if you were unaware of the existence of subjective consciousness, no observation of the physical processes of organisms and their world—no inventory, however precise and comprehensive, of the operations and structures of the brain, no empirical investigation of the body's systems of stimulus and response—would apprise you of its existence. Really, this isn't much different from the old problem of other minds: How do you know that you're not surrounded by automata who merely seem to have inner worlds of their own? You may have good reason to think this isn't so, but you actually have no irrefutable evidence against it. And, again, couldn't you imagine a robot so cunningly crafted that its every behavior was indistinguishable from the behavior of a conscious being? Of course you could. Well, then, the functional system and the inner "what it's like" of a subject are two formally distinct logical objects.

HEPHAISTOS: I refuse to concede any arguments based on mere conceivability. As often as not, all they do is take advantage of an insufficiency of information; we may find many things conceivable because we don't as yet understand why they're impossible. Anyway, I think you're missing my point. My claim is that perhaps any system of input and output of sufficient complexity would naturally include certain operations whose character appears to be subjective to the operator.

HERMES: *Appears* to be subjective? What does that mean? If something appears to me as subjective, that's what it is. How else could it *appear?*

HEPHAISTOS: I'd almost forgotten you were there. What I mean is precisely what I've been saying since this conversation began: perhaps the difference between the third- and first-person vantages is not nearly so absolute as at first it seems.

Psyche: And yet it is. As I've said, to think there's some intelligible way for the former to give rise to the latter is to fall prey to the pleonastic fallacy. Anyway, let's leave it there for now and move on. What's most important is the abiding mystery of qualitative experience: that such experience, that is, remains subjective in precisely the way that material *quanta* are not. The redness of the rose—whatever else it may be—exists for me as a private feeling of "what it's like," and not as any part of the rose itself or as some aspect of an electrochemical brain event. If our discussion of functionalism, or of any other theory of mind, should oblige us to revise that judgment, we'll cross that rainbow bridge when we come to it.

II
Subjectivity and Unity of Apprehension

EROS: My soul.

PSYCHE: Yes, my love?

EROS: While we've probably said enough about the qualitative *contents* of experience, I can't help but feel we've still failed to do particular justice to the mystery of experience as such, as something intrinsically subjective. I mean to say, Hephaistos wants to suggest that, in order to erase the absolute demarcation between third- and first-person knowledge, we need only establish that *qualia* have a function in the larger system of stimulus and response by which organisms interact with their environments. Well, frankly, that—quite apart from being an example of what you call the *cui bono* fallacy—indicates a failure to grasp what we're really talking about. As yet, he's under the impression that the issue is one of negotiating the difference between two radically distinct but still analogous modes of natural knowing. But surely that doesn't capture the deeper enigma of subjectivity itself. The issue isn't just the uniqueness of the "what it's like" of subjective experience; the essential question must be whether subjectivity in itself can fit within the prevailing picture of physical reality at all.

HEPHAISTOS: Surely we've been talking about nothing else.

EROS: Have we? Yes and no. I admit that you've discussed the subjective vantage of qualitative consciousness. But by itself, as I suspect will prove to be the case when you defend functionalism, that vantage might still be characterized as just the way in which an organism processes information about its world when registering stimulation from without. But what truly makes subjective private consciousness mysterious—what makes it consciousness rather than merely receptivity to data—is not just that it "knows," in the way a sensitive thermometer might improperly be said to "know" the temperature or a neural network might be said to "know" a shock of pain, but that it *knows* that it knows. Consciousness is an awareness of being aware: an illumination from within, a mysterious reflexivity or doubleness, not merely registering impressions from without, but experiencing itself as experiencing.

HEPHAISTOS: I'm failing to see the distinction you're trying to make. We've established that consciousness *seems* to be qualitatively unlike mechanical interactions.

EROS: Yes, I grant that. But I want to urge still more radically is that the very structure of subjectivity is an impossibility within a physicalist account of reality, because if it were physical it would have to rely on an infinite regress that a truly mechanical natural order could never, ever accommodate. Rather than resting on an objective material basis, like some neurological mechanism, subjectivity can only ever rest upon itself. It's its own foundation. And, if that's so, you can't get around the problem by talking about its function or the evolutionary advantage it confers.

HERMES: He's right, you know. A structural paradox can't be resolved by a genetic narrative. In fact, there's the genetic fallacy for you in its purest form. If you're dealing with a phenomenon that can't fit into the frame of nature as you understand it, it's pointless to say that it evolved very, very slowly. That's just to defer the dilemma to some earlier and unimaginable episode in the tale, in the hope that it might conveniently disappear from view altogether in the mists of the epic or mythic prehistory of the various species. That's just . . . well . . .

PSYCHE: The pleonastic fallacy again.

HEPHAISTOS: That particular principle is beginning to look like a barricade strategically erected to thwart any attempt at grounding the mental in the physical.

PSYCHE: Or it's a principle that reveals how impossible it is to ground the mental in the physical, at least if the latter is conceived mechanistically.

What my husband is saying is that between the psychological self—the empirically available "you" known to us and to yourself—and the transcendental "I" underlying that "you," and also underlying your and our knowledge of that "you," there's an incommensurability not of degree but of kind . . . in fact, of ontology. A physicalist collapse of this difference isn't merely a practical impossibility; it's conceptually meaningless. Simply said, subjectivity isn't just the condition of passively registering the effect of the world on an apparatus of perception. A computer or recording device can register data, and maybe the brain can as well at many levels that aren't immediately conscious. But the actual experience of subjectivity is always also, and primordially, a reflective experience of one's own act of knowledge "in here." Each of us is a "me" to whom the world is presented, but within each "me" there's also an "I" that knows that "me," and that renders it aware of itself—a kind of light that illumines the "me" from within. Or, in Kant's terms, there's a transcendental ego that abides in our conscious states, and it illumines the empirical ego—this psychological self—for itself. This recursive or specular structure to consciousness—this consciousness of oneself as conscious—is an old conundrum, of course. Even Aristotle took note of it.[5] To be an actual subject of experience, rather than a mere recording device made of neurons, your awareness of yourself as aware is an absolute necessity; which means you must also be capable of being aware of yourself as aware of yourself as aware, and so on *ad infinitum.* Well then, conceived of as a structure whose foundation is physical, consciousness simply couldn't exist in real space and time. It would have no beginning to which we could retreat. It would be like one of those M. C. Escher images of the interior of a house folded in upon itself so that its ground is everywhere and nowhere. No physical mechanism can undergird an infinite regress. If awareness had to keep retreating to an ever yet more original vantage to become itself—an ever more basic neuron or cerebral module, perhaps—it would never emerge from the oblivion of sheer objective materiality.

Hephaistos: Twaddle. Place two mirrors before one another, and *voilà:* an infinite regress.

Hermes: Which would be a compelling riposte, I suppose, if mirrors actually looked at one another, and especially if two mirrors could look at one another from some single, magically fused perspective. We're talking about personal perception, not about optical geometry.

Hephaistos: Well, isn't an infinite regress a paradox under any circumstances? Why would it be any less inexplicable in non-physical terms?

Hermes: Because in a non-physical context it wouldn't be an infinite regress; it would be a regress to a first principle. Consciousness may have a kind of infinity about it, of course, but just not of the impossible physical kind. If you don't have to ground the subjective in the objective, but allow instead that the subjective as such might be the ground of reality, then you don't have to explain subjectivity's absolute openness to everything . . . its openness even to itself. Consciousness as a pure act of simple awareness, free from material constraints, might be metaphysically simple—pure immediacy, pure transparency to itself as much as to the world. Indeed, it seems to me it must be so. But as a function of a material system it would have to be grounded in physical composites, almost certainly in a modular fashion. One part of your neurology would have to be responsive to stimulation from without, another part aware of that experience, another aware of that awareness, but then also another aware of that awareness of that awareness. . . . Do you see what I mean? Yes, I concede that even in non-physical terms it's all very mysterious. The point is that, in purely physical terms, it's not merely mysterious; it's utterly impossible.

Eros: You know, there are centuries of reflections on this very issue in Indian philosophical tradition, my good Vishvakarma.

Hephaistos: [*With a small groan, rubbing his temples:*] Have pity on my dissipated state. I haven't the strength right now to shift into one of my divine alter egos.

Eros: Well, I certainly wouldn't want to take advantage of your diminished condition . . . or your debauched wits. But much of this is very easy, really. I recall a simple mental exercise I once heard recommended by a Kashmiri Śaivite scholar, oh, perhaps a millennium ago or thereabouts. It goes rather like this: Pause to reflect on your mind; for a moment your mental functions come to a halt, and you stop thinking about whatever you were thinking a moment ago; then allow your thinking to resume. All right. Who was it who was aware of that momentary stilling of your thoughts? Who was that silent "witness"—that *sākṣi*, to use the Sanskrit term—who from within your mind observed your mind pause and then begin moving again along its otherwise continuous cogitative path? Doesn't the capacity to do that by itself suggest a knowing "I" beyond the empirical self? There's a term for the experience: *vimarśa*, "detached reflection," and it's often taken as an indication that consciousness isn't just a passive mechanism of response, but an active power that goes forth from itself to illuminate the mind—a *prakāśa* or "shining forth" that's never an object itself, but always and only an absolute primordial subjectivity, more basic than any physical ground of reality. This is just evident from any good phenomenology of mental agency. I don't know if you've read much Husserl, but he's very precise in distinguishing the living unity of consciousness within the flow of experience from the objective unities that experience encompasses, like the unity of simple facts or simple essences. A physical object is disclosed to consciousness as a successive, shifting multiplicity of aspects; but the unity of its "essence," as it were—its whatness—is an instantaneous apprehension of the mind; it's the latter, that conceptual dimension of perception, that gathers those aspects together and constitutes that object as a single discrete thing. Inside that experience, moreover, consciousness presents itself to itself as a continuous flow rather than as a sum or aggregation, and what gathers that flow into one is the unity of the "I" that abides within, which is never reducible to the psychological self. Husserl likens it to a ray of light that immediately illuminates both the thing thought and the act of thinking about it. . . .[6]

HEPHAISTOS: How very mystical and vague.

EROS: Quite the contrary.

HEPHAISTOS: Look, all this tells me is something I stipulated long ago: the powers of the mind are remarkable and complicated. As for this inner "witness"—well, my first response would be to say that you're describing a kind of redoubling of perception, which may just be a form of internal regulation for a complex system. I mean, just as our brains perform a constant proprioception—a constant inner surveillance, that is—of the operations of our own bodies, some of it conscious but most of it probably not, so too the brain conducts an internal proprioception of its own functions that at times, when it takes note of its actions, merely seems like a mysterious subjective depth.[7]

Hermes: Oh, come now. We're back at mirrors looking at one another; but mirrors don't look at anything—they're just the surfaces where something appears for consciousness to look at. Mirrors don't *experience* reflection. You can't dispel the intractability of subjective consciousness for physicalism with airy hypotheses about the mechanical functions consciousness might serve—certainly not by "pleonastically" (as our dear Psyche would say) multiplying the problem. The mystery of how a material brain might be aware of the world subjectively isn't solved just by positing another, smaller brain—or brain-module—within the brain that somehow makes one aware of the larger brain's activity. This just circles us around again to the same insoluble problems: How is this inner conscious perspective possible at all in a world of ostensibly intrinsically non-mental matter? How does this module possess subjective awareness, or at least induce it simply through doubling a mechanical operation? And how does this proprioception, as a function of a physical system, avoid the charge of infinite regress?

Hephaistos: All right, I won't dispute the point now. I think you're all making certain questionable assumptions, but I may need some time to formulate a response.

Psyche: Well, we can proceed in the meantime. Actually, this issue of subjectivity as founded on itself naturally brings us to the next matter I was intending to raise: that of the *unity of consciousness.*

Hephaistos: You've mentioned that already.

Psyche: Only in passing, and it's of more than passing importance. After all, the mechanical view of matter tells us that the physical realm must be devoid of any real simple unities. Everything real is material, and what we solecistically call material "unities" are really only composites and aggregates and coalescences, all of them spatially and temporally extended and decomposable, at least in principle. And yet consciousness—the field of awareness—seems to be one and indivisible, and necessarily so. At least, it seems clearly the case that this field isn't just a collection of extrinsic associations, like a box of tools; it's a radically singular mental experience concentrated indivisibly in one place, as one act of a single mind. At any given moment, the mind is holding together an incalculable diversity of sense impressions, stimuli, qualities, ideas, concepts, associations, memories, anticipations, intentions—things present and things absent—not to mention auto-affection and proprioception and, once again, that ever-mysterious reflective inner awareness of one's own thinking; the full richness of the phenomenal structure of subjective experience is nothing less than the intensely concentrated and yet elaborately organized—even opulently orchestrated—oneness of the world and the self; and we can have neither world nor self except through that unity. It's a continuity in time as well: a dynamic flow of perception and thought in which reality's utter diversity—not only that of the sensible world but that of the psychological and conceptual worlds as well—is constantly being organized and synthesized in the indivisible uniqueness—the vanishing point, as it were—of the individual mind, both as something present and as a temporal totality, with attention turned toward both past and future—that is, with both retention and protention, to use the technical jargon. A piece of music exists as a piece of music, for instance, only because the mind's attention and perception, as well as its powers of memory and of anticipation, hold the totality of the composition's discrete notes and intervals together in a sustained continuity—a profound unity in fact—rather than merely registering those sounds in a series of disjunctions. And this is a dual mystery: the unity of the world "out there" as experienced "in here," and the unity of the mind "in here" experiencing that world "out there."

HEPHAISTOS: Why call it a unity rather than a coordination of plural faculties? What's unique about it, that it should be regarded as radically different from any other form of natural integrity?

PSYCHE: Of course there's a coordination of faculties, but that's irrelevant. Their merged operations still have to come together *as one* within a single, indivisible point of perspective in order to constitute an act of awareness on the part of a self. That's simply what subjective consciousness is. In fact, one definition of objective, third-person, non-conscious reality might simply be the absence of such unity. That's not to deny that there might also be unconscious dimensions of the mind's activities in addition to that concentrated unity. There are many things that don't reach the surface of ordinary consciousness. Just as consciousness isn't directly in control of all the body's physiological functions, so many of its higher or ancillary functions might also exceed the scope of direct awareness. But where there *is* consciousness, there's a unity that nothing in physical nature can explain.

HEPHAISTOS: So you say, but I have my doubts.

PSYCHE: I eagerly await hearing them. But let me try to be yet clearer here. You mentioned "natural integrity." Surely you must know that integrity and unity are very different things. When I speak of the unity of mind, I'm speaking not merely of something rare, but of something unique. More than that, in fact. It's not merely the only such unity found in nature; it is itself the unity of whatever physical world there is, as known by and intelligible within experience. The physical order may contain a vast collection of organized properties and things, but all of these are ultimately combinations of parts—mereological totalities, that is. The actual unity of any given phenomenon, and of the world of phenomena as a whole, has its real existence not in those physical arrangements taken by themselves, but rather in the awareness, intentionality, and singularity of the mind. Only there are there any truly *unified* wholes.

Now I, of course, think that the very same unity found in the mind also indwells the world, as the formal cause within each thing, and as the oneness of the one divine mind in which all things live and move and exist. But, even if one doesn't hold such a view, one must grant that true unity—as opposed to mere integrity—is a mental, not a physical, reality. No order of causal relations among the parts of an organized totality can in itself achieve that oneness. The atoms, molecules, elements, and mechanical parts of a lamp do not constitute the lamp as a singularity enfolded within the singularity of the world. It's that inner "witness" of which we earlier spoke that binds all things in one, even in our experiences of multiplicity. The witness gathers and arranges diverse sensations, aspects, cognitions, thoughts, and so forth in a single present that's also the continuously changing meeting point of a past always already departing and a future always already arriving, each of which comes with its own remoter horizons of memory and expectation, and it refers all of this simultaneously to "me." Consider what that entails, just at the level of sensory experience. When you pluck a rose from a rose tree, the neurology of your brain necessarily distributes various aspects of countless stimuli throughout its system. The rose's several features occupy various parts of the visual cortex: shape, pattern, redness, and so forth are all apprehended in particular regions of neural competency. Then too there's the fragrance of the blossom, and of the leaves, and of the breeze blowing through them; there's the sound of birds, the sound of the wind, maybe a glimpse of blue wings flashing out against the greenery beyond; and so on and so forth. And yet all these sensory impressions come together for you in a synchronized totality that, of itself, can be known to none of your individual neurons involved in their separate operations. Do individual neurons have a past and future perspective?

HEPHAISTOS: Oh, come. A camera feeding images into a television monitor does as much, and produces a unified representation of those images.

PSYCHE: It most certainly does not. That unified representation is your mind's perception of the pixels and pulses and radiations of that screen. In the camera and monitor themselves, as mechanisms, there aren't any representations at all; there are only luminescent multiplicities, countless electrical and photoelectrical events. It's only in an intending mind that a picture appears as a coherent image of something in particular.

Again, please, consider just how constant and pervasive and singular this mental power of unification is. It synchronizes even temporal sensory disjunctions: there's a flash of lightning at a great distance, for example, and the sound takes longer to reach your ears than the light does to reach your eyes; yet even the delay between the sight and the sound is apprehended by you as a unity of experience within an organized dynamic flow of awareness. That isn't the function of any single faculty, much less of several distinct faculties operating in concert; it's a unified act that must be in place prior to all such functions, limitlessly hospitable to all of them, indeterminately open to every determination of mind, and able instantaneously to orchestrate their innumerable voices into a single coherent chorus. And this unity of apprehension is utterly unlike, even contrary to, the composite, successive, and discordant constitution of physical objects and events.

HEPHAISTOS: Very well, so the unifying power of the mind is a special feature of . . . well, of minds. I can grant that much without being obliged to abandon a physicalist model of reality. That's simply what the function of the neural apparatus of the brain and body is: a navigation system, so to speak, that maps the environment out as an intelligible continuum occupied by particular kinds of things. I grant also that the mechanism that accomplishes that experiential synchronization or orchestration or whatever you'd call it is a very impressive piece of neural technology. Again, though, a technology it is.

PSYCHE: That still doesn't explain the existence of unified subjectivity. The technology isn't itself the subjective experience *of* that technology. Does a map read itself? The real enigma that your view of things fails to capture lies not simply within the field of perception, but on the other side of the phenomenal spectacle, in that place from which the mind looks outward: not simply in the unity the mind imposes on the world, that is, but in the mind's own inner power of unified apprehension. It's that, I submit, that suggests the inadequacy of the physicalist model.

HERMES: This is a very old observation, after all—almost a metaphysical commonplace throughout the world, Eastern and Western, ancient, mediaeval, and modern. Consider, oh, let's say the great Sunni philosopher Fakhr al Dīn al-Razī; much of his brilliant *Book of the Soul and the Spirit and Their Faculties* is constructed around this paradox of a unified "I" associated with a composite brain. The indivisibility of mind is even one of those few points on which Descartes's reasoning is unassailable.[8]

Goodness, even Kant, while rejecting Descartes's attempt to deduce the soul's immortality from that unity, nonetheless insists on that unity's reality, and even notes that it renders the reduction of subjective thoughts to physical events logically impossible: Every composite thing, he acknowledges, is an aggregate of several other things, and all its actions are aggregations of diverse actions and accidents. This sort of composition of powers, he says, poses no obvious problem for physical effects, like the movement of the body, but it's an insurmountable obstacle to a materialist account of the act of thinking. If it's the composite thing that's doing the thinking, then each part of the composite possesses only a part of the thought, and only in the aggregate is there a complete thought—but then who or what is having that thought? Where does that thought as a unity occur? Can it be just another part of the brain, with its own diverse parts and its own necessary inner coordinating facility? But then that too is made up of partially competent . . .[9]

HEPHAISTOS: It seems to me you're confusing two different things. You're assuming that, because a thought must be unified, the machinery of thinking must be as well, rather than just—as I say—coordinated.

HERMES: No, I'm assuming that the machinery of thinking obviously *can't* be unified, and so even its coordination *can't* be identical to the unified experience it facilitates. That's a logically impeccable conclusion. A thought or perception in its entirety must be more than the multiplicity of its parts, at least if that thought combines all the various deliverances of its diverse faculties. You, I would counter, are confusing the contents of knowledge with knowledge of those contents. Mere coordination of data is sufficient if all that's at stake is the accumulation, organization, and storage of information; but it's entirely insufficient if we're talking about the actual subjective knowledge of that information. A computer is capable of the former—or, rather, is capable of storing binary code that can be interpreted as information by the mind of the computer's user—but it's entirely incapable of the latter. A computer *knows* nothing; there's no unified subject to whom that information is referred and presented; there's no inner "witness" illuminating that information and transforming it into personal knowledge. And, if we insist on treating our own organisms as machines, then we find the same mereological paradox obstructing our path to any coherent account of subjectivity.

I mean, the composite of the body is no doubt extremely efficient at relaying data from one part of its system to the next—through its cells and tissues and nerves, through its senses and all its various percipient faculties—but at no point in that flow is there a unified apprehension of reality. Even if we think of each of the various parts of the system as somehow possessing a discrete knowledge of some part of the whole, as if our organisms could be decomposed into vast colonies of independent homunculi, each somehow aware of its own little field of cognitive competency—a shudder of pleasure, a bar of colored light, a tone, what have you—even then, in the aggregate, they would no more *know* the full contents of a thought or perception than a room full of children, each separately aware of only one word from a poem, could be said in the aggregate to know the poem. Even that picture is misleading, because, even if we were composites of little homuncular functions that were somehow partially cognizant of the whole, each of those little imps would itself presumably be a material composite, acquiring its tiny morsels of cognitive data by way of its own internal structure of parts, each of which would have its own distinct competence, and so on in an infinite regress into ever more minute divisions, down perhaps to the Planck scale and sheer quantum potentiality. It's absurd. Thinking isn't a collaborative activity. Something must grasp these partial grasps of reality as a unified whole, and somewhere the *whole* must be the property of the *one*.[10]

HEPHAISTOS: I'm not convinced that a supremely competent executive module in the brain wouldn't be sufficient to coordinate all those sources of information, at least well enough for a functional sort of intermediary operation that allows our systems of cognition to negotiate our environment by assuming a kind of "first-person" appearance.

Hermes: Will you continue to revert to the issue of function, even if it can't explain how consciousness is causally possible? And to talk of the *appearance* of subjectivity?

Hephaistos: I shall, yes, until such time as I'm dissuaded from doing so. As I told you, I've more to say on the matter.

Psyche: As you should. But, as for the matter of this central module, it simply won't do, Phaesty my dear. This is the old familiar "binding problem," as it's often called. Neurologists, almost to a man and a woman, say that no such central processing facility can be isolated in the brain. But it wouldn't matter if one could be found. One more time: Let's say, as seems to be the case, that the information the brain processes from the world around it is distributed "holographically," as it were, around the cerebrum's neural architecture. Let's then say there's some privileged, supervisory panopticon located in some executive module of the brain's neurology where all the faculties of brain and body converge. As a physical entity, that module would still have to enjoy a kind of unified perspective over and beyond its own composite nature. Its power to unify experience still couldn't result from its various parts and functions; the unified perspective would have to be there already, so to speak, logically prior to that variety, organizing it—or, rather, *fusing* it—into a single point of view. Not only would that same power have to synthesize the disparate kinds of data received by the brain and nervous system and cognitive intellect through its own internal faculties; it would already have to be at work organizing the variety of its own inner faculties' functions, and would have to operate as a kind of intentionality that already somehow "knows" the difference between the partial impressions those faculties form and the complete representation or perception they convey. I repeat: that unified and unifying inner agency cannot, at least at its ground, be a physical thing. If it were . . . well, as we've said, it would constitute a regress into an infinite series of ever more occult central faculties.[11]

Hephaistos: Then let's not pursue it just now; if it's infinite, we're unlikely to reach its end before teatime. But let's also take a step back. What was it that you said about this central module needing to "know" in advance the difference between data and what the data represents . . . ? You skipped over that with alarming nimbleness.

PSYCHE: Surely it's obvious that there's a remarkably adaptable intentionality at work in this labor of mental synthesis. If nothing else, the mind has to be able to perform this marvel of unification for every kind of experience, even novel experience, and do it more or less instantaneously, or with only minimal delays. How can it, though, without some prior grasp of what it's translating from neural data into mental perceptions?

HERMES: That's right. I hadn't thought of that. No one can translate a poem without already knowing both languages, and without knowing what the poem means in its original language. Translation occurs—at least, if it's producing a result intelligible to an attending consciousness—only where there's a kind of prior understanding of both sides of the act of translation, transcending them both.

PSYCHE: Yes, and in the case of interpreting the world through the apparatus of the brain, that means the mind must already know the difference between sense-perception and its semantic or symbolic representation in thought, and have complete command of the "code," so to speak, for effecting the conversion of the one into the other, and in an efficiently useful way. But how could a physical faculty that receives all its knowledge only at the end of countless diverse neurological and cognitive stimulations ever come to possess a concept logically prior to that storm of data that would allow it to discriminate among and arrange what it receives, or allow it to provide paradigms into which to integrate those data? This is no mere system of stimulus and response, of even the most refined variety. How would it be capable of an empirical grasp of the diverse realities it gathers into a single experience apart from a more "transcendental" grasp of—and intentionality toward—a consonant totality of things within which those realities have their specific meanings and references? Though I suppose I'll need to go into further detail regarding mental intentionality to make perfect sense of that.

HEPHAISTOS: Yes, indeed you will. But tell me, if I were to note that the mind suffers constant disruptions of cognitive coherence, and were to offer this as evidence against the unity of consciousness, you'd accuse me of the psychologistic fallacy, wouldn't you? You'd tell me not to confuse the empirical self with that mysterious transcendental "I think"—that "witness," that detached vanishing point of pure perspective—that you insist is immune to the vicissitudes of bodies and brains and psychologies.

PSYCHE: [*After a reflective pause:*] Why, yes, I would. At any rate I'd insist that what I'm saying in no way requires us to believe that brain states can't be altered, interrupted, divided, or confused. It requires only that both the discontinuities of experience—or of reasoning, or of subjectivity—occur in relation to a background of unified awareness. Even confusion is experienced from a point of indivisible unity . . . of the presence of the mind to itself . . . that vanishing point, as we've called it. When you're confused, you still don't dissolve into a plurality of perspectives, each unaware of the others. You witness your own disorientation from some imperturbable place still more inward than your cognitive faculties.

Again, I don't believe in the Cartesian soul; I don't believe in a monad where all the forms of mental reality are concentrated in a single mode. I believe the mind is a contraction of some larger reality, so that at its heights it opens out into something more than itself, and in its depths too it opens out into the natural world at large. And yes, I believe in that witness—that *sākṣi* or *Ātman*—or *nous* or *intellectus* or spirit, or the transcendental "apperception" or "I think," or what have you. Call it what you like. Without that luminous continuity and oneness of consciousness there could be no self-awareness, no coherent perceptions, no thought or items of knowledge or recollection . . . and there couldn't be anything like organized experience. That's where all the diversity of experience becomes the awareness of a subject, in a unity that couldn't have arisen from that diversity. And yes, also, that unity's not the psychological self. It's logically prior to that. It's something anonymous, really—so anonymous that it doesn't differ from one person to another. And I, of course, believe it's really one and the same in all of us: the same divine spark shedding its light on all that the mind contains—the single flame burning in the lanterns of all our souls. Psychological integrity can disintegrate, personal memory can fade or be destroyed, the physiology of the brain and its cognitive apparatus can be impaired; but it's not the psychological integrity of the empirical ego that renders physical reductionism absurd. It's that abiding unity of pure, singular, incommunicable awareness as such.

HEPHAISTOS: [*Remaining silent for several seconds, then stretching out a hand and conjuring a crystal goblet of nectar into existence:*] Excuse me. Hair of the dog. [*Drinking deeply and then languidly waving the goblet away into nothingness again:*] So far, I'm not entirely impervious to your argument. At least, you've presented me with certain novel considerations. For instance, the argument about subjectivity being founded only upon further subjectivity hadn't occurred to me before, and will require further reflection on my part. I'll have to decide whether it's an illusion of grammar or a real problem. But I've also, I think, foolishly placed myself at a dialectical disadvantage in this debate. My tactical error, of course, was in gallantly consenting to that catalogue of popular fallacies you presented me with yesterday. I fear I may have inadvertently signed an armistice and submitted to terms of surrender before the battle was ever joined. Look where it's left me. You confront me with an absolute rhapsody of personal incredulity at the brain's—excuse me, I mean, the *mind's*—seemingly miraculous powers and complexities. I answer that minds may be capable of such feats because an extraordinary mechanism of control exists somewhere in the neurological labyrinth of the brain, and that such a mechanism, for all its marvelous competencies, had many millions of years to evolve. Straightaway, you arraign me for taking refuge in the genetic fallacy or the *cui bono* fallacy or both. You rehearse in stirring cadences all the ways in which the mind seems to exhibit an infrangible unity. When I note that cognitive functions are in fact subject to confusion and fragmentation, you rebuke me for succumbing to the psychologistic fallacy. If I protest that you're giving short shrift to the generative power of the gradual, epochal co-evolution of the faculties of brain and body, you'll reprehend me for falling prey to this blasted pleonastic fallacy of yours. I'd like to get out of this labyrinth you've constructed by simply forging ahead, of course, but you've sealed all the routes of escape. Do recall, though, Psyche my dear, that I have certain, ah, *daedal* gifts, as it were; if I have to confect pinions from feathers and wax to ascend out of the maze, I will. There are different kinds of physicalism, after all, and it may be that you've merely posed problems yet to be solved within a physicalist frame of reference rather than insurmountable paradoxes.

Eros: Now, don't prevaricate. Your disadvantage in this debate isn't the result of a cunningly set dialectical trap. It's the result of your taking the weaker logical position.

Psyche: [*Raising a hand and smiling tenderly at Eros:*] Wait, my love. Perhaps Phaesty's right. I think my argument still has to be considerably amplified in order to be convincing. So far we've considered consciousness chiefly as the recipient and internal curator of the reality of the world "out there." Perhaps we should begin to emphasize the mind's agency in, so to speak, venturing out into that reality.

III

Intentionality and Ecstasy

Hephaistos: How so?

Psyche: Well, let's begin simply by distinguishing between the mind's powers of unified apprehension and the prior mental agency that allows it to achieve that unification.

Hephaistos: That seems a very fine distinction indeed.

Psyche: But a vital one. Part of the mystery of the mind is that, in order to know or experience anything, it must already "will" to do so; but, in order to will something, it must somehow know what it's willing. We don't merely *receive* the world mentally; we must in a sense go out in search of it, though we may not be consciously choosing to do so; and that's possible only because we know what we're seeking, even if only in a very general way. This mysterious inseparability of knowing and willing is *intentionality.* Really, the mystery here is all rather elegantly comprised in the Latin term *intentio*—an act of being directed to or of reaching out toward some end. Already, in putting the matter that way, we find ourselves confronted with a phenomenon that seems to defy the mechanical philosophy's deepest principles; there's no more conspicuous example of teleology in nature—of final causality, or antecedent finality, or intrinsic purposiveness, or whatever you choose to call it—than the directedness of mind and will toward an end. This is the diametric opposite of the mechanistic understanding of nature. Nor is this a rare or marginal phenomenon; arguably it's necessarily present in every conscious state. Each act of thought and volition, of perception and judgment, even of simple recognition is dependent upon this initial going-forth of the mind toward the world.

HEPHAISTOS: [*With a laugh:*] That sounds like the "extramission" theory of vision.

EROS: Really? How so?

HEPHAISTOS: Well, you know: I mean the antiquated notion that, in order for the eye to see, it must project a kind of inner light outward toward the objects of vision. But, of course, we now know vision is actually wholly "intromissive"; it receives its light, and the world that light illuminates, from beyond. By the same token, I don't see why it's not enough to say that the mind receives the world of the senses . . .

PSYCHE: But is that right? Yes, of course, eyes take in light. In some sense, too, the mind takes in knowledge from the world; but can it do so simply as the *passive* recipient of some mental . . . well, "intromission," as you call it? Does it receive *the world* or does it receive only sensory impulses that it must actively interpret in order for the world to come into consciousness? Maybe the older theory of vision was an expression of a true intuition . . . a mental truth displaced, as it were, into an ocular theory. Actually, I don't think we can even *see* the world—if that means seeing it in such a way that we recognize it as an ensemble of discrete objects, each of which can be discerned as a specific kind of thing—without this prior "extramission" of the intending mind. We never perceive unless our perception is also always an interpretation, an act of understanding, and understanding is always *about* something in itself; it's never simply a passive impression. Remember, by talking about "intentionality," philosophers of mind aren't speaking merely of conscious exercises of private, elective volition. They're speaking of the mind's fundamental power of orienting itself toward a given end. It's the mind's capacity for "aboutness," the constant agency of the mind toward reality, by which it perceives, thinks, wills, imagines, discerns, desires, believes, resolves, judges, understands, communicates, contemplates, expects, fears, hopes, symbolizes, indicates, interprets, or in any other way moves itself toward a specific purpose or object.

Hephaistos: And yet, even so, what you call the mind's capacity for "aboutness" could just as well be described as world's capacity for impressing its contents upon cognition, followed by cognition translating stimuli into representations by way of a kind of neurological filtration process rather than through some special intentionality.

Psyche: No, no, no. The contents of intentionality aren't features of the physical world that affect the mind, and they certainly can't be produced just by neurological operations. They're first and foremost *meanings*, which don't exist anywhere in the physical environment. They're "aspectual," to use the philosophical jargon.

Hephaistos: Which is to say . . . ?

Psyche: Which is to say they're the intentions of things "under the aspect of" this or that. We dealt with this yesterday, didn't we? When I see a certain statue of a beautiful and majestic woman drawing a bow, I may or may not know that it's a statue of the goddess Artemis. If I don't, then the meaning with which I invest it differs from the meaning it would have for someone who knows whom it depicts. Then too, its meaning for me differs according to whether I'm disposed to see it as a religious artifact, a mere piece of civic ornamentation, an actual commemoration of some particular event, and so on. None of these meanings is there physically, prompting my intentions; the physical object remains the same in every instance. And what if, instead of the statue itself, I were presented with a picture someone had drawn of it? For me, it might be a picture of a woman drawing a bow or a picture of the goddess Artemis, while for the artist it might be only a picture of the statue: not of a real woman or goddess or of anyone else, but only of that cultic or civic artifact. The meaning of the drawing is dependent upon the intentionality of the person drawing or looking at it. Or take a simpler example: consider a picture of a single geometrical figure with three sides and three angles; you can think of it as either a trilateral or a triangle; but there's nothing in the physical composition of the figure on the paper that determines which of these meanings you impose upon it.[12] It's all rather like that wonderful Borges story about Pierre Menard's version of *Don Quixote:*

in every physical respect it's the same novel as the one Cervantes wrote; but it can never mean the same thing as the original novel because it's been so enriched or altered by countless additional layers of recollection, irony, critical history, cultural change, social history, and intertextuality, all of which the book acquires simply in being written in the twentieth century, long after Cervantes's more naïve—more innocent and unreflective—labor of writing the original.

HEPHAISTOS: From which you deduce what?

PSYCHE: That intentional ideas aren't impressed on the mind by physical causes. Wasn't it Wittgenstein who said that the image of a man walking forward up a hill is physically indistinguishable from the image of that man walking backwards down the hill, and yet the thought of a man walking uphill isn't the same as the thought of a man walking downhill backwards?[13] The aspect under which we perceive something simply can't be reduced to a third-person account of the physical interaction between our neurology and that thing, without a simultaneous act of interpretation. But let's begin at the beginning.

HEPHAISTOS: I'm beginning to tire of learning that we're still always at the beginning.

PSYCHE: I mean only of this topic, which begins in a sense with Franz Brentano. He was the one who introduced the category of intentionality into modern philosophy—or the philosophy of psychology, at least—though he was drawing on scholastic precedent. For him, intentionality constitutes the very "mark of the mental," and is a phenomenon entirely absent from any merely material physical order. In his view, there's no real act of consciousness not informed by intention, however elementary. And I daresay no one has isolated its features any more precisely than he did. He names four in all: that an intentional state of the mind or its products is always directed beyond itself toward some object; that this object might be either real or imaginary, since in neither case is it the efficient physical cause of intentionality; that this object can be indeterminate in many of its details, since the determination of intentionality comes from the mind; and that many intentional states of mind may be rather imprecise as regards reference, or as regards the truth contained in their apprehensions, because the act of intending isn't contingent on all the concrete facts about its objects. Basically, that is to say, intentionality comes from the mind *as* mind, not from the environment; it's a kind of primal active openness *toward* reality, in the form of purposive expectations about what's out there to be discovered—though, as I say, it doesn't require a physical object "out there" at all, as opposed to something wholly imaginary or conceptual or prospective. It's miraculously free of determination by any of the physical realities or relations of the world or the brain. Brentano calls this the "inexistence" of the intentional object, which means both that it exists *as* an intentional object in the mind's agency, whatever its ontological status in other modes, and that a mental act exists by virtue of having within itself some aspect of an intentional object. Intentionality is only mental, and the mental is always intentional.[14]

And yet, without this mental orientation, though we might have something vaguely like experience, of the most nebulous sensory kind—and I'm not convinced of that, to be honest—we wouldn't experience a world. Intentionality is what allows us to possess and act upon conscious meaning, to refer to objects, to understand them or present them to ourselves as particular things. I mean, you're seated there upon what for you is a bench; benches are features of your world, with a purpose and a nature. A squirrel who might come across what to you is a bench would in fact experience only a kind of solid object, and even then only to the degree that something vaguely like a concept of "object" or "solid" might be available to him. Rather he'd probably experience just a mode of solidity or obstruction. Benches, as far as we know, aren't part of his intentional world's furniture, part of his world of "meaning," if he has one, and so simply don't exist as such for him.

EROS: Actually, my soul, all the squirrels here in the Metakosmia are divine. They talk, and have all sorts of clear concepts about things . . .

PSYCHE: Yes, of course, my love.

EROS: Many of them even write poetry . . .

Psyche: Yes, yes, it was foolish of me to slip back into my human way of speaking. And who knows even what terrestrial squirrels think? One mustn't make assumptions. But I trust my point is clear.

Hephaistos: You're lucidity itself, dear lady. As yet, however, you've not convinced me that intentionality poses some insuperable difficulty for an intelligent naturalism. All right, the mind acts purposefully. Its ability to do so is an emergent feature of its neurology, which may be remarkable, but which is nevertheless the remote consequence of innumerable prior non-intentional causes—physical actions and reactions, stretching over countless millennia, until at last there appeared a system of stimulus and response so sophisticated that it could direct its own activity toward its environment, or could seem to do so . . .

Psyche: Ah . . . no. That won't do. Not unless you can explain to me how something utterly contrary to the principles of physical causation can emerge from physical causation without that constituting something on the order of a miracle—which may be what the word "emergence" often really means—as well as how a mechanism can be said to "direct" itself toward an end. An eye doesn't focus itself on something understood *as that thing*. An organism with a mind focusses its eye on something out there, under a particular aspect and with a purpose; and aspects and purposes aren't mechanical forces.

Hephaistos: And you're certain that intentionality is *utterly* contrary to physical causality?

Psyche: As always, to physical causality *conceived mechanistically*, which is the point of contention, I believe. Not only could intentionality not have evolved out of a mechanistic material order; it couldn't function at all within such an order. The issue isn't just that the mind directs its own activity; the issue is *how* it does so and toward *what*. The camera eye, for instance, may have evolved from what was initially little more than some sort of photosensitive neural cluster in the cutaneous tissue of some organism in the remote past—in fact, apparently it's done just that on repeated occasions—and then only over time acquired the mechanisms necessary for seeking the light and focusing on this or that object. But could the organism to which that eye belongs have acquired the power of intentionality in the same way, so that it would willfully train that eye upon, say, a bench or a squirrel in order to see it as, specifically, a bench or a squirrel? Considered just as ophthalmic machinery, could the eye seek out anything as "that kind" of thing? Or is that possible only for a different kind of agency—a mental inclination toward a purpose, which exists under the aspect of "purpose" only because of that mental inclination? In the one case, the eye developed in response to physical forces and constraints within the environment and within the physical structures of a long succession of organic phenotypes. In the other case, though, if physicalism is true, there could have been nothing external prompting the development of an intentional capacity. There's no "meaning" objectively present in a mechanistically physical world, nor can there have been some inchoate physiological sensitivity to "meaning" that fortuitously appeared in some nervous system. So there's nothing there in the world of physical interactions for natural selection to fasten upon. Even if I could grant that subjectivity could emerge out of absolute objectivity, which I can't, I still wouldn't be able to believe that intentionality could emerge out of mere sensibility.

Hephaistos: Again, as with consciousness, so too with intentionality: certain systems of stimulus and response, especially very complex systems, might naturally entail the appearance of intentionality.

Psyche: And, as with consciousness, so too with intentionality: such a claim is pointless unless it also explains how such a transition from pure quantitative, mechanistic causes to qualitative, subjective agency is possible. It's also pointless if it doesn't explain what that interior private dimension—consciousness or intentionality—adds to a functional system that would not be present in the operations of an unthinking automaton or "zombie." And where too, in phylogenic history, was this threshold crossed? Because, like consciousness, intentionality is either there or it isn't. Where and how was that abyss leapt over? At what point was there suddenly, as there had never before been, mental agency interpreting the world, knowing it as an ensemble of meanings—meanings of which it somehow already had some intentional grasp before ever encountering the world?

HERMES: If I may touch on the first point, I'm not sure why you continually revert to this language of "appearance." As Psyche says, intentionality is either there or it isn't; and, if it isn't, then nothing appears as anything at all. How could something merely *appear* to be intentionality? To think of something *as* intentionality—to think of your experience under that particular aspect—is already an act of intentionality.

PSYCHE: Precisely. Really, we're talking about much the same thing. Subjectivity is already "semantic"—that is, it's always already an awareness of things under the aspects of meanings or purposes, signs and significances—and yet semantics exists only for a subjective awareness. Though a good deal of analytic philosophy of mind blunderingly separates consciousness and intentionality into distinct faculties—the one concerned only with sense experience, the other only with propositional content—they're in fact inseparable. One doesn't experience a *quale* without the mind attending to it as a sensation, indicating some source—identifiable or not—of that sensation. To be conscious involves recognition, being aware of what is and also of what might be but isn't—affirmations of what things are and negations of what they're not. Meaning and awareness exist each in such intensity as the other does; and, as either fades away, so the other disappears with it. I think, if I were asked to determine these things, I'd speak of this inseparability of consciousness and intentionality simply as "attention," just as, for instance, Nicholas of Cusa does.[15] And I'd identify this attention as the mind's fundamental act. As we've discussed, to be subjectively aware is to be aware of one's own awareness, and so one's every act of conscious thought toward the world is also already an intentional directedness of the mind toward its own agency.

HEPHAISTOS: [*Throwing up his hands in mock helplessness:*] Now you're being anything *but* lucidity itself, my good Psyche. I mean, yes, I understand that awareness of a thing increases to the degree that one is specifically thinking of that thing as what it is. One is more aware of a tree in the moments when one is attending to it mentally *as a tree* and as a tree that happens to be standing *just there*, rather than when perceiving it in passing, as some background feature that one isn't thinking about directly. And perhaps one is still more conscious of it under the aspect of, say, an elm, rather than merely under the general designation "tree." And I understand that one can perceive that tree as a tree, and reflect upon it both in its general "arboreality," let's say, as well as in its individuality as a concrete object only to the degree that one's consciously aware of it. That all seems undeniable, and I follow you to that point. But then there are experiences that don't seem to correspond to any prior intention at all, such as, say, an unexpected shock of pain or a feeling of generalized anxiety.

PSYCHE: Both of which are conscious experiences only because the mind directs itself at them under finite aspects. Moreover, as far as conscious experience is concerned, the unexpected is experienced as unexpected only because it's a modality of a prior expectation: to wit, the failure of that expectation to be correctly fulfilled. You must have intentional expectations, after all, for them to be thwarted. That a momentary experience can fail to correspond with one's intentionality is itself the effect of that intentionality.

HEPHAISTOS: [*With a wince of amused incredulity:*] And what, pray tell, does that mean?

PSYCHE: It seems to me obvious that we experience anything as something particular only either through a prior expectation that the experience confirms or through an expectation that it fails to confirm. I think it's obvious that we receive the world through a kind of constant expectancy—a kind of "active patiency," so to speak, that reaches out to the world. And I think this is both specific and general. There's an expectancy regarding, say, that tree we were talking about. Perhaps I expect it to be an oak, and only when it fails to fulfill that "meaning" do I have to revise my expectation according to another meaning, and finally assign the tree to the category of "elm." And then there's a more general expectancy, turned toward the world as a whole—an expectation . . . an intention toward truth, toward the world as understandable, which causes my mind always to venture forth into the world in search of the aspects of things, under which I might grasp that truth. Without that . . . that ecstasy toward the world as an intelligible whole, we could experience nothing as anything at all. I mentioned Husserl earlier. He was brilliant in his analysis of how intentionality—how a kind of constant purposiveness, attentiveness, and expectancy—is necessary even to interpret the content of sense-impressions, through both the harmony of expectancy and experience and the dissonance between them. You know, even a shock of pain takes a moment to register as *pain*, doesn't it? A moment in which the mind turns toward that shock and interprets it so that it fits within an intelligible ordering of experience . . .

HEPHAISTOS: It's interesting that you think pain needs to be interpreted.

PSYCHE: To the degree that's it's fully conscious, it does. I don't even think this is all that extraordinary an observation, or that it concerns anything unique to supposedly higher organisms. I'm quite sure that animals too must adjust their intentionality in accord with experience properly to make some kind of sense of it. For us as conscious users of signs, of course, who interpret things according to meanings in the fullest sense, the experience comes to have specifically the meaning "pain," which we understand in a more abstract sense, even when we can't immediately identify it. For us, there's that additional level—or those several additional levels—of intentionality. But nothing that counts as real cognizance—real recognition—is possible apart from some level of intention. Again, even cognitive dissonance isn't wholly non-intentional. You experience it precisely as a disruption and failure of a prior intention within a continuum of intentions. And to overcome that dissonance, you have to rely on your memories of successful intentions, at some level of generality or specificity. I mean . . . well, take for instance, that goblet you summoned up a little while ago. Nectar, I assume. What though would you have tasted had you brought it to your lips expecting nectar but instead, inexplicably, it had been filled with goat's milk?

HEPHAISTOS: [*With a shrug:*] I'd have tasted goat's milk—which I heartily detest.

PSYCHE: No, as a matter of fact, you wouldn't have—at least, not at first. Your first impression would have been sheer cognitive dissonance. Your initial sensations wouldn't have immediately coalesced into a recognizable flavor. At first, you would have registered only that part of your original intentions had been fulfilled—it was liquid—while the rest of them had been thwarted, and your intentionality would have interpreted the dissonance for you as somehow wrong. Only after mentally retreating from the experience and approaching it again with new, broader expectations, severed from the specific intention of tasting nectar, would you have been able to recognize it and integrate it into a remembered series of past experiences. Till that moment it wouldn't even have tasted like what it was to you; the sensory data conveyed to your brain would not yet have assumed the form of the flavor of goat's milk in your mind. Even the qualitative character of your experience is dependent on mental intentions.

And the same is true, once again, of your perceptions. Consider optical illusions, such as that one you can see either as two human profiles in silhouette facing one another or as a vase in outline, as you choose to see it. You will it to have the meaning it will have for you, and then in consequence you see whichever of the two objects you consciously intend; and, of course, you can switch back and forth between them as you like. To me, that fact is impossible to make sense of in physicalist terms alone. Again, the mind knows nothing in pure passivity, simply as the recipient of a physical cause. It's always at work investing perception with determinate content. Consciousness is a kind of artistry actively, purposefully composing its perceptions out of what would otherwise be an undifferentiated storm of sense-impressions incessantly impinging upon our senses, sheer cascades of causal sequences without discrete aspects or clear delineations, and without any exact beginnings or endings.

Hephaistos: You're really certain, are you, that all of this is intrinsically irreconcilable with a physicalist narrative of reality?

Psyche: If that reality is understood mechanically. Can't you see how even this small but singular fact—that you can direct your mind to perceive an image as one thing or another—renders a mechanistic picture of intentionality almost perfectly preposterous? You physicalists are the ones who say the material order is intrinsically devoid of purpose and meaning, or of intentionality or final causes. It's all just infinite undifferentiated eventuality for you, incessant exchanges of energy between instances of mass, infinite change at infinite speed. Intentionality is the opposite of all of that. It's finite, for one thing, directed at things under very particular aspects, with very particular limits; it partially halts or crystallizes the pure flow of sensation, containing it in stable islands of enduring form amid the flood of sensory experience; that's how it isolates objects of attention, and interprets events and things in determinate ways. It's also entirely purposeful, an agency elicited by final causes, both individual and general.

HERMES: If I might interject something . . .

PSYCHE: Please.

IV
Language

Hermes: The effect of intention on sensory data is interesting, no doubt, but surely the most conspicuous expression of intentionality of all is language. Yes, we interpret everything. We see a plume of smoke as a sign of fire. We see an expression crossing the face of a friend as indicative of displeasure. But in these instances it's easy to mistake what we're doing for something continuous with a mere system of stimulus and response. It's only in the full range of our semeiotic capacities that we see the obvious difference between intentionality and anything reducible to the physical interactions of our neurology with our environment. Language is nothing but intentionality, purposive meaning communicated in signs. It's a world alongside the world, so to speak, or a plane of reality continuously hovering above the physical plane, a place in which meaning is generated and shared entirely by meaning. We can talk about—and so conceive of—realities that aren't present in any physical sense at all. We can discuss abstractions that have no material existence, let alone the power to impinge on our nervous systems. The very reality that I can use signs to communicate something to you, or can receive a message from you by understanding the signs you use, seems to me more than enough evidence of intentionality's transcendence of physical causality.

Psyche: Quite so. I didn't want to begin with language, however, because of that aforementioned habit on the part of some analytic philosophers of segregating conscious experience and intentional meaning into different, unconnected faculties. But you'll get no disagreement from me. The world of signs and symbols and meanings and purposes—the world we inhabit and can't really depart from, except perhaps in moments of psychosis or delirium—simply isn't the world of mechanical causality, and simply couldn't have emerged from it without violating the mechanical laws supposedly underpinning it.

HEPHAISTOS: Well, I'm glad the two of you are in agreement—or the three of you, I have no doubt. Let me not to the marriage of true minds admit impediments. I, however, as yet demur from Brentano's judgment that intentionality is the singular "mark of the mental." I mean, I know that you think physical nature isn't mechanistic and that it actually *is* full of a kind of intentionality, since mind underlies and pervades all things, and the physical world is somehow thought made concrete . . . or something like that.

PSYCHE: Something very like that, in fact.

HEPHAISTOS: Whatever that may mean. All right, then, let's for the moment presume that intentionality as you describe it actually exists, and can't be reduced to non-intentional explanations. For argument's sake, I'll temporarily grant the premise. What, though, if one were to argue that signification—meaning—is in some sense present in physical systems even in the absence of mind?

PSYCHE: Such as?

HEPHAISTOS: Well, if nothing else, certain phenomena are so causally connected to one another that perhaps one could say in some cases that one "means" the other. For instance, smoke in a sense "means" fire, even in the absence of any putatively intending intellect. Paul Grice, if I recall, used precisely that example. Or perhaps any device that carries information of any kind exhibits a kind of intentionality, if only of the barest kind, as Fred Dretske has suggested: perhaps the mercury in a thermometer rising to the mark for 75° Fahrenheit or the needle in a compass pointing toward magnetic north might constitute a purely physical instance of elementary intentionality, since it already "means" or indicates something beyond itself. Perhaps the intentionality of mind, if freed from the mystifications in which you're trying to wreathe the question, might be a far more developed expression of this same capacity on the part of physical systems to be oriented toward specific ends, or at least significantly—*signifyingly*, as it were—attached to them.[16]

Hermes: I must assume you already know how poor such arguments are.

Hephaistos: Please, be so good as to instruct me on what I know. I'm often several paces behind even myself, poor lame-footed god that I am.

Psyche: No need to be snide—either of you. But no, Phaesty, I can't grant what you say. I still insist that intentionality is situated uniquely and incommutably in minds. I don't even grant the propriety of John Searle's seemingly benign attempt to extend the proper designations of the word outward from the mind.

Hephaistos: I'm not familiar with that.

Psyche: Searle speaks of three kinds of intentionality. The first, the sort of mental orientation we've been discussing, he calls "intrinsic." To this, though, he subjoins the categories of "derived intentionality"—that is, the significance a mind directly invests in external objects like words, signs, maps, diagrams, or thermometers and compasses, which other minds can discover by correctly interpreting those objects—and then "as-if intentionality"—which is little more than the pathetic fallacy or mere fancy: a metaphoric ascription of purposiveness to intrinsically non-intentional phenomena, such as when a poet speaks of the rivers "seeking" the sea. Not that Searle is unaware that maps and diagrams and the like, considered purely as physical objects, mean nothing, or that rivers—at least, according to the mechanical picture of nature—intend nothing, and merely flow as gravity dictates. Still, even that attenuated use of the word seems like a solecism to me, as it might suggest that somewhere, somehow there's some subtle continuity between what the mind does in intending and what mindless physical forces—if such things exist—are doing, and that the two are to be distinguished not absolutely but only by ontological degrees. That's nonsense.

So, if I'm unwilling to concede the legitimacy of that kind of, oh, "diffused" intentionality, even as a seemingly harmless *façon de parler*, then I'm certainly not prepared to entertain the claim that smoke *means* fire in the absence of an intending mind, or that one can mystically dilate that kind of supposedly purely physical indicativeness into something somehow proto-psychic, which agonizingly, over epochs of unimaginably numerous epochs, was alchemically transformed into purposive thought. Smoke may *result* from fire, but it *means* fire only in the mind of someone observing it and interpreting it specifically as a sign of something other than itself. There's no such thing as what Grice calls "natural meaning." And as for "information," that too, if we're not using the word equivocally, exists only in the intentionality of a mind. The notion that a thermometer or a compass somehow exhibits elementary intentionality is about as obvious an example of the fallacy of displacement—of Narcissus—as I can imagine. As physical objects, the mercury in a thermometer and the needle in a compass indicate nothing at all. Thoughts can be directed at physical things; but, if physical things are mechanical, they can't be reciprocally directed at thought. Not even brain events "mean" anything apart from that mental directedness. As I said, intentionality is there or it isn't; and it isn't anywhere except in mind. That "aboutness" truly is the "mark of the mental," and it indelibly marks the mental as irreducible to the physical.

HEPHAISTOS: Well, if language is the purest expression of intrinsic intentionality, what of instances of natural language that have been divorced from any conscious subject? I mean, would you deny that a sentence printed on a page possesses intentional content—and therefore intentionality—apart from any mind? That it still means what it means even when no one's reading it?[17]

HERMES: Of course not, at least not intrinsically. Excuse me, Psyche, I don't mean to answer for you; but, for myself, I have to say that the question simply repeats the same error of displacement. In the absence of an intending mind, there's no such thing as a sentence. There may be physical marks on physical pages, but they possess no meaning whatsoever, let alone some kind of incipient form of intentionality. Sentences have meaning within an intentional space of meaning, but not "out there" in the physical order.

Hephaistos: So, if a book falls open in a forest and there's no one there to read it, does it constitute a text?

Hermes: Not if by "text" you mean the intelligible content of words and phrases with meanings. In that case, then no indeed. As a purely physical event within a mechanistic universe, a book is no different from a stone.

Psyche: I agree.

Hephaistos: What, however, if we talk not about natural language, but about something still more basic? What if there really is, as you insist there isn't, a kind of physical substrate to the use of language right within the neurology of the brain and body? Or at least within its functions?

Psyche: Functions? That's a rather flirtatious sort of word, isn't it? I mean the way it remains in the general proximity of the language of intentional agency while teasingly staying just out of reach. Are you saying there's some sort of impersonal linguistic function at work in our brains that's already in some sense intentional, from which our language-use emerges . . . ?

Hephaistos: Something like that. You know of the "language of thought" hypothesis, I assume—the idea that thinking is a kind of linguistic structure of relations processed in the brain, a representational system with semantic and syntactical properties, and that thoughts are like sentences encoded by the brain, in something rather like computer code, though not sentences of which one is conscious strictly *as* sentences; and that, once those sentences are formed, one can adopt a propositional attitude toward the representations this mental language produces, such as "I believe" or "I want" or "I imagine." That is, let's say the brain produces the mental symbols that we can translate as "That tree over there is an elm." In conceiving that thought, your brain also proposes it, as something you believe or don't believe or suspect or . . .

Psyche: I've heard of this, yes. I've never thought it a particularly interesting idea. I fail to see how it helps us here.

Hephaistos: I'm only suggesting that this quite impersonal brain function of processing data—of turning inputs into outputs—may come *before* the supposedly subjective experience of what you call intrinsic "intention." Maybe there's a computational system in the brain that only latterly expresses itself as a personal propositional or "assertoric" attitude. Maybe that basic symbolic content is the ground of intentionality.[18]

HERMES: Oh, what an altogether preposterous inversion of logic. All that that amounts to is an effort to ground the proper use of the word "language" in its improper use.

HEPHAISTOS: The terminology isn't important . . .

HERMES: It most certainly is. I agree that thought has the structure of language, because that structure is the forming cause that directs thinking and unites it to the mindlike structure of the world . . .

HEPHAISTOS: Yes, but that's simply your particular metaphysical bias telling you that.

HERMES: Well, also my aversion to double-talk. By speaking of physiological or quasi-physiological processes as containing "symbolic" functions or "representations" or "language," you're illegitimately importing the terminology of intentional agency into a sphere prior to intention, just so you can then reverse the process and demonstrate how the former transparently emerges from the latter. But all you've done is employ those terms equivocally. There's no such thing as a neurological "symbol" of a tree, or even a neurological representation. Representation exists only in the "eye" of the beholder, and symbols exist only in the mind of the interpreter. There's no such thing as physiological semantics. Instead, there's a mental agency that crafts symbolic meaning out of neurological processes. There's an inner "witness," that is, and an inner agency at work that imposes and interprets meanings. Thought may very well have a linguistic structure—I tend to think it does—but only to the degree that a higher operation of intentionality is already at work, directing the brain toward the world, and interpreting semeiotically what the brain detects neurologically, endowing it with semantic and syntactic structure. But semantics and syntax both exist only in a semeiotic space, a space of interpretation—a *hermeneutical* space, if you'll permit me the vanity of putting it that way—which is found only in minds, not in brains as mere neurological mechanisms. All symbolic thought is already intentional in the fullest sense. And so, if thought is language, that simply tells us what we should already know: that thought is created by intentional agency, not that intentional agency arises from some non-subjective "functional" level of thought. Nothing can be created by its own contingent effects. The sun isn't the product of sunlight, and language and thought alike "arrive" in reality already allied to symbolic intentionality. So, by all means, speak freely of the "language of thought"; but don't imagine you've naturalized language by doing so.

PSYCHE: Would you at least grant, Phaesty, that the very concept of "language of thought," if it's understood as something generally below the threshold of consciousness, gives us at best an equivocal model for thinking about intentionality and language both, and that it doesn't help us at all to understand how subjective, unified consciousness is possible in the first place? Perhaps thought is like language, granted; but who's "reading" it or "speaking" it or "hearing" it?

HEPHAISTOS: What I'll grant is that, if subjective, unified, intentional, conscious mind really exists and is as you say it is, then of course nothing in the physical order explains it. *If*—as the Spartans told Philip.

HERMES: But you won't grant the conditional, will you—that it really does exist?

HEPHAISTOS: Certainly not at this point.

HERMES: If it's all an illusion, then, to whom does that illusion appear?

HEPHAISTOS: Oh, is it my turn to hold forth?

PSYCHE: Not yet. We haven't finished our inventory of objections to the physicalist reduction of mind. We're only . . .

HEPHAISTOS: Only just beginning?

PSYCHE: I was going to say, we're only halfway there.

V

Concepts and Reasons

PSYCHE: Since we've introduced the issue of the structure of thought, we might as well move on to *rationality*—I mean, that is, the normal processes of consecutive reasoning, and of forming concepts and of conceiving rationales and of reaching reasoned judgments.

HEPHAISTOS: [*With a faint groan:*] Is that all?

PSYCHE: Probably not. But let's start with the obvious. We've already said that the mind understands its world by, in a sense, composing that world in its intentionality. Well, then, what's the grammar, so to speak, by which it does this? What structure does it give to the world to render it intelligible? In very large part, it organizes experience by way of disembodied concepts. It unites the particular to the universal, the empirical to the transcendental, the concrete to the abstract. If I may draw again on Kant, the mind relies on *a priori* categories of reasoning—categories, that is, already there before any process of ratiocination or cognition can take place, which physical reality can't impress upon the mind, but which must always already be in place in order for coherent empirical experience to be possible.

HEPHAISTOS: Haven't we addressed this?

PSYCHE: We've addressed the role of intentionality in forming experience; we haven't yet noted that it does this through a relation with non-physical objects.

HEPHAISTOS: Non-physical?

Psyche: Well, certainly. Universal categories and concepts occupy no region of space or time, and yet they're everywhere and always available to reason. At every level of intention, the mind in some sense "interacts" with something outside the material manifold. Otherwise there'd be no such thing as continuous and intelligible experience, and that in itself is a formidable problem for physicalist reductionism. Some of these concepts are of such universal range and elevated abstraction that they're justly called "transcendentals"—truth, goodness, and beauty, for example, as well as unity and being—because they can in some sense be applied by degree to everything there is while remaining themselves irreducible to particular objects. These create an index of values by which one can form judgments about things—"that's true," "that's false," "this is good," "that's wicked." . . .

Eros: "You're beautiful."

Psyche: [*With an amused smile:*] So are you, my love. [*After a moment's distracted reverie, followed by a tender sigh:*] Yes, anyway, the transcendentals are especially obvious examples, because they're such general criteria for making broad judgments of value. But there are concepts no less abstract and no less universal at work in all judgments, in regard to every kind of propositional content. You mentioned, for instance, smoke being a sign of fire. Well, what's involved in reaching such a judgment? You see smoke rising from beyond a ridgeline, your brain arranges these impressions according to a syntax of relations, your mind conceives something like the proposition "that smoke indicates a fire" at a higher semantic level of meanings, and your reasoning faculty consciously judges this proposition to be correct. At least, that's how a certain "language of thought" theorist might describe the process. I prefer other terms. Whatever the case, though, your senses have at most registered an impression of smoke, but you—you've made a rational deduction, based on a prior concept of causal order. Or say, rather, that you see both the fire and the smoke at once and don't have to deduce anything about the latter's source. Even then, your senses merely register a certain spatial contiguity and perhaps a certain temporal sequence of impressions—or, rather, your intentionality arranges the storm of sense data into discrete, articulated impressions organized in continuous spatial and temporal order—but your mind then also synthesizes that experience into the judgment that the smoke is caused *by* the fire, rather than, say, the reverse; and this it does only because its conceptual repertoire includes such abstract notions as "cause," as well as a concept of the difference between a primary cause and its secondary effects. What the senses, regulated by intentionality's "aspectual" agency, deliver to the mind as spatial and temporal juxtapositions and sequences the reasoning mind understands as causes and their consequences.

HEPHAISTOS: And given the grand assertions you've already made regarding intentionality, I imagine you'd scoff if I suggested that such abstractions are just that: concepts *abstracted from* empirical experiences—noetic residues, so to speak, of countless sensuous experiences that, as they accumulate, naturally arrange themselves into sets of resemblance.

PSYCHE: Scoff I would, and then frown in scorn to boot. The mind has to interpret reality simply in order to have a reality to interpret. It can't abstract anything from experience without already having abstractions in place. For sensuous experiences to arrange *themselves*—whatever that could possibly mean—they must first be coherent experiences of certain things as such. And that requires the mind to make judgments that unite individual objects to universal concepts, as such concepts are the very substance of our knowledge of reality; they supply it with its structure, though they themselves have no material form.[19] Yes, sense-impressions may arise from a mechanical interaction between our neurologies and our environments; but knowledge belongs to the world of those rational judgments—a world that, in relation to the physical order, is a kind of intellectual heterocosm, accessible only to thought. Honestly, just you tell me how any sequence of physical interactions could have invested the mind with immaterial abstract concepts, or tell me how any physical system of stimulus and response could organize itself into universal categories that grant us a real grasp of the world if those categories weren't already present at hand to guide the process. Do you remember that rose blossom I showed you yesterday?

Hephaistos: How could I forget it? The bright lure that caught me on your hook. Now I can't wriggle free from this debate no matter how hard I try.

Psyche: And here I thought it was my personal charm that held you captive. But look: when we were all engaged together in staring at that humble flower, it presented itself to us as an object of recognition within a limitless but organized spatial and temporal range of discrete objects and moments precisely because, at every level, our minds were imposing conceptual categories upon the empirical data. Even to think of a given flower as an individual specimen of a natural kind requires abstract concepts of the singular and the general, of roses, of rose trees as opposed to bushes, of flowers, of vegetation, of biological systems, of organic nature as opposed to inert nature or human—or divine—artifice, and so forth. And that's only the beginning, since all around these immediately present eidetic and taxonomic concepts there hover innumerable other associated concepts, in a huge variety of types, such as the symbolic meanings of roses, or the ideal beauty of roses in comparison to this particular rose, or this rose considered as either a triumph of horticultural art or an expression of nature's irrepressible variety and vitality, or roses in general as motifs or subjects in literature and painting, or perhaps personal memories of the roses that once grew in the garden of one's childhood, and so on. There are conceptual dimensions to even the barest recognition of a rose as a rose, and then ever richer dimensions of association and significance, and all these together create the experience of the rose.

Now, I can't speak for you, but for myself it seems self-evident that the rich palette of intentional and conceptual pigments that my mind uses to compose its world must far exceed anything mere sensory stimulation could occasion in me; and it's no less self-evident that a merely mechanical material system could never, out of some pre-conceptual void, produce so much as a single abstract concept. There's no feasible series of steps—evolutionary or physiological, even over vast epochs of time or by way of the most complex modular neurological concrescences—that could cause conceptual abstractions to arise from concrete sensory encounters. Even the work of sorting out and comparing the objects of experience to one another, and then of arranging them into sets and categories and natural kinds, requires prior conceptual categories. In that process, there could never actually be a pre-conceptual moment, because *comparison* and *resemblance* and *kind*—these are themselves already abstractions. So is the very notion of discrete objects *as* discrete objects, as is the notion that one object might be compared to another according to certain rules, distinguishing between general likeness and particular difference. Even an infinite number of brute encounters between purely physical objects and one's physical sensory apparatus couldn't produce the faintest intuition of the likeness between two things without some universal absolute—some concept forever "absolved" of any particular empirical attachments—mediating that encounter, whether it be a concept as broad as "resemblance" or as narrow as "flower" or as specific as "rose" or as particular as "this" rose—for even the notion "this" is a kind of abstract absolute. The entire universe exists as a composed whole only in the heterocosm of the eternal reasons of things, and yet that entire universe as a physical event is impotent to have generated so much as a single one of those reasons.

Hephaistos: Such magisterial confidence. Are you so very sure, though, there are no intermediary realities between the conceptual and the empirical? Can't you imagine simple patterns of resemblance imposing themselves on the brain, until a succession of similar sensory impulses condense themselves into what you'd call abstractions?

Psyche: Like what? Describe such an amalgam of the empirical and the abstract to me—of general type and particular instance—and tell me how it could be produced from mere physical impulses? Or, rather, don't try. That very condensation, as you describe it, would still be a feat of conceptual synthetic reasoning, dependent on prior categories. You're never going to be able to retreat to a point in the process of mental recognition where the synthesizing work of comparison between distinct sense-impressions is possible without some conceptual grammar in place, and you're never going to be able to devise a plausible account of mere physical forces generating immaterial categories of relation, or of a brute succession of similar nerve-impulses miraculously coalescing into an immaterial concept. Again, even "similarity" is an abstraction, and without it no organism could possibly arrive at the reflective knowledge that one sense-impression is "like" another. Just as subjectivity rests only on subjectivity, and signs are invested with meaning only by signs, so abstractions are sustained solely by abstractions, and the attempt to find a more basic physical ground for any of it is nothing but the inauguration of an infinite regress toward an eternally elusive first cause. And then, too, the world of concepts is far vaster than any mere inventory of taxonomies and sets of physical resemblances. If I may for a moment wax pompously axiomatic: never a cogent "percept" without its corresponding concept, but many a concept without a corresponding percept.

Hephaistos: Oh, you could never be pompous; but you can at times be a tad peremptory in your pronouncements. I'd gladly wager that, at least in principle, the genealogy of any abstract concept could be traced back to some empirical original.

Psyche: I don't even think that's true of abstractions that apply to physical things, if only because the abstractions invariably exceed any of their physical occasions. Yes, a concrete image over many centuries can come to have a more abstract meaning; the notion of "glory," for instance, might have evolved from meaning something merely very bright to meaning all sorts of more impalpable things. But that evolution of sense was guided by the prior surfeit of one or more abstract concepts over the physical phenomenon to which the word originally referred. It's precisely that excess that the physical facts can't explain.

Hephaistos: You're losing me, I fear.

Psyche: Well, consider something as basic as simple geometrical shapes. Perfect circles, triangles, straight lines, unextended points—of these we have clear geometrical concepts, and we're in the habit of applying those concepts to physical objects, even though they don't really exist in their ideal perfection anywhere in nature. I tend to think we find, say, triangles in nature by synthesizing experience through the prior geometrical concept; at least, it's hard to say how the mind could abstract "triangularity" from the rough approximation of triangles in the physical world when the mind would presumably first have to discover them, and their resemblances to one another, by way of the pre-existing concept. And, then, consider far more complex mental objects—say a symmetrical polyhedron with a thousand faces. Not only do we never encounter such an object in the world around us; we can't even summon up a picture of it in our imagination.

HEPHAISTOS: Well, we can extrapolate mental objects of that kind from more elementary figures.

PSYCHE: And that act of extrapolation is an entirely abstract operation, isn't it? An operation of reasoning anchored neither in empirical impressions nor in any actual physical connection between the simpler concept and the more complex . . . which is a problem in itself. But we needn't confine ourselves to mystical geometries, after all. Pure mathematics—one of the highest imaginable employments of reason—exists in a realm of abstract meanings and entailments that has absolutely no genetic continuity with any kind of physical object of experience. And don't tell me that you think mathematics is just an amplification of arithmetic, and arithmetic an amplification of counting . . .

HEPHAISTOS: I wouldn't dream of it. I'm not just a blacksmith, you know. I'm a fairly accomplished engineer, and not a bad mathematician in my own right. Believe me, I know that mathematics is a language, and the most abstract of languages at that. No doubt, though, you know there've been many attempts to naturalize the origin of mathematical thought.

PSYCHE: None of which comes near to explaining the range of mathematical applications in every sphere of quantitative reasoning: physical, scientific, statistical, economic, or what have you. And it's especially absurd to try to make developments in mathematics conform to an evolutionary logic. Advances in the language of mathematics arise from mathematical premises, not from physical causes, because mathematical truths are necessary truths, true in every possible reality, and would be true if there were no physical reality at all. Yet the mind is capable of really interacting with these strictly immaterial entities—mathematical principles, that is . . . and logical principles too—none of which can be grounded in physical or even psychological processes. Just consider truly immense computations . . . or consider the capacity of the mind to conceive of infinity, and even to employ the infinite as a function within mathematical reasoning, even though no sensible representation of what we're thinking about is possible for us. Well really, Phaesty, even you must at times be amazed at the mind's obedience to necessary abstract laws and principles, far beyond anything a physicalist or psychologistic reduction of thought could possibly explain.

Hephaistos: I grant that it's remarkable. Amazing even. I grant that the rational mind's capacity for abstract concepts like "beauty" or "goodness" is as well, and that its capacity for unrepresentable ideas like indivisible geometrical points or "infinity" is positively astonishing. So are its capacities for speculative reasoning and imagination and inspired innovation. But nature is overflowing with things remarkable, amazing, and astonishing. Perhaps you underestimate what nature can accomplish.

Hermes: And perhaps you fail to see that nature can accomplish so much only because it's suffused with powers that exceed the merely natural.

Psyche: Or, at the very least, that nature isn't the mechanical economy you take it for. Really, we needn't take wing into the otherworldly mysteries of mathematics to show as much. Why, just consider what we're doing here.

Hephaistos: Bickering?

Psyche: Reasoning. The very act of rational thought, however elementary, is already a contradiction of the physicalist narrative. Reasoning involves sequences of premises and conclusions, semantic content regulated by a logical syntax rather than by material causality, ideas connected to one another by logical entailment rather than by exchanges of physical energy. The entire sequence of any rational reflection is determined by meanings and their conceptual implications. The simplest equation—2 + 2 = 4—is something utterly unlike any kind of physical event. The simplest syllogism—"All men are mortal; Socrates is a man; therefore Socrates is mortal"—is a dynamic process outside of and contrary to the laws of mechanism.

Hephaistos: Different, perhaps. But contrary?

Psyche: I would say so. Mechanical processes are series of brute events, determined by purely physical causes, obedient to impersonal laws, whereas thinking is a process determined by symbolic associations and rational implications. Yes, perhaps the electrical events in the neurology of the brain can serve as vehicles of transcription for thoughts; but they can't be the same things as the semeiotic and logical contents of those thoughts. The firing of one neuron might induce another neuron to fire, which leads to another firing in turn, as a result of physical necessity, but certainly not as the result of logical necessity. The strictly consecutive structure of a rational deduction—that simple equation, that elementary syllogism—simply isn't, and can't be reduced to, a series of biochemical contingencies, and the conceptual connections between a premise and a conclusion can't be the same thing—or follow the same "causal" path—as the organic connections of cerebral neurology. One can't be mapped onto the other. Nor, by the same token, should the semantics and syntax of reasoning be able to direct the flow of physical causes and effects in the brain. Not, at any rate, if anything like the supposed "causal closure of the physical" is true. So, really, the syllogism as an event in the brain should, by all rights, be quite impossible. And, while we're at it, I might note that consecutive reasoning is irreducibly teleological: one thought doesn't physically cause its sequel; rather, the sequence is guided by a kind of inherent futurity in reasoning—the will of the mind to find a rational resolution to a train of premises and conclusions—that elicits that sequel from its predecessor. Teleology is intrinsic to reasoning and yet repugnant to mechanism.

Oh, really, don't you see the problem here, Phaesty? There can't be both a *complete* neurophysiological account of a rational mental act and also a *complete* account in terms of semeiotic content and logical intentionality; and yet physicalism absolutely requires the former while every feat of reasoning consists entirely in the latter. The predicament becomes all the more utterly absurd the more one contemplates it. If, for instance, you seem to arrive at a particular belief as a result of a deductive argument—say, the belief that Socrates is mortal—physicalist orthodoxy obliges you to say that that belief is actually only a neurological event, *mindlessly* occasioned by some other neurological event. On the physicalist view of things, no one has ever really come to believe anything based on reasons; and yet the experience of reaching a conclusion tells us the opposite.[20]

HEPHAISTOS: So, at least, it appears to us.

HERMES: Oh, not this again.

HEPHAISTOS: Yes, O fleet-footed god, *this*—as you say—*again*. Whenever we reach the end of this interminable inventory of imponderables, I'll have occasion to make my case for what's called "functionalism" at greater length, I hope. Here, though, I'll just say that I find it perfectly conceivable that a highly efficient functional system of input and output—that is, an "informational" system of stimulus and response—in processing data and converting it into behavior, just might, as a kind of economical user-interface, generate the illusory representation that one is "reasoning along" with a sequence of logical entailments rather than being carried along by the impersonal flow of operational algorithms converting data into behavior . . .

HERMES: This computational jargon is insufferable.

HEPHAISTOS: Well, screw your courage to the sticking place and suffer it long enough to tell me why what I'm saying is so implausible.

PSYCHE: Well, there's the not insignificant fact that you yourself don't believe it. Your very words betray you. You engage in reasoned argument because you believe semantic meaning generates logical entailments, which can be followed and can yield reasonable conclusions. And you trust those conclusions. This you prove every time you adopt a course of action dictated by reason—say, the solution to an engineering problem in designing one of your lovely automata.

HEPHAISTOS: I may, as a matter of habit, proceed on the assumption that I actually believe what I believe. That's the whole point of that user-interface I just mentioned: to spare me the task of arduously synthesizing the flow of data for every discrete action I undertake. Very well, I may be doomed to believe that I believe. That too is just good engineering: I'm constructed to function efficiently. Moreover, I can trust that countless epochs of evolutionary attrition have winnowed away less efficient functions, killing off less well-adapted systems of input and output, and that therefore what I believe that I believe is optimally suited to my environment, and allows me to act with extraordinarily successful predictive confidence. Who cares if I really know what I'm doing? What's true knowledge of reality, after all, other than control over one's environment? Knowledge is the ability to act. Knowledge is power.

HERMES: There's something altogether bracing in an epistemic nihilism that radical, I must say.

PSYCHE: And yet something distinctly absurd as well. I mean, for one thing, since there are many ways in which illusion might prove more evolutionarily beneficial than a correct apprehension of reality, what you're saying obliges you to grant that your so-called functional system might have very little to do with the true nature of things at all.

HEPHAISTOS: Yes. And? Call me a pragmatic Kantian: all I can know are the conditions that allow for practical action. I don't have any grasp of things in themselves—not even of the true thing-in-itself that might hide behind what I perceive as my own rational thinking. Where I'm confronted with the manifest image of a reasoning mind, the true scientific picture may be of nothing other than the functional mechanical processes of a brain.

PSYCHE: And yet that too won't do, my dear obstinate friend. I don't mean to be tediously repetitious, but you can't found a reductionist physicalism on an infinite regress. If you believe that you believe, then you have a belief; and, if you want to argue that that too is just a condensation of functions into—forgive me, Hermes dear, for the vulgarity of the computational argot—into a *user-interface*, then you must account for how it is that you believe that you believe that you believe. And so on *in infinitum*. You'll never escape the foundational reality of semantic intentionality. And this is just a general law. Every time you claim that some self-evident aspect of mental existence is illusory—whether consciousness or intentionality or rational thought—you necessarily presume the operation of the very faculty whose existence you're denying in describing the supposed illusion.

Hephaistos: And if that infinite regress is more an impression than a reality? Let's dip our toes for a moment in that seemingly bottomless abyss. I'm not done with the metaphor of mirrors mirroring mirrors. I can imagine a kind of feedback echo within a system—a strange loop or tangled hierarchy[21]—that creates the sense of the self watching itself watch itself, forever and ever along an infinite corridor of ever more original selfhood, whereas in fact all that's happening is a kind of constant oscillation between and circulation among hierarchically interrelated faculties . . .

Psyche: No, you're missing the point. It's not simply a personal sense of endless reflective regress that's at issue here, impossible as that is, nor even that it's clearly meaningless to say that physical and functional loops and tangles somehow generate conscious awareness. No, the regress in question is logical. You can't get outside of the prior reality of the things you're trying to explain away. Let's say thought is, as you suggest, simply a functional flow of input and output (to use that rebarbative language), which the brain then represents to itself as a logical sequence of connected ideas, accompanied by judgments of belief or disbelief or by an impulse of further curiosity. First of all, to whom is this representation appearing if it must assume the qualities of personal subjective experience? Why would it have to do so if there weren't really a subject there to be deceived into believing it believes? And how can the brain fabricate the illusion of continuous, unified, intentional consciousness except by way of continuous, unified, intentional consciousness? An illusion of consciousness must be a consciousness of that illusion. But that's only the beginning of the problem. In order to represent the flow of information in a functional system as though it were actually a semantic and syntactic economy of logical premises, conclusions, concepts, and entailments, all expressed symbolically, the brain would still have to possess a real semantic and logical faculty capable of imposing the "appearance" of semeiotic meaning on that flow of stimulus into response, and capable too of making that imposed meaning hold together as a rational "narrative." That very faculty would still remain an inexplicable reality—the very same inexplicable reality as before—in a putatively mechanistic universe. If you can reconstruct or represent a physical process in terms of reasons rather than of physical causes, and arrange those reasons in a coherent logical and conceptual sequence, then you're in fact already really reasoning, in the most non-physical of ways. Even the ability to be deceived on this score depends on a coordinating intentional faculty that merges perception and ratiocination under the *aspect*—the intention—of logical entailments rather than of physical effects, and hence a faculty that possesses a mastery of logical consequents, even if its conclusions are flawed. Your supposed "user-interface" must still employ a completely semeiotic, completely linguistic, completely intentional, completely rational system, as it were, in order to produce this supposed "illusion" of a semeiotic, linguistic, intentional, rational agency. It requires mastery of the very grammar of meaning it denies exists. I don't see how you can explain the paradox away. A successful explanatory reduction of any mental phenomenon to physical causes would have to reduce even its *appearance* to something that could not appear as it is; to reduce consciousness solely to appearance is in fact to affirm its reality. It makes no sense.

HERMES: And how very vacuous this language of "strange loops" and "tangled hierarchies" really is—as if mere repetitive oscillations and circulations and twisting lemniscates of physical processes could somehow explain the qualitative chasm between mindless third-person events and first-person subjectivity . . . as though thought were a physical object, like a Möbius strip in which inside and outside are one continuous surface. These are nothing but placeholder concepts, promissory notes on a theory that will never ever come. Geometrical complexities and qualitative complexities are not two versions of the same thing.

PSYCHE: Let me ask you, Phaesty: Are you willing to say that perhaps reason itself is an illusion?

HEPHAISTOS: [*Pausing and lowering his eyes to his hands before speaking:*] That's a hard question to answer, because I know what your next step will be if I simply say "Yes." You'll say I've rendered all my own arguments null and void. You'll say I can't even really honestly embrace materialism, since materialism is a *reasoned* position—a conceptual edifice constructed from semantic bricks and syntactic mortar. And, naturally, you're well aware that any metaphysical naturalist's self-understanding is most vulnerable just here, in his or her conviction that naturalism is an austerely rationalist position. None of us likes to play the role of the glad absurdist purveying paradoxes. So, *touché;* I won't deny that it's a hit, a very palpable hit. But, once we've awarded that particular pass to you, let's come again *en garde.* Let's say yes, I think it's arguable that what we experience as reason may be a kind of epiphenomenal or instrumental disguise on the part of a physical system that processes stimuli into behaviors; but I would also argue that there are evolutionary imperatives at work at all times, as a result of which those intrinsically illusory consecutive logical connections aren't so much illusory as, oh, I don't know, *allegorical.* They're morphologically correct, as analogies of the relations between different things—*a* is to *b* as *x* is to *y*—rather as a fabulist might try to impart a moral lesson by personifying slander as a thief and depicting lost reputation as a stolen purse, and might do so with such deftness that the listener thinks he's really hearing a story only about a thief and a stolen purse, though all the while the real meaning is subtly implanting itself in him. And these analogies or allegories are useful because, in each case, evolution has progressively conformed the representational narrative to the shape of the physical process underlying it. They're successful representations, even if the true import of the little dramas they enact on our private cognitive stages escapes our comprehension.

PSYCHE: But even that rationalization can't be anything other than another dissemblance, surely. Even that explanation can't be asserted strictly as a truth. In fact, it can't be true at all, since there wouldn't be any rational truth to speak of in that case.

HEPHAISTOS: Even so. I must here trust simply in the verdict of evolutionary efficacy. And I'm willing to do that while acknowledging that I only imagine I have reasons for doing so. So, yes, perhaps when I juxtapose the premises "Every man is mortal" and "Socrates is a man," as though they're connected semantically, I'm really only describing a representation of the physical juxtaposition and connection of two neural electrochemical events in my brain; and then, in seeming to conclude that "Socrates is mortal," I'm really only representing a physical conjunction as a logical entailment—a processing of data as an understanding of meaning. So be it. And maybe my introspective sense of having formulated a coherent syllogism merely represents another electrochemical event that somehow fortifies and further synthesizes that flow of data. And, yes, maybe even the reasoning of the argument I'm making to you now is just one more performance of a representational allegory.

HERMES: In which case, nothing really *means* anything at all. All seemingly intrinsic rational connections are just extrinsic neural associations, tricked out in masquerade costumes. No argument employs a logical syntax, because no such thing as a syntax really exists. Words mean nothing . . .

HEPHAISTOS: They *mean* precisely what they accomplish. They discharge their part in a functional system, and do so as viable "tokens" of a process that can't be directly known in all its details, but that can generate cognitive correlates in the forms of apparent rationales . . . again, as user-interfaces or practical tools of navigation.

HERMES: Why would it need to? Why can't the process operate without such . . . allegorization?

HEPHAISTOS: For reasons . . . excuse me . . . as a result of *causes* I've already mentioned: perhaps certain complex systems naturally produce the illusions of consciousness and intentionality and rationality as part of the larger process of input and output. Maybe those illusions are also the most convenient and economical user-interfaces possible.

HERMES: I must say, this is the damnedest thing I've ever heard. You're so committed to a physicalist picture of reality and to a physicalist reduction of mental agency that you're willing to deny the self-evident realities of mind—consciousness, intentionality, unity of apprehension, and now even reason itself—if you can't force them into the confines of your materialist dogmas. How can you believe such preposterous claims?

HEPHAISTOS: Excuse me, I didn't claim to believe them. In fact, if what I'm saying is correct, belief itself is an illusory or, at any rate, merely allegorical representation of a purely physical process. All I said was that I find it possible to entertain such notions, and see no reason why I shouldn't.

HERMES: I see. Well, if you're truly willing to embrace irrationalism, which every coherent sentence issuing from your mouth seems to belie, you'll have won an altogether Pyrrhic victory here today. You'll have revealed yourself—and by extension inculpated all physicalists—as the forthright irrationalists in this engagement, whereas on our side of the field the banner of reason and enlightenment will remain proudly unfurled.

HEPHAISTOS: How very stirring.

PSYCHE: As I doubt I have to point out, even your trust in the power of evolution to conform your rationalizing allegories to the physical flow of data through your neurology is only an empty posture at this point. If reason is illusory, perhaps total illusion is often more evolutionarily beneficial—more prone to survival—than the sort of morphologically parallel representationalism you presume. Maybe the content of your beliefs is utterly false precisely in order to aid in your survival—say, in the way one might be kept away from a neural toxin secreted by the skin of a particular Amazonian frog by being convinced that a deadly curse has been cast by a witch on all frog-kind. And maybe the representation is even more radically deceptive than that. Really, outside the realm of the immediately practical, such as procuring food or sex, or asserting dominance over another organism, whenever your *apparent* reasoning *seems* to move into the ever more abstract realms of ideas and principles and logical entailments—well, there you obviously have no basis for confidence whatsoever. Actually, your own commitment to causal closure makes such confidence impossible. What could evolution "see," so to speak, other than physical processes, upon which conscious states have no effect? It could never select true beliefs as beliefs; it would at most have the power to preserve, quite by accident, fortuitous parallels between behaviors in thinking organisms and any beliefs that those organisms might have. Then evolutionary epistemology more or less denies itself . . .[22]

HEPHAISTOS: As I've already conceded. As I say, I'm not staking the game on this point. I see its inherent weaknesses, but I also see that it's a theoretical possibility to be left open.

HERMES: Only because it creates its own conditions of irrefutability, and does that only because it's so perversely incoherent.

PSYCHE: I think you also know what my response will be. Not the obvious one about your argument's contradictoriness, since that's as much a confirmation as a refutation of what you're saying. Inasmuch as the claim that "all is nonsense" is itself willfully nonsensical, to my mind it constitutes an abdication of any and every real argument. But that's not important to me. Once again, I'll assert that the supposed illusion of reasoning must still be a coherent act of reasoning, and therefore can be no mere illusion. Your allegory must still—even in dissembling its physical basis—exhibit and preserve a rational coherence, one that you can also communicate to others within a community of discourse. I mean, who's writing it? Where does it get its narrative continuity from? The faculty that permits all of this is still one that works in a wholly semeiotic, intentional, and logical way, and as such produces a continuous mental activity that structurally exceeds the merely physical facts you say it only allegorizes. It produces *and imposes* a real level of meaning—even if that meaning is somehow false or illusory in relation to the physical facts—and that level of signs and logical entailments and syntax enjoys an ontological autonomy that can't be reduced to its physical substrate, or to a merely physical sequence of contingent events. Reasoning is still really occurring. So, no, I don't grant the solvency of such a theory. I see it as yet another invitation to retreat with you down an infinite corridor of explanatory insufficiencies.

HEPHAISTOS: [*With a loud sigh:*] At this rate, our infinite regresses will soon constitute an infinite regress of their own.

PSYCHE: A *bon mot* is the last refuge of the dialectical scoundrel, Phaesty dear.

HEPHAISTOS: Oh, I'm merely holding my fire, dear Psyche, till I know my powder's dry and yours is exhausted. Or are we at the end of our inventory?

PSYCHE: No, not quite.

VI

Free Will and Purpose

HEPHAISTOS: What else, then?

PSYCHE: Freedom—of the will, of the imagination, of creativity . . .

HEPHAISTOS: Oh, *that:* the oldest illusion of all.

PSYCHE: Such a cynical old Lemnian.

HEPHAISTOS: I'm simply growing impatient. Free will is a supposition that we can't prove or disprove, but one that seems . . . let's say *doubtful.* Cause is followed by effect, each effect becomes the cause of other effects, and so on, and it seems highly unlikely that the actions of an individual organism somehow escape the causal interconnectedness of all things, going back to the first event—whatever that may have been.

HERMES: And once again you presume as true all the things we've already shown to be arbitrary convictions, without either empirical or logical support: the causal closure of the physical, the brute mechanistic nature of all causation, the reducibility of mental intentions to mindless physical forces . . .

HEPHAISTOS: Yes . . . but also no. Even if thought isn't reducible to, say, electrochemical impulses devoid of content, still one thought causes another, one impulse of the will prompts the next—everything is a consequence of something else, and the chain of causes and effects goes back to some point far earlier than any particular seemingly free choice.

PSYCHE: One thought may be the *occasion* of another, but it isn't its *cause*—not in the sense you're implying. The intentional content of thinking, as we've been discussing, isn't a physical force initiating other physical events. Again, a rationale and a mechanical cause are two very different things.

HEPHAISTOS: That remains a point of debate between us. At least, the issue of whether rationales have consequences entirely of their own is a point of disagreement.

PSYCHE: Well, if intention is indeed inherently teleological, rational purposes would seem to operate as final causes, which—far from being produced by prior efficient causes—are themselves the motives that bring those efficient causes into being. There really isn't any good reason to deny the experience of freedom of the will . . . even if one must acknowledge that it isn't absolute.

HEPHAISTOS: And yet, still, your perception in the present of what you see as a purpose drawing you freely toward a desired end might itself be no more than the effect of a chain of causality leading up to this moment. It might, once again, be a kind of user-interface, or an allegory of what in reality is just an irresistible physical momentum, determining all your deeds and all your ostensible desires and intentions.

HERMES: A notion that hasn't become any more plausible or any less incoherent in the last two minutes.

HEPHAISTOS: If you say so. To my mind this is the very definition of an inadjudicable dispute. If you can prove to me that physicalism is false, then I'll reconsider the evidence of my own experience of free volition. Until you do, I retain the right to regard my experience as simply an impression created in me by the absolute determinism of the physical forces that shape me.

HERMES: If you're not really free, why would your nervous system need to convince you that you are? What would it gain in functional terms? I suppose you'll just say again that it's all an accidental concomitant of the system's complexity, or that it's the most economical functional interface. I'm curious, though: you grant your metaphysical commitments greater authority than your own immediate experiences?

HEPHAISTOS: Don't we all do that? Don't we all feel we should yield to the iron dictates of our deductions, even when our common sense urges us to do otherwise?

HERMES: But . . .

HEPHAISTOS: And please refrain from introducing another blasted regress. Don't tell me that, by choosing to believe my reasoning rather than my own lying eyes, I'm proving the truth of free will. That one simply won't work; it's not a paradox in the way that, arguably, it's a paradox to think that reasoning is an illusion—which I grant.

HERMES: I had no intention of doing so. I was simply going to say that an experience that's constant and immediate should be rejected or disbelieved only if there's some contrary evidence of comparable magnitude.

HEPHAISTOS: Perhaps. But can you really say you *experience* freedom? Is that really true? What's the nature of that experience? You seem to want to say that freedom is a rational faculty, one that involves the sovereign power to elect one purpose rather than another, as a final cause, and then to pursue it. But why do you choose one end rather than another, except as the result of some impulse or other that, followed back to its ground, seems utterly without rationale—just a brute stirring of the will? Yes, you may form a purpose now as the result of having formed another purpose before now, and so on back through an immense series of purposeful actions. But at some point back there something without rational motive prompted you toward one end or another. You can choose either to follow or to resist a desire; and, in the latter case, you resist one desire because there's something else you desire more strongly: perhaps you refrain from drinking a liquor you love because you desire sobriety even more, or refrain from a wicked deed because you have a stronger longing for a clear conscience. Very well: rationales within rationales; rationales at war with other rationales. But, once you've accounted for all of them, you ought to conclude that, yes, maybe you were able to do or not to do what you desired; but you were never free to choose *what* you desired, or to choose which desire in you is stronger than another. When you come up against *that* issue—when you realize that you're a creature of impulses that precede your conscious rational deliberations—then it's only a short step further to realizing that perhaps all your free actions are reducible to brute, unreasoning impulses, no more free than any other spontaneous physiological or psychological event, like a heart-attack or a spasm of anger at a sudden pain in the sole of your foot caused by a sharp pebble.

There's good empirical evidence, you know, that conscious choice might be just an epiphenomenal impression produced by unconscious physiological forces. Think of all those experiments that follow the model Benjamin Libet established several decades back, and that have grown in sophistication ever since. I mean, experiments like the one in which test subjects are asked to perform some minor motor action, such as twitching a wrist or pressing a button, whenever they feel the desire to do so, and then to try to report—maybe in regard to an oscilloscope timer—precisely when they had been aware of deciding to act, while electrodes attached to their scalps or MRI scans were recording the electrical impulses presumably motivating the decision. The exact method has improved over the years, but the point is that the researcher can determine that the neural impulses prompting the choice actually precede the conscious act by several seconds. The researcher can even reasonably predict whether the twitch of the wrist—or whatever's been agreed on—will occur as much as seven times out of ten. This has led some to think that the very existence of free will is, well, again, *implausible.*

Psyche: Only persons with a poor grasp of logic, I should think. Neural impulses prompting the choice? Surely you mean the neural impulses that the test subject then *chooses* to indicate by twitching a wrist or pressing a button. That's what's happening after all. How you phrase these things—how you think about them—makes quite a difference in how you interpret your experimental results.

Hephaistos: Why do you feel the need to introduce an additional step—this moment of deliberate choice—between the physiological impulse and the physiological response?

Psyche: I'm not the one introducing it. It was explicitly introduced within the terms of the experiment, which dictated that a choice be made in order to mediate between a felt impulse and a deliberate act, apart from which the one wouldn't have yielded the other. There would have been no *natural* twitching of the wrist or pressing of a button or what have you. It's not as if the neuronal event and the conscious act were identical, or as if the mechanical impulse had been spontaneously expressed in a mechanical action. The subjects undertook in advance to move their wrists to indicate their awareness of having felt an urge, and then did so. In fact, there was no connection, as far as the terms of the experiment were concerned, between the two physiological termini of the event except the conscious semantic and purposive operation of the subject's free intention . . . free will.

Really, what a silly, even staggeringly foolish conclusion to draw: that, since certain kinds of conscious choices are typically preceded by certain unconscious neuronal actions, free will must be an illusion—that the *real* cause of action must just be some autonomic electrical flicker in the brain, while the supposed conscious decision is just some posterior impression, like the lingering afterimage from a lightning flash. But there's absolutely no logical connection between the experiment as actually conducted and that conclusion. It's a total *non sequitur.* All this tells us is that a researcher's interests frequently dictate what he or she thinks has been observed. In this case, the researcher goes looking for a mechanical transaction, and so artificially extracts the data of the experiment from their actual context of intention and interpretation, and then miraculously discovers what he or she has thereby predestined the experiment to disclose. If you write your conclusions into the way you phrase your question, the answer is predetermined, no matter what the evidence. It's really quite absurd; the researcher is interpreting the data as one would if the experiment were performed upon a mindless mechanism, with absolutely no regard to the reality that there's an actual agent involved, with a prior history of intentional commitments. Well, when you pretend that the phenomena of conscious volition aren't there at the beginning of your experiment, even though they clearly constitute its very basis and operative principles, then you're not going to recognize them thereafter in the fabric of the experiment, even though they're ubiquitous. In fact, the more logical conclusion to be drawn from the entire exercise would have been just the opposite one: that the results confirmed the reality of rational freedom. My only hesitancy here is that, if the subjects were *absolutely* free, one should be able to predict their actions in that situation with perfect accuracy, rather than merely seven times out of ten.

HEPHAISTOS: Now, how do you arrive at *that?* I was following you till then.

PSYCHE: Because the subjects did exactly what they had freely agreed to do: to act, that is, of their own volition when they became aware of an impulse—one, in fact, that they'd also agreed in advance to summon up within themselves. But the researchers worked by the bizarre fiction that they were witnessing an isolated mechanical process without any prior premise, rather than—as was actually the case—a premeditated act prosecuted willfully, and so they inevitably arrived at the monstrous fantasy that they'd proved the whole act to be reducible to a spontaneous physical urge. What should truly have amazed them was the power of the rational will to command the body to behave "spontaneously" at a specific future time and place, under conditions carefully arranged ahead of time. The whole structure of the experiment was teleological. What a splendid vindication, then, of intentional liberty and of the power of final causality to induce real physical effects—even unconscious neurological agitations.

HEPHAISTOS: I see.

HERMES: Really, of course, the very notion that data this trivial—concerning neural agitations and minor physiological behaviors, whether spontaneous or premeditated—could really tell us anything about free will at the level of actual choices made on purpose is rather silly. A real act of personal deliberation, such as whether or not to propose marriage to someone, occurs at a level of such intentional and conceptual complexity that there's little if anything these trifling investigations into stimulus and response could possibly tell us about it.

PSYCHE: Quite. But, even at the level of those trifling investigations, the researchers were simply deceiving themselves. The experiment they imagined they'd run isn't even logically possible in its own ridiculous terms, as there's no visible intentional or mental content in any given electrical impulse in the brain that identifies it with any particular act.

We haven't any notion of how these electrical firings in the cerebral cortex relate to the conceptual contents of a decision to do something; we certainly can't say that they themselves constitute the act of decision, or that they are anything more than physiological tendencies or potentials for action that the deliberative will might either obey or suppress. It's not as if one could observe the electrochemical activity of the brain, without already knowing how the subject chose *in advance* to translate it into an action, and predict what's to come. The urge doesn't go directly to its goal without crossing the interval of consciousness. And the researcher can never retreat to a more original moment in which a physical urge exists wholly outside that free movement of the mind. That object just isn't found in nature. Only if one starts from the assumption that all natural causality is mechanistic and that all human actions are mechanical events, can one imagine that it makes sense to take a single physical act in isolation from any larger context of actions and determinations, look for a discrete physiological concomitant, isolate it as a kind of spring of action within the mechanism, and then claim that one has found a physical explanation of the act that renders all the prospective, conceptual, and deliberative powers of the will—as well as the whole continuous context of intentional activity—causally superfluous. To reach this conclusion, though, one must ignore everything one is actually doing in preparing the experiment.

In the end, then, what's been proved? Perhaps that we often feel an urge before we freely decide whether to act on it. Well, you don't need electrodes on the scalp to prove that. But even then the brain event visible to researchers is never isolated, because at both ends—impulse and act—there's a decision of the conscious mind that defines it. In between there's some raw physiological agitation, which those free intentions have shaped into an accomplished deed. Let's just say that that agitation of neurons is the material substrate, and that the intellect that makes the choices is a kind of formal cause: it's always shaping impulse into intentional action—prospectively, retrospectively . . . synoptically. It's always imposing determinate order upon the otherwise inchoate promptings of our neurons.

Hephaistos: As it happens . . .

Psyche: I mean, no doubt such experiments might call into question the direct constant supervision of human actions by a Cartesian homunculus within. But so what? We already know that most of our physical actions aren't determined moment to moment by our conscious minds. When we go for a walk, there isn't some executive sprite in the cerebral cortex issuing a ceaseless stream of conscious instructions to our nerves, sinews, joints, limbs, heart, and pulmonary system. The question of our freedom correctly posed, however, is whether going for a walk is, at the higher level of awareness, something we've chosen to do as a conscious intention and then done in accord with that final cause. Free rational activities involve complex behaviors, comprehending a great many moving parts, some conscious and some unconscious, but all of them are comprised within a coherent totality of purposive operations. Our free actions look like purely physical effects only when artificially separated from one another and then viewed through the incredibly narrow lens of a mythical mechanistic universe devoid of . . . spirit.

Hephaistos: Psyche, my dear good friend, I keep trying to tell you that I agree. Well, except for that invocation of "spirit," whatever that may be. But, yes, you're absolutely right: such experiments are ill-conceived and have been ineptly interpreted. You convinced me of that almost immediately—chiefly because I was never particularly persuaded by them to begin with. But that doesn't alter my other argument: that the choices we make are themselves the results of prior choices and impulses that reach back toward still earlier causes that long antecede our conscious agency; hence, they may be guided by desires that we may have the capacity to "choose" *to follow*, but that we do not have the capacity to choose *in themselves*.

Psyche: A gracious concession; I'll not prove recreant to the reciprocal courtesy. I concede your point too, to the degree that such things can be assessed. But that has no bearing on the matter at hand, really. It seems to me you're talking now about not a physical, but rather a metaphysical, reduction of rational freedom. I'll admit that the full dimensions of rational liberty may be impossible to discover, but what matters here is whether the *structure* of rational freedom is teleological and intentional and semeiotic, as opposed to mechanistic.

HEPHAISTOS: Determinism is determinism.

PSYCHE: Tautologies are irrefutable, so I can't demur. But not all determinisms are of the same nature. A physical determinism is a brute event composed of mechanical causes, to which rationales might attach as illusions or epiphenomena but not as the true sufficient reasons for what happens. By contrast, an intentional determinism of the sort you've described is composed of rationales and logical entailments and purposes and deliberations and decisions and semantic contents and syntactic structures. Whether rational freedom is partly libertarian or, according to a more classical model, wholly "intellectualist"—guided, that is, by an irresistible final causality, a natural desire for some Platonic "Good beyond being"—doesn't really change the calculus here. If rational freedom really does function as it seems to do, then the physicalist model of mind and cosmos is still false; and, for me, that suffices.

HEPHAISTOS: Even if it could be traced back to pre-conscious causes somewhere in the dark backward and abysm of time?

PSYCHE: I have a hard time granting the premise. I don't believe real intentionality and consciousness can emerge from mindless matter or mindless causes, as you know. But it's the very existence of intentionality and consciousness—and so forth and so on—that matters, and the real efficacy of irreducibly mental realities in bringing about consequences in the physical world. There may be causal streams flowing below the level of conscious life, but at the level of consciousness itself we act toward elected ends, according to our rational understandings of those ends and of our own wills. A subordinate officer receives written instructions from a superior officer and obeys those orders. Abstruse considerations of the physiological substrate or prehistory of his acts in no way qualify or diminish the wholly semeiotic character of that transaction, which produced the result that the intentions of one man were put into action by another. That semeiotic disjunction can't be written back into the physicalist story. The whole causal power in that sequence of events was the meaning present in the written commands, and meaning isn't a physical property. Maybe the superior issues his commands based on some unknown deterministic materialist history; maybe the subordinate is disposed to obedience based on another such history; but the act of translating the commands of the one into the actions of the other crosses a purely linguistic, purely hermeneutical, purely intentional interval, without which those two alleged material histories could not combine into the accomplished deed. It seems to me the matter's as simple as that.

HEPHAISTOS: Nothing's ever that simple.

PSYCHE: Well, let me put it this way. If we're to take seriously a truly reductive physicalism, we must believe that intentional consciousness could be subtracted—or, at any rate, effectively discriminated—from the world's web of physical relations while leaving those relations wholly intact. Even the sort of functionalist model of mind you seem disposed toward presumes only a system of input and output, with all the seemingly distinctive phenomena of consciousness and unity of apprehension and intention reduced to the realm of mere appearance—mere useful dissemblance.

HEPHAISTOS: I see more clearly than ever that we're destined to revisit the issue of functionalism.

PSYCHE: Yes, no doubt, but all I want to establish here is that there are clearly physical events—physical transactions—that could not occur apart from the intentional and conscious content of minds, including such things as intentional perception, axiological judgments, acts of semeiotic communication . . .

HEPHAISTOS: All of which might yet be reducible to physical causality.

EROS: Would that mean that all purpose or final causality is only an appearance too?

HEPHAISTOS: Yes. Or, at the very least, it would mean that what we think of as purpose is the product of a long, non-purposive physical history, from which it emerges as a kind of subalternate function. Whatever the case, it too would be reducible to physical causes within a closed causal continuum. All actions are, at some level, the results of their prior physical causes; and what you think of as final causality is something determined entirely by that history: an inexorable physical momentum transcribed, as it were, into the user's illusion of a purely rational and voluntary end, beckoning our minds and wills into the future.

Eros: Determined entirely? *Now* who's the peremptory one? Emergence is a nebulous concept, of course, which is why it's such a convenient one for materialists and metaphysical naturalists: it obscures everything just enough to render the explanatory inadequacies of materialism or naturalism invisible. But to me it still looks like an invocation of magic, made out of desperation, which you'd never venture but for your ideological aversion to formal and final causes, or to any concept of causality other than the mechanistic. Yet all the evidence of personal agency says we do in fact think and act according to purposive rationales, which means that such agency remains an obviously teleological reality within a universe that, according to the mechanical paradigm, admits of no teleology.

Hephaistos: We can trace this same logical circle forever if you like. An infinite recurrence might be a pleasant break from all our infinite regressions. I'm happy to see that you've *emerged* from your silence, however.

Eros: [*Arching an eyebrow:*] Only because I was prompted to do so by a purpose.

VII

The Irreducible

Eros: Honestly, how can you cling so to this arbitrary fundamentalist belief in the causal closure of the physical? It's a purely metaphysical commitment, with no logical or empirical warrant, or any warrant at all other than want of imagination. It does amaze me, I have to confess, that so many philosophers of mind accept a premise—this impoverished picture of causes as always only mechanical exchanges of energy between distinct material forces within a closed continuum—that's not merely unnecessary, but obviously irreconcilable with mental acts. Goodness, there are learned scientists who talk as if—at least, once reality passes over the quantum threshold into the realm of classical mechanics—something like Laplace's fantasy holds true: a demon of superlative intelligence, knowing at a given instant the precise location and momentum of every subatomic particle in existence, could both reconstruct the entire physical history of the universe and foresee its entire future.[23] True, they might all grant that thermodynamics or quantum indeterminacy probably dictates that this wouldn't be literally possible purely from the evidence of the present dispositions of things; but still they speak as if, in principle, all events at higher levels of physical organization must be reducible without remainder to lower, more particulate causal moments. Hence, if our demon could somehow account for irreversibility or quantum indeterminacies—maybe by a perfect grasp of maximum entropy thermodynamics or by an occult knowledge of quantum hidden variables, or whatever—he could, from the dispositions of all the atoms and molecules and other corpuscular entities composing me and my environment a week ago at noon, have infallibly predicted my presence here today and the words currently passing through my lips, since everything we do must be the inevitable macroscopic result of the ensemble of impersonal physical forces underlying our formal existence. And yet we know this to be false. To whatever degree I'm a physical system, I'm also an intentional system, whose mental events take the forms of semeiotic determinations, and whose actions are usually the consequences of purposes I've conceived for myself. And these, precisely because they're irreducibly teleological, could appear nowhere within a reductive account or comprehensive inventory of the impersonal antecedent forces and processes composing me as a physical event. Simply said, I have *reasons* for being here, and any complete phenomenological description of my choice to be here would be one that could never be collapsed into a physical description of atomic, molecular, or even neural events. Even when I merely do this . . . [*Snapping his fingers:*] . . . it's clear that the action wasn't simply caused by the prior flow of material and energetic forces impelling my actions to that point. Yes, my action was consonant with those forces, but the same would have been true had I not done it. There was no physical determinism in any mechanistic sense, and certainly none at the atomic level. What caused it to happen was my free purposive decision to do it, just so I'd be able to make the point I'm making now. The meaning of my words caused the action.

That qualitative difference, as my beloved Psyche says, is sufficient to expose physicalism as a preposterous prejudice and nothing more. And, as she also says, the illusion of intentionality would still be an intentional phenomenon. Yes, of course, at the physical level of the exchanges of matter and energy—or of their interchangeable mathematical values—perhaps the natural order may always even out into an inflexible equation. But the movement of those material and energetic forces is also directed by rational relations existing at a higher level, causalities of a different kind that impose on the flow of physical events formal and final determinations that aren't merely phenomenal residues of those events. Your belief that free will and conceptual purposes would violate some law of physical causality if they had real effects, or would somehow add to or subtract from the conserved energy of the universe, is absurd. And your claim that all intentionality is in some sense illusory, reducible to complex electrochemical brain events, in turn reducible to molecular description and then to atomic description and so on, is frankly childish. Higher order operations aren't the determinate effects of lower order physical explanations. A dog fetching a stick isn't the causal effect of all the atoms in his body behaving in a certain way.

HEPHAISTOS: It seems that we'll need to interrogate the notion of emergence also.

PSYCHE: Indeed we shall, because that word often indicates the same error in its reverse form. I know modern philosophy of science is often torn between the ideas of absolute reductionism and strong emergentism—between, that is, the belief that all higher effects are reducible to physical causes without remainder and the belief that novel properties somehow emerge irreducibly from purely material causes—but both are nonsensical.

HEPHAISTOS: Ah. I know why you say that about reductionism—you've all been quite clear on that score—but I'm not sure what analogous problem you see in emergentism.

EROS: Equivocation, for one thing. All too often we allow the word "emergence" to obscure a crucial distinction: that between, on the one hand, synthetic properties that naturally arise at a higher level of organization out of the discrete properties of their ingredient parts and, on the other, properties that appear at that higher level without any plausible causal connection to the properties of its ingredients. That is, it often neatly hides the crucial distinction between quantitative and qualitative transitions from lower to higher levels of order—or, in the fashionable jargon, between weak and strong emergence. And what we've been discussing here is a perfect example of precisely the kind of problem that vague talk of "emergence" only allows us to evade. Mental intentionality is clearly a part of nature, one whose structure is irreducibly teleological and therefore contrary to the mechanical picture. Simply to speak of it as an emergent phenomenon, in the way that, say, we recognize the solidity of this bench I'm sitting on as emergent from an atomic and electromagnetic substrate, is to conflate two very different kinds of causal narrative.

I might add, moreover, that every act of intentionality is of its nature transcendental in both its most original movement and its most ultimate aspiration, and so clearly irreducible to the logic of physical causality. I'd go so far as to assert that rational intentionality as such is, in its most basic structure, a movement of self-transcendence whose ends are simply infinite, and so a movement impossible to confine within any mechanical picture of reality.

HEPHAISTOS: Now you're verging on the mystical, and I'm not prepared for that just at the moment. I take it, though, that you're claiming there's some basic, original, natural intentionality of the mind toward . . . what?

EROS: A transcendent end that makes all other mental actions possible. You yourself described the matter quite well not so long ago, when you noted that one desire often displaces another, and one purpose is elected over another, simply on account of a stronger attraction. I think your example was desiring to drink something inebriating but refraining from doing so out of a different and stronger desire for sobriety. I would say that the reason for the existence of all these desires, as well as for our ability to deliberate among them, is that all of them together are comprised within a more primordial desire for those transcendental ends we discussed earlier. Although I should add that I'd prefer to describe that intentionality—that constant natural orientation of the will toward its transcendent horizon—as . . .

HEPHAISTOS: [*After a moment's suspense:*] Yes?

EROS: As love.

HEPHAISTOS: Ah. *Natürlich.* I should have seen that coming. [*Looking up to the sky with a shrug:*] So much to discuss. Especially this hard-and-fast distinction you draw between weak and strong emergence. But the day advances apace. Unless my eyes deceive me, it's noon or thereabouts. I propose we adjourn for the day, go about our several tasks, and gather here again at, say, noon tomorrow, or slightly after. Otherwise we're just courting mental fatigue and increasing irascibility. I think I can summarize where we stand. Basically, you three have—laboriously—presented me with a simple syllogism. The major premise is that, if any of the apparent phenomena of mental life—consciousness, subjectivity, unity of apprehension, intentionality, language, reason, or what have you—are really the irreducible things they seem to be, then physicalism is false. The minor premise is that one or all of those phenomena are most definitely precisely what they appear to be. And the ineluctable conclusion is that physicalism is false.

PSYCHE: That's a fair summary.

HEPHAISTOS: I won't pretend that your arguments have been feeble; but I won't concede that they've been irresistible. And so now it falls to me, I suppose, to attempt to show how we might still reduce mental phenomena to something physical, or at least something compatible with a physicalist paradigm, or to show how those phenomena might have emerged from a physical basis—in my sense of "physical."

PSYCHE: So it would seem.

HEPHAISTOS: [*Rising from his bench and stretching his arms:*] Very well. I look forward to whatever comes.

[*Exeunt omnes.*]

DAY THREE
Brain and Mind

I

Emergence and Form

A little past noon in the same garden, bathed in the clear light of the Intermundian sun, under the impossibly blue vault of the crystalline sky, stirred constantly by fresh and gentle breezes blowing down from the western hills and from off the aetheric sea beyond. Enter HEPHAISTOS, *deep in thought. A few moments later,* PSYCHE, EROS, *and* HERMES *also enter and—at his back and unnoticed by him—take the same seats they occupied yesterday.*

PSYCHE: [*After several moments of expectant silence:*] Phaesty, my dear, your audience eagerly awaits.

HEPHAISTOS: [*Turning about:*] Why, you furtive little deities you, I should have heard your approach.

HERMES: Not mine, surely.

HEPHAISTOS: I was simply pondering how we should resume our debate. What's clear to me is that we'll have to revisit such matters as causal closure and emergence and so forth, since that's the most elementary level of our disagreement.

EROS: I'm certainly agreeable.

HEPHAISTOS: Yes, as a rule you are. [*Also seating himself on the same bench he occupied yesterday:*] So let's start with some very basic terms, just to set a clear boundary to what I'm arguing. I think it fair to say that the simplest definition of the naturalist or physicalist project with regard to mind, whatever variations or qualifications one might add, is that it's a thoroughgoing metaphysical materialism. That is, it tells us that the basic reality underlying all things is matter, which may be understood in any number of ways so long as it's always taken to be a wholly physical and intrinsically mindless stuff, and that mind is a fundamentally physical reality, reducible to or emergent from that mindless substrate; thus every mental function is, at least in principle, explicable by the same physical laws that explain chemical reactions, geological tectonics, cellular biology, and whatever else the hard sciences explore. At least, it can't exceed those laws.[1]

PSYCHE: Which already starts from the assumption that all physical laws can be reconciled with a strict materialism. As I've already confessed my quasi-Aristotelian belief that that's not so . . .

HEPHAISTOS: Quite. We needn't rehearse any of that now, though. I just want, before we voyage into deeper waters, to make a quick survey of the shoreline, and of our point of departure. Principally, I want you to tell me why it's really insufficient to assert that mental phenomena *emerge* from material causes, when nature is full of emergent properties. In the natural world, new realities and new powers continually arise at higher levels of organization, and then exert a kind of "top-down causation" upon the very forces from which they emerged. Why do you insist that mental properties can't be emergent in the same way?

HERMES: Would you give an example?

HEPHAISTOS: Nothing could be easier; nature more or less entirely consists of such properties. Take, for instance, water, at least of the terrestrial variety: it's composed of two very combustible gaseous elements, hydrogen and oxygen, and yet it possesses the emergent properties of liquidity and the capacity for extinguishing fire. Moreover, its liquidity is a top-down *cause* with regard to the elements composing it; each of its molecules contains the two hydrogen and one oxygen atoms composing it in covalent bonds, and then the liquidity of those molecules in the aggregate contains and directs those molecules in a cohesive totality that behaves in novel ways—that is, in turbulent or laminar flow, or in vortices, or in relative calm, or even in the courses of those small agitations that produce Brownian pedesis. If you want a somewhat more abstruse example, consider long-range topological order in quantum systems, which we can say *emerges* from quantum entanglement . . . or even, perhaps, topological order at the level of classical physics, as in certain polymer systems . . .[2]

PSYCHE: Now you're getting *too* abstruse. You've areas of specialized knowledge that we lack, remember.

HEPHAISTOS: Yes, sorry. Well, consider the structure of a wheel, then: even though it's an artifact rather than a naturally occurring phenomenon, its solidity and roundness emerge from its atomic and molecular and electromagnetic substrata; and yet it's the wheel that determines the motions of its ingredient elements, not the other way around. There are any number of powers that reside in composite totalities that can't be found in any of their parts in isolation. It seems to me that you might be guilty of what's called the *compositional fallacy:* the error of thinking that the properties of a complex reality must also be properties found in its individual parts. But of course the special properties of a wheel *as* wheel exist nowhere except in the wheel as a whole, and you'd never argue that its properties are anything other than physical results of physical causes. You'd never say that, though a house is made of bricks and mortar and timbers and glass and so forth, its physical properties as a house aren't found within any of those ingredients as such, and so those properties are inexplicable in physical terms. And yet you seem to think that precisely such an argument can be made with regard to the physical foundations of mental properties. As I understand the arguments of many dualists—and yes, I know that's not how you characterize your position—they consist in a simple failure to think through the difference between mereological accumulation and mereological composition: that is, the difference between a whole consisting in simply an uncoordinated assemblage of individual parts and the whole understood as an integrated system. Thus the antiphysicalist argues that, since subatomic particles can't think and individual molecules can't think and so forth, then nothing composed of them will be able to think merely by virtue of the physical interactions of those particles and molecules and whatnot.[3] It's really just Leibniz's mill, isn't it?

HERMES: Is it?

HEPHAISTOS: Surely you know it. Leibniz's argument was that, if what enabled a rational being to perceive and think were the mechanical structure of its physical parts, then we should be able to explain thought in mechanical terms. Thus, if we enlarged the machine of the brain to the size of a mill and entered it, we'd be able to find, among all those material mechanical parts exerting extrinsic forces upon one another, something like perceiving and thinking, or something that would explain them. But we wouldn't. We'd find just mindless machinery.[4]

HERMES: Yes, I'm familiar with the allegory. I'm simply unconvinced that it's only about composition . . .

HEPHAISTOS: Why? What Leibniz is saying seems plain to me: the juxtaposition and physical functioning of the intrinsically mindless parts of the brain, however intricate their arrangement, can't exhaustively explain the presence of perception and thought in the mind. Well, yes, that's true. Identifying certain properties as emergent doesn't *explain* them exactly, I admit it; but it does place them within our ordinary experience of physical phenomena. If we could enter into a water molecule and observe its parts free from the effects of their covalent ligature, so to speak, we'd see nothing remotely like liquidity; and, if we didn't already know the result of that covalency, we wouldn't be able to predict it. And yet we don't doubt that the physical bond of two hydrogen atoms and one oxygen atom is the sufficient reason for water's special properties. It may be that the exact cause of any given emergence eludes us as yet. It may even be the case that it will do so forever in some cases, as those who identify themselves as "mysterians" claim will always be the case with consciousness.

EROS: But can you provide a definition of "emergence" that covers *all* presumed cases?

HEPHAISTOS: *Das ist ganz einfach:* There are in nature composite realities whose peculiar properties and capacities emerge from the interaction of their elements, even though these properties and capacities don't reside in those elements themselves. An emergent whole, in other words, is more than—or, at any rate, different from—the sum of its parts; it's not simply the consequence of an accumulation of discrete powers added together in a sum, but rather the effect of a specific ordering of relations among those powers, which produces something entirely new within nature. And, given enough complexity in the composite structure, the range of the novel powers may exceed anything we could possibly imagine in advance. Consider, for instance, a computer: it's composed wholly of silicon, metal, plastic, electrically conductive elements, and so forth, and yet not only are its operations not present in any of its discrete parts; they're qualitatively different from any mere aggregation of the properties of those parts. I see no reason to reject, say, John Searle's arguments for seeing mental activity as basically a biological product of neurophysiological structures and processes, no different in principle from digestion and metabolism, or from enzyme secretion, or for that matter from liquidity in water, or from solidity in atomic and electromagnetic composites. Mental events are what he calls "system-level" operations, not identical with any of their lower-level constituents but emergent from them nevertheless, and able then to exert top-down causation upon them. That's not even a strictly materialist position, since one can grant—as Searle does—the real subjectivity and intentionality and such of consciousness, which aren't physical *things*, just so long as one acknowledges that it's all the natural consequence of physical *operations*.[5] Mysterious, yes, but not supernatural. What makes you so very certain that mind isn't an emergent property in just that way?

PSYCHE: Ah, you've raised several different issues, in fact, so this may take some time.

HEPHAISTOS: As you've noted, we're gods. Time isn't in short supply.

PSYCHE: I'll say upfront, however, that I've little patience for "mysterianism." Those who say we simply can't understand how consciousness arises from material causes but that we nevertheless *must* presuppose that it does so really mean only that they can't account for consciousness in a way that fits into the materialist metaphysics they arbitrarily adhere to; but they don't want to confront the fact. That should make them reconsider those metaphysical commitments rather than deceive themselves that they've any right to a picture of reality that can't intelligibly accommodate the only phenomenon that no one can sanely doubt. In fact, consciousness *in itself* is the one thing we most definitely do understand: we can enumerate and comprehensively describe its features, as we did yesterday, and immediately confirm them for ourselves. It's quite easy. Consciousness is reality as such for us, and it presents us with no obviously insoluble enigma if we don't dogmatically presume it must be grounded in an entirely mythical realm of pure mechanistic matter.

The real problem with what you're saying, though—if you'll forgive me saying so—is that your use of the concept of emergence does more to confuse issues than to elucidate them, because you speak as though it were a single univocal concept, even though many of the "system-level" operations you want to class under it are only barely analogous to one another. Moreover, let me say, one of the reasons I can't grant that mentality is an emergent property is that it isn't a property at all. Weight, mass, spin, atomic composition, velocity—or, for that matter, liquidity, solidity, magnetism—*these* are properties: discrete aspects of a thing, measurable in isolation from one another in the way physical attributes always are. What the mind does, by contrast, is a form of agency, a specific kind of act that exists only *in* act, and in which willing, consciousness, ratiocination, perception, subjective awareness, unity of apprehension, and so forth are all present as different dimensions of an indissoluble whole.

HEPHAISTOS: All right. I'm indifferent to the terms we use. Let's call it an emergent phenomenon, then—an emergent system.

PSYCHE: That's a very different thing, though. It requires greater explanatory detail. I mean, liquidity is a property and therefore easily accounted for in terms of other properties in combination. But a form of activity—not just of action, like water flowing, but a real form of agency that in some sense determines itself toward various ends—is something much harder to reduce to an arrangement of physical ingredients. If it's produced wholly physically—even if it's emergent (whatever we take that to mean), and even if it's a "system-level" operation—it's still bound by physical law and by logic to behave in a way consonant with the base from which it arose. It mustn't be able to do more than its physical constitution enables it to do. Yes, a "system-level" operation may be more than the sum of its parts; but it can't be antithetical or repugnant to the properties of those parts, or wholly unrelated to them.

Hephaistos: Surely water's capacity for extinguishing fire is antithetical to the combustibility of either hydrogen or oxygen.

Psyche: No, not antithetical to, only different from. Yes, water's properties aren't *identical* with any properties resident in either hydrogen or oxygen, but they're most definitely reducible to those special properties that, in a particular combination, cause hydrogen and oxygen to negate one another's combustible propensities and gaseous structures. Physical properties derived from other physical properties—no great problem there. So long as this is all that's meant by "emergence," then the concept is as inoffensive as it is obvious. But there's a point at which vague talk of emergence is just another way of talking about something that you might otherwise justly call magic. You spoke just now of the compositional fallacy; but that's invariably a failure to appreciate how a structure of relations can elicit new *quantitative* properties from the things related. It has no bearing at all on issues of *qualitative* discontinuity. Your example was of a house as I recall, and indeed it's true that a house is more than the sum of its parts. But it's also dependent upon those parts, with all their attributes. A house made of bricks and mortar and timbers can't, for instance, occupy no space, or lack composition, or be utterly devoid of mass, or be a non-composite unity, or—to return to our central topic—experience itself as a profound subjective and intentional unity. More to the point, its existence as a house isn't an emergent state; it's a formal determination imposed upon its physical elements by architects and builders.

Hephaistos: And for you it's clear that mental agency is a property—sorry, a *phenomenon*, an *activity*—as qualitatively discontinuous from physical causes as all that?

Psyche: Yes. At least from physical causes of the mechanistic sort you presume.

Hephaistos: But why?

Psyche: For goodness' sake, my darling Phaesty, for all the reasons we spent much of yesterday laying out. Listen, when you invoke Leibniz's mill, do so with some respect. The point he's making isn't an instance of the compositional fallacy. It's a perfectly correct observation that the third-person, composite, mechanical arrangement of mindless material parts is not merely quantitatively different from mentality, but is actually qualitatively opposed to it. There's not merely a missing causal narrative uniting the two; such a narrative is a logical impossibility. And it's this impossibility that's conveniently obscured by the—forgive me for saying this—wanton imprecision with which you apply the concept of "emergence" to a range of phenomena that obey radically different causal logics. We really need some clear distinctions here—chiefly between "weak" or "structural" emergence, on the one hand, and "strong" emergence, on the other. The former is merely an expansion of physical propensities into other, more developed, physically consequent propensities; the latter would be the appearance of entirely novel propensities that are wholly unrelated to the properties whose conjunction resulted in them—rather like the chanting of certain words, conjoined to certain herbs and eyes of newt and the light of a full moon, producing a magic castle. If we properly distinguish weak from strong emergence, what we'll find is that instances of the former abound—as you say, nature more or less consists in them—but that instances of the latter are absolutely nowhere to be found, and that what might occasionally look like a case of strong emergence is actually a case of formal causation.

Hephaistos: Well, hold on, don't you think everything's a case of formal causation? Isn't form one of those rational relations that you think can be identified in the structure of anything—even, presumably, weakly emergent phenomena?

Psyche: Indeed, I do; but you don't. So we needn't become overly metaphysical here. Even in terms of the mechanistic view of reality you cling to, one can differentiate between cases of wholly natural emergence and cases of physical composites that have to be given form by some adventitious agency or causal force. All too often, talk of "emergence" is just an expedient way of evading that distinction. As for emergence in the abstract, it's all quite true in a general sense; but it's also a limited truth. In order to close the devilish explanatory gap between mechanism and mind, your model of emergence would somehow have to allow for the appearance of new physical realities that, even though they remain dependent upon the native properties of the elements composing them, nevertheless possess characteristics entirely *irreducible* to those properties. But this makes no sense. At least, as a claim made solely about physical processes, organisms, and structures in purely material terms, it can't possibly be true. From a physical perspective, emergent properties can't be discontinuous from the properties of the prior causes from which they arise; anything, in principle, must be reducible, by a series of "geometrical" steps, to the physical attributes of its ingredients. Obviously, this poses no problem in the case of a purely physical phenomenon, like the liquidity of water. But things are very different when one tries to explain away causal gaps like the difference between, say, a computer's physical elements and its functions, because the latter don't naturally emerge from the former at all. What distinguishes a computer's powers from those individually possessed by its various material parts isn't any *emergent* property, but rather the causal influence of a creative intellect acting upon those parts from without. So, while it's true that nothing that physically characterizes a computer is anything more than a mathematically predictable result of certain physical antecedents, those operations that actually involve computing in the full sense have been imposed upon the computer's physical constituents by a further, more eminent, *formal* causality, which is itself directed by a final causality—that is, the intentions of a designer and a programmer and a user. At the purely material level, anything truly emergent is also reducible to what it emerges from; otherwise, "emergence" is merely the name of some kind of magical transition between intrinsically disparate realities.

Hephaistos: As significant a difference as that is, it doesn't actually weaken my argument. Here you're making far too much of the difference between emergence and formation. All right, so a computer doesn't emerge from its elements; it's assembled by a designer and programmed with software. Well, that's just a secondary level of emergence as far as I'm concerned. Conscious organisms are also designed, by epochs of evolutionary attrition and retention. So what? That's also how they emerge. The issue is whether, once all of something's physical parts are in order, an emergent phenomenon arises upon that physical basis. The computer may be an artifact; but its functions and processes are purely physical results of physical causes. The same may well be the case with mental phenomena and their organic basis.

PSYCHE: Ah, no. Even in the case of computers that's clearly not the case. Yes, the electrical and mechanical processes of a computer are physically dependent on and reducible to an ensemble of material elements. But the full operations of a computer involve the use of digital processing to produce representations of intentional content—words, numbers, images, meanings, semeiotic systems—all of which exist *as* intentional only in relation to minds, in a hermeneutical space entirely distinct from the physical space inhabited by the computer. That hermeneutical level doesn't rest upon the physical facts about the computer at all. But this all leads into the issue of computational models of mind, which I'd rather defer for now.

HEPHAISTOS: By all means. For once, I'm happy to wait, as I'm still not convinced you're not making a distinction without a difference.

PSYCHE: In a sense, at the material level, you're correct. And therein lies the problem with all your vague talk of emergence. Isn't it rather obvious that when one describes such things as liquidity or solidity—or, for that matter, topologies of the sort you mentioned earlier, whether of quantum or of polymer systems—one isn't describing an effect that bafflingly arises out of and in addition to a structure of physical relations? Rather, one's simply describing that structure itself. So too, when one describes a composite artifact, like a wheel or a house, one isn't speaking of anything above and beyond the special arrangement of its physical ingredients; the wheel or the house simply *is* that arrangement. That's what I mean by structural emergence: not a new property in addition to a synthesis of elements—not an effect following mysteriously upon a combination of parts—but quite simply the structure of that synthesis or combination as described in formal rather than material terms. So you're right, at that level the distinction between emergence and formation doesn't make a difference. There it's simply a matter of descriptive reversibility: one and the same phenomenon can be described in terms of its material constitution—the iron of an iron wheel, say—or in terms of its formal configuration—the wheel made from that iron.

This is crucial, though. For, along with that descriptive reversibility, there comes a certain reversibility as regards what one calls "top-down" and "bottom-up" causal explanations—at least, in the case of any property or phenomenon that's truly emergent from its physical ground. This is simply another way of stating the supposed "causal closure of the physical": a truly reductive physicalism requires, as an inviolable maxim, that all effects can be *physically* reduced to "bottom-up" causation, and this includes even the *effect* we call "top-down" causation. "System-level" entities are still just composites of lower-level forces, and so are merely extensions of those forces; otherwise, their operations would violate the most basic laws of physics. Take that iron wheel: yes, when it turns, it causes all of its material parts to rotate; and yet there's an ambiguity here, because it's no less true that the wheel turns only *because* all those parts—down to the threshold of the particulate level—are rotating in concert with one another and "propelling" the wheel. What a very obscure word "because" turns out to be here. All the constituents of the wheel are in motion *because* the molar totality of the object they belong to is moving. In this sense, the chief causality of the operation is "top-down." And yet it's also "bottom-up" in a more than defective sense, since the molar totality's movement is dependent on the motion of its molecular constituents. The wheel's roundness allows for rounded behaviors to be imposed on its material parts precisely because those material parts allow for its roundness; base and superstructure are one and the same action, described from opposite vantages. I submit that any truly emergent phenomenon is entirely a structural extension of its parts in just this way, and must exhibit just this ambiguity, just this descriptive aporia, just this *complete* reversibility of explanation without any remainder of causal objects or forces. Nothing emerges that is not virtually present in what it emerges from, nothing emergent can exceed the causal potentials resident in its parts, and whatever "top-down" powers it possesses are still physically predictable in principle. The mereological hierarchy, in physical terms, is a closed totality: one and the same equation in either direction.

But none of this is so—for all the reasons we gave yesterday—of the relation between mind and, say, physical neurology. In fact, far from being inverse descriptions of one and the same causal structure, the causal powers peculiar to each sphere—the material and the mental—aren't even vaguely similar to one another. Each operates in ways radically discontinuous with—even contrary to—the ways in which the other operates. Recall what we said yesterday about, for example, the incommensurability of sequences of electrochemical events in the brain and ratiocination's sequences of consecutive logic. A simple syllogism, in its very structure, is already a miracle from a mechanistic perspective. Or consider the intrinsic teleology of intention, or the unity of apprehension, or subjective awareness. You can call all of this "emergent," but there's no other case of a relation this occult anywhere in nature. "Strong emergence" is a myth; to invoke it is to say nothing. You're merely projecting the unique mystery of mind backward into the realm of physical nature, to make it seem that it's not unique; but material nature comprises only structural extensions of expressed powers, novel mechanical complexities, acquisitions of new amplitudes of expression, new configurations and patterns—but it yields no truly new, qualitatively discontinuous powers or phenomena.[6]

Hephaistos: None whatsoever?

Psyche: None. Try to name one. Wherever you encounter any physical phenomenon that seems to exceed the purely physical powers of its ingredient causes, you'll find that you've merely isolated an instance of formal causality, as in the case of that computer of yours. That takes us back to yesterday's discussion of free will as a real causal force: certain actions aren't reducible to their physical antecedents; but the physical powers expressed in those actions are ones to which those antecedents are wholly adequate. Within any mereological hierarchy, downward and upward causation are strictly proportional to one another—are even, as far as physical closure is concerned, identical. Even in living organisms—and I say this as someone hostile to the notion that life can be reduced to purely material causes—the actual *physical* operations that sustain life are characterized by this same explanatory reversibility. Enzyme secretion, for instance, is possible at the physical level entirely as a structural extension of such things as an enzyme's ingredient proteins. Therein lies the futility of Searle's argument that we should treat mental phenomena as analogous to other emergent physical and physiological phenomena. All the supposed analogates he adduces—whether mere properties, like liquidity or solidity, or advanced system-level processes, like metabolism or digestion—are specimens of structural emergence and the formal organization of physical elements and entities, such as molecules. By contrast, to say how first-person mental operations arise *physically* from third-person biochemistry, if your mechanical model of nature is correct, we really would have to talk about magic or miracle . . . or "strong emergence," if you prefer—some marvelously inexplicable transition from the undirected, mindless causality of mechanistic matter to the intentional unity of consciousness.

Hephaistos: Some of this sounds suspiciously like a formula for absolute physical determinism after all. I mean, if top-down causation is just bottom-up causation expressed at the system-level . . .

Psyche: Pay attention, Phaesty dear. It would be such a formula *if* I believed in the mechanistic view of nature. I'm speaking here solely about the principles that would necessarily follow from a consistent physicalism. I myself am no physicalist. I believe that there really are instances of top-down causation that can't be reduced to their bottom-up causes. I believe there are countless natural phenomena that are products of formal causality, and so not *simply* reducible to physical causes.

Hephaistos: Yes, I know. You do grant that there are instances of irreducibility in nature while also denying the logical coherence of strong emergence. I was paying attention; I simply wanted to be clear on your picture of nature.

Psyche: Certainly I grant the reality of irreducibility in nature, no less than I did in the case of a computer. Hence physicalism is impossible for me. I don't believe the chemical level of nature is necessarily exhaustively reducible to physics, and I'm quite sure the biological level isn't exhaustively reducible to the chemical, or the neurophysiological to the biological, or the psychological to the neurophysiological, or the social to the psychological, or so on. At least, not at the formal level. I think we've covered this already. I believe that, in the hierarchical structure of life or mind, every lower level is, as it were, a "material" or "potential" level in relation to the next level up, and that the lower level is subsumed into the higher quite often as a result of the plastic powers of higher causalities—formal and final, that is. The subvenient reality is the material cause for the immediately supervenient, and the supervenient reality is the formal cause of the immediately subvenient. There are some very good philosophical and scientific arguments, after all, against regarding higher-level physical processes as merely the calculable results of the lower-level systems on which they supervene.[7]

HEPHAISTOS: Which is the point I was trying to get at. If there are such discontinuities between levels, which I thought was what you were saying don't exist in nature, why insist on formal causality instead of emergence? Why prefer one ghostly, mysterious causal language to another? Why call the one logical and the other magical?

PSYCHE: Because of the laws of physics. Because of the laws of logic. How often must we rehearse these arguments? I'm not the one who denies the existence of formal discontinuities between levels of causality; you physicalists do. That's why you contradict yourselves when you simply throw your hands in the air and invoke the principle of emergence—though you then conceal the inconsistency from yourselves by making the principle so vague that it hides the difference between structural emergence and the sort of fantastic emergence that would be needed to fill in the gaps in your view of reality. Discontinuities of the sort I'm talking about, by contrast, aren't simple magical saltations between incompatible realities. They have a rational structure. They're discontinuities only at the formal level. They're still continuities in another sense, at the physical level. They represent no breach in modal possibility, as your view does. They're different aspects of the rational relations resident in everything; hence, there are always ties of rational dependency among them, and those lower or subvenient laws I mentioned always constrain the higher levels physically. While chemistry may relate to physics as a kind of formal cause, at its physical level it possesses no concrete substance in addition to its physical substrate; it's wholly dependent on physics. Or, if that's not absolutely obvious, take a step further up: biology constrains chemistry formally, chemistry constrains biology materially. This is a logical truth, it seems to me. Lower, subvenient laws always constrain the higher levels materially and the higher, supervenient laws always constrain the lower levels formally. None of that, of course, need suggest any disruption in the quantitative continuum that unites these levels; even mental agency is susceptible of physical measurement, in that it requires an expenditure of energy in physiological functions. But, as one ascending tier of the hierarchy of nature surmounts another, the qualitative disproportion grows, until one reaches a point—mind—where the physicalist or mechanistic narrative of causality clearly falls apart. And this very difference between the discontinuous and the continuous, rather than being a logical lacuna that must be hidden behind the meaningless invocation of "irreducible emergence," is what allows for hierarchical causal structures of ever greater complexity and power.

So yes, I believe in formal causes, and believe they're logical rather than magical in all the ways that strong emergence can't be; but obviously formal causes aren't going to be visible within the *physical* history of any given phenomenon; they appear only in the difference between system and material substrate. Then again, neither is the law of absolute mechanism visible. Those who assume it to be true merely apply their prejudices to the phenomena they observe. Hence, the physicalist will assume that somehow physics *must* yield chemistry, chemistry *must* yield biology, and so forth, even if the terms of that necessity are difficult to establish. *Post hoc, ergo propter hoc:* one of the most venerable of logical errors. Sooner or later, we're told, even mind will turn out to be only another physical result of physical causes—neurophysiology will explain consciousness. But all of that, curiously enough, is irrelevant to the specific point we're dealing with here. Once again, I'm not a physicalist, but I can agree with the physicalist that, *to the degree* any phenomenon is physical, all its physical powers must be reducible to—which is to say, incapable of exceeding the potentials of—its physical basis . . . its physical ingredients. A formal cause is limited by its material conditions. But any truly qualitative difference between the lower and higher levels, rather than a difference merely in degree or in structural relations, requires another explanation. And mind is just such a qualitative difference.

HEPHAISTOS: You know, there are schools of "non-reductive physicalism" or "dual aspect theory" that say otherwise—that claim that non-physical qualities can emerge from physical elements as secondary properties that, while remaining non-physical, are nevertheless entirely dependent on their physical foundation. That is, all *things* must be physical, but not every *property*.

HERMES: How preposterous.

PSYCHE: How, I wonder, can that possibly be reconciled with the physical explicability required by materialism or naturalism?[8] Once again, we're in the land of magic and miracle, the arcane realm of the "mysterians" and the naturalist fundamentalists. No: mind is not physically emergent from mechanistic matter.

HEPHAISTOS: And still you resist characterizing your position as a dualism because . . .

PSYCHE: Because, once again, I don't believe in mechanistic matter to begin with. The only kind of material substrate I believe in exists always as one rational relation within an indivisible totality of rational relations, all contained within a mindlike—or mental—order. Matter for me is an aspect of thought in its full range of expressions. It's one dimension of the structure of real things, which is to say the structure of mind made concrete in nature. So I'm quite at one with Leibniz, not on the grounds that atoms and molecules and tissues don't think and therefore can't compose a thinking thing, but on the grounds that mechanism and mind are irreconcilable in principle. That's not the fallacy of composition at all; it's the recognition that physical ingredients, understood mechanistically, can't be combined to produce non-physical realities. And, as mind is an undeniable reality, pure mechanistic naturalism must in the end prove to be a fantasy.

Hephaistos: [*After a long sigh and a longer pause:*] Very well, then. It seems to me my course is clear. Or, rather, I see two possible courses: either I must demonstrate that mental phenomena can, despite all appearances, be described mechanistically, or I must demonstrate that matter can be described in a non-mechanistic way without abandoning physicalism.

Eros: So you've identified our point of departure to your satisfaction?

Hephaistos: More accurate to say, to my vexation.

Hermes: But we can embark?

Hephaistos: We can.

II
Identity and Eliminativism

HEPHAISTOS: Let me start, just for completeness' sake, with what I suspect will be the arguments you'll dismiss with the most impatience.

EROS: Which are . . . ?

HEPHAISTOS: The ones that say there's no actual mystery to consciousness to begin with, and only our own bad habits of language make us imagine there is. I'm thinking of identity theory and eliminativism.

HERMES: [*With a groan:*] Must we?

HEPHAISTOS: I'm leading the dance just now, so yes, we must.

EROS: I know what "identity theory" is, at least. At least, I assume you mean the claim that mental phenomena and the physical events we think of as associated with them aren't actually two distinct and correlated realities, but instead one and the same thing. Yes? So, rather than saying "this pain is the *result* of the firing of this neuron," we should say "this pain simply *is* the firing of this neuron," because our customary division between a physical event in the body and a subjective experience in the mind is just a figment of grammar. Right?

HEPHAISTOS: Exactly. Mental properties are perhaps simply material properties. Much of this we've already covered in principle, I admit, but let's be as exact as we can. After all, we're aware that a single phenomenon can bear two very different kinds of description, sometimes to the point of misleading us into thinking we're referring to two different objects, such as describing the planet Venus as both the Evening Star and the Morning Star.

Psyche: Which, in either case, is to speak of a star. Obviously that's very different from saying a third-person electrochemical discharge in the brain simply *is* a first-person thought or a perception or a qualitative impression. That there's a correlation between the two is almost certainly true—but an identity?

Hephaistos: Admittedly it's a different sort of identity. But take the classic example of what Saul Kripke called *a posteriori* necessity: the terms "water" and "H_2O" refer to the same object necessarily, by definition, and yet that identity isn't a logical or an *a priori* truth; it's one we come to know through experience and study. Is it so absurd, then, to suggest that one and the same physical event might be severally described as both a "brain-state" and a "mental state" while in fact being simply one and the same thing?

Psyche: [*Shaking her head gently:*] No, no, no. Surely you see how bad an analogy that is, Phaesty—as even Kripke would tell you, given that he saw his argument as militating *against* the identity of brain and mind. In the case of water or H_2O, we're clearly talking about a single uniform phenomenon under two different descriptions that aren't analytically identical, but that we've found empirically to refer to the same thing. In the case of, say, a neuron firing and a thought forming, the logic is the reverse: we're clearly talking about two distinct phenomena whose descriptions are identical neither *a priori* nor *a posteriori*, and whose identity we can neither see nor conceive but only assert, more or less paradoxically. Are we really going to say that this or that sequence of biochemical and electrochemical events in the cerebral cortex is *identical* to the quadratic equation, or to the thought of the quadratic equation? Identical in what way? In the case of water, we can see how its molecular description merely amplifies our understanding of what in either case has exactly the same attributes and properties, qualitative, quantitative, and phenomenal. We already know that water has a physical constitution; the concept of "H_2O" merely fills in the blanks at the molecular level, and so it poses no conceptual difficulties for us once we're aware of it, because we're dealing with two third-person descriptions of a third-person referent, and both descriptions apply to that referent in analogous fashion.

In the case of physical and mental events, however—as we so laboriously discussed yesterday—we're still presented with two descriptions that remain conceptually irreconcilable: uniquely so, in fact, as here alone we're confronted with the absolute qualitative disjunction between a third-person and a first-person phenomenon. Think about it. In speaking of a neural event, we're talking about an observable object in the physical world; I can, with the proper apparatus, observe electrical activity in a material brain. When, however, we're discussing a mental event, we're talking about a private pathos or percept or concept that I most certainly *can't* observe. That being so, every version of identity theory is sheer empty assertion. It answers no questions. It's just yet another restatement of the problem of mind. In the end, we're left, as always, with a correlation, not an identity, for which we have no causal narrative.

HERMES: Anyway, isn't identity theory out of fashion?

HEPHAISTOS: Well, yes. At least, theories of "type identity" are—that is, theories that say a certain mental event like pain is directly convertible with one particular kind of brain event. I mean, taken far enough, that would mean that every type of experience would be identical to a single particular neurology, as no two brains are exactly alike. Most philosophers of mind now like to hold open the thesis of "multiple realizability" or "token identity." That is to say, there are certain "types" of both brain-states and mental states—say, a certain kind of electrical activity in the former case and a certain kind of experience of pain in the latter—and there may be a functional correlation between them; but we needn't think that either of these types exists in only one form, or that the correlation between them comes in only one form either. Rather, each type may be expressed in an indeterminate number of particular "tokens," and thus the same structural correlation between *this* type of brain-state and *that* type of mental state may occur in a number of different ways. Not only can two different persons be said to experience pain in the same fashion, despite having different brains; the same pain-function is possible for neurologies radically different from the human. There need only be the same correspondence between a certain token of a certain type of brain event and a certain token of a certain type of mental experience; and neither need be identical to the tokens found in another organism. A certain token of electrical activity in the neurology of an octopus may also occasion a token of pain, for instance, though its neurology could scarcely be more unlike a human's. So the question is one not of identity at the physical level, but only of identity in function, in the system of the organism taken as a whole. If it walks like a duck and quacks like a duck, it still might experience the feeling of water in the same ways as an otter or a sea-nymph. It may be that certain mental states supervene upon radically different neurologies in the way that the figure in a statue of Artemis might supervene upon either granite or bronze.

Psyche: Now who's talking about formal causality? That would be the very definition of an absent physical causal relation, wouldn't it? If the same phenomenal function can be achieved by radically different physiological systems, then physical reductionism has no plausible basis. If a mental state and a brain-state can't be identified with one another by isolating a set of necessarily shared physical predicates, then they aren't the same thing.

Hephaistos: Well, once again, we're talking about functional states, ways of processing data, not about ontologically concrete objects. I know we've yet to address the issue of functionalism, but suffice it to say here that there's more than one way of skinning a . . . banana. That does raise a question though: What might you make of the argument that we mistake the relation between brain and mind for a causal problem because we're thinking of mental operations as things or substances, whereas we should conceive of them merely as activities in which the brain engages—in the way, say, a dancer's body may engage in dancing? Thinking is merely the brain engaged in mental activity.

Psyche: That may be an even more vacuous argument than identity theory. First of all, I'm not sure why the language of causality would apply only to things and substances. Activities are caused too and, if physical, they must have a physical cause in some sense. And if what the mind does is intrinsically unlike what a composite physical object in a supposedly mechanistic universe does, then the problem most certainly persists. How does a physical object engage in an activity that defies physical principles?

HEPHAISTOS: Let me phrase the matter differently. What if we're describing mental activity as a thing in itself that, in fact, it isn't? What if we've constructed for ourselves a concept of a single kind of object, when in fact what we're presented with is an ensemble of operations that, decomposed to their most basic elements, lack any of the properties you think you can identify as irreducibly mental phenomena?

HERMES: [*With a groan:*] I thought you were jesting. Are we really going to pretend to take eliminativist materialism seriously?

HEPHAISTOS: Well, I rarely take anything totally seriously. But the issue here is what's conceptually coherent. Whatever the dialectical disadvantage at which I may have placed myself in this debate, the one great advantage I continue to enjoy is that I don't have to prove any particular theory of mind to be true; I need only demonstrate that your position isn't the only rational one on offer—or the most rational, for that matter.

HERMES: But *eliminativism?*

EROS: Excuse me, but I have to confess that I'm a bit hazy on the details here. The little I've ever heard of the theory made it sound too absurd to bother looking into any more deeply.

HEPHAISTOS: The idea is simple enough. As Paul Churchland, one of its principal proponents, defines it, it's the view that commonsense notions of psychological phenomena—like beliefs, intentions, motives, desires, consciousness, and so forth—constitute a "radically false theory," so defective in its principles and ontology that it's not sufficient to attempt to reduce those phenomena to purely physical causes. Rather, our commonsense picture is mere "folk psychology" and has proved utterly inadequate as an explanatory or predictive model of behavior and cognitive activity, and so must be totally eliminated in favor of a more scientific, wholly impersonal neuroscientific theory, entirely purged of such mythical entities as the personal subject, intentional states, and the like, in the way that the sciences have also purged themselves of such fantasies as phlogiston or vital spirits, or that medicine has purged itself of belief in demons and demon-possession.[9]

EROS: [*After a prolonged pause, with knitted brows and a scowl of incredulity:*] That sounds positively . . . ridiculous.

HERMES: You needn't be so generous.

HEPHAISTOS: Let's not be polemical now.

HERMES: Why not, pray tell? You're not really asking us again to entertain the idea that consciousness can be an illusion?

EROS: Honestly, how can such a view be stated without contradiction? I mean, how can one take seriously the *belief* that there's no such thing as belief? How can one act in a way consistent with such ideas, or even formulate them without invoking the very entities they're supposed to banish, like beliefs? Isn't that a kind of cognitive suicide?[10]

HEPHAISTOS: Oh, that's not a serious objection. The eliminativist need only reply that even his or her belief in eliminativism isn't really what folk psychology tells us it is, but is instead a neurophysiological fact for which we'll eventually find a better paradigm and terminology. The eliminativist is more than happy to eliminate the commonsense meaning of his or her own conventional language.

PSYCHE: Which is a bit absurd, but which is also, I have to admit, not entirely contradictory. [*To Eros:*] I agree, my love, that eliminativism is ludicrous, but not so much because of its performative inconsistency—something of which we're all guilty from time to time, since we're forced to use the words and ideas at our disposal—and not even because of the unpleasantly patrician ivory-tower sneer concealed in that term "folk psychology," but rather because it's inherently nonsensical, and in fact based on demonstrably false claims. [*To Hephaistos:*] As for you, Phaesty, since I know you don't really believe a word you're saying, I feel no compunction in seizing the reins from your grasp.

HEPHAISTOS: [*Raising his hands in mock helplessness:*] Just so long as you leave me the whip, for defensive purposes.

PSYCHE: *Pshaw.* We're all friends here. [*To Eros:*] But yes, my love, the fully developed eliminativist position really is that there's no such thing as consciousness at all, and that all talk about persons, subjects, consciousness, thoughts, intentions, ideas, convictions, and so forth, as commonly understood, is simply a quaint and primitive patois that a more scientific account of the brain will one day render obsolete and so eliminate, when we've learned instead to speak of psychological phenomena solely in terms of discrete biochemical and physiological processes. Once those figments of folklore are banished from our conceptual world, we'll recognize them as illusory—like the seemingly concrete images in a pointillist painting when viewed from a distance, which dissolve into a haze of tiny motes of pigment when one draws close enough to the canvas to see what's really going on. At that point, the problem—the illusion—of mental agency will have been dispelled. [*With a labored but longanimous smile:*] One doesn't have to engage such ideas at a particularly rarefied intellectual altitude to recognize them as nonsense.

For one thing, there's the sheer childishness of the picture of the sciences they presume—I mean, the crude notion that a properly scientific theory is one that recognizes only bottom-up causality, rather as Laplace's poor simpleton of a demon does. It's positively eighteenth-century, the way the eliminativists speak. We've already noted that the philosophical arguments against that sort of unilinear reductionism are formidable. Biology must be compatible with chemistry, but it can't be reduced to chemistry; chemistry must be compatible with physics, but it can't be reduced to physics. In fact, the whole reductionist project has proved something of an embarrassment, especially when applied to system-level phenomena such as, oh, organisms and minds. As ever, a physicalist reduction is worthless—little more than a survey of a phenomenon's minimal limit-conditions—if it can't be complemented by a reconstruction of the phenomenon from the basic laws to which it's been reduced. Alas, systems don't simply emerge from their ingredients. And, of course, I've also told you why I think it impossible to decompose mental agency into a collection of separate faculties, let alone separate physical parts. But that's of only secondary concern, since eliminative materialism isn't a scientific proposal to begin with. The whole eliminativist premise would mean that no empirical phenomenology would be properly "scientific," and would always have to be replaced by a bottom-up causal narrative without remainder. Every higher-level or system-level phenomenon would have to be decomposed into lower-level causes in order to be an object of scientific scrutiny. At which level do we stop, though? Which is the truly "scientific" rather than merely phenomenal level—the scientific rather than merely manifest image? This is utterly arbitrary. By that logic, taken to its end, none of the real sciences other than physics would be sciences at all; nothing dealing with systems of causation or mereological structures would be seen as explaining anything. Alongside folk psychology, we might as well talk about folk botany, folk chemistry, folk biology, folk engineering. Only physics would have explanatory value—or perhaps only quantum physics, which is the one field of course that *explains* nothing. Eliminativists may speak of replacing folk psychology with a complete neurophysiology, but by their own premises that too would ideally be replaceable by a complete biochemistry, and that by a complete basic chemistry, and that by a complete physics, and still we would never reach the ultimate "why" underlying it all. This isn't a scientific perspective. It's a superstition, based on a crude confusion of a system's functions with its physical parts. It's the genetic fallacy exaggerated to the point of a psychosis.

Hephaistos: Oh, come now. I acknowledge that many eliminativists have a somewhat naïve view of scientific explanation—probably a bit nineteenth-century, to be more exact—but don't use that as an excuse for avoiding the question of the explanatory insufficiency of, quite specifically, our commonsense view of mental agency. The specific issue we're dealing with here isn't whether every empirical phenomenology needs to be reduced to a physical narrative; we can cross each bridge as we come to it. Here the claim is that, in this instance in particular, the empirical phenomenology is defective and haunted by mythical monsters.

Hermes: Such as beliefs? Intentions and ideas? Subjectivity?

Hephaistos: To name some of the more feral and voracious.

Psyche: But that's where eliminativism is most absurd of all: it's a program to correct a problem that doesn't exist, and that there's no reason to think exists. There's nothing obviously deficient or misleading about our commonsense understanding of mental agency. When eliminativists say there is, they mean only that it can't be explained in wholly physical terms, which is an entirely circular argument. In fact, that commonsense understanding is grounded in direct empirical evidence, more surely than is our knowledge of anything else. What the eliminativists really find galling is, once again, that this phenomenon, uniquely, exhibits characteristics that are formal rather than physical, and that therefore escape that explanatory reversibility of purely physical phenomena we talked about earlier. Mental agency's top-down structures of causation—consciousness, intentionality, unity, freedom, rationality—simply exceed the bottom-up potentialities of any purely physical system, from which what we should actually conclude is that the regular successes of commonsense mental categories are proof of the inadequacy of physicalism.

And those successes are self-evident. What the eliminativists call "folk psychology" isn't, in fact, a defective theory; it's not a theory at all; it's merely a set of direct observations of objective realities, which may require some explanation and deeper investigation here and there, but which certainly can't be explained away. It has survived over the epochs, moreover, because of its all but perfect predictive and explanatory accuracy. It may not explain everything, but when someone tells me, for instance, that he intends to do something, I can predict from that with fair certainty what he will do. Even if he's lying to me, if I can deduce that he's lying, I can still make a good guess at what he will do next, based on his intentions and what I might know of his psychological characteristics—his beliefs, dispositions, temperamental impulses, and such. Moreover, if I know someone believes something to be true, I know also how he'll regard a challenge to its truth. Conversely, if I disagree with an assertion he makes, no one can understand my actions in contradicting or disbelieving him without knowing the intentional content both of his assertion and of my response. He wants to convince me, perhaps, that Schubert's *Winterreise* is the highest achievement of Western music; I wish to convince him that that distinction belongs to Bach's second unaccompanied violin partita. The noises and gestures that pass between us, the nervous agitations that our relative degrees of emotional investment might excite in us, as well as the animosity that springs up between us over this small dispute—all of it can be described in purely physical terms, right down to the lowest levels to which our sciences can penetrate, but none of that would ever provide an adequate explanation of *why* any of it is happening. No description of the physical states of anyone's neurophysiology, be it ever so comprehensive, could possibly supply the sort of predictive accuracy that so-called "folk psychology" provides us with in every moment, precisely because intentionality is real and precisely because it isn't mechanical, and thus can't be found within the material structure of things. Actually, our common and ordinary perceptions of and suppositions about mental agency routinely meet with comprehensive predictive success. Far from constituting some corrigible or dispensable theory about psychological states, they're often in fact a precise, perspicuous, exhaustive, and almost infinitely verified phenomenological account of the primary data of experience. They're reality at its most fundamental, to which any aspiring scientific theory must prove itself adequate in order to be taken seriously—not the reverse.

HEPHAISTOS: And those who believed in phlogiston would have said much the same thing about it.

PSYCHE: If so, they'd have had no right to do so. That's a wholly specious analogy. Phlogiston isn't and never was a phenomenon; it was a postulate devised to explain phenomena that couldn't be denied, such as combustion and rust, and it had to be abandoned only because it failed to accord with the evidence; hence, it was ultimately eliminated and eventually replaced by the theory of oxidation. That's actually how the real sciences work: when the theory doesn't adequately account for the phenomenon, it's the theory that's eliminated. Eliminative physicalism, however, performs exactly the reverse operation, and attempts to rescue the theory—mechanistic materialism—by eliminating the phenomenon. And not just any phenomenon: rather, the one phenomenon—our commonsense or immediate experience of mental agency—that both declares itself as absolutely indubitable and openly reveals its properties in every single instant of experience. Beliefs, desires, intentions, consciousness—these are themselves the very things we can't deny, but must explain. Phlogiston doesn't exist. My *belief* that phlogiston doesn't exist, however, self-evidently does, and has demonstrable, phenomenologically observable consequences for the things I say and think on the matter, which no inventory of mere material and physical events could ever account for.

Anyway, I know you don't really think there could be some causal account of mental states that could supplant our understanding of intentionality or beliefs or consciousness or what have you without any empirical remainder. I'll admit, though, that in one crucial sense eliminativism is logically consistent. Not internally, of course; in itself, it defies parody. But it's the inevitable terminus of the physicalist or naturalist project, in that it follows impeccably—and more so than does any other theory—from an unfailing adherence to naturalist principles. If one on principle can't grant that the formal structures of mental life and experience are real causal powers in themselves, then they must be not only reducible to, but genuinely eliminable by, more fundamental descriptions of a purely physical and impersonal variety. One must really think it possible imaginatively to dissolve mental agency into ever smaller particular elements until the barest material substrate has been reached, and then conceptually to reconstitute that agency again from that substrate without ever needing to invoke any higher or immaterial principles. For all its intrinsic absurdity, eliminativism is the only truly consistent physicalism. Or, rather, precisely *because of* its absurdity.

III

Behaviorism and Epiphenomenalism

Hephaistos: Oh, that I definitely deny. I'm starting from the extreme position, I admit, but only so as to move on to what I hope is a more plausible synthesis. I bring up identity theory and eliminativism—just as I want to bring up behaviorism and epiphenomenalism—not to identify my position with any of them, but only to demonstrate that they explore certain possible perspectives that, adopted in more moderate form and in varying combinations, might produce a perfectly reasonable physicalism. I'm not trying to scale any of the individual theoretical mountains to its isolated peak; the air's always too thin to breathe up there. I'm trying to find the pass that leads through them into a less imposing but perhaps habitable valley. My own view tends to be that mental activity can be reduced to just a functional system; all that's required then is to show how the seemingly anomalous phenomena of mental activity—the things that seem so contrary to mechanism—might be associated with that system without violating physicalism's limits.

Psyche: I wish you well with that, even if I don't see how four errors can combine to produce a truth. But let's linger a little here. I still say that every materialism must become an eliminativism in the end. I recall reading a book not long ago by an American philosopher named Rosenberg that wasn't very good but that was oddly mesmerizing even so, precisely because its author's materialist fanaticism—what he proudly called his "scientism"—was so intense that there was nothing he wasn't willing to argue in its defense. The result was a bizarre combination of absolute irrationality and absolute logical consistency. For instance, he spent several pages arguing that no material system could really produce intentionality as we experience it; and many of the arguments he adduced were the very ones I might make to disprove reductive physicalism. Your brain can't actually think *about* anything at all, he says at one point; it can't even really entertain the proposition "Paris is the capital of France" as a real intentional statement regarding Paris, because your brain consists in neurons and neurons can't really be *about* anything at all; they certainly can't be about Paris in a representational sense, in the way a postcard might be said to be, or in the indirect way in which a stop sign means "stop"; neurons can't even *interpret* something as being *about* something else, since they draw support only from other neurons, and so are no more *about* anything than are the inner workings of a computer, or the configurations of pixels on its screen, which merely process input and output without thinking about them.

Well, to this point, needless to say, I was able to agree with him: neither neurons nor computer functions are themselves *about* anything. To me, though, it seems obvious that the next step in the argument is to affirm that meaning exists at another level of agency, distinct from the merely physical, and is therefore irreducible to a physicalist description. Leibniz's mill again: none of the mere machinery of the cerebrum by itself produces a thought about anything, and so physicalism is false. And yet our author concluded instead that it is intentional thought itself that's intrinsically impossible. How this could be he never makes clear. Instead, he simply heaps one absurd assertion atop another: Just as a computer doesn't think about anything, so neither do you, for your brain's just a computer too, and it's an illusion that thoughts and language are really about things, or that there can be thoughts about the future, like dispositions, plans, or purposes. Like sea-slugs, he says—though why he assumes he knows whether sea-slugs are conscious or not I can't say—we're simply systems of stimulus and response. He even rejects every attempt to frame a naturalist account of intentional states, as he can't grant that such states are real entities to begin with. There simply can't really be a subjective point of view that belongs to a self, he insists, as such a reality would be a fact not fixed in place by physical facts; but this is impossible, because physical facts fix all other facts in place. Thus there can't possibly be such a thing as real subjectivity, or a self, or personhood, or a soul—all of which are simply illusions generated by our fallible powers of introspection. QED.[11] Of course, this would also mean—as there's no intrinsic intentionality—that even the book in which all this gibberish appears is not really *about* any of the things it seems to be addressing, or about anything at all; but our author grasps the nettle all the same and accepts the premise that he's not actually saying what he's saying; and therefore, apparently, what he's saying is true.

It's all easy to mock, of course, and mock it I did; and yet, on reaching the end of the book, at least once my laughter had subsided, I was struck less by its argument's absurdity than by its inevitability. Yes, it was ridiculous; it was even a little appalling. Simply to deny the evidence of one's own experience on purely doctrinaire, abstractly metaphysical principles—well, this is an abdication of reason. But to produce an entirely intentional artifact like a book arguing that intentionality is an illusion isn't merely odd; it's stirringly perverse, almost to the point of a kind of mad heroism. And to venture claims that are so thoroughly contradictory not only of what we all experience to be true, but even of the most basic conditions necessary for those claims to be true is . . . well, tragic, in a grandly irrational way. But, really, how can the physicalist project reach any other terminus?

Hephaistos: Well, I'll try to avoid being *tragic.* Admittedly, I can see a certain analogy—a certain conceptual continuity—between the sea-slugs-and-computers view of the mind and behaviorism. And . . .

Eros: I'm sorry to do this again, but I'm afraid I'll need you to explain. Is this the behaviorist school of psychology we're talking about—B. F. Skinner, *Walden Two*, that sort of thing?

Hephaistos: Not as such, no—though there are resemblances . . . [*Clearing his throat:*] To be precise, in philosophy of mind, behaviorism *was*—and I emphasize the past tense, since it's a largely abandoned theory—the notion that all statements about psychological states or conditions are really only condensed descriptions of behavioral states—physical actions, that is, or the disposition to perform those actions. Thus, to talk about someone's "pain" isn't to refer to some inner feeling or pathos on his or her part, but only to indicate certain behaviors, such as crying out or writhing. To speak of someone's "belief" that it's too cold outside is to refer not to some private psychological state, but rather only to that person's disposition to such behaviors as, say, donning a winter coat and a hat.

EROS: Really? Well . . . well, what about beliefs that are purely cognitive rather than behavioral? I mean, what behavior is indicated by declaring my belief that, in the solar system we used to inhabit, the largest planet was the one called Jupiter?

HEPHAISTOS: That too is the description of a behavioral disposition: say, a disposition to answer the question "What's the largest planet circling Sol?" with the phonemes "It's Jupiter."

EROS: I see. That's, of course, inane. But couldn't such statements be associated with any number of behaviors? I mean, if I say I believe it's very cold when I'm out for a walk, I might be about to wrap my coat more tightly about me, but I might instead be about to take it off and place it around the shoulders of my dear Psyche for fear she'll catch a chill . . .

PSYCHE: He's very old-fashioned sometimes. It's sweet.

EROS: The point is . . .

HEPHAISTOS: The point is that there's no one-to-one correspondence between any given proposition and any behavior. Quite. I understand.

EROS: And how could any of that possibly tell us anything about inner experience?

HEPHAISTOS: It doesn't. For those, and any number of other reasons—as I've said—it's something of a cashiered theory. But, for all its inadequacies, it pointed the way toward functionalism: toward, that is, the idea that mental activity's chiefly a means of processing data, and especially of translating cognitive or sensory input into behavioral output.

HERMES: That odious jargon yet again.

HEPHAISTOS: [*Paying no attention to this:*] *Which* hypothesis, if it can be justified, provides any number of explanatory paradigms. It tells us what thought does, why it's associated with the brain's neurology, why it was selected by evolution, how it became visible to evolutionary selection . . .

EROS: But what about consciousness? And intentionality and all that?

HEPHAISTOS: As I said back when this conversation began, those—or their appearances—may be inevitable concomitants of the system's sheer complexity, or might be functions within the system that we mistake for intrinsic states . . .

HERMES: [*With a note of disgust:*] "User-interfaces."

HEPHAISTOS: Quite so. Or, alternatively, they might be entirely useless in themselves while still being inevitable byproducts of the process—like the sparks thrown off from burning steel under a blacksmith's hammer-blows.

PSYCHE: You're talking about epiphenomenalism.

HEPHAISTOS: I am, yes.

HERMES: Ah. Now I'm the one who might need some clarification. As I understand that term, it would have something to do with the generation of entirely accidental secondary effects by a primary phenomenon.

HEPHAISTOS: Right, but in philosophy of mind it refers to epiphenomena that aren't only accidental, but wholly nugatory—wholly ineffectual. Specifically, it suggests that consciousness may be real enough just as we experience it, as a non-physical phenomenon in addition to the physical processes with which it's associated, but that it arises from those processes even so. Moreover, though consciousness is physically caused, it is itself totally physically impotent; it causes nothing; it's just the phenomenal residue of physical realities it can't reciprocally influence.

HERMES: I see. And the appeal of this bizarre notion is . . . ?

HEPHAISTOS: The same as the appeal of eliminativism, albeit from the opposite vantage. Both claims—either that consciousness can be eliminated in favor of purely physical non-conscious causes or that consciousness can be regarded as a powerless aftereffect of such causes—follow from one and the same commitment to the causal closure of the physical, as well as to the sort of Neo-Darwinian perspective that most physicalists presume. The difference is that eliminativists don't believe in evolutionary spandrels—that is, accidental but pointless byproducts of the evolutionary process—or in any such non-physical entities as consciousness in itself, while epiphenomenalists are willing to entertain the possibility that, though all real physical events belong to a closed causal continuum, some have the curious effect of generating the ghostly aftereffect of personal consciousness, which is real enough in itself but which also—not being material—can't enter back into the causal continuum. It can't even be an object of evolutionary selection, as only what's really efficacious makes a difference from the vantage of phylogenic survivability—which is to say, only the mindless physical processes themselves.

HERMES: I see. So a kind of post-Cartesian dualism, so to speak: one in which the ghost has no control over the machine, or any agency at all. A very ghostly ghost indeed, it seems. And so we're to suppose that somehow this does away with the embarrassment of admitting the undeniable reality of the extra-physical features of mental experience? So long as the physical continuum remains intact, the noetic shadows it casts in our private little experiential worlds don't violate physicalist maxims? There's just some occult extra potency in matter that overlays that continuum with a phenomenal surface?[12]

HEPHAISTOS: If you like.

HERMES: I don't like—not in the least. So, let me be clear: This means that, while I might imagine that my consciousness of a desire for the taste of nectar is what prompts me to fill a goblet and drink, the reality is that all of my actions are the results of mindless neural machinery at work, and my consciousness plays no causal role whatsoever?

HEPHAISTOS: Precisely.

HERMES: And when, say, a human blacksmith, not blessed with your divine invulnerability to material harm, burns his hand and pulls it away from the fire, it's not his consciousness of the pain that induces the action—that's simply epiphenomenal all the way down—but merely a physiological mechanism by which his body preserves itself against damage?

HEPHAISTOS: Two for two.

HERMES: Then what's the point of consciousness at all?

Hephaistos: It has none. It's a surd, so to speak. As I said, a residue.

Hermes: Well, this is a very tenuous physicalism indeed, I must say. [*Knitting his brows quizzically:*] Doesn't that also mean that it's not even a conscious belief that prompts you to say you believe in epiphenomenalism?

Hephaistos: I haven't said I do. But, yes, in fact that is an implication. Consciousness does nothing: it can't make you withdraw your hand from the flame, or raise a goblet of nectar to your mouth, or open your mouth to utter words. Those are all blindly mechanical events, confined to the realm of physical forces and systemic processes.

Eros: Does that mean that when we're talking about epiphenomenalism we're not actually talking about epiphenomenalism? Rather, physical causes, devoid of intentional content, are causing noises to emerge from us that have nothing to do with our conscious perception of a meaning in them?

Hephaistos: One might say that they possess meaning only in the sense that functions might be called meanings; the meanings we're conscious of are something altogether illusory. That too would seem to follow—especially if, as our dear Psyche insists, consciousness and intentionality are inseparable.

Psyche: They clearly are, just as both are inseparable from unity of apprehension, reasoning, and reflective subjectivity. If your consciousness isn't fully invested in your intentional acts, then the meanings of those acts—their semantic and purposive content—aren't there either.

Hephaistos: Not necessarily. Not entirely. The physical system processing data in your neurology might well have a "purposive" structure, so to speak, in the sense that it turns input into output—stimulus into behavior—and maybe it's that structure that's reflected in your epiphenomenal illusion of intrinsic intentionality.

Psyche: Which again means that there's no real intentional content. It's a fetchingly perverse theory. Its chief defect, it seems to me, is that it's self-evidently false. I mean, I see no reason for being coy about this. Beliefs, desires, intentions, and so forth all do affect your behavior at both the mental and the physical levels, and do so precisely because you're conscious of them.

Hephaistos: Ah, well, if you're going to be doctrinaire . . .

Psyche: I'm being logical. I *could* be doctrinaire if I chose. I could argue that you can't reject a self-evident truth of experience without a compelling reason for doing so, and that a dogmatic commitment to a metaphysics of physical causal closure simply doesn't constitute such a reason. But that's not my principal objection. There are simply too many logical flaws in epiphenomenalism for it to be granted any credence. When you say that a blacksmith who's burned his hand pulls it away from the fire not because of his consciousness of pain, but because of some pain-stimulus reaction—or some physiological defense reaction, if you prefer—you're saying something for which there's absolutely no evidence. I mean, there's no evidence that the consciousness isn't what's causal as far as behavior's concerned. I think it was Raymond Ruyer who asked whether it's imaginable that human beings would ever have invented anaesthetics if epiphenomenalism were true.

To me, it's evident that consciousness is an actual efficacious agency simply from the way in which willful intention can determine perception. If consciousness were simply the inert, passive residue of physical processes, then how could I will myself to perceive an optical illusion under one aspect or another, as we've already discussed? My consciousness in such moments—and, really, in all moments that involve active engagement with the world—is modulating itself according to mental intention. Rather than passively receiving the world as an ensemble of physical impulses that it's merely translating into the vacuous spectacle of phenomenal representation, my mind is actively determining what it will impose upon and extract from the world available to the senses, and in so doing actively determines how I—body and mind—will comport myself toward reality. I admit, you could program an automaton devoid of consciousness to "react" to its environment, but only as a simulation of conscious activity, guided by the conscious intentionality of the programmer. And, too, what of delayed awareness . . . delayed reactions?

Hephaistos: What of them?

Psyche: Well, consider. Let's say you're at a large gathering of people, and amid the din of all their voices someone cries out in pain, but you fail to register it at first, and so you don't react. Then your conscious mind informs you, retrospectively, that what you heard a moment ago—maybe several moments ago—wasn't a laugh or a shriek of merriment, but a genuine cry of distress. You then, moved by conscience, stop what you're doing, seek out the person you think may need help, and find that someone on the other side of the room has had a heart-attack. Happily, you're a physician . . .

Hephaistos: Yes, yes, I see: your consciousness in that case, you'd argue, plays a vital role in motivating your actions—in causing them, in fact. I'm sure, though, that one could easily argue in the opposite direction—that your delayed awareness was an aftereffect of the slow adjustment of your neurology to confusing data, or something like that.

Psyche: Ah. All right. But then, even if epiphenomenalism were true, how would it provide us a plausible causal narrative of mental states? As we said yesterday, even the illusion of consciousness or intentionality must possess the features of consciousness or intentionality, and those features remain acutely inconsistent with a physicalist account of reality.

Hephaistos: Well, we'll see about that. As it happens, I'm willing to accept your basic claim, because I agree that the evidence that consciousness has a role in behavior is simply overwhelming. But, you see, that's where I'm heading in the end anyway. As I said, I don't recommend the extreme positions—eliminativism, behaviorism, epiphenomenalism—and I admit that, by themselves, they're fairly absurd . . . eliminativism especially. But my aim is to stake out a plausible middle: to physicalize mental agency in a rational way, without gravitating toward any of those childish extremes. And here you're making my point for me. In that last example of yours, you show how consciousness might be described chiefly as playing a role within a larger functional system; and it's that function that chiefly matters. All else—such as the illusion of a continuous intrinsic subjectivity—is secondary or subordinate to it. And in fact, in certain cases, that quantum of consciousness, whatever it is, turns out to be a negligible one within the system.

Hermes: You're talking nonsense.

HEPHAISTOS: Ah, the true believer speaks. Consider the phenomenon of "blindsight": it's been established, in humans and other primates, that blindness as a result of damage to the visual cortex doesn't necessarily make it impossible to perceive what the color or shape of an object before the eye is. That is, even a person rendered incapable of the qualitative inner experience of vision by a cortical injury or surgery can often still somehow report that something to which his eyes are turned is yellow, or that it's square. Such a person can even sometimes report whether an interlocutor's facial expression is happy or sad, angry or kind.

PSYCHE: What do you imagine that implies?

HEPHAISTOS: That consciousness isn't even a necessary part of cognition; it may merely be one function among others for amplifying or enhancing the essentially unconscious process by which data are translated into behavior. This suggests that our sense of a privileged sphere of mental agency, where reason and consciousness and cognition all exist together, is probably quite illusory. Even if consciousness isn't merely an epiphenomenon, neither is it more than just one operation of a far more complicated organic machinery. I mean, our own introspection tells us that we need qualitative consciousness in order to know that something's yellow, and yet it's wrong . . .

PSYCHE: No, it tells us nothing of the sort. Really, I'm going to become as impatient as Hermes in a moment. There are so many errors in what you just said that one could fill a book with them.

HEPHAISTOS: [*With a shrug:*] Why, then, please rescue me from my waywardness.

PSYCHE: I've encountered this argument before, you know.[13] But it's wrong in principle. Our private introspection most definitely *doesn't* tell us anything about the absolute necessity of qualitative consciousness with regard to what we know about things; it tells us only that, when we're experiencing *qualia* subjectively, that's what we're doing. Therein lies the still insoluble enigma for the physicalist, whether qualitative awareness has any function or not. It doesn't oblige us to claim that other avenues of knowledge about an object's qualities don't exist and can't be used by the mind. Part of the problem here, obviously, is that you're once again taking issue with a Cartesian model of mind, and so you imagine that we're talking about some kind of dualism of substance, according to which the soul alone would be the seat of knowledge and the body just a machine, and the soul could only ever know things in an intuitional way while the body would simply function as its sensory instrumentation. How often do you need to be disabused of that crude and very modern picture of things? That's not what I believe. You're still trying to prove that some faculty of the mind, like qualitative awareness, can be distinguished from all its other faculties, hoping you'll thereby demystify the mind. Even in those terms, it's a silly argument. Blindsight might just as well be taken as evidence that the mind transcends physiology, because it's capable of knowing things that the neurology of the cerebral cortex can't reach through its normal sensory apparatus. But that scarcely matters, because your far more egregious error is that you're confusing consciousness with sensation—that is, you're confusing the subjectivity of the experience of *qualia* with the objects of that experience. In my experience, that's an error one all too often encounters in philosophy of mind.

Hephaistos: That you'll need to explain.

Psyche: Let me ask you: Do you believe a blind man is less conscious than a man with vision?

Hephaistos: [*After a pause:*] Well, I believe he's not conscious of *as much* as a man with vision is.

Psyche: That, dear Phaesty, is a meaningless statement. Consciousness isn't a matter of brute quantity, but of qualitative subjective awareness. Otherwise, consciousness would be nothing but a third-person inventory of impressions, differing in quantity from one sentient being to another. I'm not asking what that blind man's conscious *of*, but only whether he's fully conscious. And, to spare you the task of stating the obvious, the answer is yes, of course he is. This is why one must be careful to distinguish subject from object in phenomenal experience. The yellow that our senses perceive isn't the same thing as our consciousness of yellow. Rather, our *awareness* of that yellow—our self-reflective subjective knowledge of seeing it and of having a sense of what it's like, which rests upon our awareness of being aware—is consciousness. And in that respect we aren't any more conscious when we see yellow than is a blind man who doesn't see it. He's just as aware of his experience of blindness as we are of our experience of vision. By the same token, the man who's aware of an object's yellowness entirely by way of the mechanisms of blindsight is still *conscious:* he's still aware of whatever he does experience, visual or non-visual, including his experience of knowing that object's color even when that knowledge has reached him by some avenue other than that of qualitative sense-impressions. Even if that knowledge is just a "report" that comes to him from some other quarter of his neurology, it's still to *him*—as a conscious subject—that it comes. He may not know how he knows, but of course neither does a person with vision really know how he knows qualitative impressions; the mere mechanics of the eye and brain don't explain the experience of the "what it's like" of yellow. In either case, there's an awareness of the experience—whether we're talking about the experience of yellow or the experience of darkness, or even the experience of knowing something's yellow without any qualitative dimension to that knowledge. It's not sensation, but subjectivity as such, that can't be reduced to physical explanations, whatever its qualitative or cognitive content. Blindsight tells us absolutely nothing about the nature of consciousness or about its centrality in mental agency.

Hephaistos: Many analytic philosophers of mind, you know, object to making any conceptual distinction between sense-perception and the act of consciousness as such.

Psyche: Which is very much to their discredit. They think that way only because they don't want to confront any reality, however self-evident, that can't fit into their physicalist model. The moment one draws the obvious and inevitable distinction between sensations and the conscious faculty—the witness, again—that's aware of those sensations, one's already lost the physicalist thread. Unfortunately for them, intrinsic consciousness—like intentionality and all the rest of mental agency's features—is still there, and they still can't account for it. As I say, I've seen this argument before. I've even recently seen a particularly inept attempt to argue from such phenomena as blindsight to the totally arbitrary conclusion that an obviously extremely intelligent, extremely *intentional* organism like an octopus is totally devoid of consciousness.[14] It's a ridiculous, barbarous, and cruel argument, and one that simply bears no serious scrutiny. Yes, an organism may possess any number of physical means for registering information about its environment; and there are such things as autonomic reactions at the most basic levels of organic activity. But for there to be such a thing as real *behavior*—complex and varying "system-level" responses to the world on the part of a cognitive being—there must be awareness of some kind, and some kind of intentionality allied to that awareness.

Hephaistos: Have you never done something complicated without thinking about it? Walked somewhere, perhaps, in a state of distraction and then found you have no real memory of having done so?

Psyche: No *memory* of having done so—yes, I've certainly done that before. But that doesn't mean the action itself was unconscious. It means other things preoccupied me sufficiently as I was performing it that it left no very strong memory behind, but that doesn't mean my awareness wasn't engaged to some degree in that action at the time.

Hephaistos: [*With a sigh and a wry smile:*] All right. You know, I'm going to grant what you say. I take your point that consciousness shouldn't be reduced to mere sense-impressions, if only because one can be conscious of things other than the sensible. I'll even grant that it seems highly unlikely that the complex behaviors of an octopus—and most especially its remarkable abilities to adjust to new situations and unexpected circumstances, and to relate to other beings—would not involve something like what we call consciousness. I freely acknowledge that organisms at every level of evolution likely possess some degree of conscious awareness. But I also think that that may fortify my position rather than yours. To me, this still seems to suggest that what we think of as intrinsic consciousness may really be only an operation within a physical system of stimulus and response. All I really need to do, as I've said, is to dissociate my position from the untenable extremes and attempt a more moderate and plausible reduction of consciousness to a physical state.

IV

Supervenience

HERMES: And what, for you, would qualify as a more moderate position? What would you find reductionist enough without it turning out to be just eliminativism hiding behind an equivocation?

HEPHAISTOS: Good of you to phrase the matter in terms of such sterling neutrality. What I was thinking of, however, was perhaps something along the lines of a theory of supervenience. I'm not sure that would satisfy me, but as yet I see no insurmountable objection to it. At least, it seems to me plausible to say, on the one hand, that mental agency really exists and really operates through its own inherent properties, and so can't be eliminated in favor of purely physical descriptions of things; but to say also, on the other, that it does so only because mind *supervenes* upon a material and physical basis, which it's never independent of or prior to or separate from.

HERMES: And how exactly does that work? I mean, how is it really mental agency in an intrinsic sense and still wholly dependent on physical processes?

HEPHAISTOS: Well, the constraints in such a view are obvious: there can be no change of state at the level of mind without a corresponding change of state at the physical level. So there's always a strict, simultaneous, necessary concomitance between the mental and the physical, even though there's not an identity between them. But, just as any physical system supervenes on a lower level of physical ingredients, and can cause nothing at its own level without a corresponding causal sequence at the lower level, so mind supervenes on the physical system in such a way that every mental event maps directly onto an appropriate causal relation at the physical level. This means you don't have to presume the sort of crude reduction of systems of top-down causation to more basic bottom-up causes that eliminativism demands; but you needn't forsake the principle of physical causal closure.

Hermes: Well, can mental events cause physical events then?

Hephaistos: Yes, but only by virtue of this necessary concomitance of the physical and the mental. Jaegwon Kim is the philosopher who's probably thought about supervenience with the greatest subtlety; and, as he lays out the theory, any sequence of mental events—say, M^1, M^2, M^3, and so on—must map directly onto some sequence of physical events—Ph^1, Ph^2, Ph^3, and so on—in such a way that any variation at one level must be exactly matched by a corresponding variation at the other level. So, if I should say that a particular mental event causes a particular physical event—say, my desire to be noticed by a passing friend causes me to wave my hand—this is because the mental event is already supervenient on a physical event that has the power to bring the resulting physical event about. That is, it's the physical event upon which the mental state is physically dependent that actually *causes* the next physical event.

Hermes: So . . . so, then, my desire to wave my hand causes my hand to wave, but only because the physical event that underlies that desire causes the physical event of me waving my hand . . . and this somehow preserves both real causal closure *and* real mental causation . . . ?

Hephaistos: Precisely. Moreover, when one mental event causes another mental event, this happens because the physical event on which the first mental event supervenes causes the physical event upon which the second mental event supervenes.[15]

Hermes: And how, precisely, does that affirm the reality of mental causation? I see how it preserves physical causal closure, perhaps, but . . .

Hephaistos: It made perfect sense to you when we were speaking about a wheel: the higher system-level causal stream of the wheel itself is simultaneous with the lower-level causal stream of the elements composing the wheel, and nothing can happen at either level without something correspondingly happening at the other. The wheel turns and, absolutely simultaneously, the molecules in the wheel move collectively in a circular pattern. That's simply a mereological truism. All one need affirm about the relationship is that there must be a covariance between the higher and the lower levels, with a complete dependency of the higher upon the lower but also a non-reducibility of the higher to the lower. And this latter is true because the causal laws of the system are emergent from—structurally emergent from, if you like—the lower. So, for instance, it really is the consciousness of pain that causes that human blacksmith to draw his hand back from the fire; that action is the physical event upon which the mental activity is the supervenient system, just as the collective rotation of the wheel's molecules is the physical event upon which the turning wheel is the supervenient system.

HERMES: I see. And how absolute is the bond between these two levels—I mean, between the mental and the physical? Do the mental properties supervene *necessarily* on the physical? And, if so, what kind of necessity is it? Is it logical? Well, no, don't bother to answer that, since clearly the answer there is no. There's no analytic convertibility between the mental and the physical—no identity. So, is it metaphysical? *Must* our mental event M^1 supervene on the physical event Ph^1 by virtue of their intrinsic natures? Or is it a nomological necessity—I mean, just a necessity as far as the actual laws of physics in this particular cosmos are concerned? Because I'm still struck by the qualitative abyss Psyche has identified between mental and physical phenomena.

HEPHAISTOS: Who knows? Perhaps it's one of those *a posteriori* necessities we've yet to discover. When we've dissolved mentality into a properly mereological hierarchy, we might find we're merely dealing with a structural emergence after all.

PSYCHE: Phaesty, my obdurate friend, that simply doesn't work, for any number of reasons. This is all, just as Hermes said, an equivocation. Unlike the case of a wheel and the material from which it's made, mind and its presumed physical substrate exhibit no necessary link at all—logical, metaphysical, nomological, or what have you. And mental agency isn't a physical structure that can supervene on a physical base;

it's a form of action. And simply saying there may be some *a posteriori* necessity of which we've yet to learn—like, say, the identity of water and H_2O—is to fall prey to a confusion we've already exposed. We've already established the limits of structural emergence. The wheel and its constituents are joined together by a physical continuity and by a shared causal logic. Again, the form of the wheel isn't a novel property bafflingly emerging from the structure of its ingredients' relations; it simply *is* that structure. Thus, as we've seen, there's a clear proportion between its top-down and bottom-up causal dynamisms—a reversibility of description. But, for all the reasons we so fatiguingly discussed yesterday, this simply isn't true of any relation we can coherently posit between the mental and the physical. The intrinsic and structural logic of each differs radically from that of the other; the qualitative abyss separating the physical from the mental is fixed in place. That being so, supervenience is simply an empty concept—unless, of course, you're talking about real formal causality, and you mean to say that the mental is a real form always being imposed upon the substrate of the physical—but then you'll have given up on causal closure of the physical as you understand it.

The possibilities here aren't exactly numerous, after all. If the mental and the physical are related by physical law, then the mental must still be a case of physical emergence, even though it exhibits properties that defy physical reduction. That would be a miracle. If, however, the relation is accidental, then we're talking not about any kind of complementary causality, but only about some mysterious, obscure, but inviolable, parallelism or occasionalism between different levels of reality. That too would be a miracle. Of course, you're assuming the former option, and so it really makes no sense to speak as if you think the different causal laws obtaining at each level equally real. Frankly, you've already conceded as much. According to you—and the causal closure you believe in demands that this be so—one mental event can cause another only if the physical reality underlying the former also causes the physical reality underlying the latter. You don't seem to want to say the reverse, however. Well, then, that would seem to mean that all *real* causality occurs at the level of the physical description, none at the level of the mental. In such a scheme, mental events merely float upon the surface of a stream of physical causality that can't actually be interrupted by any power from above. Such a picture, no matter how subtly conceived, surely succumbs to all the problems we've already discussed. I mean, just consider again the logical syntax and semantics of rational thought: if one mental state is induced by another through a purely logical sequence of thoughts—in the course of a syllogism, for instance—it simply can't be the case, in purely physicalist terms, that this sequence of rational entailments literally *causes* the sequence of physical effects underlying it. And yet the two streams of causality are supposedly exactly correlated. How? If mind is formally causal, certainly: no difficulty there. But that's precisely what you deny.

No, Phaesty, I'm sorry, this is just epiphenomenalism again, masquerading as something else. Even if that weren't the case, supervenience theory would explain nothing. All it really accomplishes is a restatement of the very problem it pretends to address. We already know that there's a correspondence between mental and physical events; what we require is a real causal narrative that can directly relate—not merely align—the two levels of operation.

HEPHAISTOS: As it happens, Kim himself has admitted that his formulations may in the end amount to epiphenomenalism. But, of course, the hope underlying supervenience theory is that the relation of mental to physical events will turn out to be a mereological one—a relation of whole to parts, that is—no less than in the case of the wheel and its constitutive ingredients.

PSYCHE: And, after two and more days of discussing that possibility—or something very like it—it should be obvious by now that that's a vain hope. The "system-level" operations of mind and the lower level of physical events obey two disparate causal logics. There's no reversibility there of the causal description uniting the levels. No equal physical proportion between the top-down and bottom-up . . .

HEPHAISTOS: We needn't rehearse the problems again. You've just stated the case with exemplary clarity. [*Taking a deep breath and thinking to himself for several seconds before speaking:*] You know, I've conceded a good deal to your position along the way . . . not out of any particular desire to be accommodating or out of some misplaced gallantry or *politesse.* I acknowledge the strength of your position. If it weren't so strong, the problem of mind wouldn't have proved so intractable a matter of philosophical debate for so very long. And I, like you, deplore any philosopher who dismisses the problem as somehow an exaggerated concern, because the mystery is quite real and it's no good pretending it's not. That said, I can't simply concede the impossibility of a mereological reduction of mind to lower, physical functions—or, if not reduction, at least *some kind* of causal reversibility between mental and physical functions—because I'm not yet convinced of the impossibility of dissolving the seemingly inseparable phenomena of mental agency into discrete parts. After all, at the system-level of operation in any composite, many faculties may be inseparable from one another. But that doesn't prove that the system itself is anything other than that composite.

Psyche: Again, that's all very true in cases of structural emergence or in cases of formal causality of things like chemistry, which operate only according to physical laws. But, for the thousandth time or so, mind doesn't exhibit a physical—that is, physical in mechanistic terms—logic.

Hephaistos: Well, let's make sure of that, shall we? Just one last time? For certainty's sake?

V

Psychological Plurality and Mental Unity

HEPHAISTOS: At the risk of falling afoul of your catalogue of fallacies, I'd like to undertake a slightly more deliberate consideration of the implications of cognitive plurality. I know you'll accuse me of psychologistic confusions, but is it really so clear that the mind possesses quite the indissoluble unity you claim? There was a time in the history of human medicine, as you know, when especially severe cases of epilepsy were treated by a commissurotomy—the surgical separation of the *corpus callosum* connecting the brain's two hemispheres. The procedure didn't induce any immediately evident signs of mental disintegration; but in time it emerged that, under certain strictly controlled conditions, each hemisphere could be "addressed" separately, and in those cases one side of the brain could recognize and respond to stimuli without the other side's "knowledge," to the point that it seems clear that there were two different centers of consciousness at work. At least, it seems clear that the left hemisphere, the principal seat of many linguistic and analytic skills, and the more comprehensively perceptive but also more inexpressive right hemisphere can each accomplish certain specific cognitive tasks without there being any conscious communication between them. Why, really, shouldn't we think of this as two distinct "minds" at work? And, if one mind can be separated into two, is it really then so preposterous to think of consciousness as somehow dissoluble into parts? And would it then seem quite so absurd to conclude that the source of conscious experience lies in the brain and nervous system? Surely, too, if we consider this alongside clinical studies of localized brain functions, and of how different parts of the brain deal with different aspects of the processing of information, we have some warrant for seeing this unity of consciousness of which you speak as in fact a kind of consortium of faculties and functions, distributed through the architecture of the cerebral cortex. Perhaps that unity is itself merely part of the phenomenal impression created by these functions in their coordination with one another.

Or consider an even rarer phenomenon, but one that's perhaps even more revealing: merged minds. Occasionally, craniopagus twins are born—that is, cerebrally conjoined twins. And among these there are a few cases where the connective tissues are located in the thalamus of the forebrain, which among other things processes sensory signals. In one case in particular, it's been well documented that two girls conjoined in that way share sensory information: that one is often aware of the other's pains or pleasures; that each can describe certain visual features of an object held up before only the other's eyes; and so forth. Well, clearly you have there a case of distributed consciousness that nonetheless, from either girl's perspective, might easily be mistaken as the unique property of an isolated subjectivity.[16]

Or what of dissociative identity disorder—"multiple personality disorder," as it used to be called? We've more or less ascertained that such conditions are genuine. At least, there are cases of persons with fully functioning eyesight with personalities that are supposedly blind; and, when those personalities become dominant, the neural circuitry of sight in the brain fails to fire. This has been established more than once in laboratory conditions. And quite often the diverse personalities of such a person are conscious of one another, in a kind of inner community of selves, even though only one expresses itself at any given time. Everywhere we look at the actual experience of consciousness, we encounter plurality—in fact, plural faculties. Is that really so irrelevant to the question of the unity of consciousness as you suggest?

Psyche: Yes, it really is.

Hephaistos: Oh, come now. How absolute a distinction are you really willing to draw between psychology and mentality?

PSYCHE: Fairly absolute, to be honest, and you should as well. For one thing, the simple fact of a plurality of brain functions could just as well be taken as evidence of a real difference between mind and brain, since—once again—the unity of the mind's experience and agency is utterly unlike that plurality.

HEPHAISTOS: You're begging the question.

PSYCHE: For another thing—though, really, this isn't very important either—many of the claims made regarding commissurotomy patients are often exaggerated. I'm familiar with the case studies, and a good deal of the time the supposedly clear clinical evidence is really just an interpretation of ambiguous data. There's no real evidence, for instance, that the procedure literally produces two wholly distinct psychological subjects, each with its own separate self-consciousness, or that there's really—as is often claimed—a kind of internecine conflict between the separated hemispheres, with the sober intentions of the left hemisphere being thwarted by the perverse and mercurial antics of the right. Quite often, the behavior that's been observed and recorded could be read simply as evidence of a single subject attempting a single task, but without the ability to coordinate his or her actions, on account of a derangement of his or her neural equipment—rather like trying to read a poem through a prism. It could all be taken as a single psychology trying and failing to integrate the experiences and behaviors or streams of information that each hemisphere makes possible.

Rather than two subjectivities, it seems better to speak of a single subjectivity forced to assume the modes of the brain's two hemispheres in a fragmented way. The flow and integration of information has been interrupted, but there's no evidence that the experience of that confusion is literally plural. If it were, it would be like the experiences of two separate persons with two different bodies, utterly unavailable to one another. Yet, as you've noted, for the most part these disruptions of the brain's functioning integrity occur only within very constrained conditions; and in those circumstances perhaps the mind is forced to divide or stagger its attention between the two hemispheres' capacities, creating a kind of parallel amnesia in which the mind can't bring about a properly continuous experience. But is that really very different from other kinds of cognitive disjunction, caused by physiological or psychological conditions? A severe blow to the skull, for that matter? Or perhaps conscious and subconscious states in a person with an intact cerebrum? Haven't we already granted that intentionality and consciousness exist in proportion to one another? That one can walk somewhere, in a preoccupied state of mind, only to arrive at one's destination without any memory of the walk itself? That when a pianist plays a piece of music, he or she isn't consciously directing his or her hands in an immediate way? If the mind must attend irregularly to abnormally separated functions, as in the case of the commissurotomy patient, how does that tell us anything about the unity or plurality of consciousness? Frankly, we already know that our mind's agency has many levels, only some of which can be the object of direct consciousness at any moment; the others fall beneath—or perhaps rise above—ordinary awareness.

And something analogous might be said with regard to what you call "merged minds"—which, as far as I can tell, are nothing of the sort. I mean, yes, it's quite clear that the two girls you mention share sensory information; but, oddly, it's no less clear that they don't share the introspective *awareness* of that information. Certain neural avenues of information have been merged in the brain, granted, but the witness in each mind that perceives and attests to that information remains distinct; neither shares the other's self-reflective consciousness. What I find most remarkable about your account, that is, isn't that two minds can be aware of the same physical stimuli—I've already insisted, remember, that one must distinguish between sense data and the subjective consciousness of those data in the form of *qualia*—but rather that each mind persists as a distinct subjective unity even when so much of the putative physical foundations of that unity has been radically compromised or disrupted. The sense data belong to a shared field of knowledge; but the consciousness of that field is the property of two different minds. How very strange this is when considered from the reductionist vantage. How is it that there remain these two distinct minds, each of whom can identify much of what the other is experiencing while still never knowing how the other experiences it "for me," as it were? The same brain-states—the same sensory stimulations that give rise to *qualia*—belong differently to two selves. But why? Why, at the points of convergence, doesn't the sense of discrete subjectivity dissolve or become a hazy superimposition of conscious selves? It seems to me that we see here something of the real distinction between mere neural patiency or receptivity and genuine subjectivity.

HEPHAISTOS: And what would you say of cases of dissociative identity disorder, then?

PSYCHE: I would say much the same thing as I did with regard to commissurotomy patients. And I would add that, as far as the clinical evidence goes, such cases demonstrate the distinction I've been anxious to make all along between the *pure* subjectivity of the inner witness, with all its imperturbable oneness, and the always fluid, finite, changing reality of personal psychology. The latter is dependent upon the former, not the reverse. Hence, you see, all of this is quite irrelevant. That's the larger point I want to make. None of it touches upon those aspects of mind that defy materialist reduction. Yes, psychology is a plural phenomenon, as is cognition; but the subjectivity, unity of apprehension, intentionality, and consciousness underlying them are still, as ever, irreconcilable with a mechanistic physicalism. So what if that subjective depth within us can disport itself in a variety of psychological masks? We already know that, at the level of finite individuality, we all contain multitudes. The problems you raise here would be quite insurmountable, I suppose, if I were trying to defend a Cartesian picture of reality, in which the mind is intrinsically a simple, disembodied "thinking thing," at once cognitive and psychological and affective, and the body intrinsically a compound, mindless machine, and in which also these supposedly radically different substances function in tandem. But functioning in tandem is not the same thing as a real unity. Stop imposing that arid metaphysical paradigm on this discussion, *je t'en prie.* The psychological self is something that occurs *within* the consciousness in each of us; but it's not consciousness as such; it's only a contracted expression of some far deeper source. The debate between Cartesian substance-dualism and mechanistic materialist monism is a relic of crude early modern reductionisms. My understanding of the soul comes from a far older and far richer philosophical grammar.

Hephaistos: Then at least locate the unity you insist on somewhere within the agency of mind, so that I can clearly see where it is.

Psyche: It's everywhere. It's not a faculty among faculties; it's more fundamental than any discrete aptitude. Consciousness isn't psychological personality; it's private, but it isn't proprietary. It's much the same—in fact, it's identical—in each of us, because it's a unity prior to any differentiation, capable of integrating diversity in its simplicity. It's something in which our individual minds participate, not a property residing in the substance of some ghost inhabiting the machine of the body. But, that said, the plural aspects of individual psychology and cognition—the functions of what we can call the empirical ego—all still depend upon it: upon that higher, more anonymous transcendental unity of consciousness, with all its irreducible, inescapable subjectivity of perspective. Even the disjoined experiences of commissurotomy patients, to the degree that they're available to consciousness, are possible by virtue of that "vanishing point" of subjective perspective; only *that* allows the diversity of reality to appear to the mind as a unified phenomenon, to which consciousness can attend. So it doesn't matter that surgery or psychosis can introduce divisions and contradictions into our psychological constitutions. Even if such interventions resulted in truly distinct conscious personalities, it wouldn't matter. The disorder of the empirical ego doesn't detract from the unity of the subjective perspective that's expressed in each "identity" to the degree that there's true consciousness present. It's that unity in itself that defies mechanistic reduction.

Hephaistos: You truly are a Neoplatonist, it seems. You really do believe that every soul or mind participates in a more original shared . . . well, soul, *psychē*, whatever . . . and that this soul is sustained by a still higher . . . what? *Nous?* Pure mind, pure intellect, pure knowing, prior to its individuation in all separate minds . . . ? And that *nous* participates in the absolute One that unifies all things as what they are?

Psyche: That's one way of thinking of it, yes. A hierarchy of relations in the mind, from the individual self to a universal source, with the unity of the latter shedding its light on every level below itself. Forgive the spatial metaphors, though. I mean, one could just as well depict it as a matter not of height but of depth—an ever more inward reality, reaching all the way down to that simple, pure, pre-psychological wellspring of consciousness where there exists no discernible difference between me and you, or between either of us and the transcendent principle in which we share. Much the same picture is offered by various schools of Indian metaphysics too, if you recall our earlier remarks on the matter. Remember? The silent "witness," the *sākṣi*, within us, resting on no ground but its own pure first-person awareness? Or our capacity for *vimarśa*, "detached reflection," or that active intentionality within consciousness, that *prakāśa* or "shining forth" that illuminates the mind to itself while never becoming an object to itself?

HEPHAISTOS: I recall, yes—though with a twinge of impatience.

PSYCHE: Isn't it instructive, though, that we—even we gods, who should know better—habitually revert to the early modern picture? That's why so much philosophy of mind has become a pitched battle between equally absurd options. Really, to ask whether it's the ghost or the machine that does the thinking—well, neither choice makes sense. It's the person who thinks, the one organism in its entirety, spiritual and material. I deny physical reductionism, but I don't doubt that the body—the whole brain and nervous system—*thinks:* not as a mechanism impersonally processing functions, but precisely as a living reality participating in that one organism, that one personhood, that one soul—that unity at once physical and mental. The body is simply the concrete manifestation of the soul, which is the forming and quickening power and rational order that becomes concrete in its living structure: not a machine, but rather spirit in its visible, tangible manifestation. And the soul, as a thinking reality, isn't a Cartesian bodiless substance, a disembodied ghost, but is rather life and mind, expressing itself and acting within the physical world as a living organism, with a living body. That's why, if you'll cast your divine mind back only half a millennium or so, you'll remember that *psychē* was at one time understood as at once the vital entelechy—the rational, mindlike structure of any living thing, the intrinsic formal cause of the body and the self—and also the principle of thought, sensation, intention, will, and consciousness within. For the last time, O irksome god of fire and iron, in us and in our mortal kith the "soul" is the formal principle—the form—of mind, life, and language at once, all of which are aspects of one irreducible reality.

HEPHAISTOS: Yes, I know, I know. I understand. All right, then, I too say let's exorcise that Cartesian ghost once and for all from our reflections. I'm not yet, however, prepared to dispense with the machine. It really is, after all, quite an impressively plural picture of cognitive functions we're discussing here, isn't it? I grant that you lot aren't claiming that the soul or the mind is some kind of bodiless sprite that, in pure abstraction from the flesh, combines in itself psychology, sense-perception, consciousness, cognition, and all the rest of the mental world. Nevertheless it remains the case that you think there's some deeper or higher unity that holds together all the strata of living mental agency, spiritual or corporeal or what have you. Perhaps you're right. But is it self-evidently the case? Daniel Dennett, for instance, proposes we undertake a "homuncular decomposition" of our customary picture of unified intentional consciousness into the disparate sensory, neurological, and discriminatory systems underlying it. He too rejects the notion of a single brilliant and omnicompetent Cartesian homunculus installed at the center of the self, but he doesn't feel, as you do, that this leads to some more mysterious, transcendental unity and subjectivity pervading and shaping both mental agency and the body's functions. Rather, he thinks of those functions themselves as a legion of rather stupid, minimally competent homunculi whom evolution has forged into a complex confederation of distinct but related competencies that, in their totality, add up to quite a competent system of behaviors.

PSYCHE: Yes, I know: the "Multiple Drafts Model" of mind.

HEPHAISTOS: Just so. That's part of the picture, at least. Rather than a unified intentional feat, one's knowledge of the world consists in a great number of information states that are never resolved into a single presentation or located in any single place in the brain; instead they spill over and modify one another continually. Not only is there no unique and indivisible spiritual subject within—no soul—neither is there some cerebral control room, some "Cartesian theatre" at the center of the brain's labyrinth, where the mind enjoys the fully composed spectacle of the represented world. Data enter the brain in many ways, in a ceaseless flow of shifting and somewhat incongruous "drafts" of reality that aren't absolutely coordinated or synchronous with one another. From this Dennett concludes that there's no single locus of consciousness, and so no such thing as subjective consciousness at all as we normally conceive it, or any real intentionality; there's only the illusion of such consciousness produced by the variegated physical and functional machinery of the body and brain. Steven Pinker says the same thing: that not only is there no ghost within the body; there's no part of the brain that plays the ghost's role. Our sense that each of us is an "I" who controls the mind is an illusion the brain works hard to produce.[17]

Eros: Why?

Hephaistos: Why what?

Eros: Why does the brain work so hard to produce that illusion? What's the need? And how does it do so, if it isn't an intentional agent? And whom is it trying to deceive exactly, and to what end? And who suffers from that delusion?

Hephaistos: Again, it's for the sake of functional efficiency. The concept of a unified conscious self is a . . .

Hermes: A "user-interface." That grotesque jargon again. Of course.

Hephaistos: As disarmed as I am by your invincible snideness, I'm going to insist we pause here and think about our assumptions. Why not take Dennett's position seriously? The brain contains a huge multiplicity of parallel processes of interpretation—a plural, fragmentary, irregularly syncopated succession and ensemble of diverse neurological stimuli—all of them in a constant state of redaction, by themselves and by one another, and there's no central panoptic faculty where they're resolved into a single lucid representation of reality or a unified field of intuition . . . no governing subjectivity judging the data of experience and arranging them into a representation of the world. There are merely countless tiny unconscious judgments being made by the neurology of the body at every moment. No inner self observes the world; that's a narrative, a fiction we construct over time, mostly based on a kind of "fame" or "celebrity" among the brain's various information states in the cerebral cortex. Various data-processes assume temporarily dominant positions in our cognitive apparatus at various instants, briefly monopolizing cognitive resources long enough to have functional effects, because they've managed to capture our attention most forcibly; only afterward do we weave this stream of functions together narratively into what seems like a singular unified perspective, for simplicity's sake. In reality, there's only the ceaseless ebb and flow of diverse information functions and discriminations.[18]

Or think of Bernard Baars's "Global Workspace Theory" of the brain, which says much the same thing: that cognition is constructed from a kind of diffuse architecture of information-gathering, all vying for attention and for the privilege of being "broadcast" throughout the whole system. This, perhaps, is all that consciousness is: these global alerts, as it were, these instances of one or another fragment of information-processing becoming known throughout the whole brain.[19]

Psyche: But surely you see how badly such a picture subverts itself. Fame? Celebrity? Broadcast? Don't you see how those very notions still rely on the same subjective, simple, single vantage they're meant to banish? All right, there are thousands of discrete processes going on in our neurology that you'd like to characterize as small, local, minimal unconscious "judgments." But there are no such things as unconscious judgments. That's all empty metaphor until those little events of physiological discrimination are genuinely rendered *as* judgments by a comprehensive and unified subject who truly does pass a verdict upon them as a whole, by extracting a unified apprehension from them. Real judgment always involves a faculty that already, as it were, "knows" what it's translating from neural data into intentional impressions; and that's something that occurs only through a faculty capable of imposing a total synthesis on all the little processes contributing to perception. Your neurological equipment may register a stimulus of some kind in isolation; but it becomes a conscious experience and a conscious judgment only because there's a person to whom the local and particular appears within a stream of continuous and indissolubly single awareness. Who cares how many discrete "homunculi" are working away at their individual tasks? They're only potential sources of awareness until they're really admitted into the unity of the one true consciousness they serve. The mystery to be solved remains how all those deliverances appear to a conscious mind as a fully unified object of awareness and comprehension; and the only solution to that mystery is the recognition that there really is an indissolubly single subject to whom they appear.

And, for goodness' sake, how can any particular function become a dominant object of attention—a temporary cerebral "celebrity," enjoying its brief fifteen minutes of "fame"—except by way of the "witness" who's doing the attending? How can the brain's workspace be "broadcast" at all except as information grasped in its global totality by a unified subject? And it's no good saying that the sense of unified subjectivity is only an emergent posterior narrative fiction, since the fiction would then have to be its own premise: there must be a continuous subjectivity to whom the narrative of continuous subjectivity appears, as well as a continuous subjectivity capable of constructing a unified narrative; there must be a subjectivity to whom the plurality of experience is referred in order for there to be anyone to tell or to hear the tale—anyone to organize all that diversity into continuity. Unity is known only to unity, and produced only by unity. As ever, the claim that some feature of mental agency is illusory invariably presumes the very faculty it's meant to disprove. The illusion of unity of mind is possible only through mind's unifying power to create an illusion. Nothing—*absolutely nothing*—you've said calls that unity into question, or suggests a plausible alternative to it. In fact, nothing you've said addresses the phenomenon of *consciousness* at all.

Honestly, I can't for the life of me understand how theorists like Dennett can imagine that arguments of that sort dispose of the role of a privileged mental subject. If anything, they strengthen the case for believing in a conscious mind, truly distinct from the physical apparatus of the brain. The notion that this concept of "multiple drafts" constitutes some sort of demystification or solvent of subjective consciousness is absurd. *Of course* brain processes are multiple and diffusely distributed throughout the body's neural architecture, and *naturally* they're not perfectly synchronized or harmonized in operation, and *of course* our modes of knowledge and discrimination are sometimes confusing and confused, and *obviously* our sensory and cognitive apparatus consist in countless faculties and functions. That's the very problem at issue. For example, different parts of the eye and optical equipment perceive hues, intensities, lateral configurations, contrasts, and so forth. Moreover, the mind often has to correct initial failures of perception based on that multiplicity of information states—when, say, you momentarily mistake a length of rope in your path at twilight for a coiled venomous snake, or a goblet of goat's milk for a goblet of nectar, and your intentionality must retreat from its initial impression and then recompose what the mind receives from the world out there. But all of that simply makes it that much more astonishing that perceptions and sensations—despite all the physical conjunctions and disjunctions they comprise—are experienced from a unified perspective, a unified subjectivity in which both the continuities and discontinuities are integrated in a single act of awareness. Your ocular apparatus may receive impressions of the world as a flood of disjoined fragments of information, but what you see with the eye is located not in the eye, but in the witnessing mind within you. As an old Indian maxim says, it isn't the eye that sees or the ear that hears, but the soul to which both belong, and which enlightens both from within. It's the soul also that makes the very different realities of the seen and the heard belong to one act of attention and awareness. It's the subject who selects among the competing "drafts," if you will. We've said this already: the eye may see something at a great distance well before the ear hears it, but the "I" in whom the two perceptions are joined in a continuous experience—even when it's a continuous experience of seemingly discontinuous data—simply abides, undivided. The unity of intentional subjectivity doesn't depend on the perfect synchrony of the senses; and yet the recognition of their asynchrony most definitely depends upon the unity of intentional subjectivity and its ability to interpret and synthesize the stimuli received by the brain.

So yes, by all means, undertake a homuncular decomposition of mental agency. Break down intentionality and consciousness and all the rest of it as best you can contrive to do into hierarchical arrangements of ever more local, subordinate, and diminishingly capable faculties; try to descend into the deepest strata of the brain's systems and subsystems, seeking out ever more basic, more limited aptitudes, ever more minimal sensory powers, ever stupider homunculi, until representation and intention both dissolve into mere physiological responses to stimulation. You'll never reach the bottom. At least, you'll never discover some mysterious threshold or mystic boundary where, if you reverse the process, the physiological mechanisms magically *become* consciousness, intentionality, unity, subjectivity. No physical stimulus amounts to a perception of anything unless there's already consciousness there to shape and interpret its disclosures intentionally. No mere sensory aptitude is a conscious intention, and no conscious intention can be reduced to a sensory aptitude. And so, if subjective consciousness makes its first appearance anywhere within the continuum of our physiological systems, it must do so all at once, without physical premise, as a transition that constitutes nothing less than a miraculous reversal of physical logic. Again, go ahead, descend as far as you like into the tangles of neurology. You'll never find a purely physiological base from which you can naturally reconstruct the totality you've disassembled. All those aptitudes and functions taken together will never add up to anything even remotely like mental experience.

For the last time, I implore you to consider the nature of the unity of mental apprehension that scrupulous introspection discloses. Consider in particular the absence of any quantitative properties in that unity. I'm not talking about a mere faculty for coordinating distinct processes in an orderly form. I'm talking about an intrinsically indeterminate capacity that gathers a limitless field of diverse impressions and thoughts and velleities into a genuine oneness. I'm talking about the mind's power, unlike any other power in nature, to confer unity on anything and everything altogether—sensations, cognitions, thoughts, intuitions, memories, and so on in a dynamically flowing present—by referring it all to the "me" within each of us, without limit and without change, no matter how much is added to or subtracted from the experience it makes possible. To talk of a methodological, "homuncular" decomposition of this profound—this *unique*—oneness is meaningless. It isn't just some mental function among others; it's not even the Cartesian subject; it's the very actuality of unity as such, prior to any possible function or self, so much the essence of mental agency that it must be present in its totality before any thought or perception can become possible.

VI

Function and Knowledge

Hephaistos: You know, it's all too easy to allow oneself to be carried away by one's own rhetoric.

Psyche: Is that what I've done?

Hephaistos: It may well be what you're in danger of doing. If nothing else, you may be listening too credulously to what you tell yourself—or, rather, what your brain tells you. Your assumption is that you have direct introspective access to your own mental agency *in itself*, but presumably that impression—which you take to be self-evident—is modulated through your brain; and that consideration should give you pause, and should prompt you to consider whether that introspective phenomenology, for all its apparent lucidity and serene luminosity, isn't just a kind of algorithmic contraction to . . . well, to that user-interface of which we keep speaking: a kind of computer icon on the screen of your brain. I mean, surely you'd acknowledge that conscious agency is full of unconscious competences.

Psyche: I'd prefer to say competences that are unconscious in their separateness, which become conscious—or become *consciousness*—when gathered into a totality by the unified intentionality of the mind.

Hephaistos: That's a subtle and a clever distinction, but also an evasion. You know what I mean: there are within your body and brain discrete physiological and neurological functions that occur below the threshold of consciousness, which are too numerous and complex for you to understand and operate directly, and so there has to be some medium—some interface—that allows you to act at the level of competence where you *can* operate, without needing to master all the intricate details of its routines and subroutines. As Daniel Dennett likes to point out, we've really no better access to our thinking than we have to our digestive processes.[20]

PSYCHE: That's clearly false, and it's a specious comparison. True, we don't have an immediate awareness of the various levels of physiological process present in either digestion or in cognition, but we do most definitely have immediate access to our thinking. Indeed, thinking is nothing but immediate inner access.

HEPHAISTOS: So you tell yourself.

HERMES: So direct and undeniable experience tells us.

HEPHAISTOS: [*Arching a single, skeptical eyebrow:*] Does it now? Let me stay with Dennett's arguments for a while. After all, he's the philosopher who's consistently made the most adventurous assaults on these citadels of subjective certitude.

HERMES: "Adventurous" might be *one* way of describing it.

HEPHAISTOS: [*Clearly suppressing a sharp retort, then smiling wryly:*] Vex me not, O god as swift as thought. Try, if only for a moment, to take an imaginative step back from your experience and view it from the outside. Then ask yourself whether your certainty of its irreducibly, intrinsically first-person character isn't the result of your prior adherence to a first-person account of mind. You'd grant, after all, that there are also a great many aspects of what your mind does that you *don't* experience, and I don't see it as absurd to wonder then whether what you do experience is far less than you imagine. I mean, Dennett would tell you that he's not denying the reality of all conscious states; but he is denying the existence of what he calls the "Cartesian Theatre" within each of us.

HERMES: Haven't we already dismissed the Cartesian self?

HEPHAISTOS: Yes, but sometimes a felt absence makes us imagine that the only thing that can fill the place it's evacuated is something with the same shape as the cavity left behind. What Dennett's complaining about, as I've said, is the tendency of even materialist philosophers still to think in terms of some little composed spectator within us, before whom the equally composed spectacle of the represented world appears in its entirety: a physiological ghost, as it were; a phantom constituted of neurons rather than ectoplasm. But, says Dennett, there aren't really any internal representations separate from all those many information states and discriminations that flow through our neural streambeds, spilling over one another, as it were, generating the illusion of a singular point of view in the brain. It's the global system of functions that "perceives" the world, and not the user-interface that redoubles this activity under the fiction of a perceiving subject. The latter is a posterior superimposition.

HERMES: This is preposterous. We've already covered this matter, several times, including just a few moments ago. Psyche has already answered this issue with devastating exactitude: the "illusion" of unified apprehension is possible only for a truly unified apprehension. The illusion of consciousness or intentionality is possible only through the reality of consciousness and intentionality. And so on.

HEPHAISTOS: Maybe you're making the same error as the materialist philosopher who thinks in terms of an inner homunculus watching the exterior world depicted for him on an interior screen; you're just making it from the other side—the side of pre-modern metaphysics, I mean—by insisting that the phenomenon of experience is anything more than one small part of the larger set of systems, which we *use* in a way that necessarily induces the appearance of a continuous, intrinsic subjectivity.

HERMES: We're going to keep circling back, aren't we? This second-order Cartesianism is a distraction from the actual issue. As Thomas Nagel noted some time ago, it makes no sense to ask what our experiences are *really* like as opposed to how they seem to us, since the seeming is itself that irreducible fact that physicalism can neither assimilate nor conjure away.

HEPHAISTOS: Yes, we've established that that's your position. Maybe you're right. But let's reach the end of this trail before we decide we absolutely have to double back; it may yet get us through the woods. Obviously, we're talking about—and I know we keep making partial approaches to the topic—a version of functionalism: that is, the view that whatever mental states may exist need not be analyzed in the merely physicalist terms of the absolute eliminativists, but may nevertheless be regarded as functions in a larger system for translating stimulus into response. As such, *how* they appear to us may very well be part of their function rather than a direct intuition of their true nature. Even what we take to be our reasoning is really just the "manifest image," slightly to misuse Wilfrid Sellars's term, but it's anything but the whole story.

HERMES: Then what's your *reason* for *believing* in functionalism?

HEPHAISTOS: Again, I haven't said that I do. But, in fact, to say something is the "manifest image" is not to say it's false; it's simply to say that it's an image suited to a particular . . . well, *function*. That's the whole point. I'm not denying reason, or beliefs, or what we think of as intention and consciousness; I'm saying that what they appear to be isn't actually intrinsically what they *do*. Function, of course, is dictated by context, as Dennett likes to insist. Much of what we take to be *qualia* are in fact . . .

HERMES: *Take* to be *qualia?*

HEPHAISTOS: Yes, much of what we *take* to be *qualia* are actually just dispositions to behave in certain ways—here's the aspect of behaviorism that's true—and what makes them "conscious" is simply the set of dispositions to which they're linked. Hence, they have no intrinsic content at all. Consider pain, for instance—or, rather, the stimulus that we generally interpret as pain. Well, its function varies, enabling different dispositional states within different contexts of action. For example, according to the specific functional process in which it's playing a role, it can become "conscious" as a disposition to either aversion or pleasure. The exact same sensory stimulation can figure in a punitive behavioral context as a very disagreeable ordeal but in an erotic behavioral context as an altogether delicious rapture. So does it make sense to speak then of the "pain" *quale* as having an intrinsic content or meaning? Or as being an intrinsic kind of conscious experience? Dennett's right to complain of those who speak as if "pain" still has the intrinsic quality of *pain* whether it's recognized by one's psychology or not, as though it were a fixed reality projected on the screen of our Cartesian theatre. In fact, once the functional relations are subtracted from our understanding of *qualia*, nothing remains. When you look at a tomato, for instance, there's no distinctive red *quale* in your mind, displayed before the curious eyes of the Cartesian soul; your brain already possesses that information as part of the global system of perception. For Dennett, there's simply no such phenomenon as the real *seeming* of things, over and above the judgments we reach that certain things are or are not the case, and our neurological reports to ourselves of those judgments.[21]

Hermes: Of course there's something more. There's the actual experience itself, right there, immediate and intrinsic and in every sense indubitable.

Hephaistos: Dennett would deny that. What does such an idea add to the whole complex of behavioral processes that perception serves, after all? Say someone down there in the terrestrial realm is driving a car and, on seeing the red of a stop sign, presses the brakes. Well, the process explains itself entirely in terms of the discriminative states that bring about the functional translation of stimuli into behaviors. There are no intrinsic properties attached to those discriminative states—no subjective, private, ineffable aspects that constitute *how* the redness of the sign appears to some subjectivity within that driver. As far as those states are concerned, their dispositional properties suffice to explain their effects exhaustively, leaving not a rack behind: they explain both peripheral behaviors, such as stepping on the brakes-pedal, and "internal" behavior, such as the brain's report that it has judged a certain object to be red.[22]

Hermes: Explaining their effects isn't the same as explaining *them.* This is absolutely absurd. This is just behaviorism again, which is nothing but an evasion of the issue. What's the point of making assertions so patently false?

Hephaistos: Even if their effects exhaust their contents? Look here, one of Dennett's more famous thought-experiments with regard to *qualia* is his little parable about two coffee-tasters whom he names Chase and Sanborn—quality-control experts, let's say, who work for a company that roasts and sells coffee—each of whom has recently discovered that over the years his attitude toward their employer's product has changed markedly, and he no longer likes its flavor. But, though both have reached the same state of dissatisfaction, they've reached entirely opposed conclusions regarding its cause. One believes that some change has occurred in the flavor of the coffee itself or in his physiological sense of taste while his personal preferences have remained constant, but the other believes the coffee and his senses are the same as they have ever been while something has altered in his gustatory sensibilities that has robbed him of his enjoyment of the coffee. How can we determine which of them is right? There's nothing in the nature of the *quale* itself that makes it possible to distinguish between an objective and a subjective alteration, or between a physiological or an aesthetic change. Introspection proves useless here. Instead, what's required is some sort of third-person investigation—a chemical analysis of the coffee, perhaps, or a neurological or psychological examination of Chase and Sanborn—to clarify what's happened. In Dennett's jargon, we need to abandon the "autophenomenological" perspective altogether and adopt in its place a "heterophenomenology," produced by a plurality of third-person reports in coordination with the supposedly first-person reports our brains issue to themselves, all measured against one another. Indeed, we should approach even our own mental operations heterophenomenologically before making any judgment regarding what seems to be the case. It turns out, we find, that we don't even have any infallibly direct access to our private sensory intuitions. So what's "intrinsic" to them other than their behavioral results? As far as Dennett is concerned, since *qualia* don't do any work in explaining behavior, we should simply dispense with the concept altogether. They're a fantasy.[23]

And he's no less deflationary in his treatment of intentionality. That too he denies is an intrinsic property of conscious organisms. Rather, it's something we attribute to others *and to ourselves* as a kind of algorithm or interface, when it's useful to do so—when, that is, it aids us in predicting behaviors. It's the comportment we take toward reality when we assume an "intentional stance" and interpret action in those terms alone. Under other circumstances, though, we can just as legitimately interpret those same activities without reference to intention at all: what we might call a "belief" or a "thought" or "desire" when judged in intentional terms we would identify from a "physical stance" as an electrochemical "brain event," or from a "design stance" as part of a system for processing stimuli. . . .

Eros: I'm sorry: did you say we merely *attribute* intentionality—attribute thoughts and beliefs and desires and so forth—not only to others but even to ourselves?

Hephaistos: Indeed. And one can see how useful it is to do so. We can't really undertake a survey of all the physiological processes determining what appear to be our intrinsically semantic behaviors, but by adopting intentional designations as a kind of *façon de parler* we create an instrument for ourselves that, thanks to epochs of evolutionary refinement, grants us a very good approximation of a predictive grammar by which to anticipate what organisms will do, and how we might react to them. And yes, that includes us: as I said earlier, we aren't aware of all those physiological systems and subsystems that produce our behaviors, so we tell ourselves that we are actually thinking, feeling, believing, desiring subjects. The notion that we're conscious creatures possessed of subjective inner worlds that can't be reduced to unconscious physical processes is an illusion, a purely practical faculty that evolved so that we can make use of it when we need to communicate our dispositions and competences—to others and to ourselves.[24]

Eros: Father Zeus preserve us!

Hermes: Again, what's the use of saying something so self-evidently false? I see now the point Psyche was making when she noted that the physicalist reductionist refuses to make any distinction between sense perception and the subjective consciousness *of* that perception. Private experience, it seems, remains the great scandal of the mechanistic paradigm. I also see why your arguments sound so circular: you want to claim that what we think of as *qualia* are really just sensory functions; but of course their sheer phenomenality remains a fact in excess of any merely functional descriptions of what the brain does. So your argument for functionalism is simply to deny the reality of *qualia* and of everything else that fails to fit into the functionalist narrative, even when what you're denying is unquestionably real. That's not an actual rational proposal. It has all the subtlety and dialectical substance of a small child's tantrum. Simply dogmatically declaring that only behavior needs explaining and then denying the evident truth of subjective experience on the grounds that it doesn't accord with that dogma is the height of philosophical fatuity. How does that differ from the attitude of a six-day creationist refusing to acknowledge geological evidence on the grounds that it doesn't accord with six-day creationism?[25] Anyway, isn't this the entire point of the so-called knowledge argument?

EROS: Excuse me, again I must apologize. What precisely . . . ?

HERMES: Oh, surely you know it—the "Mary" argument . . . ?

EROS: Surely I *don't*.

HERMES: Oh, all right. It's simply the argument that qualitative consciousness—the "what it's like" of private experience—can be shown to constitute a kind of knowledge that the physical facts of neurology by themselves can't account for. It comes in various versions, but one of the more famous is a thought experiment originally devised by Frank Jackson: a story about a brilliant neuroscientist named Mary who has lived her entire life in a black and white room, connected to the world beyond by a black and white monitor, perhaps wearing spectacles that drain everything of color—I forget some of the details—but, anyway, a woman who basically has had no experience of color at any time in her life, but who as a scientist of uncanny genius also has complete knowledge of all the scientific facts regarding the physical mechanics of perception. Then, one day, she leaves her room and experiences color for the first time. Could anyone deny that, in addition to her knowledge of the physical facts, she would also now acquire another kind of knowledge altogether—an immediate, incommunicable knowledge of what it's like to see yellow or green or blue?[26]

EROS: I see. That's rather ingenious.

HEPHAISTOS: Perhaps, but it isn't unanswerable. Even Jackson, I believe, has abandoned it.

PSYCHE: Imprudently.

HEPHAISTOS: Really? I can think of any number of objections to it. There are those who see the parable as a failure to distinguish between the contents and the modalities of knowledge. They argue that Mary on leaving her room acquires not any new *factual* knowledge, but only a new way—perceptual rather than descriptive, that is—to understand or conceive of facts she already possesses. For some, this is simply the acquisition of a new ability—a kind of *savoir-faire*, so to speak—for imagining or recognizing colors.

PSYCHE: Which is a silly argument, and one that weirdly misses the point. Call it a new ability if you like, but it's still one acquired through a new kind of knowledge, a new *qualitative* experience, beyond what the physical facts convey. Pointing out that her experience doesn't constitute a new kind of *factual* knowledge merely reinforces the argument against physicalism, which is precisely that there's a species of knowledge radically different from the purely quantitative, third-person variety—not the contents of experience, but the experience of contents—and that neither form of knowledge is reducible to the other or to some more basic form of knowing comprehensive of both.

HEPHAISTOS: Well, what if I were to say that Mary's first direct sensory encounter with color would be rather like a mathematician of extraordinary range encountering the Hindu-Arabic numeral system for the first time? Again, what's the difference really? It's just a new . . .

PSYCHE: No, no, no. That's the same error. In that case, the mathematician before her encounter with Hindu-Arabic numerals is simply as yet unacquainted with just another item of a kind of information she already completely possesses: a different system of notation than she's already familiar with. The encounter with Hindu-Arabic numerals simply corrects a quantitative and structural deficiency in her knowledge by supplying a purely quantitative and structural extension of information. Someone could exhaustively describe the shapes and functions of those numerals to her before she's ever actually seen them, and she'd be able to construct their visual representations from that description. But no one, before she's ever seen the color blue, could describe the experience of blue to her in a way that would prepare her for the radically, qualitatively novel experience of actually seeing it and coming to possess it as a privately intuited *quale*.

Hephaistos: You know, Dennett would deny the very premise. He argues that, if Mary actually were in possession of *all* the physical facts, she would know how colors appear to our sensory apparatus, even without having yet seen colors for herself. She'd have no need of direct experience. On first seeing blue, she'd recognize it as blue.

Psyche: Which is so obviously false that I don't know how to summon up enough scorn to reply to it properly. It's at best a rhetorical trick and nothing more. The consciousness of color—the "what it's like" of blue—isn't a quantifiable sensory perception and so isn't a physical fact; it's the private experience of that perception, the qualitative sense of the color "for me" granted solely by immediate acquaintance with the object of perception and the perception of the object. There's the pleonastic fallacy at work yet again. All the physical factual information in the universe couldn't bring you a single step nearer to that kind of knowledge apart from that acquaintance. Dennett, of course, knows that no one could reasonably demand that he prove his claim by supplying all the physical facts that Mary supposedly possesses, thereby showing how they would enable her to know what the conscious experience of blue would be like without her ever having seen blue. But one doesn't need to play along. One need only demand that he say precisely what *kind* of physical factual knowledge could possibly, in the absence of immediate experience, convey the contents of immediate experience, and so close the qualitative chasm between that sort of knowledge and that experience. All he need do is supply something analogous—something vaguely conceivably imaginable—to the kind of knowledge it would require. And, of course, he can't, because his claim—that pure experience, transparent only to itself, can somehow be known wholly by way of a comprehensive grasp of corresponding physiological states—is essentially meaningless.

Hephaistos: [*A note of asperity entering his voice:*] Such assurance! Persons are often mistaken about what they themselves are actually doing. You know, Dennett has addressed just this issue of interior certitude many times. For instance, there's his little parable about a robot named Shakey—a machine with a computer for a brain and a video apparatus used by its software to identify the physical objects in a room, assembling images on a screen from a series of separate functions for picking out the different contours of objects. Now, the screen is for Shakey's human users; he—it—doesn't look at the screen and, as far as the robot's functions are concerned, the screen could be switched off without it affecting the system at all; Shakey just goes on translating pixels from his camera in binary notation, nowhere actually producing what we would think of as a direct visual representation or image. Really, this may be what brains do as well, perhaps: maybe they don't produce a real visual replica of objects, but they encode information that can, as utility dictates, be perceived or manipulated as images. After all, if Shakey also had diagnostic software installed so that it could report its operations, whether the screen is turned on or not, it might merely provide an inventory of each of its mechanical and digital processes; but it also might, if its software dictated that its report be algorithmically reduced to a usefully concise description, tell everyone that it possesses the images of the objects in its room, and even that to "him" it "seems" as if those objects are what they are. In that latter case, one could interpret the report as evidence that Shakey "believes" he has experienced those images, even though all that's going on in his computer brain is the coordinated storage of the information that, were the screen turned on, would appear in the form of images to his operators. If we assume the heterophenomenological vantage, we can accept that, from Shakey's perspective, he does indeed believe he sees images in a privileged mental space; but then our third-person perspective also allows us to relativize the intentional and qualitative stance that tells us how things seem to Shakey and to recognize that what he reports to us as images that he's perceiving are really, described from another stance, only so many binary notations. Well, so it may be with our brains: what we report to ourselves as real images somehow *in* our minds might really be just the various flows of information that the global neural system stores in our brain to be used as needed, without there really being some sensuous depiction of *qualia*—which themselves, after all, would need to go through yet another process of qualitative discriminations in the brain's central homunculus, and so on and so on. We might all really be computers, in a sense, since computers show us how seemingly intentional systems can consist entirely of unconscious competences—competences without comprehension, that is, but with full "cognitive" and "intentional" functions. Or we might be those affectively empty zombies we discussed before, merely convinced that we have inner conscious experiences.[27]

HERMES: This is utter gibberish.

HEPHAISTOS: Is it, now? And is that how the rest of you see it?

EROS: Yes.

PSYCHE: Actually, it doesn't rise to the level of gibberish.

HEPHAISTOS: [*Arching his eyebrows:*] I'm alarmed. You sound as captious as Hermes now.

PSYCHE: Only because you sound like a lunatic. This really is the most abysmal nonsense: *non sequitur* upon *non sequitur*, floating in an ocean of conceptual confusions. I don't know if anyone, even Descartes, actually believed in something like the Cartesian theatre that Dennett describes. Maybe certain materialist philosophers do, inadvertently, but I don't care. If so, it just means they, as we already know is the case, have no coherent explanation for subjective mental states. Yet we know that those states exist. Yes, if belief in real consciousness and intentionality and unity of apprehension and so forth really involved a homuncular pleonasm, so to speak—a retreat from one large neural module called the brain to some smaller central module within the brain—then we'd be involved in an infinite regress. But we've already said as much. Indeed, it was one of my better arguments against a purely physical basis of consciousness, I thought. Of course, it hadn't occurred to me that instead it might be used as an argument against the existence of consciousness, but that's only because the suggestion that consciousness merely *seems* to exist is ridiculous. As I've pointed out, those of us of a classically metaphysical bent in these matters don't think of consciousness in terms of a Cartesian ghost absorbing representations of a mechanical material order. Instead, we merely believe that mind and subjectivity are founded upon themselves, that the material world is a modality of a deeper mind-like or spiritual constitution of all reality, and that we—as organisms, living mind, animating and forming bodies—participate in and know reality by sharing in the same forms that shape the world about us. Dismiss all of that if you like. All language on these matters is an attempt at description of something very mysterious, I admit, but my view of things isn't incoherent in the way yours so spectacularly is. Again, if your theory can't accommodate the phenomenon at issue, eliminate the damned theory, not the phenomenon. And no phenomenon is more ineliminable than phenomenality as such.

HEPHAISTOS: "Damned theory?" Goodness. For you, dear Psyche, that's practically a tirade. If I've done anything to rob you of your composure, I'm sincerely sorry.

PSYCHE: Oh, I'm only beginning.

VII

The Turtle Principle

Psyche: I understand perfectly well how exhilarating it can be to indulge in boldly counterintuitive claims. It can make one feel so daring. I also recognize, however, that it's a temptation that as often as not produces pure nonsense, and this is definitely nonsense. I agree with the philosopher Galen Strawson, who's hardly a champion of supernaturalism, that the denial of the reality of intrinsic consciousness constitutes the single strangest and silliest aberration of reasoning ever to have occurred in the whole history not merely of philosophy, but of human thought as such, and that by comparison even the most outlandish of religious beliefs is scarcely less sensible than the claim that grass is green.[28] If I sound impatient, therefore, it's because there's something demeaning in having to argue that nonsense is nonsense; it's like being asked to reason with a small, angry, obstreperous child as if addressing a calm adult.

Don't misunderstand me. I can see how Dennett must have arrived at his idiosyncratic understanding of these things, and can even sympathize up to a point. It's almost certainly all the result of an especially circuitous version of the Narcissean fallacy, one induced by an exaggerated credulity with regard to the Turing test, or to its underlying assumptions. Imagine, that is to say, a computational system whose algorithms have become so exquisitely refined that, when that system is "addressed" from the outside, its responses are genuinely indistinguishable from those one would expect from an actually conscious agent. Your interactions with that system would be, for all intents and purposes, the same as your interactions with a person. And, as you imagine this, surely you'll find yourself wondering whether a system of such intricacy would have to command so formidable an array of internal information states and finely calibrated operations that perhaps this indistinguishability extends all the way into a kind of interiority in the machine. What's the real difference? Or so you'll ask yourself. Inevitably, you'll wonder whether the machine's ostensibly cognitive functions—including its internal "report" of the data it has collated and arranged from the world beyond—might be so complex as perfectly to imitate conscious and intentional mental states, and whether it may in fact be meaningless conceptually to separate external behavior and internal awareness. Well, then, having reached this point, all at once it seems plausible to you to reverse the picture and ask the same question of yourself: "How do I know that I'm not merely an ensemble of information states and functions with an algorithmic basis?" It's not an unreasonable question to entertain, at least for a few moments. But, once those moments have elapsed, it requires only a little further reflection to realize that there are no information states in a computer that constitute information *for* the computer, and that this is the same as any other version of this galling fallacy: the imposition of a false equivalence on two phenomena that are utterly dissimilar (as we've already shown), based on a beguiling simulacrum and on a fervent desire to believe.

That said, I'm not entirely unsympathetic to certain other of Dennett's concerns too. I also understand the appeal of insisting upon third-person verification in cases where it's appropriate to do so, such as in the collection and accumulation of scientific data; but one makes a mockery of real science by allowing that insistence to become a mystical fanaticism that denies both the authority *and the reality* of intrinsic first-person experience. And it's self-defeating, of course; it undermines the very foundations of objective verification. As I've also already noted, there's no such thing as an actual third-person perspective; that's the most redoubtable of all of modern science's useful methodological fictions. What we call the third-person vantage is really just the unanimity—or really, as often as not, the statistical mean—of an indeterminate number of first-person testimonies; the third person—*homo tertius*—is a phantom "subject" generated out of a milling congress of numerous real subjects; we describe him or her as making an observation in the way we might describe a deliberative legislative body as making a decision. This is all to the good, of course. The more the merrier, I say, and merriest of all when those testimonies are in agreement regarding the evidence of repeatable experiments and scrupulous observations. But there's no mystical juncture at which all those first-person vantages are transformed into an actual third-person vantage, whatever that might be. Whatever heterophenomenology might or might not entail, it certainly can never be more than a structural extension of the power of "autophenomenology." To imagine otherwise is yet another instance of the pleonastic fallacy. In the end, it's the trustworthiness of the unified and intentional subjectivity of private *witness* that renders all "objective" knowledge credible. If somehow subjective consciousness isn't even really subjective consciousness, but only a functional "interface" and narrative fiction constructed as a convenience from multiple brain-states—who can say how or by what faculty?—then the mind certainly can't be a vehicle for establishing scientific truths.

Not that anyone really needs to rely on such an argument to answer Dennett. He's well within his rights to lavish contempt, as he so often does, on those who believe in realities beyond the physical; but it somewhat weakens his position if this obliges him to deny the reality of things that unquestionably *do* exist. One really isn't obliged to pretend that there's anything intellectually respectable going on here. This is all just a fantastic exercise in attempting to make an irrational fundamentalist adherence to an absurd picture of reality sound somehow rigorously rational. But the belief that there aren't really such things as beliefs, the conviction that there are no intrinsic convictions, the denial of *qualia* on the utterly irrelevant grounds that they seem to have no fixed function, the bizarre notion that consciousness can't both comprise a number of uncomprehending competences and also have intrinsic existence—all of it's absurd. All those leaps of logic, and all those circular arguments, and all the further little epicycles of reasoning within each of them . . .

What, for instance, is the point of speaking of subjective, intentional consciousness as a user-interface or computer icon or anything of the sort when these very metaphors refer to implements employed by subjective, intentional consciousness? Implements that exist for no other purpose than serving the ends of an intrinsic intentionality? Logical circles aren't explanations.

Moreover, Dennett's arguments against the intrinsic reality of *qualia*—than which nothing could possibly be more obviously real—defy my best powers of ridicule. Again, the baffling question posed by qualitative subjective experience isn't what purpose it might conceivably serve, evolutionary or physiological or what have you. That's interesting but hardly obscure. Yes, it's very useful to have a mind; so let's stipulate the truth of that *astounding* discovery and move along. The question is how it is that such experience is possible at all—how, that is, the alleged aimlessness and mechanistic extrinsicism of matter can produce the directedness, self-presence, and introspective depth of the personal vantage, the pure perspective of the I. Somehow Dennett continually shifts the focus here from phenomenal experience to utterly subordinate and largely irrelevant issues of epistemology and behavior. Those are matters of function, within specific contexts; but function and context neither explain what consciousness is nor explain consciousness away. As Hermes says, the experience remains, and it remains irreducible to its physical concomitants, functions, contexts, or uses. That ineffable, private, intrinsic, directly accessible sense of "what it's like" whose existence Dennett denies not only really and indubitably does exist; it's the foundation and medium of everything we know and are. Frankly, it's an embarrassment, and something of a philosophical burlesque, even to have to debate such things. Especially bizarre are the ways in which Dennett's failure to address the actual question of consciousness in terms other than the functional or epistemological or behavioral produces such garbled arguments. The one you cite—the one about the coffee-tasters—is a perfect example, because it's also a perfect loop: it starts from the sheerly dogmatic assertion that all mental states must be merely functional processes; therefore, mental states that aren't merely functional, like intrinsic qualitative experience, can't really exist; hence, they don't; and, as they don't, then all mental states must merely be functional processes. This is positively mystical in its circularity. And somehow, supposedly, it gets us past the rather significant reality that intrinsic qualitative experience *does* in fact—inconveniently, it seems—exist. So his proof of functionalism is to assert its reality, and then to deny reality itself because of its failure to confirm his assertion. There's a nimble feat of dialectic for you.

HEPHAISTOS: Well, I don't . . .

PSYCHE: And *of course* qualitative states of consciousness can be altered by changes in the objects of perception or in one's organs of perception, or for that matter can remain unaltered despite such changes. So what? This entire debate of ours began with a red rose blossom plucked from a tree, and I freely admit that, if I should suddenly find that it appeared to be yellow instead of red, I could not be sure whether it or my optic apparatus had been altered. Conversely, if I continue to see it as red, I can't really know from that alone whether it truly is still red, or indeed ever really was red to begin with. In fact, simply by perceiving it, I can't be certain that it really exists and that I'm not hallucinating the entire episode. Yet the one thing of which I can be *absolutely* certain is the immediate, private, intrinsic, subjective qualitative experience itself. All functional, representational, psychological, and behavioral issues can be set aside here, since they have no bearing whatsoever on the matter that remains inexplicable in purely physicalist terms: first-person consciousness. I'm not even sure what point Dennett imagines he's making, since his putative proof that *qualia* aren't intrinsic subjective states is simply to complain that they don't correspond to objective causes—which suggests that he's attempting to disprove the intrinsic reality of *qualia* by demonstrating their independent reality. If anything, what he's saying only reinforces the claim that the qualitative dimension of experience doesn't exhaust itself in any mere function; it's something quite distinct from whatever objective information it may or may not be associated with, in regard either to the world or to my own neurological structures; rather, it's thoroughly subjective—*subjectivity as such*, in fact—ontologically distinct from any of the objective physical processes or behaviors with which it might be associated. A particular *quale* in the present may not tell me whether it's my coffee or my aesthetic standards that time has altered, but it certainly attests to itself in a wholly immediate, private, and undeniable way. This is a primordial datum—the primordial datum *par excellence*—which it's a degrading nonsense to pretend isn't real.

We see the same basic irrelevancy in Dennett's point about the various ways in which pain might be experienced. Here his argument is nothing more than the psychologistic fallacy at its most elementary—a failure, that is, to distinguish between the qualitative experience itself and one's psychological appropriation of it. Yes, the same thrill of pain might in one context induce aversion and in another erotic pleasure, but the subjectivity of the experience is no less mysterious as a result, and the pain is still a private experience, even when it's not associated with a behavioral "pain-function." Frankly, we can subtract psychology altogether from our reflections on *qualia*, since they're present in each of us even when there's no egoistic appropriation of them as psychologically "mine." At times, they can even be disruptive of one's preoccupation with oneself. A ballerina may lose herself in her dance, precisely because her qualitative awareness has in a sense liberated her from herself, and allowed her to submerge her consciousness in the pure flow of sensuous and emotional impressions, and to achieve a rare immediacy of encounter with the phenomenal realm. There are moments of transport—artistic, mystical, what have you—that utterly subsume function in experience; but the qualitative privacy of the experience remains constant. Why not draw exactly the opposite conclusion, then? Why not see all of this as proof that awareness and intentionality are independent of any mere function as such, and enjoy a kind of ontological liberty from the mechanistic properties of mere stimulus and response? That, in fact, *qualia* aren't merely dispositions toward one behavior or another, but possess an intrinsic nature indifferent to whatever behavioral dispositions might at any given juncture rely upon them? That this is intrinsic to the powers of living souls?

Then, of course, there's the nonsense about the "intentional stance." Well, surely I shouldn't have to point out to you that any such a stance would itself be a specimen of intrinsic intentionality. I'm not even sure this rises to the level of a good logical circle, it's so very, very inane. I might be able to extend my sense of my own intentionality to some inanimate object, as a result of the pathetic fallacy perhaps; but I certainly can't attribute intentionality to myself except as an intrinsically intentional act.

HEPHAISTOS: It's turtles all the way down, then?[29]

PSYCHE: If you like. I've already said as much, haven't I? Let's call it the "testudinal principle"—the *principium testudinis:* mind in any of its aspects—unity, subjective consciousness, intentionality, rationality, what have you—can rest upon no foundation but itself, and there's no way into that self-subsistence from outside. That's why Dennett is forced to use rhetorical sleight of hand—albeit not very deftly—to make his arguments seem cogent. Note how he extracts a reductionist account of "belief" from his little parable about the robot precisely by first introducing the notion of belief *into* his description of the robot's functions, like a dove concealed in a magician's hidden pocket, so that, having first rhetorically animated the machine, he can then reverse his tropes and transform the computer into a metaphor for the inanimate mechanisms he thinks minds to be. After all, so his argument goes, if a computer can be programmed to "believe" it has a visual experience . . . and so on and so forth. Except, of course, it can't. Computers have no beliefs, whereas we most definitely do. Moreover, we don't merely "judge" and then "report" to ourselves—whoever those selves might be—that we're conscious after a sequence of unconscious judgments—whatever that means. Rather, we're directly, infallibly conscious of being conscious, and for precisely that reason we're capable of making judgments—epistemological, moral, propositional, and so on. The *sākṣi*—the witness—within each of us is a pure subjectivity, a pure awareness of being aware, and were that not so we too *would* be like machines, entirely devoid of mind, judging nothing, reporting nothing, believing nothing. This isn't matter for any kind of meaningful debate. It's directly and indubitably self-evident. We may make epistemic judgments regarding perception, but we don't make phenomenal judgments regarding experience. We possess the phenomenon *in se*, without need of any propositional supplement, as a private experience that's irreducible to the functional information available to our neurology. Neural signals may convey all the sensory data there is to convey; but only the subjective mind possesses the phenomenal impressions.

Actually, the analogy is defective at both poles, because computers not only have no beliefs and make no judgments, but also because they don't "report" that they do, even if we've programmed them to produce reports to that effect—any more than an abacus with varicolored beads "reports" that it "believes" that $(2 \times 10) + 5 = 25$. Computers can't tell themselves they see colors, nor can they tell us. They merely process code that, for them, never comes to possess any semeiotic content whatsoever. It is we alone, through them, who make reports of their functions to ourselves, in a semantic form that possesses content only in a hermeneutical space belonging to minds, into which no machine process can ever enter. And it is we alone who make judgments; computers can't. Judgment is a deliberative act based on a discriminating knowledge that also exists only in the hermeneutical realm. Computers don't even employ words; they generate electrical operations that we're able to understand as words because, unlike computers, we possess minds. And, of course, it doesn't matter whether the computer is creating visual representations on a screen or not, because representation too is a matter of intentionality. Purely physical systems can translate physical realities into different kinds of data: a camera, for example, stores patterns of light and color in an analogue or digital form, and a recording device can do the same thing with sounds, but nothing that either device produces constitutes a representation of anything at all unless there's a subjective consciousness present directed toward the picture or the recording *as* representing something beyond itself, and toward the thing depicted *as* represented, all of which is an act of awareness—of subjective attention. When Dennett tells us that, for all we know, we might be "zombies" who only believe we're conscious, he's talking twaddle. Belief isn't data; judgment isn't an unconscious operation of physiology. Each requires an intention and also an immediate *affect*, an actual "what it's like": to believe is to experience oneself as believing; to judge is to experience oneself as thinking. A "zombie" could never experience thought, could never be aware of being aware, and so couldn't think—just as, in fact, no computer has ever entertained a single thought of any kind.

HEPHAISTOS: [*After several moments of pensive silence:*] As it happens, I do want to discuss computational models of the mind. You've made a great many assertions, after all, as to why they're defective. I'm going to require a more substantial argument before I concede the point. But the day is passing swiftly.

PSYCHE: Yes, it is. Tomorrow, then. We can . . .

HERMES: Wait, please, let's not dissolve our little parliament yet. I want to know whether our friend Hephaistos is now ready to grant that subjective experience really is what it is—really is subjective consciousness with its own intrinsic properties, irreducible to mere physical facts.

HEPHAISTOS: [*With a sigh:*] You're unrelenting. [*Considering for a moment:*] What I'll acknowledge is that Dennett's arguments to the contrary are circular, as you say, and largely unpersuasive as stated. And yet I find myself unable simply to grant that anything just is as it seems, without absolutely ruling out every other possible angle upon it. Something still tells me that it's not wholly implausible to say we're essentially dealing with information states that, through a certain structural arrangement of relations, can generate an appearance of intrinsic subjective experience, above and beyond the information itself.

HERMES: An appearance *to whom?*

HEPHAISTOS: To themselves, perhaps. I don't know. Whatever the case, computers are, after all, very impressive analogies of minds, it seems to me. As I said some hours ago, however, I must demonstrate *either* that mental phenomena can, despite all appearances, be described mechanistically *or* that matter can, without any violation of physicalism, be described in a non-mechanistic way. If you convince me that the computational analogy fails, I'll abandon the former task and take up the latter. But first you must convince me.

HERMES: And if . . . ?

HEPHAISTOS: Tomorrow, however. Let's say around teatime.

[*Exeunt omnes.*]

DAY FOUR
Machine and Soul

I

Language, Thought, and Code

Late afternoon, verging on early evening. The angle of the Intermundian sun's rays is already markedly oblique. The breeze, coming from the direction of the rose arbors, is especially delectably fragrant. Psyche, Eros, Hermes, *and* Hephaistos *are now seated at the garden's center in chairs of wrought-iron filigree embellished with ingenious floral designs, arranged around an elegant but intimate table whose circular top is of blue marble resting on an ornate base of the same dark iron. The tea-things have just been cleared away—or, rather, waved away into nonexistence—and everyone seems quite at ease.*

Hephaistos: That was delightful, as the hospitality of this house always is. I can't say I'm especially eager at the moment to resume our conversation of yesterday, but I expect I should. Or would someone else like to start?

Psyche: No, you go ahead, please. You're still the chief inquisitor here.

Hephaistos: I'm not sure I relish that title, but thank you. Yes, then. Remind me, did we discuss the "language of thought" hypothesis of mind?

Hermes: Yes. We talked about it in relation to intentionality. You made it sound like just another version of functionalism?

Hephaistos: Similar—aligned, perhaps—but with certain distinctive features. It's not an especially interesting theory in general outline, because all it really says is that there's a structural continuity or similarity between reasoning and speaking, which is hardly an earth-shaking proposition. What's important about it, and what makes it relevant to computational models of mind, is what it says about language, and therefore what it says about mental states. In a sense, it's a kind of reverse reductionism: not of language-use to physical events, but of physical events to the structure of language—but, of course, on the premise that language already exhibits properties that aren't, as such, mental.

HERMES: Then it's a false theory. All language-use is intentional and conscious.

HEPHAISTOS: You're somewhat missing the point. I'm not talking about the use of language, but of its basic structure. Yes, when I say, "That was a lovely tea," I'm aware of what I'm saying and why I'm saying it, but that's all in a sense consequent upon linguistic functions that precede any intrinsic intentional content. Language is composed of symbols, such as phonemes or graphemes, which in isolation have no essential properties beyond their physical embodiments; they mean nothing except by virtue of their relations to other things—other symbols, objects, processes. There's nothing actually tea-like in the word "tea." There's nothing intrinsically porcine in the word "pig." So it is, this theory tells us, that there are neurophysiological equivalents of linguistic functions—neural symbols, as it were—that are combined in representations of the world. They have no inherent intentional content, obviously, but they take on an intentional character through our acts of propositional or assertoric judgments—judgments such as "this is true" or "this is false," that is. Call it "mentalese": a "syntax" of brain-states that realizes neural symbols in a way that processes . . . well, input into output. Mental states, however—*qualia*, reasoning, beliefs, and so forth—come afterward, and belong to an emergent, second-order reality; the first-order series of realizations are brought about through the interactions of the semantic properties of this "language of thought" with one another and their environment, and all the actual transitions within this functional process are more or less computational in nature. Or, to put it very simply, none of these mental mechanisms in itself understands the representations it produces; but at the level of second-order processes the mind is a system that, as a whole, *does* understand. In fact, at that level, producing those understandings simply is the production of representations. That's what it is to entertain mental "concepts."

HERMES: So mental states—states we call consciously intentional—emerge from this "language of thought," which itself emerges from an aggregation of neural "symbols" in interaction with one another and with the world, just as meaning emerges from the interactions of the otherwise inherently meaningless signs composing natural language?

HEPHAISTOS: That seems a fair summary of what many theorists claim.

HERMES: Well, then it also seems wrong.

HEPHAISTOS: Does it now?

HERMES: Don't misunderstand me. I'm perfectly prepared to grant that thought and language are . . . isomorphic, let's say. Indeed, I believe thought *is* language. But I don't believe language is even vaguely similar to "neural symbols" in interaction with one another, principally because the very notion of "neural symbols" strikes me as just another vague metaphor—a transference of terms from a context in which they have a meaning into one in which they don't. It might make a kind of sense, I suppose, if language actually arose from symbols that somehow existed in themselves prior to meaning and then, only latterly, combined into meanings through structural relations and interactions. But of course that's not what happens. Language doesn't arise from the parts of language; rather, language in its totality, as an intentional semeiotic system, is itself the source and ground of the parts that compose it.

HEPHAISTOS: Is that a structural or a genetic claim?

HERMES: Both. Structurally speaking, language isn't a bottom-up product of a more primordial level of symbols without intentional content. Genetically speaking, language didn't evolve out of an ensemble of discrete linguistic functions that somehow pre-existed the languages that give them meaning. Symbols never exist in isolation; they exist only within an entirely replete semeiotic ecology, a complete language, in which syntactic and semantic functions are wholly in operation, both of them sustained by a fully realized capacity for symbolic thought. To understand anything as indicating something else is always wholly dependent upon a complex system of signification. Language is structurally a top-down hierarchy, descending from intentional thought through a system composed of semantics and syntax—neither of which can exist in abstraction from the other—to particular instances of meaning.

HEPHAISTOS: Ah, of course. I almost forgot: the three of you think of language as a kind of formal causality, fashioning the material order "from above."

PSYCHE: Language, life, and mind, to be precise. None of these things evolved. They're eternal . . . well, forms.

HEPHAISTOS: Oh dear.

PSYCHE: Rather, material reality has evolved over time into an ever richer participation in their power. They're the formal reality shaping material reality "from above" into ever more diverse and complex living, thinking, and communicating organisms.

HEPHAISTOS: Oh dear, oh dear.

HERMES: At least we'd agree that thought is language; we'd merely add that language doesn't arise from any kind of mechanistic system, while thought is always already intentional, and intentionality can't emerge from the non-intentional. So, what are we talking about here? Neurophysiological symbols? What could that possibly mean? How do neural processes *refer* to anything as that particular thing? Symbols exist as *nothing but* intentional content, whatever their physical accidents. That's their whole ontology. Simply seeding one's account of the brain's operations with linguistic terms—symbol, semantic content, syntax—doesn't render the claim that non-intentional processes are somehow essentially linguistic, or that language rests upon a non-intentional foundation, even remotely credible. I mean, look, when I say—and say sincerely—"That was a lovely tea," my understanding of what I'm thinking can't be the posterior effect of physical relations between differing neural functions distributed about my brain. My knowledge of my meaning—which is also my subjective *awareness* of my knowing my meaning—is a hermeneutical, interpretive act, a top-down formal determination that assumes the lower neural states into the higher mental states. It's a semeiotic process: I'm using signs meaningfully.

HEPHAISTOS: And yet computers give us a very compelling model of the opposite process: of thought, that is, arising from a host of uncomprehending competences.

HERMES: They most certainly do *not*. That's not what computation is. Quite the reverse: a prior semeiotic content on the part of a programmer or a user encodes or interprets the computer's functions, but those functions—as far as the computer's concerned—have no meaning at all. A computer neither uses symbols nor thinks.

HEPHAISTOS: Ah, well tell that to the chess-masters and masters of *Go* who've been defeated at their games by these supposedly unthinking mechanisms. Look, before we start freighting our account of things with language about intrinsic meaning, why don't we proceed from the evidence before us? It's hard to deny, after all, that computers seem to behave—and ever more so—as if they were thinking machines, which means there's at least nothing inherently absurd in suggesting that thought might be, at base, mechanistic. Maybe the brain too is only a computer, and mind only a kind of software—just so many flows of data, processed into behaviors by functional connections and discriminatory filters, all erected upon a kind of digital platform in the neurology of the body. Maybe, as Dennett argues, all the brilliance and powers of comprehension that define our mental states and capacities simply emerge—or, rather, develop—out of countless little uncomprehending competences compounded over epochs of evolution into ever more competent—and so ever more comprehending—systems.[1] If we were to undertake our aforementioned "homuncular decomposition" of the mind in purely computational terms, we might descend through a symbolic level of operations down to a level of something like simple binary functions, then down further to the even simpler "switches" in the brain that produce binary processes. Now, it's a matter of indifference to me whether one concludes from this either that one day computers of sufficient complexity might become conscious or one concludes instead that thinking beings like gods and humans and Intermundian squirrels are in fact only computers who merely imagine they possess intrinsic consciousness. Those are really just two different ways of saying the same thing: that what we think of as intrinsic mental states are, in their origins, only functions. You've just described the process perfectly, in fact, albeit inadvertently: your seeming "mental states" really just translate certain brain-states into the behavior of saying, "That was a lovely tea." Yes, yes, I know that doesn't explain *how* consciousness exists or seems to exist, but it does explain *what* consciousness does. We're accustomed to think we, say, experience a pain state and then, in consequence of that experience, perform this or that action. All that functionalism asks us to do is to entertain the possibility that the reverse is actually the case and that we "experience" a certain state as painful only as a result of its function in the larger system of translating outputs into inputs—the software of "thought." We experience it as pain, that is, because such an "experience" is part of the process of producing, say, pulling one's hand away from a fire.

HERMES: Yes, we've been over this.

HEPHAISTOS: And you've rejected it, I know, because you claim the experience exceeds the function. I'm not yet convinced, however.

EROS: Excuse me. If thought is software and the brain a computer, could the thinking that goes on in my brain be extracted from it, theoretically at least, and then made to run in some other brain, just as software can be run on more than one computer?

HEPHAISTOS: Yes, indeed, if that other brain were structurally compatible with that software. Or, rather, thought can be run on any platform capable of accommodating its functions. It needn't be a brain at all, perhaps. That's one of the necessary implications of functionalism, as it happens: that what each of us thinks of as his or her intrinsic inner world is really a kind of data stream and coding, which might just as well be installed on a cybernetic platform composed not of cells and tissues but of silicon and transistors. In practice this may prove an impossible technological achievement; but in principle it's a logical entailment. And who knows? Maybe it is technologically feasible, or will be.

The philosopher David Chalmers, for instance, has proposed what he calls the "principle of organizational invariance" or—when he's being less grandiose—"mental structuralism." He finds it very plausible that thought—consciousness, intentionality, and so forth—is the result not of the physical substance or substrate of the brain, but entirely of a structure of relations and functions. If so, any system of computation structurally isomorphic to the processes in a living brain will produce the same experiences as that brain would, no matter what the platform or physical medium by which that system is enacted. Any simulated brain that precisely mirrored a biological brain would be no less conscious than its organic counterpart. One of his arguments for this is what he calls "fading *qualia*." That is, one can imagine one's brain being gradually transformed into a silicon rather than organic object through the substitution, one at a time, of a computer chip for each neuron; it seems unlikely that in the process our consciousness would gradually disappear along with our original neurons, given that the structure of the emerging silicon brain would produce the same behaviors as the neurological brain it's replacing. And maybe, in this way, one's mind could be gradually uploaded into a simulated brain without any loss of personal consciousness; this in fact might be the safest and surest method for transferring one's mind to a virtual platform.[2]

Psyche: What a very curious supposition. I mean, quite apart from the question of consciousness and whether *qualia* would persist in a brain gradually transformed from a collection of neurons to one of silicon chips, why does he simply presuppose that the brain is basically a computer and that the mind consists entirely in the electrical impulses passing through its structure? Does he really believe that those impulses convey transcriptions of some kind of operational system, recorded in some form of electrical coding? And is that code something distinct from the electrical impulses themselves, a kind of layer of supervenient digital meaning? Why does he assume that neurons are simple electrical conduits that can be replaced with neural prostheses, so long as the latter allow those electrical transcriptions to continue to flow unimpeded? Don't bother to answer; the last question probably answers itself. I suppose he must. That's quite a leap of logic, wouldn't you say? I mean, it's only so long as one accepts this odd dogma of organizational invariance, however, that one can confidently assert that all the features of conscious experience would simply emerge or be duplicated within a virtual brain . . . including even the sense of unified, intentional, subjective experience that, as far as our knowledge of nature goes, is uniquely an attribute of living creatures. What's the evidence, though? *Why* is he so certain that a brain replaced piecemeal with circuitry would continue to yield the same behaviors as its original neurology? It seems far more likely that the process of replacing one's neurons with computer chips would be little more than a very slow process of suicide, producing not the same behaviors as a living mind, but only progressive derangement and stupefaction, culminating in an inert mass of diffusely galvanized circuitry. And why think that structures in the abstract are what account for thinking, without regard to the actual physical occasion of thought? This seems to me as sickly a dualism as it's possible to imagine. Really, does he believe that we need only build a model of a brain and it will conjure consciousness into existence once we turn on the electricity? Structures and systems as such, of their nature, have as far as we can tell no unified and simultaneous view of anything, let alone any of the mental capacities that would be contingent on them.

Of course, I have my own prejudices. I see mind, in both its structure and its operation, as being inseparable from life, and so see this metaphor of mind as a kind of software—indifferent to the distinction between organic and inorganic platforms, merely carried along on the living electricity of the brain's neurology in the way a digital code is carried along on electrical currents in a machine, or from one machine to another—as simply banal. I can fully appreciate the frustration of an old-fashioned materialist like John Searle at the oddly inverted Cartesianism in computational accounts of the mind, and especially at this curious dualism that so easily separates mentality into, on the one hand, a kind of functional software and, on the other, the purely structural hardware or "platform" where it's realized. Mental agency has never been discovered anywhere except in organisms, where it appears to be associated with brains and nervous systems and nerve tissues and organic cells and all sorts of other biological realities. So what precisely justifies this belief that mental activity resides entirely in code, or that it could be sustained wholly by electrical transcriptions and circuitry? What could unify any of that into an actual "I think"? Wouldn't it make more sense to assume that the brain's capacity for mentality has some connection to the cells and tissues and enzymes, synapses and axons and myelin, composing it, and to an organism's unique history of continuous growth, development, catalysis, regeneration, and constantly developing and changing neural pathways, and to its complex relations with the complete neurology, biology, organs, and history of the body as a whole, as well as to its organic relations to the environment around it? In fact, the very notion of "structural invariance" is an oddly telling one, because organisms aren't stable structures through which information flows, much less a bare architectonics that can be reproduced in static silicon infrastructures; they themselves *are* the flow of what informs them. Brains change constantly over time, often in coordination with intentional employments of the mind, forging new neural connections and causeways. Brains may be the physical occasions of mental agency, but they're also constantly being shaped and refashioned and renewed by that agency; the two are a single inseparable action, at once noetic and corporeal. All organisms are composed by their own continuous narratives; they're composed of time, in a sense, as processes of learning and expansion and alteration and self-revision, right down to the cellular level, and surely that dynamic flow of retention and protention in relation to various environments is continuous with the affective and intentional processes of mind. It makes much more sense, that is, to think that the dynamism of mind and the dynamism of the living organism are at base one and the same process of . . . well, of rational vitality, let's say . . . or vital rationality. What sort of neural plasticity, one has to wonder, would a network of silicon chips possess? Why assume that neurophysiology is simply one expression of a more general neurotechnology that might equally well be expressed in some other physical medium, or imagine that mind, rather than being something bound to the unique properties of organic life, is simply a pattern of coded activity that could be realized in a cybernetic simulacrum or digital phantom of a brain? If we take it for granted that thought and experience and all the features of mentality are simply a matter of connections and conductivity, with no relation to the physical ingredients and processes and individual history of the brain and body, we've already entered a kind of quasi-Platonic otherworld, albeit a drearily dispirited one: a realm where abstract patterns are all that's *really* real, and where structures—rather than organisms or persons—are the seat of mental agency, and where abstract paradigms are more real than their organic instantiations.[3]

No, no, Phaesty, to me it seems this is nothing more than yet another of the many *reductiones ad absurdum* that the early modern paradigm of reality has bequeathed those poor mortals down there who labor away over these questions. Ever since their picture of their own humanity was reduced to a comically awkward dualism between the machine of the body and its resident ghost, they've been confronted by the false dilemma of trying to determine which of the two is really the seat of the mind. For a short time, the ghost enjoyed that grand eminence; but ghosts are rather ineffectual in the physical order, and the tendency of the modern mind is not to believe in them to begin with, so in fairly short order the mind came to be assigned instead to the machine. But machines don't think, or experience anything; they possess no inner coherence of any kind; they're composites of inert parts extrinsically organized to perform functions imposed on them from without by beings who *do* think and experience things. This is true even of machines that obey coded programs, which are nothing but more sophisticated and flexible mechanical systems, producing results that in themselves are still nothing in excess of the mechanical. Before the modern epoch, no one was aware of this version of the "mind-body problem" as such. No one would have thought it sensible to ask to which part of the living organism—the living person—mental states belonged, not because the prevailing paradigm of human life was dualistic, but precisely because it wasn't—at least, not in the modern mechanistic sense.

HEPHAISTOS: But you're not a physicalist because . . . ?

PSYCHE: Because, for the thousandth time, I don't believe in mechanistic matter. Matter is mindlike—or, rather, matter is one rational relation within the mindlike structure of nature, and physical reality is merely mind as expressed in a certain kind of concrete mode or phase—as you well know to be my opinion. Really, I do think sometimes you're just trying to provoke me. I believe in . . . well, *psychē:* at once both the principle of life and the principle of mind, an inherently integral rational structure, informing both the bodies of living organisms and thought itself. Modern dogma, I realize, holds that biological life is reducible to mere chemical interactions, and that surely human beings will one day be able to summon living organisms out of their Petri dishes as though from a magic cauldron. As yet, however, despite all their understanding of biochemistry, whatever that final dash of henbane or last mystic incantation is that has the power to transform chemical volatility into organic vitality continues to elude them. All one can say with certainty for now is that the unity of organic life—with all its "mindlike" order and teleology, its faculties of self-movement and reproduction—is always present, perhaps to the point of identity, wherever the unity of the conscious and intending mind is found; and, so, to assume that organic life and living mind can be *physically* alienated from one another and continue to exist separately is nothing but a wild leap of fantasy.

Hephaistos: Ah, now, be consistent. I happen to know that you don't believe the soul or mind or what have you perishes with the body.

Psyche: No, as it happens, I don't—not, however, because it's a kind of software, but because it's life and form as such, and gives life and form to the material body, and so doesn't depend on a strictly material body to exist, even if the material body is its way of being *this* particular mind *here* at *this* moment within the physical continuum. But I don't want to be drawn off along that path, since my personal beliefs aren't the issue here; and, anyway, if I'm deceived on that score, I'm still not as guilty of magical thinking as you are. You've dwelt so long among those automata of yours that your workshop is becoming a factory of delusions. This is a perfect example of what I called the Narcissean fallacy. Computational models of mind are nonsensical; mental models of computer functions equally so, but computers produce so enchanting a simulacrum of mental agency that sometimes those who use them fall under their spell and begin to think there must really be someone there, just on the other side of that mesmerizingly glowing screen. It's probably only natural that humans should be so easily seduced by shadows and stupefied by their own beguiling reflections; but you're a god and should know better. They're just clever apes, after all, who've impressed themselves on the world around them far more intricately and indelibly than any other terrestrial animal could ever do. They've mastered countless ways, artistic and technological, of reproducing their images and voices and visions, of giving expression to and preserving their thoughts, and of reshaping their physical environment. And now, in this late modern age of theirs, they've come to live at the center of an increasingly inescapable house of mirrors. They've even created a technology that seems to reflect not merely their presence in the world, but their very minds. So, like Narcissus bent above the waters, they look down at their computers and, captivated by what they see reflected there, imagine that another gaze has met their own. That's sad enough, but then many of them go further still and redouble—by inverting—the folly of that young, beautiful Boeotian idiot: rather than mistaking their own shadows for other selves, they instead mistake themselves for other shadows; having first imposed the metaphor of an artificial mind on computers, they now reverse the process and impose the nonsensical notion of a thinking machine on their own minds.

[*With a long sigh:*] Yet these are all only so many empty figures of speech. One speaks of computer memory, for instance, but of course computers recall nothing. They don't even store any "remembered" information, in the sense of symbols with real semantic content; they just preserve certain electronic notations for their users. Not only are computers unaware of the information they contain; in themselves, they don't actually contain any semantic information at all. Those notations—those transient binary traces inscribed on silicon parchment with electrical ink—yield semantic content only in respect to our intentional judgments of their meanings in our minds. A computer no more remembers the files stored in it than the paper and print of a book remembers the contents of its text. Nor can one say that there are "higher order" functions in the computer's software, at some other mechanical level of functional integration, that transform those notations into coherent meanings. There are no higher functions *in* the computer; those higher levels exist only in the living minds the computer serves. Even the programs that computers run don't exist *in* the computers themselves as intelligible purposive systems. In a computer, considered as a physical object in which physical processes occur, there are neither symbols nor algorithms; there are only inactive material parts, electrical impulses, and binary patterns without reference. A computer programmer can translate meanings or functions into algorithms because, being intentionally conscious, he or she is capable of imposing a semeiotic formality upon all of that intrinsically aimless matter and energy, and is then also capable of representing the operations of the computer not merely as physical events but as intelligible symbolic transcriptions of something else. It's solely in the consciousness of the person who programs or uses a computer, or in the consciousness that operates through the physical apparatus of the brain, that symbols reside.

It's all rather silly, when you think about it, this computer analogy. Computational models of the mind might make sense if what a computer does could be characterized as an elementary version of what the mind does, but there isn't even a remote analogy between them. A computer doesn't even really compute; it's the user who does all the computing, using it as an instrument for his or her ends, just as one might do with that abacus we mentioned earlier. A programmer can program a computer so that it will produce an image on a screen that a user reads as meaning 2 + 2 = 4; but those luminescent figures have mathematical content in their minds only, not in the computer itself. In there, 2 + 2 = 4 isn't a mathematical sum, or any kind of thought at all. One could program the computer reliably to produce figures on its screen declaring that 2 + 2 = 5, and there would be no violation of logic on its part in doing so.

HEPHAISTOS: A brain can produce errors too.

PSYCHE: A *mind* can produce error; error is a privilege reserved for intending agents, and neither neurons (conceived mechanically) nor circuits enjoy that singular dignity. A purely physical system can be neither right nor wrong, but only efficient or inefficient. Software no more thinks than that abacus thinks, and its coding is only a set of protocols for physical processes. No computer has ever used language, responded to a question, or intended a meaning. No computer has ever played chess or *Go*. No computer has ever added two numbers together, let alone entertained a thought. The only intelligence or consciousness or even illusion of consciousness in the whole computational process is situated in living minds, and anything in computers that appears to us to be analogous to minds will turn out to be, on closer inspection, pure projection on our parts. [*Another sigh:*] It's so simple, really. The problem of mind for us is the correlation within us—within *us*—of physical and mental actions. There are physical actions in a computer, but all the correlated mental actions that may or may not be associated with them are still in *us*.

Frankly, I don't even see *how* mechanical computation could be said to resemble mental agency. It seems obvious to me that computers function as efficiently as they do precisely by virtue of the absence of anything like mental states. Much of their power lies in maintaining discrete operations that need never achieve—indeed, *must* never achieve—unity except at the representational level: that is, at the level of a conscious person looking at images on a screen or something of the sort. At the level of the processing of data, there are merely segmented files related to one another only occasionally, by way of algorithms, in as many separated parts as possible. Even in their physical design, computers are austerely modular systems with very few complicated connections. Neither do computers produce streams of consecutive reasoning; their processing speed isn't a more efficient form of thinking. By the same token, a chess-player considering his or her strategy—imagining, calculating, deliberating risks, contemplating possible future configurations—isn't engaged in a less efficient form of computation. He or she is doing something qualitatively completely different—and, for that matter, infinitely richer. Actual thought requires a kind of phenomenal reflexivity, a kind of awareness of thinking that refers everything back to the knowing subject; when one is thinking, one *experiences* that thinking as a phenomenal flow of impressions, sensuous or imaginative. All of that's absent from the diverse, segregated, unconscious functions by which the algorithms in a chess-playing program eliminate statistically less successful courses of action and then, over the course of countless, mindless reiterations of all possible moves running in several discrete simultaneous operations, produce a *representation*—and a representation only, and then only when presented to us—of the move least likely to lead to a tactical disadvantage. There's no intelligence there, no consciousness, no choice—no *move* actually made by the computer. If it "wins," it does so precisely by *not* playing chess and by *not* contemplating the board.

HEPHAISTOS: And yet, from all that welter of intrinsically meaningless physical competences and forces, meaning still emerges.

HERMES: Hardly. Rather, *upon* all that welter of intrinsically meaningless physical competences and forces, meaning is adventitiously *imposed*—as a formal cause.

II

Functionalism, Computationalism

HERMES: [*To Psyche:*] May I take over again? As you know, the issue of language is one especially dear to my heart.

PSYCHE: Please. I'd be grateful.

HERMES: My thanks. So, then, let me try to define the logic of functionalism as I understand it. It's the claim that the brain is what Daniel Dennett calls a "syntactic engine," which more or less as a phylogenic fortuity or hypertrophy was selected by life's Darwinian logic, and which over the evolutionary epochs has come to function as a "semantic engine." That is, the brain's a machine platform, something like a Turing device, one that began its existence as a physiological organ for translating stimuli into responses but that now runs a more sophisticated program for translating "inputs" into "outputs." In Dennett's version of the story, this happened in part as a result of the brain's gradual colonization by "memes"; but, whatever the case, supposedly this program has come to incorporate in its functions a number of brain-states that, in order to serve as useful interfaces between us and all those computational processes, appear to us to be conscious or intentional states with meanings, though in essence they're nothing of the sort. The governing maxim of functionalism would be something like "Once the proper syntax is established in the neurophysiology of the brain, the semantics of thought will take care of themselves." That is, once the syntactic engine begins running its impersonal algorithms, the semantic engine will eventually emerge or supervene.

Eros: Sorry, can we pause to refresh our memories? I've more or less forgotten what "memes" are supposed to be—assuming I ever bothered to find out.

Hermes: Oh, it's a term coined by Richard Dawkins, indicating a kind of cultural analogue of genes. A meme is supposedly a unit of shared behavior or thought, like a style of clothing or an architectural fashion or a tune or an idea or a turn of phrase, that's transmitted from one person to another by imitation and variation. More to the point, memes supposedly replicate *themselves* in some sense, colonizing the ecology of the brain, adapting, surviving, and displacing less robust memetic populations, and thereby creating and determining the contents of consciousness. It's a largely worthless concept. I mean, as an ironic metaphor it's not a bad way of describing the genealogy of popular culture, but as a serious proposal regarding how intentionality is formed it's vapid. Not that I don't see its appeal for those devoted to a computational model of mind. If it made sense, it would certainly constitute a convenient conceptual bridge between the uncomprehending physiological competences of brains and the apparent intrinsic intentionality of minds; but, alas and alack, it *doesn't* make sense. The basic idea—the notion, that is, of some pre-conscious form of intentional content that proliferates on its own, and that's situated in the brain the way DNA is situated in the cells of the body, contributing "information" to consciousness in the way that genetic codes contribute "information" to organisms—is impossible to state cogently. Genetic materials are propagated physically because they're physical realities. "Memes," however, if such things exist, are composed entirely of intentional content. They couldn't be "selected" by nature, in the way the units of biological evolution are said to be, but would literally have to be chosen, if perhaps a little passively, by conscious minds. They'd be objects of intentionality, as well as intentional artifacts, but they certainly couldn't explain intentionality; the existence of a cause can't be explained by the existence of its own contingent effects.

Hephaistos: For what it's worth, the versions of functionalism I'd be disposed to defend wouldn't include "memes," which I too see as an inane notion.

Hermes: But you'd still agree, I assume, that for any functionalist model of thought—and most especially any computationalist model—one would have to accept this model of a basic syntactic engine or system and then a secondary semantic engine or system that runs parallel to it, in dependency upon it? I mean, you'd accept this idea that semantics supervenes upon syntax, not only in computers but also in brains? And you'd say it's this parallel stratification of functions that *mechanically* yields thought and meaning—that thought and meaning are, so to speak, parasitic upon the brain's computational functions?

Hephaistos: A fair *précis* of my position.

Hermes: Well, that's something of a problem, then. I see that you want to show how thought can arise from a purely mechanical substrate; but I also see you can't accomplish this by reference to mechanical computation. If you really want to suggest a model for how a system of physical "switches" or operations can generate a syntax of functions, which in turn can generate a semantics of thought, which in turn can produce the reality or illusion of consciousness—well, then you've got your argument totally backward. None of that's what a computer actually does, and certainly none of it's what a brain would do if *it* were only a computer. If that's functionalism, then it really is, as Psyche says, a collection of vacuous metaphors. Worse, they're metaphors based on a phenomenon that doesn't and couldn't actually exist. Software isn't the composite result of uncomprehending competences. Its functions are imposed from above, and are dependent on a higher order of semeiotic content, which is itself dependent upon a fully present teleological and intentional structure of meaning, already containing both syntax and semantics. In any intentional structure, meaning is the ontological ground, not the causal result, and the ontological ground of meaning is the intrinsic intentionality of a mind. It's all an entirely top-down causal hierarchy: from mind down to a fully formed semeiotic system, then further down to coding, then further down still, all the way to those physical switches whose operations the coding determines. The theory you're advancing is worthless. To repeat a point we keep returning to, a physicalist reduction of a phenomenon to purely material forces explains nothing if one can't then reconstruct that phenomenon from principles wholly inherent in that material basis, without invoking any higher causes; and this no computational picture of thought can ever do. Intentional contents—*symbols*—don't emerge from the physical processes in a computer; they inform those processes, and arrange them according to a rational rather than physical order. It is they that create the system's ensemble of competences, not the reverse. Looking from the opposite direction, hoping to discover a causal order rising up from below, one finds instead only the untraversable abyss that separates the intentional nullity of matter—matter as mechanistically conceived, at any rate—from the intentional plenitude of mind. Rather than meaning supervening secondarily upon mechanical functions, those functions are subvenient, so to speak, to meaning. Simply said, computation is ontologically dependent on intentionality and consciousness, so it can't possibly be their foundation.

HEPHAISTOS: As I think I admitted . . . oh, two days ago, it's true that computer software has a human programmer, whereas the mind was programmed by evolutionary history. You're confusing my structural analogy with a genetic analogy.

HERMES: Have you listened to nothing I've said? The issue of the dependency of computer functions on higher causes isn't just a genetic matter of where the software comes from. It's a structural issue through and through. In a computer, nothing like meaning or intelligibility ever *arises from* the coding. Look, you're familiar with John Searle's "Chinese Room" argument?

HEPHAISTOS: I am.

EROS: And I once more, sad to say, am not.

HERMES: Well, the Chinese Room argument is simply meant to show that even a computer capable of passing the Turing test—that is, a computer able to convince even a diligently skeptical human interlocutor that it's in fact a conscious agent—would never actually possess subjective awareness or understanding of its own operations . . . at least, not on the basis of its computational processes alone. It's a simple thought-experiment: Say we designed a program that allowed for an entirely convincing "conversation" in Chinese between a computer and a native speaker of Chinese; would this be the same thing as the computer in some vague sense "knowing" Chinese? To answer this, imagine that instead of a computer there were simply a room in which we've installed a man who knows not a word of Chinese, but who's been equipped with an absolutely infallible set of instructions that allow him, on receiving "input" written in Chinese ideograms through a slot in a door, to produce perfectly appropriate "output," also in Chinese ideograms, even though he has no idea what any of it—the input or the output—means to readers of Chinese. Manifestly, that man would have no grasp at all of the semantic content he's supposedly processing. And that, says Searle, means that there's no intentionality and hence no thinking going on in the translation process, either in the computer or in the Chinese Room, purely on the basis of those syntactic protocols and operational processes.[4]

Eros: And its importance here is . . . ?

Hermes: Well, for functionalists, thought is essentially a kind of computation, and computation, according to this scheme, is the manipulation of symbols purely in terms of their syntactic, rather than semantic, properties. Semantic content comes after. But how can this be, Searle prompts us to ask, when the program is only mechanical and syntactic while thought is also mental and semantic? How does the former become the latter?

Hephaistos: Don't neglect, while you're at it, to mention that it's an argument that's been subjected to some fairly excoriating critique in the past.

Hermes: And none of it successful, really.

Hephaistos: Oh, really? You've complained of Dennett discreetly introducing intentional and mental language into his description of a robot's computational functions, only then to use that language to suggest that what we think of as mental states might be generated by such functions. I take your point. Rhetorical sleight of hand is to be avoided. But note here how Searle has introduced the figure of an already complete conscious self into his little fable, but sealed it off from the systems in which that self is embedded. As many have argued, however, the whole point of functionalism is that it's the system as a whole that understands—that in fact the processing of those symbols by way of their syntactic properties is what yields or accommodates the supervenient semantic stratum of meaning.

Hermes: Which, for reasons already laid out in detail, is absurd. That's simply not what computers or brains do. Systems don't and can't understand anything; only agents can. As for Searle starting with the image of a completely competent mental agent at the center of the system, that's precisely the point: even if the processing of those ideograms were performed by an unquestionably conscious mental agent rather than by a programmed machine, there still wouldn't be any semantic knowledge involved *at any point in the process*, and there'd be no occasion or logic dictating that such knowledge could arise *from* or supervene *upon* the process. This isn't an instance of the "fallacy of composition" either. It's true that you can't deny that a system as a whole has consciousness simply on the grounds that one part of the system lacks that capacity. But the man in the Chinese room isn't part of the system; he *is* the system, and one totally competent to understand semantic information. He's the recipient of "input" and the producer of "output"; even the rules he obeys exist only in his mind, even if they're written down for him somewhere, since the physical medium of ink traces on paper isn't where that information has a functional existence either. Searle really didn't need the conceit of the room at all. The point of the story is simply that a system can manipulate syntactic correspondences and equivalences forever and ever, but this will never produce semantics. That said, though, I'd agree that the Chinese Room argument isn't wholly adequate—unless I'm much mistaken, Searle himself has concluded as much—but only because it still concedes too much to functionalism. In actual fact, computation is devoid not only of semantics, but of syntax as well. This is a problem in most information-theory, as it happens: the failure to distinguish between syntax in the proper sense—that is, the organization of semantic functions in a coherent order—and the mere physical vehicle of information—the physical traces that convey letters, numbers . . . the "bits," that is. A program doesn't run on symbols and meanings, true; but neither does it run on syntactical symbolic relations. It runs simply on bare juxtapositions of tokens of code that, from the "perspective" of the computer (so to speak), have neither semantic nor syntactic features of any kind. There are no grammatical functions in a computer—no verbs, nouns, or predicates, no indicative, subjunctive, or optative moods, no imperatives or interrogatives, no conditional forms. Thought and language are semeiotic processes, yes, but computation is, as we've said, nothing even remotely like such processes.

In the end, neither computers nor brains are either syntactic or semantic engines; there are no such things as syntactic or semantic engines; syntax and semantics exist only as intentional structures, inalienably, in a hermeneutical rather than physical space, and do so only as inseparable aspects of a single semeiotic system. Syntax can't exist prior to or apart from semantics, and neither exists except in the intentional activity of a mind. We can talk of syntax in the abstract, but what we're talking about then is always only an artificial distillate of the complete language of signs that generated it; it can't *produce* a semantics because it's ontologically dependent upon semantics, just as semantics is ontologically dependent on it; it functions only within the system of signs it shapes. Now, of course, to phrase the matter in terms of the "structuralist" school of linguistics, the signifier within any given sign—the actual word in its concrete written or spoken form—may be variable and somewhat fortuitous, but the signified within that same sign—the concept or meaning it indicates—is largely invariable within any given syntax. And, to phrase things in the terms of "poststructuralism," signs possess their meanings only within and by virtue of all other signs. Or, as C. S. Peirce liked to say, signs are interpreted always by other signs, in an infinite web of signification. But what's important is that all of it—all language, all semeiotic functioning—exists only by virtue of the prior reality of intentional mind.

As for the operative structure of computer coding, moreover, even the distilled or abstracted syntax upon which that coding relies has no actual existence within a computer. To imagine it does, as dear Psyche likes to say, is rather like mistaking the ink and paper and glue in a bound volume for the contents of its text. Meaning—syntactical and semantical alike—exists in the minds of those who write the code for computer programs and of those who use that software, but not for a single moment does any of it appear within the computer. The software itself, for one thing, possesses no semeiotic unities of any kind; it merely simulates those unities in representations that, at the physical level, have no connection to those meanings. And, as we've also said, the results of computation that appear on a screen are computational results only for the person reading them. In the machine, they've no *significance* at all. Even the software's *code*, as an integrated and unified system, inhabits no physical space in the computer; the machine contains only notations, binary or otherwise, that cause mechanical processes to produce simulations of the representations for which the software was written. So the functionalist conceit that thought arises as a posterior effect of semantics, and that semantics emerges from syntax, while syntax is generated out of a purely physiological system of stimulus and response—this entire nonsense of an emergent, causally bottom-up hierarchy of meaning and agency—could scarcely be more backwards. When one decomposes intentionality and consciousness into their supposed semeiotic constituents, and signs into their syntax, and syntax into physical functions, one isn't reducing the phenomena of mind to their causal basis; one is dissipating those phenomena into their ever more rarefied, remote, and impotent dependent effects. Meaning isn't a physical result of lower functions; it exists in minds that can extract patterns from their own operations and employ them to produce instruments—books, abacuses, Turing devices, what have you—of notation and information-processing. But this happens within what must remain forever an entirely top-down and indissoluble hierarchy of dependent relations, unified at its apex by intentional mind, or all at once it will disintegrate. In any intentional structure, the more "eminent" reality of realized meaning is the ontological ground of the operations that the structure creates and sets into motion. Simply said, as with language, so with intentional agency in its every dimension: it can't arise from its own contingent consequences.

Hephaistos: That's what you mean when you deny that language evolves, then? I suppose you must, since it's hard to see how language *could* evolve if it must exist as a complete system in order for any of its individual elements to exist. Yet can't you grant that some very primitive primordial form of signification—say, one troglodyte pointing at the rock he wants his fellow troglodyte to hand him so that he can fling it at yet another troglodyte's head—could develop over time into a system of signification that possesses a syntax and a semantics?

HERMES: I can't. I mean, I can grant that the troglodyte's gesture of indicating a rock with an extended forefinger might be a very primitive expression of intelligent life's evolution toward deeper participation in semeiosis. But, to the degree that that primitive gesture really *indicates* something, then symbolic thought is already present in it, as is the semantics of the sign—the symbolic act of "indication"—and also the syntax of relations uniting those signs to a wider intentional context. What can never have been the case is that the syntax pre-existed the semantics, or that either ever existed apart from a system of symbolic thought.

HEPHAISTOS: That's a painfully broad assertion.

HERMES: It seems self-evident to me. Any act of indication is already . . . well, *in the indicative*, so to speak. In the case you adduce, it's certainly an already wholly symbolic capacity that allows the one troglodyte to communicate his meaning to the other: by pointing, he means, "Look at the first physical object to which an imaginary straight line extending down along the length of my finger and then continuing from its tip might extend, and then recognize what action I am attempting to prompt from you in regard to that object rather than in regard to my finger, and then perform that action." There's a subject, an object, an intention . . . even an implicit predicate: "That rock *is* the rock I desire." There's even an implicit verb-function in the act that's transitive in regard to the rock—"Look at . . ."—and so a differentiation between verb and substantive. The entire gesture, moreover, in context, functions as an imperative and has the form of a purposive proposition. All of this, moreover, is subject to both correct and incorrect interpretation—comprehension and misprision.

HEPHAISTOS: A dog can be trained to pick up an object when you point at it. And I don't mean one of our talking Intermundian dogs, but one of those sublunary, terrestrial dogs who cheerfully consort with humans.

Hermes: Yes, because dogs too—like all living things—participate to the degree they can in mind, life, and language . . . in the mental, vital, and symbolic structure of nature. Goodness, even honeybees communicate with one another through an elaborate system of semeiotic gestures. Don't keep slipping back into Cartesian models of animate life; you've come so far, after all.

Hephaistos: Well, I'm certainly not going to convince you that language is a mereological or emergent phenomenon if you're willing to say dogs can talk.

Hermes: Not quite what I said. Dogs can participate in the semeiotic structure of reality in their own mode. Whether they actually talk, as such—well, one doesn't like to speculate, but I like to think they do. You understand me, though: the mereological emergence of semeiosis is unthinkable. This very problem, as it happens, bedevils every attempt by human linguists down there on earth to provide a plausible account of the evolution of natural language. We discussed this, though in a very hasty way, on the very first day of this little colloquy of ours. For one thing, there's an embarrassing absence among human cultures of any such thing as a "primitive" or evolutionarily more elementary form of language—even in communities, such as certain Amazonian tribes, that have had no contact with the wider course of human cultural history for countless generations. Dennett and others have argued that there must surely have been more inchoate forms of language that have simply disappeared—prelinguistic missing links, as it were—but I defy him or anyone else to give a coherent account of what such systems could possibly have consisted in. As yet, no philologist has succeeded even in reverse-engineering any kind of merely "proto-glossal" system of communication that could actually operate on its own, without secretly summoning the powers of fully realized language to its aid. Every attempt to reduce fully formed semeiotic economies to more basic syntactic algorithms, in the hope of further reducing those to proto-syntactic functions in the brain, and those to physiological systems of input and output, founders upon the reefs of this indissoluble top-down hierarchy of language. No matter how basic an algorithm the linguist isolates, it exists solely within the sheltering embrace of a complete semeiotic ecology.

Take, for instance, what theorists such as Noam Chomsky and Robert Berwick think might be language's *most* basic algorithm: the strictly dyadic function called "Merge," which allows two lexical objects to become a single lexical object: the power, that is—conceptual and grammatical—of combining two semeiotic units into a single syntactic set, and then of taking the latter as a semeiotic unit in itself capable of further such combinations. Such mergers can occur between any two kinds of word—noun, verb, adjective, adverb, preposition, article—or between two words of the same kind, but then also between any two merged sets, or between a word and a set, no matter the degree of complexity, so long as the process is a systematic accumulation of purely binary pairings. Most important, these mergers are conceptually connected rather than sequentially, composed from structural rather than spatial proximities, and this allows for hypotactic rather than merely paratactic linguistic arrangements. Thus any syntactically replete sentence—say, "That tall man over there is, as far as I can tell, very old"—consists in a structure of several such "merged" sets, including a few whose contents are not spatially contiguous—such as that containing "man" and "is" or that containing "is" and the merged set "{very old}." I'm grossly simplifying things here, but you get the point. And this triumph of structural over immediate association, whenever it occurred, was something quite novel with regard to normal cognitive processes, and the capacity that permitted it must have appeared rather suddenly within the evolutionary history of language-using animals, more or less all at once.

All right, this seems persuasive enough to me. But, if all of it's so, what was it then that so abruptly appeared in nature? Not a prelinguistic capacity that only gradually developed into a repertoire of linguistic functions. Quite the contrary. It must have been a fully linguistic capacity that could have had no actuality apart from the prior reality of language in its totality. I mean, Merge may be a simple mechanism within a system of signification that's already fully discriminated into verbal and substantive semeiotic functions, each with its distinct form of modifiers, as well as prepositions and declensions and conjugations and all the rest of the apparatus of signification, all necessarily sustained by symbolic thought. The seemingly simple binary structure of the operation in no way qualifies this reality, and makes it no more explicable than a triadic function would be; every act of association between one sign and another is already part of a semeiotic totality. Nor does it make this linguistic capacity's "natural" emergence within what must have been a community of rational natures—since language is never merely an internal psychological reality but must take the form of real communication—any more plausible. So, yes, considered as an algorithm *within* a language, Merge is indeed an elementary process. But, imagined as some sort of mediation between prelinguistic operations of the brain and language-use, it would be a miraculous leap across an infinite qualitative abyss. It can help explain the extravagant fecundity and power and limitless expressive range of language, perhaps, but it definitely can't explain anything about the *origin* of language.

HEPHAISTOS: I'm beginning to think you three are obsessed by an abhorrence of all theories of emergence.

PSYCHE: I think it truer to say that we're convinced that irreducibly formal structures require irreducibly formal causes.

HERMES: Look, if you can devise a model of syntactic and semantic functions absent symbolic thought, or of syntactic processes absent semantic content, or of semantic content absent syntactic relations, or . . . well, please, be my guest. To me, it seems obvious that the parts of language are dependent for their meanings on a hierarchy of associations, but that that hierarchy is possible only because of the prior reality of those meanings. Neither can precede the other in the order of being. And consider how these associations work: Any given sign already has a kind of bifid or dual consistency—the linguistic structuralists were right about that—comprising both a signifier and a signified, in a relation that's somewhat arbitrary *apart from*, and that makes sense only *with regard to*, a prior symbolic intentionality. Then, too, these same signs are meaningful only within that web of interdependent signs we mentioned above—and the poststructuralists were right about this—secured within the system of meaning in part by their differentiations from one another as signifiers. Moreover, only within this system can signs possess that triadic relationship—and here the semeioticians have always been right—of language-user, sign, and thing signified. And all of this is possible only within a community of language-use in which these relations of meaning are shared between intending minds. There's no bottom-up causality rising from the physiological seat of the Merge algorithm up to the pinnacle of this fully realized semeiotic hierarchy. If Merge is the most basic linguistic operation, it's primordial only structurally, not genetically. It's the complexity of language that generates the simplicity of the operation, and not the reverse.

HEPHAISTOS: Well, you just mentioned Chomsky. What would you say of his idea of a universal human grammar—that innate human capacity for absorbing and using language in all its complexity—if not that it's a kind of abstract syntax embedded in the brain, which only secondarily produces semantic content?

HERMES: Produces? Hardly. A child *learns* semantic content. But I still wouldn't call the capacity that makes that learning possible a "syntax" as such. I would call it a predisposition toward both syntax and semantics in their inseparability, a natural semeiotic organ of the soul, so to speak. It's simply the capacity for articulate symbolic thought.

HEPHAISTOS: But wait, surely it's still the basic syntax that's invariable in that capacity? That's what remains the same whether a child learns to speak French or English. In either tongue, what constitutes a substantive function, or a verb function, or a prepositional function . . . whatever you like . . . *that* remains constant. The semantics, however, come afterward. A French child learns to say "*arbre*" where an English child would learn to say "tree," but the underlying grammar of associations and linguistic types precedes that difference and remains unaffected by it.

HERMES: Learning signs isn't the same thing as producing them. Yes, at the level of signifiers, every language differs from every other, but the semantic *content* of a sign, once again, lies chiefly in the signified—the object of symbolic reference, which is fairly stable from language to language, whether that object's called an "*arbre*" or a "tree." Of course, certain words in any language have ranges of conceptual association—nuances, implicit connotations, and such—unique to that particular language, with meanings partly generated by the way those words relate to other words in that tongue's special verbal ecology. Still, though, neither the syntactic nor the semantic dimension of that capacity actually exists in separation from the other, either in a latent or in an expressed state. Look, let's put this as simply as we can. Let me propose four simple rules: First, signs literally can't possess any semantic content except as they're related in syntactic structures. Second, syntax possesses no structure except as a system of organizing existing semantic content. Third, neither syntax nor semantics can exist at all except by way of an intentionality grounded in symbolic thought. Fourth, symbolic thought is impossible apart from the prior reality and inseparable relation of syntax and semantics.

HEPHAISTOS: I see. So language is what? An eternal reality? Wholly irreducible? A collection of Platonic ideas preexisting in the realm of mind? Meaningfulness in itself, communication in itself . . . divine mind in its eternal act of self-expression?

HERMES: Ah, see, you do understand. You merely feign incomprehension.

HEPHAISTOS: Well, I don't feign my incredulity at the metaphysical pretensions in claims so enormous. Leave it to the god of language to turn linguistics into mystical theology.

HERMES: Again, if you wish to contest my claims, do so by demonstrating to me how one can perform a single genuinely linguistic act without the entire superstructure of language already implicitly present within that act.

HEPHAISTOS: [*Throwing his hands into the air:*] You're asking me to use language to get behind language. That may very well be an impossibility.

HERMES: No, I'm asking you to recognize *why* it's an impossibility.

EROS: Excuse me, you two, but we're becoming horridly repetitious here. This whole debate has been diverting, I admit, but what are we really talking about? I've listened and I've tried to suspend judgment when I could, but I still can't see how anyone can take functionalism or computationalism seriously. And I'd say the same, Hephaistos, of any of the other theories you've launched out on the water these past few days, apparently just to see how long they can remain afloat. All I find are bad metaphors, inept analogies, vague similitudes . . . but nothing at all that draws us one step closer to explaining the mysteries of consciousness and mental agency. Is this really what's become of philosophy of mind down there in the terrestrial sphere? Thought as code? What could that possibly mean if translated into a literal claim? What are the coded "bits" in the thought that today's tea was lovely? How are they transcribed or read? Why does that code become aware? And are we really supposed to waste our energies pretending that it makes sense to deny the intrinsic reality of consciousness and intentionality and unity of apprehension, or of beliefs and *qualia* and consecutive reasoning? Are we really being asked to entertain the preposterous notion that what a computer does is even remotely similar to thought and awareness and desire and experience? This is all claptrap. To deny something self-evident is irrational; to deny everything self-evident at once is psychosis. You, Hephaistos, accuse Hermes of mystifications, yet I can imagine no more unreasonable fanaticism than what you've advocated—who can say with what degree of conviction. Does your "rationalism" truly oblige you to doubt the reality of rationality, or to believe that reason is parasitic upon purely irrational physical events, and that it may well be the case that our nonexistent consciousness is only deluded in intentionally believing that there is such a thing as intentional belief? How odd it is that those who hold to such ideas imagine themselves to be the champions of reason and science, when in fact they're obviously nothing but fideists who'd deny their own ears and noses if they thought their odd materialist dogmas demanded it of them.

Computers, forsooth! As my beloved Psyche says, you may as well say an abacus calculates or a book reads or a clock knows the time of day. And Hermes is obviously right: functionalism is an empty metaphor and computational models of mind are just a reversed narcissism. But all of that's an almost trivial concern, given how obviously impoverished a picture of mental acts such theories require. What truly appalls me is how completely they must omit any mention of all those dimensions of mental life that no machine analogy can even obliquely reflect. I mean such ordinary things as dreams and daydreams—the latter especially, perhaps—as well as frissons of aesthetic bliss, or humor, or willful nonsense, or even coherent nonsense of the Lewis Carroll variety. And, of course, I mean the arts, which resist every physicalist philistine's attempts at evolutionary or utilitarian reduction, and the infinite elasticity and subtle variations of creative intelligence, as well as the always changing palette of private sensibility, and the ability not only to make rules to follow, but to violate those rules creatively in ways that somehow make sense—all of which is possible because living minds can understand what they're doing with a tact that no machine could imitate, and with an implicit awareness of more than their immediate context of operation, whatever it is. We can ponder counterfactual or conditional claims; we can reason by way of judicious violations of reason followed by deductive reconstructions of our arguments. We can intuit a truth in its entirety before we've established it ratiocinatively, and then act upon that imaginative prompting to discover things we might never otherwise have considered. Think of Einstein's discovery of relativity in a sudden flash of insight while gazing at a clock-tower from a moving tram. And then there's our power of evaluation, of judgment, in light of transcendental values that appear nowhere within the physical universe but that guide us in every moment of mental life—the Good, the True, the Beautiful. . . . I agree with every point Hermes has just made about the ontological priority of intentionality in regard to semantic content and syntactic structure, and agree also that it tells us a great deal about the structure of language and of meaning, and hence of meaningful thought. I agree also that thought is semeiotic and computation absolutely is not. Yet there's an even more radical sense in which intentionality informs mental actions, and any truly scrupulous phenomenology of mental acts discloses it: the most basic dynamism of thought—clearly irreducible to physiological processes of stimulus and response or, to use that ghastly jargon, input and output—is a kind of *a priori* orientation of intellect and will toward the totality of being as infinitely desirable intelligible truth.

HEPHAISTOS: [*Shaking his head morosely:*] Ah. Here we go round the metaphysical mulberry bush . . . again.

EROS: Even the most ordinary mental acts, like recognition or judgment or simple attention to some object in one's surroundings, depend on this rational appetite for the absolute, this full orientation of the thinking and adjudicating intellect toward a total intelligibility at once more original and more ultimate than any proximate object of knowledge, any propositional attitude, any inquiry, any finite project of the will; and yet, it's only in the light of that finality beyond finite finality, and the indeterminacy that it sets free within the mind, and the incessant further longing that it prompts in regard to every finite step toward fuller understanding, that recognition and judgment and engagement in the world become possible. Neither, moreover, this transcendental appetite nor the necessary openness of mind and will it produces is a form of computation. Indeed, both are in principle repugnant to computation, as they're the very antithesis of the controlled algorithms of input and output that alone constitute—and, of course, limit—computational processes. No machine ventures out from itself in desire—in love—toward the whole of reality, engaging with all the particular things of the world under the canopy of transcendental yearnings and acts of judgments. In living minds—gods, mortals, what have you—knowledge becomes actual only as a result of that prior orientation toward the absolute. In rational natures, there's an immanent and indeterminate power of discovery that's prompted into action by the rational will's transcendent determinacy toward being as a whole and as one—toward an immaterial but always urgent realm of *values*—and for this reason we're capable of discoveries for which no algorithmic potency could possibly prepare us, and we enjoy an intrinsic capacity for unlimited novelty of apprehension, without any prior constraints on what we may find or create. We can come to know because we want to know, and we want to know because we already know more than we understand. This is also why gods and mortals write poetry and compose sonatas, why we're both able to invent things that nothing in nature adumbrates, why we can always revise even our most fundamental understandings of reality, and so forth. Simply said, thought isn't computation, not only because computation is an abstraction produced by intending intellects out of a prior semeiotic system, but also because thought in its essence is an "open system" of discovery and therefore precisely what computation is not.

HEPHAISTOS: And leave it to the god of love to make all thinking into an erotic ecstasy.

EROS: But that's exactly what it is.

HEPHAISTOS: Then I've definitely been doing it wrong.

III

Panpsychism

PSYCHE: [*To Eros:*] My love.

EROS: [*To Psyche:*] Yes, my soul?

PSYCHE: He's not yet ready for this topic.

HEPHAISTOS: Indeed I'm not. Perhaps if instead of tea we'd had cocktails, I might be, but as it is . . .

PSYCHE: [*To Hephaistos:*] But don't think you can avoid the issue. Sooner or later, we'll have to address the structure of mental agency in its totality if we're properly to understand how mind, life, and language constitute one irreducible phenomenon.

HEPHAISTOS: I'm all atremble with anticipation.

PSYCHE: Are we finished, though? I mean, with this incessant argument? As far as I can see, in four days we've taken not a single step in the direction of a convincing physicalist reduction of mind to lower causes. All we've done is find a large variety of ways to arrive at the same *impasse.* Must we continue going around and around *ad infinitum?*

HEPHAISTOS: [*Gazing off ponderingly into the sky for several seconds, then turning his eyes to Psyche again:*] No, it's time we stepped off the carousel. I see that your conviction regarding the irreducibility of mind is quite imperturbable. And I grant that all the obvious evidence favors your position. I mean, I can't really claim to believe there's no such thing as belief, or to think my consciousness illusory, but at the same time I also see the problems inherent in viewing such mental phenomena as emergent from a non-mental physical reality. Moreover, I grant both that functionalism is impossible to prove and that, even if it could be proved, it really wouldn't explain how inner experience or any other distinctive feature of mental agency is possible. It probably is, as yet, more metaphor than clear concept. And you're right, I don't really believe that computers can think or have experiences, whereas I'm quite certain I do both. And, since you roundly reject the Cartesian view—"substance dualism" I think it's usually called—I can't use its deficiencies against you. So yes, at the dialectical level I admit defeat—or at least am willing to make a strategic withdrawal—and so we may indeed bring this phase of debate to an end.

PSYCHE: Well, then, if I've actually convinced you of the logical solvency of my arguments against physicalist reductionism, then it seems you're now obliged to let me attempt to argue that mind is the ground of reality, and that infinite mind is the source and end of finite mind, and . . .

HEPHAISTOS: Not so fast.

PSYCHE: That *was* our agreement.

HEPHAISTOS: Ah, but recall also that I proposed *two* paths away from the arrant supernaturalism you defend: *either* a convincing mechanistic account of mental phenomena—which I concede I can't provide to your satisfaction, or even to mine perhaps—*or* a non-mechanistic account of matter that doesn't require the abandonment of physicalism. The latter course is yet to be pursued.

EROS: [*With a groan:*] And how long is that likely to take?

HEPHAISTOS: Let nothing you dismay, my pinioned friend. It shouldn't detain us very long at all. There's really only one possible theory here, and it comes in only a few variants.

HERMES: Panpsychism?

HEPHAISTOS: *Précisément.* After all, you three have worked so tirelessly to convince me that the concept of a phenomenon irreducibly emergent from the physical order is incoherent, and that mental agency would have to be just such a phenomenon in a mechanistic cosmos, that you've damned near convinced me. But for me this still raises the question of whether we might abandon physicalist reductionism not by vaulting upward into the empyrean of the Platonic ideas or by diving down into the fathomless depths of the mind of God, but simply by replacing the mechanistic paradigm of nature with another still situated on the immanent plane. I think we've established that none of us here has much affection for Cartesian dualism, even if we don't agree on why. I'm perfectly prepared now to jettison mechanistic materialism along with the immaterial soul, so long as it doesn't oblige me to take leave—premature leave, at any rate—of my commitment to metaphysical naturalism. You, dear Psyche, mentioned some censorious remark of Galen Strawson's not long ago regarding those who call intrinsic consciousness illusory. Well, as you also know, he's as thoroughgoing an antagonist of supernaturalism as there is, and he regards panpsychism as the most rigorous, plausible, and logically parsimonious form of naturalism. Moreover, you said something a few days ago that I've come to appreciate more and more as our debate has proceeded. You said that you object in principle to all dualistic answers to any questions for the simple reason that, if there remains within any phenomenon a duality that can't be resolved into a more original unity or shared principle, then nothing has been explained, because a paradox isn't an explanation.

PSYCHE: Indeed. Unless we can name a more original ground of non-repugnance that dissolves the duality, we've only invited an infinite explanatory regress.

HEPHAISTOS: Very well, then, you've persuaded me of that too. Once we get past the Cartesian picture altogether, and all the dilemmas generated by the concept of a material nature inherently contrary to mentality—and vice-versa—what forbids us from considering panpsychism . . . or "panprotopsychism," as some prefer to call it? What obliges us to deny that matter in itself might *naturally* possess a kind of consciousness, or at least a kind of inchoate disposition toward consciousness, that's qualitatively continuous throughout all the levels of material organization, and that merely achieves a particularly complex and capacious order and intensity in brains? Mind need not *emerge* from matter in the strong sense if matter's always already invested with consciousness. Perhaps consciousness is, as they say, "equiprimordial" with matter, never wholly absent from any of the elementary constituents of the world—because, that is, it's a fundamental physical property of the universe, a brute fact like electromagnetism, rather than a late product of mindless machine forces. Maybe there's always some degree of awareness, some very simple form of inner pathos, present wherever one physical reality affects another. Perhaps, when one stone strikes another, that inner vibration that passes through each isn't strictly a third-person event as we're accustomed to thinking it is, but is also a kind of faint inner first-person shiver of experience. Perhaps there's an elementary level of physical interaction where any strict division into the objective and the subjective hasn't yet become possible.

HERMES: I'm not even sure what that means.

HEPHAISTOS: Aren't you? And you claim not to be a Cartesian dualist. It seems to me there can be—and, as it happens, there are—any number of ways of conceiving of the matter. One has simply to see all material things as possessing, in addition to all their other attributes, a "pathological" *property*, the power of registering a dim inner apprehension or affect—the barest phenomenal agitation, that is—as a result of outer realities. You might speak of this as a psychical property or as only proto-psychical, depending on how closely you imagine it must resemble consciousness as experienced in fully developed cognitive structures like organic brains and neurologies. And perhaps it's simply this pervasive basic property of physical reality—neither purely mechanically objective nor purely spiritually subjective, neither wholly third-person nor wholly first-person—that accounts for the reality of mind in organisms. There's then none of the mystery of strong emergence here; there's only what Psyche calls structural emergence. That's one way of thinking of it, at least.

Another is to think of consciousness as a necessary concomitant of any information-state. After all, a pattern of neurons firing constitutes an information-state in a brain, and that state is naturally realized in the form of conscious experience. Perhaps this isn't unique to cerebral events. David Chalmers, for instance, has speculated that maybe every such meaningful configuration of material reality is—or is accompanied by—some kind of experience, whether elementary or developed. And then, of course, IIT—that is, "Integrated Information Theory"—is all the vogue today.

HERMES: What's that?

HEPHAISTOS: Well, its principal inventor is the physician Giulio Tononi, but it's won the support of a great many prominent scientists. Max Tegmark is a robust promoter. It's even made an avid convert out of the neuroscientist Christof Koch, and persuaded him to abandon his long arduous expedition through the ganglial forests of the cerebral cortex in search of the headwaters of consciousness. It's not a theory about the *origins* of consciousness, however, since it starts from the panpsychist premises that information is always already consciousness and that, since any integral relation of matter qualifies as information, consciousness is ubiquitous. That also means, so the theory goes, that consciousness can be measured quantitatively, since it's directly proportional to the degree of information that exists in integrated systems. The greater the complexity of the system, the greater the awareness it contains. Tononi calls the quantum of measurable consciousness "Phi," and has proposed ways of objectively determining how much Phi any composite system possesses. As far as he's concerned, *any* truly integrated system—a brain, a computer, the internet, but also a barometer, a photodiode, a geranium—has *some* calculable Phi value. That means that consciousness is qualitatively the same in all things in its essential nature, differing only in terms of intensity and capacity, which naturally increase along with the complexity, synergy, richness, and ordering of cognitive information in organized wholes. Or, more simply, the greater the degree of integration, the greater the "Phi-value," and the greater the Phi-value, the more conscious the system. This means also, perhaps, that higher-level integrated systems are concrescent totalities that subsume less conscious levels into themselves, so that, say, a brain comprises smaller integral unities that on their own would be, so to speak, lesser instances of consciousness; but the consciousness of any system lies at the level of greatest integration, so those potentially independent instances of consciousness are, as it were, absorbed into the fuller functions of the brain.[5]

For myself, however—taking my cue from Psyche and seeking to avoid so much as the appearance of an unresolved dualism—I think I prefer to formulate panpsychism in a more explicitly monistic register: something along the lines, perhaps, of the physicist Arthur Eddington's argument that consciousness and perhaps other mental states may very well be the intrinsic nature of what the sciences can measure only extrinsically, in terms of physical properties. That's to say—let me be clear—not that consciousness is a property in addition to other material properties, but rather that those attributes physics knows from the outside, under such aspects as mass or charge or momentum, simply *are*, from the inside, fundamental forms of consciousness. Physics, that is, can measure only behaviors, not essential natures. Bertrand Russell said something very similar: that from the physical side our sciences discern merely the extrinsic structural relations and dispositions of things, but not their intrinsic, categorical natures; those we know only in our own experience of consciousness. And so he proposed that the most basic reality of all things was neither mind nor matter, but rather some single *tertium quid* that encompassed the properties of both.[6]

PSYCHE: I'm glad you made that distinction. I mean, I'm glad you qualified your view as a monism, as otherwise one might think you were talking about some occult propensity within matter, merely hidden behind its properly material aspects. Still, one does wonder with respect to all these formulations whether it's anything more than a residual habit of thought—the tendency to imagine the fundamental reality of all things as a kind of objective *stuff*—that qualifies any form of panpsychism as a metaphysically physicalist or naturalist position. For myself, I have considerable sympathy for real panpsychism, at least in its classical form, as a kind of idealism and cosmic animism and vitalism, and I've been quite open about my belief that all that exists, the material no less than the mental, has the structure of thought and is most originally mind, and that mind is the ground and end and pervading source of all that is.[7] In a sense, classical theism necessarily implies a kind of panpsychism, since in that picture everything exists within and is pervaded by an infinite mind, and so there's a kind of spiritual depth—a kind of *logos* or rational ground—that knows every individual thing from within; and surely that inward knowing is also, necessarily, a kind of self-consciousness within that thing. At least, that's my metaphysics and I'm sticking to it; but that's not something you need worry about. What I find odd, though, is your ungainly attempt to produce a panpsychist view of reality that somehow also qualifies as a physicalism or, at least, naturalism—which, I have to say, I find no more plausible or coherent than the physicalist reductionism I've spent these past few days rejecting. Does such panpsychism really escape the contradictions of dualism and materialism? Or does it simply prevaricate and equivocate its way past those contradictions without actually solving them? I find it especially mystifying when one phrases the matter in terms of mental "properties" inhering in matter. I mean, why is that more coherent than it would be to reverse the equation and say that the "physical" or "material" subsists as a property of mind? Given the mysterious nature of the alliance, how can we tell the substance from the mode?

HEPHAISTOS: I suppose I could try to answer, but I sense that those are only rhetorical questions.

PSYCHE: Look, Phaesty dear, I expect basic misunderstandings from analytic philosophers—indeed, I expect little else from them—but you've existed for aeons and should have a more judicious perspective on these things. Obviously, the physicalist panpsychist is still thinking in residually Cartesian categories, and so simply can't imagine that something as *concrete* and *substantial* as matter could be derivative of something as *ghostly* and *ethereal* as mind. As I've noted, this is the reverse of the antique notion that mind or spirit, as the source of being and form and purpose, is infinitely more powerful and substantial than matter, while matter, the more it's reduced to itself alone, is ever more shadowy and abstract and evanescent . . . even essentially nonexistent as anything more than pure potency. You mentioned Galen Strawson, who's a fair-minded critic of the reductionist project; but he too grows strangely censorious about what he calls "fairytales" regarding "immaterial souls." For him, souls can be conceived of only as Cartesian "thinking substances" merely haunting the bodies they animate, while matter is to be understood as an extended substance invested with strictly physical or quasi-physical "properties." But then Strawson wants to speak of consciousness simultaneously as a fundamental reality, neither an emergent nor a composite phenomenon, and yet also as something discretely present in individual sentient beings as subjective mental agency. *Alors, mon ami, voilà: l'âme elle-même.* What's he talking about if not the soul? Really, at this point we're discussing dispositions or potentials in matter so far outside the mechanistic paradigm that terms like "physicalism" or "naturalism" have been rendered otiose, since apparently they exclude nothing—except, perhaps, some hazy pictures of an anthropomorphic God and an ectoplasmic soul inherited from the religion of the nursery or the philosophy of Descartes. It seems rather pointless so vigilantly to guard one's metaphysics against incursions of supernaturalism in a world that can accommodate sentient sand.

HEPHAISTOS: Now, now, caricature isn't an honorable dialectical method.

PSYCHE: All I mean is, if you're willing to concede that matter is already in some sense mind, what then is your vaunted "naturalism" other than an arbitrary prejudice—an obstinate resolve to believe that the primordial ground of mind is not a mind, but only some mysteriously "physical" property? Why is this a more plausible position than a straightforward idealism, or than an Aristotelian picture of reality as a mindlike structure of inherently rational relations? What remains in this picture of matter, in the case of the first version of panpsychism you mentioned, that makes matter the most plausible candidate for the most basic of cosmic principles?

More to the point, as I think I've said, it doesn't make any sense to speak of consciousness as a "property." It isn't one of an object's various specifiable or measurable aspects, such as mass, spin, extension, liquidity, charge, and so forth; it's not merely a fixed quality, mode, accident, disposition, or potency, which is perhaps expressed in differing degrees—as mass is, for instance, according to different magnitudes of gravity—but which otherwise is simply another way of describing that substance or event. A property is an invariant fact about something—what its potentials are, principally. Consciousness is at least conceptually severable from the substance with which it's associated. Not so, say, mass. A croissant devoid of mass is simply a nonexistent croissant. A brain devoid of thought, by contrast, is easily conceivable—and often encountered. This is because consciousness is always a specific *act.* When I kiss my husband, that fact isn't a physical attribute inhering in me, but is instead a very particular moment of agency, with a beginning and an end, possessing clear phenomenological contours. And we've already discussed what the contours of mental agency are: an indivisible apperceptive unity and intentionality, a logically prior and transcendental simplicity that organizes the many into one, a subjective vantage formally constitutive of the totality it perceives, particular movements of intentionality toward particular objects under specific aspects within the embrace of a transcendental movement of intentionality toward absolute values, subjective awareness in the form of *self*-awareness, abstraction and conceptuality, and so forth and so on.

Consciousness *never* exists in the abstract, much less as some kind of discrete physical property—any more than running across a garden or writing the libretto of *Don Giovanni* is a physical property. And, as it's an act, it's also always something accomplished by an agent, with a real private interiority. It's not merely a pathological or affective disposition or potency in material things that may or may not be actualized. Even if there were such a potency, it still wouldn't explain mental agency in all its indivisible dimensions; we'd simply have yet another story of "strong emergence" before us, no less fabulous and incredible than any other. Even if something inchoately disposed to consciousness could exist in the absence of the whole structure of mental agency, the arising of that structure from that mere affective potential would still be miraculous. I mean, none of us thinks matter is inherently contrary to thought; none of is a Cartesian, as we've already established *ad taedium;* so presumably we all assume that the *potentiality* for thought isn't something extrinsic to the physical. Fine. But, for panpsychism to serve as a truly physicalist rather than classically idealist theory, it would have to posit the presence of real agency all the way down. Is every proton a kind of "micro-psyche" then, with some natural predisposition toward a horizon of transcendental values, and an intentional orientation toward other protons under specific hermeneutical aspects, and a unity of apprehension that composes the plurality of cognition into a unified and unique subjective vantage? I shouldn't think so. But, if it were, this fact still answers none of our questions. We're merely deferring the question of mind to the subatomic level without fundamentally qualifying it, in the vain hope that it may grow so very small that it will vanish away altogether. We're left with the same paradox: one and the same atom, say, possesses two seemingly radically disparate aspects, each of which is the logical inversion of the other: to abuse those terms again, a "nomological" and a "pathological" dimension. One side of the thing (that bound by physical laws) is objective, deterministic, mechanical, and empirical, while the other (that possessed of qualitative awareness) is subjective, intentional, teleological, and transcendental. But the interaction between the two sides is no less mysterious for being atomized; the terms of unity remain as mysterious as they are at the macroscopic level. That's a paradox I can barely tolerate when applied to myself—but to my breakfast?

Hephaistos: Again, beware of caricature. Few naturalist panpsychists, if any, believe every brute amalgamation of matter to be conscious. There has to be some kind of systematic integration of the parts that's capable of creating a distinct information-state.

Psyche: But there'd also have to be some kind of combination of discrete subjectivities as well, wouldn't there? As I say, it's meaningless to speak of consciousness as anything other than mental agency, in all its glorious intentionality and subjectivity and so forth, so we can't simply be talking about the integration of diverse material things into enclosed systems. If a thermometer is in some sense conscious, however dimly, it must also have some unified vantage from which to *experience* information. Wouldn't that require that higher integrations of information must somehow involve some strange, magical merging of countless private vantages into a single private vantage? Integration? Well, a brick wall is an integrated composite of bricks; but composition isn't combination, and combination (as far as we know) doesn't produce indivisible simplicity and unity. Isn't this the same thing as the idea of "mind-dust" that William James once considered, and doesn't it suffer from the same deficiencies? James himself used the wonderfully apt metaphor of a hundred distinct feelings arranged together like a deck of cards: no matter how often the cards are shuffled and rearranged, they never admit of any violation of their several privacies. How could all those incommissible interiorities be fused into some organism's interior self? How can all those micro-psyches become a single soul?[8] Diverse agencies can, of course, produce a unified *effect*—as when, say, forty voices are gorgeously blended and interwoven in the polyphonic totality of Tallis's *Spem in alium*—but the agencies producing that unity remain obstinately plural and discrete. And there's really no way around this. If my consciousness is the product of the accumulation of something really like consciousness in each particle of matter, then there are only two possibilities for how this works, both of which are incoherent. Either my consciousness is the fusion of all those lower "minds" or my consciousness is a kind of supervenient effect produced *in addition to* all those combined "minds." In the former case, the privacy and unified integrity that makes consciousness what it is would be entirely violated and "mind" would vanish from the physical ingredients upon which my mental agency supposedly relies. In the latter, my mind would be an instance of strong emergence, and so something like magic.[9] No, as ever, mental unity and simplicity can't arise from physical plurality and divisibility; that unity must be the prior reality—the formal cause, the radical source—that imposes a single perspective upon the material aggregate. And this "combination problem," as I believe it's known, seems to me an absolutely insuperable barrier to any physicalist version of panpsychism.

Hephaistos: Perhaps. But the very term "integration" is ambiguous.

IV

Integration and Neutral Monism

HEPHAISTOS: Look, I suppose you've adequately made your case that a purely mechanical integration of the physical constituents of the brain wouldn't yet constitute mental unity, and also wouldn't seem to account for the mind's natural states and operations. But IIT isn't a theory about mechanistic matter, and the combination of the inner pathos within one material thing with the pathos within another needn't work according to the logic of mechanism. After all, the supervenient level of mind in this theory is arguably something that occurs at the level of the information-state of a system, not at the level of its material composition. That integration of inner states of consciousness could operate by degrees not of complexity but rather of intensity, in the way that an increase in the sheer number of photons in a closed room increases the illumination of the room.

PSYCHE: Oh, that's a dreadful analogy. The intensity of the light in the room is still a third-person, physical, quantitative *effect*—and one that's composite rather than combinatorial. Photons don't blend into larger photons. By the same token, an increase in the number of persons in a room may quantitatively increase the total amount of consciousness present, but it still doesn't combine their minds into a single yet more intense consciousness. Don't mistake aggregation for real integration. And, anyway, we aren't talking about photons; we're talking about instances of mental agency, each of which depends upon a subjective simplicity and unity more radical than the mere physical indivisibility of a photon, and one that's also indivisible from all the other features of mentality. This is why the claim that the most complex instance of integration in any given system subsumes lower levels of consciousness into itself is essentially absurd; it's a magical notion. None of this gets us past the division between the nomological and the pathological, or between quantity and quality, nor is it any more plausible than tales of brute emergence. Not that this matters very much. The most basic flaw in Integrated Information Theory, understood as a theory of *mind*, isn't its failure to overcome the combination problem (though it certainly does fail), but chiefly its dependence on an elementary verbal confusion.

HEPHAISTOS: [*With a placid scowl:*] How so?

PSYCHE: It seems fairly obvious. The very notion that there's some sort of necessary concomitance between "information-states" and consciousness is just a category error occasioned by an enticing homonymy. It's a venerable rule of predication, you know, that certain words—or certain homonymous terms—admit of univocal, equivocal, and analogical acceptations. And, if one fails to make these distinctions properly, one's liable to arrive at fairly specious conclusions. I know the word "information" is in great currency these days—in physics, the life-sciences, philosophy, computational theory, and so on—and many of its uses are remarkably nebulous. But at least two senses of the word can easily be isolated: sometimes "information" means simply "data," objective facts given "out there" concerning things, processes, events, and so forth; at other times, it means the cognitive contents of subjective knowledge "in here" *about* those things, processes, events, and so on. If there's any analogy between these two uses, it's of only the most tenuous kind. Really, they're probably equivocal. In nature, structure, and logic, objective "information" and subjective "information" are radically distinct, but IIT depends upon their tacit conflation in one largely undefined concept. This isn't a meaningful theory; it's just a bizarre amplification upon a trivial lexical happenstance.

It's also not a project for scientific research. Really, the equivocity here at the level of what the sciences can investigate is absolute, and goes well beyond the difference between objective and subjective knowledge.

In physics and the sciences generally, integrated "information" doesn't as a rule refer just to data; it means also any negentropic order able to maintain the past and constrain the future, which is to say, structural systems capable of persisting by temporarily resisting entropy and functioning with some kind of circumscribed internal coherency in controlling the exchange of internal order for external disorder. In matters cognitive, however, "information" is intentional meaning, aspectual perception, semeiotic content, private experience, and so forth. Now, admittedly, both kinds of information can be attributed to one and the same phenomenon, but never—as the schoolmen used to say—*in unica voce.* A bound volume of *Paradise Lost* can be described as a physical integration of materials and molecules, with a certain structure that can be measured in terms of such properties as mass or charge; in that sense, its "information" as a physically integrated system is objectively constant and uncomplicated. The letters on the page can even be quantified as a kind of physical "syntax"—at least, in the problematic information-theory sense of that word. Then, however, there's the very different subjective knowledge not just of those facts, but of the purely intentional and semeiotic "information" that constitutes the actual book as a book and poem as a poem in a hermeneutical space. There's absolutely no point of connection, real or possible, where these two meanings of "information"—the negentropic and the epistemic—achieve identity with one another; and neither of them *explains* subjective knowledge as such. When David Chalmers or the champions of Integrated Information Theory suggest that every information-state might be accompanied by some kind of consciousness, they're really saying nothing except that negentropic arrangements of matter are also instances of mental agency. That's simply not a rational intuition, or even an assertion with any intelligible content; it seems to be to them only because they've confused the objective and subjective senses of the word "information," collapsed an equivocity into a univocity, then simply failed to see the disjunction that their theory has obscured. Yet it's precisely that intractable difference in meaning that, in a sense, *is* the philosophical problem of mind, and it can't be conjured away by a supposed "science" based on a verbal confusion. No information theory can be also a theory of consciousness. To think you can get from the one to the other is, yet again . . .

HEPHAISTOS: Let me guess: the pleonastic fallacy. It's so good to meet old friends again.

PSYCHE: There is, of course, a radically different kind of integration, one that doesn't simply give rise to conscious mind, but that's actually identical with it.

HEPHAISTOS: Let me guess: life.

PSYCHE: Even so.

HEPHAISTOS: See? You've been singing this song for so long that I've learned *all* the lyrics. [*Breathing deeply and momentarily gazing up into the now darkening sky:*] Look, I can see how the specter of an unresolved dualism in any physicalist theory of mind—emergence, supervenience, even the kind of panpsychism that talks about consciousness as a property or that posits an integration of discrete *quanta* of consciousness—makes your preference for the language of formal causality reasonably defensible. I accept all that.

HERMES: Then you've come a long way.

HEPHAISTOS: Exactly what "form" is, of course, is as unclear as what "information" is. Even so, I also mentioned neutral monism. Why can't we say that what we identify as the material and the mental are only *apparently* different orders of being, and that the properties we ascribe to them are in fact, respectively, the exterior and interior aspects of a single reality?

PSYCHE: It's an attractive alternative in some ways, but one that seems to me still to be hampered by an unreflectively materialist prejudice.

HEPHAISTOS: In what sense?

PSYCHE: Just that it's still an attempt to resolve the difference between the mental and the material by way of a metaphysics of "stuff"—of some kind of element or basic, extended cosmic constituent—which is a strategy already incompatible with any plausible account of mental states. In a sense, every attempt at a unified philosophy of mind involves some kind of monism. I mean to say, unless one really embraces substance dualism, one's likely to be either an idealist or a materialist, and yet what does either metaphysics really mean in regard to our normal understandings of either matter or mind? The idealist must believe in a concept of mind and of mental experience vastly unlike our usual concepts of such realities, one that probably erases our commonsense distinctions between the physical and the mental, and even our sense of what qualifies as "real." The materialist, by the same token, implicitly advocates an understanding of matter that's anything but genuinely "materialist" in the modern sense, however he or she might resist that conclusion, inasmuch as no truly mechanistic materialism can explain the generation of mental phenomena out of mindless extension and energy. But let's set all of that to one side. The truth is that I've come to think that neutral monism is more an evasion than a serious proposal, and probably just another unresolved dualism concealed. It's also a strategy for rescuing *something like* materialism—that is, again, a metaphysics of "stuff"—from the seemingly inescapable immateriality of mental phenomena. It's still a theory about the "properties" of some extended substrate of reality. But it doesn't work. The unity of mental agency, for instance, is just as repugnant to fusion in some hazy intermediary substance poised meaninglessly between matter and mind as it is to straightforward materialist reduction. Mind can have no basis that isn't simply mind itself, and trying to get around that fact by a retreat to some undefined and intrinsically undefinable quasi-material *something* gets us nowhere. Here again, a restatement of the problem of mind masquerades as its solution. We may want to say that outward, measurable physical properties *just are* mental properties in their essential, inward nature—that, say, this much mass at this velocity *just is* this kind of experience—and yet we can't describe either in terms proper to the other, so we still have to ask how their unity is grounded, and in what, and whether that ground is simple or complex, subjective or objective . . . I mean, which side of the seeming antithesis is better able to accommodate the other? Or, failing that, what could possibly accommodate both?

HEPHAISTOS: Would you have the same reservations regarding, say, the wave-particle duality of quantum physics?

Psyche: No—another defective analogy. Yes, of course, the wave-particle duality is a great mystery, but it's also one firmly situated within the realm of quantifiable physical entities . . . or potentials, at any rate. The most essential principles of the quantum landscape, with all its fantastical topographies, may forever elude the comprehension of human beings and gods alike, but in principle we can imagine a physical ground or context somehow simpler than and comprehensive of both wave and particle functions; at least, we can coherently imagine it *as* a physical reality. In the case of the sort of neutral monism you're advocating, by contrast, we're dealing with a paradox not of structure or measurement, but of the entire governing logic of the phenomena in question; and that's not so much a paradox as a bottomless rational chasm. I doubt, though, that you want me to rehearse all the arguments of the past four days again. The more I think about it, truth be told, the more convinced I am that whatever this neutral *something* is that seems to possess the characteristics of both matter and mind while being reducible to neither can't, logically speaking, resolve the contradictions between our commonsense notions of material and mental qualities. Once one's posited neutral monism, one's still obliged to say how it annuls those contradictions without also annulling those qualities. For, if it can't, then we've merely produced an empty paradox: somehow this *je ne sais quoi* is mental without being mind and material without being matter while also somehow being simultaneously mental and material without inherent contradiction. And yet, even after we've made that dazzlingly dissonant claim, the difference between the mental and the material refuses to slink away in shame; rather, it remains there before us, defying us, proudly mocking us with its obdurate insolubility. And *this* means that one's still obliged to wonder whether this unnamed something's inherent properties are more like those of "mind" or those of "matter." And *this* means that one's simply presented anew with the choice between idealism and materialism. Yet there's no choice to make: in the end, idealism, in its classical forms, is the only possible answer. Panpsychism on any other terms is simply a distraction.

Hephaistos: [*Tapping his fingertips meditatively upon the tabletop for several seconds before speaking:*] What if we were to abandon this "metaphysics of stuff" as you call it, and instead were to try to reconceive nature not in terms of substances at all, let alone substrates, but as composed from events, moments of experience, comprising both objective and subjective dimensions, but . . .

Psyche: I'm more than willing to consider all forms of panpsychism that start from the side of experience and thought; but do realize that all of them will just turn out to be more an idealism than a materialism, once again, and so effectively just idealism.

Hephaistos: [*Nodding:*] Come to think of it, you're right. Let me curtail my own line of reasoning there. And yet it seems to me that the idea of something more original than the distinction between subject and object is conceivable.

Psyche: Yes, indeed, but that something will always turn out, on final analysis, to be something like mind rather than something like mechanistic matter, as only the former can unite subject to object. Subjectivity can "objectify" itself—for instance, in taking itself as the matter of thought—but objectivity can't "subjectify" itself. As Russell says, the physical is the realm only of extrinsic structural relations. Nothing on that side of things, so to speak, can overcome the difference between subjectivity and objectivity, the pathological and the nomological, physical quantities and phenomenal qualities . . . "it" and "I."

It's so much easier if you're willing to entertain the idea of the One or God or *Brahman* or what have you. This current generation of naturalist or physicalist panpsychists—Galen Strawson, Philip Goff, perhaps David Chalmers in certain moments—they're all quite perceptive when it comes to the failings of the reductionist and eliminativist projects, and it's wise of them to want to find a better naturalism, hospitable to actual mental phenomena. But they must first rouse their sessile imaginations out of the conceptual swamp created by the mechanical philosophy; they must move beyond thinking that the only possible alternatives to their views are mechanistic materialism and Cartesian dualism; because, even in rejecting those alternatives, they allow the barren general morphology common to both—mechanical nature, bodiless mind—to continue to constrain the alternatives they propose. Hence, they get only as far as the idea of what Goff calls a "physical universe whose intrinsic nature is constituted of consciousness,"[10] whereas their only real hope for a solution to their quandary is to think instead in terms of a *phenomenal* universe whose intrinsic nature is constituted by *mind*—not, that is, a physical order composed from some sort of fabulous mind-element, but a spiritual and physical order that subsists in one infinite mental agency.

HEPHAISTOS: The mind of God. Again.

PSYCHE: The very one. You know me. I regard that indivisible unity—that simplicity—that makes subjective consciousness and intention and thought possible as one and the same in all minds, and I believe that it's by virtue of that indwelling spark that we participate as subjects in that infinite source in which all things exist and consist. All things, that is, both as objects and as subjects, are as it were contractions or crystallizations or prismations, facets or modes or phases, of that one light. How, though, is that more improbable than what naturalist panpsychists propose? They're willing to grant the presence of consciousness in all things, and they believe that it can somehow be gathered into personal unities. All to the good. But, as we've said, consciousness isn't a property that exists in abstraction from mental agency as a whole, and so the only coherent panpsychism is one that acknowledges the ubiquity not just of some kind of receptive inner pathos in things, but also of mind in its every aspect—the one divine mind, reiterating its own oneness and intentionality in each finite mind's unity and intentionality, repeating its inexhaustible rational order in the concrete structure of the universe, expressing itself in countless emanations, of limitless variety, while remaining ever one. It's all or nothing, you see. I don't believe that minds can be composed from atoms of mentality, so to speak, or that the profound unity of mental agency can arise from a prior diversity fused into one; either view is contradictory. I certainly do believe, however, that infinite mind can produce countless reflections and manifestations of its inexhaustible richness in finite things, and that one and the same "I think" can produce all the diversity of finite, conscious minds, and can constitute the indivisible depth of subjective unity within each of them.

Hephaistos: I don't need an entire metaphysics. I already know you're a kind of Neoplatonist or Vedantist or what have you. I'm not capable of being quite so exotic in my thinking. For me, the issue comes down to a set of far humbler questions, such as whether the fullness of mental agency in all its dimensions *really* has to be present for there to be any glimmer of awareness in a thing. If I were fully convinced of that, I might very well at that moment retreat from the field of battle.

Psyche: I don't think you need to be convinced; I think you merely need to admit to yourself what you already know. I think it's clear that intentionality—simply in the form of *attention* to a specific end—has to be present for there to be consciousness. In fact, as I mentioned some days ago, to be conscious is always also to *attend* to one's own awareness; to be aware of anything is simultaneously to be aware of oneself as aware, and that's already an intentional act. So too, reciprocally, intentionality requires consciousness; and then both depend upon the absolute unity of subjective apprehension; and so on. If you can imagine any of the features of mental agency as existing in real isolation from all others, please tell me how, because to me it's something on the order of trying to say how the squareness of a square box can exist in the absence of shape, substance, and spatial extension. This intrinsic indivisibility of mental agency may be the best proof of all that mind can never have a material basis. Mind, in its true depth, as actual subjective consciousness, is necessarily based only on itself *as* subjective consciousness, logically prior to any objective ground.

Hephaistos: Ah, we're back to that "testudinal" principle of yours.

Psyche: We are. It's turtles—or the inner "witness"—all the way down. Mind can rest only upon mind; it can have no other foundation.

V
The Witness

Psyche: I don't mean to sound doctrinaire. I simply believe we've exhausted all other possibilities, and I think that logic and experience alike, when consulted honestly, lead to only one sane conclusion. Somehow we habitually fail to see—or train ourselves not to see—just how . . . how *uncanny* the structure of consciousness truly is. Mind you, I take your point that we'd probably never accomplish anything at all if we allowed ourselves constantly to be seized by wonder at that uncanniness. Even so, it *is* wonderful. This doubling of mind in the mirror of its own nature, this illumination from within, this reflexivity of the mind's knowledge of itself in knowing the world, without which there could be no consciousness at all—well, it's all so inexplicable in physical terms that, at least in those moments when we lower our defenses, it should simply overwhelm us with its obviously numinous nature.

Hephaistos: Numinous?

Psyche: Nothing less. At the ground of mental agency there's a pure knowing, a pure "I think," a pure subjectivity that you'll never ever reach by way of cerebral modules or neurology or any other physical vehicles of consciousness. As Coleridge noted, in every mind there are two seeming certainties: that I am aware of a world existing outside myself and that I am aware of myself perceiving it; and, while the former can perhaps be dissolved by analysis, the latter cannot.[11] And I'd say it's indissoluble precisely because it's the most original reality of all.

Hephaistos: Because you think any other ground to that doubling, as you call it, leads to an infinite regress?

Psyche: Yes. Look, I know it isn't especially novel to observe that conscious mental states are always necessarily conscious of themselves. Even Aristotle took note of how the mind grasps itself as an accidental concomitant of the act of thinking of something else.[12] And certainly the phenomenological tradition put great emphasis on it; Franz Brentano and Edmund Husserl, for instance . . .

Hephaistos: I hope you'll excuse me if I admit that I still fail to find quite the profound significance in it that you do. Really, I'm not even sure how constant a reality it is; I'm fairly certain that, when I'm thinking about something, the thought "Ah ha, by Jove, I'm thinking!" doesn't typically cross my mind, and if it did, I'm fairly sure the experience wouldn't strike me as *numinous*.

Psyche: [*With a deep sigh:*] I'm obviously not talking about a propositional judgment regarding your actions, much less a psychological preoccupation with yourself. Brentano, for instance, always differentiated this inner perception of perception—or, rather, this "apperception"—from any sort of psychological introspection, which is of course quite fallible. When we're thinking or perceiving, we don't focus our minds on some concrete *thing* in addition to that thought or perception within us, as though our mental agency were just another object of the senses; rather, we perceive our perceiving immediately in perceiving anything, and it's because of this always more original field of simple pure awareness that we're actually present to ourselves as knowing and thinking selves, in the way that an automaton or threshing-machine isn't. For Brentano, this double intentionality simply *is* the structure of conscious mental agency.[13] And that's what I'm talking about: of its nature, the conscious mind is always at once transparent to itself and also somehow detached from itself. I maintain that the attempt to treat this as some sort of product of physical systems is simply a fantasy. The "I" of the "I think" within each of us has a depth that can't be the effect of some exterior impression upon a material organ; rather, that "I" is the very light that converts such impressions into the private awareness of a living mind, as at once consciousness and intention and unity.

HEPHAISTOS: I expect you know that many philosophers of mind—at least, among those who acknowledge this apperceptive redoubling in consciousness—ascribe the phenomenon to some "higher order" function or process within the brain's operations. That is, sensory impressions become conscious experiences in us precisely when we make them an object of a "higher order thought" of an assertoric kind—that is, a judgment that something is or isn't really the case. Or maybe they're rendered conscious by a "higher order perception" that monitors lower order processes of perception. Or a "higher level experience" that, on attending to the lower order, conceives an affective awareness of it. In any of these cases, the higher order function itself remains unconscious unless it's made the object of a still higher order assertoric judgment or proprioceptive perception or autoaffective experience . . . or whatever. For some, like Dennett, that "illuminating" operation is probably just a higher order "representation," a kind of report by the brain to itself regarding what it's doing in something like narrative form, and so is entirely dependent upon the possession of language.

PSYCHE: Each of those higher order theories still implies an infinite regress toward a ground of subjectivity that can never be reached. But, tell me, do those who think in terms of higher order representation then deny that animals have consciousness—presuming, I mean, that language isn't found among animals?

HEPHAISTOS: Many "higher order" theorists deny phenomenal consciousness to animals, and in fact to human infants. Some deny it even to persons with autism, but I would never . . .

PSYCHE: How very obscene. It amazes me that anyone could fail to tell the difference between automatic responses to stimuli, on the one hand, and behaviors that clearly entail affective experience and emotional responses, on the other. But I'm not going to dignify that sort of moral obtuseness by dwelling on it at length. I'll simply say again that these are all versions of an infinite regression in pursuit of an explanatory principle precisely where it can never be found. How could any higher order function or faculty render anything conscious except by being itself already conscious? And what would explain that, except a higher conscious function or faculty, and then another higher still, and so on forever? To me, these attempts to ground private awareness in something somehow prior to consciousness or to treat subjectivity as the posterior result of some kind of objectivity are all still rather on the order of saying that a room full of mirrors sees itself simply through the accumulated force of all its specular recapitulations. Consciousness comes first or it comes not at all.

I'd also note that it can't simply be the *objective* act of taking perception as a cognitive or propositional object that makes perception also conscious of itself, any more than one makes a wall aware of itself by thinking about it or talking about it or experiencing it. This "double intentionality"—this perceiving or thinking about one's own perceiving and thinking—is a unique attribute of consciousness precisely because consciousness already subsists in its own act of self-awareness, and not in any source of another kind. As the great Ādi Śaṅkarācāryaḥ insisted, the non-conscious can never be the cause of the conscious; presentations are known to the mind only in the light of the *Ātman* within us, whose nature is pure self-illumination, absolutely simple, flooding the mind with its own radiance. The inner witness, the *sākṣi*, the apperceptive "I"—*that* can't be perceived as an object, because its whole nature is absolute subjective knowing; it doesn't exist as an object, but only as subjectivity: pure self-illumination, pure pellucid awareness as such—*caitanya*—revealing itself in revealing everything else, a light that's known solely in making all else shine forth.[14]

HEPHAISTOS: Whenever you shift into a Sanskrit idiom, I know your heart is taking wing.

PSYCHE: Well, I do believe Indian philosophical tradition addressed the conditions and mysteries of consciousness far earlier in history, and with considerably greater subtlety, than its Western counterpart did. Not, that is, to discount Western traditions regarding the mind or *intellectus* or *nous* or spirit within each person, and its relations to the absolute or God or what have you. As we've repeatedly said, I'm a

Neoplatonist if I'm anything. When, say, Meister Eckhart spoke of the "little spark" of the divine at the soul's center or, say, Suhrawardī wrote of the *isfahbad* light of self-knowledge reigning over the soul and underlying consciousness—or, for that matter, when Kant spoke of the transcendental ego, which is only the condition of knowledge and never its object—and so on and so forth, and when they all repeatedly differentiated this inner ground of awareness from any material organ of perception . . . well, the same basic intuition was being expressed.[15] But Indian thought at a very early date was already considering the specific issue of subjective self-awareness, and of its dependence upon itself, at a depth as yet unexplored elsewhere. Śaṅkarā was especially brilliant on the matter, but so too was Rāmānuja—who was perhaps better on intentionality—and so in different ways was Kumārila Bhaṭṭa, especially his treatment of the *svaprakāśa*—the self-illumination—of mind, as well as so many others, including theorists in the Kashmiri Saivite tradition; but the question of the inner witness appears in Indian tradition as early as the Upaniṣads . . .[16]

Hephaistos: Where that inner light is *Ātman*, spirit, which is one with *Brahman*, godhead. Yes, we're all familiar with these things. And that, of course, is where you want to lead this conversation in the end, isn't it? From the irreducibility of mental states to the indwelling light of mind to the infinite mind of God in which we all live, move, and have our being?

Psyche: I won't deny it. But, of course, it's not just the interior mystery of consciousness that informs my convictions regarding the real nature of mind. There's also the mindlike structure of the world, and especially of life—which, I think, it's time at last for us to discuss again, more thoroughly than before.

Look, my dear good friend, sweet Phaesty, days have now passed and it seems to me that we've come nowhere near to a plausible physicalist explanation of consciousness: certainly none coherent enough to occasion any doubt in me regarding the nature of mind. You've offered me plenty of charmingly vapid metaphors and nimble verbal tricks, a veritable cornucopia of circular arguments, one or two items of nonsensical metaphysics, but absolutely nothing that seems to me as rational, as logically parsimonious, or as in accord with the evidence of experience as is a forthright idealism that recognizes mind as the primordial ground of all else. So, then, can we draw the curtain on this part of our debate? Have I convinced you that my views—the views of the three of us—are sufficiently reasonable that we've won the right to argue *for* mind, in its fullest expression, as the very foundation of reality?

HEPHAISTOS: [*Pondering briefly, looking upward at the sky, and then rising from his chair:*] You may proceed. You haven't convinced me that you're right, but you have convinced me that you've cogent reasons for thinking you are, and I suppose that that's all you had to do. I've been working under the assumption that I needed only to achieve a stalemate to win the day, if not the board. Now, though, that my gambits have failed to pen you in, I see it was to your advantage all along that I try to play to a draw. On these issues, every ambiguity redounds to the benefit of the commonsense view of things. But let's adjourn for now and begin again tomorrow afternoon. The evening's come, the stars are shining overhead like an ocean of gems, teatime seems an age ago now, and the goblets of the banquet-table call out to us in dulcet tones. I'm weary, thirsty, and eager for the pleasures of the night.

[*Exeunt omnes.*]

DAY FIVE
Soul and Nature

I

The Semantics of Life

The garden is awash in the mild light of early afternoon. Psyche *is alone at first, standing at a slight distance from the benches and evidently deep in thought, idly holding her rose blossom so that its petals gently touch her lips. Enter* Eros, Hermes, *and* Hephaistos *at a leisurely pace; after a moment, each seats himself on the bench he occupied on the first day of the debate. A butterfly of exquisite rainbow-hues—quite unlike any earthly butterfly—drifts languidly across the garden on outstretched wings and then disappears amid the shadows of the trees beyond.*

Hephaistos: [*After two minutes or so of waiting:*] Is that the same flower that started this interminable colloquy of ours?

Psyche: [*Turning around with a smile:*] The very one. If it were a terrestrial blossom, of course, down there in the death-haunted world, it would have begun by now to fade and wither. I have to say, it continues to inspire a number of thoughts in me.

Hephaistos: Naturally. We've already established that it's a boundlessly suggestive flower. One need only glance at it, apparently, to discover God hiding among its petals.

Psyche: All living things are boundlessly suggestive, if only you're willing to heed them. [*Crossing to the bench where Eros is resting and seating herself beside him:*] Contemplating it again—its color, its fragrance, its sheer beauty—has made me think that perhaps one good definition of the modern era might be "the reign of pure syntax."

Hephaistos: [*With an ironical smile:*] Which means what?

Psyche: It means the dominance of a syntactical ontology, as it were, which is an ontology of death. It's the prejudice—as we discussed some days ago—that the really real is the realm of abstract quantifications and unyielding structural laws, and that realms of higher organization and relation and agency—the semantics of life, so to speak—are secondary and accidental, and can be understood only by reduction to those more general abstract laws. Well, what's that if not the metaphysical triumph of syntax over semantics, of dead matter over organism—and, for that matter, of physics over biology? At the dawn of modernity, the full nihilism of that vision of things was held in abeyance only by the fanciful and fragile contrivance of substance-dualism: alongside the universe of dead mechanical matter, early modern thought posited a parallel universe of living soul and divine spirit . . . but there's no need to rehearse that tale again. The dissolution of that gossamer-thin partition was inevitable, just as it was inevitable that one side of the division came to devour the other. And there's where things stand now. Just as certain theorists find it possible to think of language—and so of rationality—in terms of basic syntactical functions, to which semantic content is only secondarily added, so we've all learned to think of the bare quantitative measurements of physics as Galileo imagined it as the foundations of the semantics of life, so to speak, and to think that the laws of life are simply emergent from the laws of physics, and even to think—most preposterously of all, perhaps—that mind is reducible to functional processes for translating stimulus into behavior. As I say, an ontology of death—of mindless mass and momentum without intrinsic qualities as the really real, and of life as merely a certain set of transient structural and chemical conventions . . . life and mind and meaning and experience as just so many ephemeral and anomalous *fata morgana* illusions hovering over an infinite ocean of death.

Hephaistos: Such bathos. If your objection is that the picture's too grim, that's not a particularly incisive argument. Perhaps reality is very grim indeed when confronted in its bare essence. It needn't correspond to our emotional needs.

Psyche: My objection, Phaesty, is that it's explanatorily empty, and indeed clearly wrong. It fails entirely to capture or elucidate a ridiculously enormous range of the phenomena of real existence, and offers no plausible account of how such an ontology could possibly yield life, mind, or meaning. A cosmos reduced to a certain set of ghostly abstractions, disembodied Euclidean geometries, impalpable magnitudes, spectral trajectories . . . well, it's all perfectly fine as a kind of abbreviated notation or useful distillation of the world's most minimal structural principles—world *qua* calculus, world *qua* syntax—but when mistaken for the really real it becomes a principle of negation and of willful obtuseness. Hans Jonas pointed out many decades ago that, from the perspective of the physics of matter, even the knower of reality knows himself or herself only as an object within a world that is pure unknowing, and so is obliged to view mind and life as somehow redundant in the explanation of nature. The mathematical and purely material world, so conceived, isn't the world of even basic persistent organic form—the form through which matter flows in constant streams of metabolism—but is instead one in which that matter's flow is calculable only in terms of discrete lines of force. In the mechanistic world, actual intrinsic unities—as opposed to extrinsic integrations—don't exist. In fact, even a unified principle or ground for such integration is impossible in such an order. Nowhere is there even, in any meaningful sense, a place for organism as an intrinsic reality—a place for form. The vital integrity of organisms is found only at another topology, so to speak, another level, altogether distinct from the continuum that can be exhaustively specified by mathematics alone; all that are visible to the mechanistic gaze are accidental events of composition, confluent lines of force, persisting amalgams, but not substances governed by inherent rationales; living, changing organic form, as distinct from transitory configurations of particles, is purely phenomenal and so invisible to the mathematical gaze.[1]

Hephaistos: Come now, physics is well aware of living systems.

Psyche: It's aware of the physical properties of their embodiments, yes, and of the matter and energy they process, but it takes account of them only in terms of its own minimalistic principles—with which the phenomena of life are necessarily compatible, naturally, but which they far exceed in their creative lawfulness. Physics elucidates organisms only as local expressions of general physical laws . . . structural amplifications of mere matter in motion . . . but that will never provide a sufficient explanation of the integrated complexities or the special laws that make life *life*. At most, the laws of physics inform us of the structural constraints governing the physical substrate of the phenomenal world. Over against all that, I propose we should seek a properly semantic ontology, an ontology of life, not simply as some Romantic protest against mechanism—though as that too—but as the only way of establishing a method that can actually take account of reality as it truly presents itself. Life, at every level of organic integrity, is composed of hierarchies within hierarchies, complex intentional and relational systems of both upward and downward causation, all in a constant state of controlled, flowing, organized becoming, sustaining itself amid change by making use of material resources for ends that aren't actually strictly material.

HEPHAISTOS: [*Grimacing:*] Purposiveness, my prophetic soul informs me, will be today's topic.

PSYCHE: Probably. And why not? You know, Robert Rosen, brilliant man that he was, argued that we should reconceive our methodological presuppositions altogether, and should cease to think of fundamental physics as providing the general framework for our understanding of nature, or to think of biology as just one special expression of the general laws of physics; instead, he proposed, we should recognize the laws of relation and organization found at the level of life as our primary and general indices of the nature of reality, so that biology becomes our general paradigm and physics is demoted to a special case of *its* expression—one dimension of life's complexity . . . its minimal limit-conditions, so to speak. So too, the machine metaphors we apply to the universe should be abandoned *in toto*, at which point we'll see that these fundamental organic principles are found at every level of the real structures of the cosmos, all the way up and all the way down—even down to the level of the apparently protobiotic. In the case of biology in particular, this would mean many revisions of method, such as abandoning the fruitless attempt at understanding phenotypes merely as the calculable results of genotypes—which, in any event, we now know not to be the case—as well as abandoning our desire to find in the gene some kind of basic "particle," as it were. And we should shed the fundamentally misguided habit of thinking of organisms—whose "non-fragmentable wholes" are far more than the sums of their parts—in terms of machines, which are eminently "fragmentable," and can be disassembled and reassembled without loss of function. Above all, we should stop thinking of life, which is an "open system" capable of creative innovations *within itself*, as if it were a closed system of physical determinism governed solely by extrinsic pressures and internal efficient forces. In the end, he argued—and with considerable sophistication—the simple, spare, elegant but minimal formalism of physical syntax can neither adequately adumbrate nor reductively explain the incalculably rich and subtle interrelations of the semantics of life.[2]

Hephaistos: [*Rubbing his brow:*] I do tend to think of the fundamental as, well, *fundamental.* If physics is the limit-condition of all things, surely in some sense it's the foundation too.

Psyche: Every structure rests upon some kind of simple foundation; that doesn't mean the foundation explains the structure—at least, not obviously any better than the structure explains the foundation. Remember my defense of the older view of causation—plurivocal causation, as it were—in which the material "cause" is at once a necessary predicate of any substance and yet also subordinate to and dependent upon the whole architecture of causation—an architecture, that is, of which by itself it can provide no adequate account but apart from which it is nothing at all. Think of physics as the science of material efficiency—the syntax of sheer physical quantity. For the fanatical physical or molecular reductionist, explanation begins and ends there, in the orderly efficiency of things that are ontologically—not just incidentally—dead. He or she believes that, since the laws of physics pertain to a world of lifeless entities, and since organisms are composed of those entities, life as such is nothing over and above those laws of lifelessness, and we shouldn't confer on organic systems any special status to distinguish life from non-life. All this really proves, however, is that the laws of life aren't contained in the laws of physics, though the laws of physics are embraced within the laws of life.

HEPHAISTOS: I still find it easier to think of life as governed by special laws wholly within the embrace of the general laws of physics than to think of physics as describing special laws embraced within the more general laws of . . . organism. A cosmic organicism . . . is that what you're proposing? Teleology as a fundamental cosmic law?

PSYCHE: I'd hardly be the first to say as much. Look, Phaesty, life is arguably the very shape of our experience of everything. I've spoken of the mindlike structure of things repeatedly, but I might just as well call that structure "lifelike." The syntax of things never really exists independent of their semantics. At every level of life we seem to encounter cognitive and intentional systems, with real content and an orientation toward meaningful ends, right down to the cellular level.

HEPHAISTOS: I won't enter into the old debate again about the difference between real purpose and the appearance of purpose produced by evolutionary attritions; I'll simply remind you of it.

PSYCHE: And I'll remind you that I think the latter notion just another variant of emergence-as-magic.

HEPHAISTOS: Of course, so let's leave the issue there for now. What I want to understand is how this cosmic organicism of yours illuminates the realm of the inorganic. What of lower levels of inert matter? What of the billions of years of cosmic history before the dawn of organic life? Is all of that also enveloped in these universal biological laws you speak of?

PSYCHE: Yes. Obviously I'd say—as I already have, I think—that matter is never, and has never been, dead; that life and mind have always been present, in the very predicable structure of all things, suffusing and quickening and summoning matter toward organic vitality and order; and that, in every epoch of cosmic existence and at every level of causality, life and mind are already always supplying the underlying and informing and guiding laws animating the whole.

HEPHAISTOS: And again I say: Oh, dear. A mystical Romanticism of the purest water.

PSYCHE: I've no objection to the description, though I regard what I'm saying also as the severest rationalism. For days, thou waggish god of forge and fire, we've been discussing altogether ludicrous attempts to explain or—more ridiculously—to *explain away* the evidently real phenomena of conscious life and mental agency; all of those attempts have been inspired not by logic or scientific discovery, but solely by an arbitrary devotion to a mechanistic metaphysics, which is itself nothing more than a positively cancerous metastasis of what was originally little more than an investigative method—and an overly idealized method at that, which could never be practiced with absolute rigor. That, to my mind, is a mystical materialism of the purest water—or, worse, a materialist fundamentalism. What I'm proposing, by contrast, is a model that, though it may look outlandish from the perspective of certain modern orthodoxies, I believe to be the only one capable of making sense of countless phenomena that are evident and undeniable, but irreconcilable with mechanism.

As I've already noted, there's no concrete ingredient to be found in the purely physical history of any organism or natural object that would look like form or antecedent finality to a skeptical gaze; nowhere in the inventory of a natural phenomenon's discrete physical causes will one discover either the presence or absence of "higher" causes. Then again, fair's fair, there's no phenomenon that exhibits the *absence* of finality either: nothing exists that doesn't possess a defining limit of its ultimate possibilities, as well as some inherent disposition toward realizing those limits; in that sense, everything has an aetiological structure that includes an antecedent finality among its inherent predicates. You can say, if you like, that this appearance of purpose is simply the fortuitous result of a mindless evolutionary process; but, then again, what could evolution select that didn't already have this structure? Why argue, though? If higher causes exist and appear to view anywhere in nature, it's at the level not of physical quantities, but of systems and hierarchical structures.

Hephaistos: This is all fairly obvious. That's precisely why talk of final causation is usually regarded as adding nothing to a scientific description of reality.

Psyche: Well, that's just the mechanical superstition rearing its misshapen head again; and it's an empirically false claim, since purpose is presumed ever and again in the life-sciences, whether acknowledged or not. The issue, however, is whether those systems and hierarchies could emerge from a reality truly devoid, at *any* of its causal levels, of the purposefulness they exhibit; and, for all the reasons we've discussed, I still say strong emergence of that sort is incoherent: if purpose is present at all, it is so from the beginning, as a real disposition or potency in even the lowest levels of reality. As to the invisibility of higher causes among the purely physical elements of a phenomenon, you're mistaken: it's certainly *not* obvious to everyone. A good number of philosophers and scientists still think of form and finality as something on the order of physical forces that, like phlogiston or the cosmic ether, have been expelled from our view of nature as the sciences have advanced. Much of the dogmatically gradualist Neo-Darwinian orthodoxy that still reigns in the evolutionary sciences, despite its many logical and evidentiary problems, is motivated by the fear that to entertain the possibility of any process of evolution less grindingly mechanical than a slow, mindless succession of isolated chance microevolutionary mutations cumulatively preserved by natural selection would be to invite something beyond the physical back into our picture of nature. Perhaps it would, perhaps it wouldn't, but there's no excuse for refusing to think the matter through. The gradualist view, as often as not, isn't a scientific truth, after all, or even a hypothesis susceptible of demonstration; it's a view obedient to a particular metaphysics that it isn't really incumbent on anyone to believe, even the most unyieldingly "naturalist" of scientists. As a reductionism, moreover, the Neo-Darwinian synthesis is a convincing alternative to the older view only to the degree, yet once more, that it can plausibly reconstruct the phenomena of life from a bare material basis without secretly relying on the very principles it supposedly excludes, which I doubt is possible.

For instance, it occurs to me that the most revealingly inept attempt at a demonstration of the gradualist view ever recorded has to be that computer program that Richard Dawkins devised many years ago, meant to show how a particular phrase with seemingly intelligible intentional content—in that case, Hamlet's "Methinks it is like a weasel"—could be produced by a succession of supposedly random, non-intentional mutations starting from a mere assemblage of uncoordinated letters. That's of course impossible, except perhaps as a random coalescence within an infinite series of iterations, which would dissolve again in an instant because it has no intrinsic principle of persistence—no actual semeiotic unity—that would prevent it from passing by like the shadow of a cloud—a weasel-shaped cloud, if you like. But, within the strictly quarantined virtual space of the program, Dawkins had written Hamlet's phrase directly into the coding as a target to be reached, and had set in place a prospective protocol for retaining or eliminating mutations with respect to that target.

HERMES: So, essentially, he'd programmed the process with a final and a formal cause.

PSYCHE: Exactly. He was trying to show that a full semantics could emerge out of a bare syntax, so to speak, and yet he very nearly demonstrated the reverse: that a syntax has no actuality except as fashioned in the service of a prior semantics. All he'd accomplished was a primitive simulation of an Aristotelian picture of the genesis of intelligible order, not the emergence of order out of sheer "noise"—to use the "informatic" term. He'd induced a negentropic result out of an apparently entropic basis through the secret imposition of a prior negentropic grammar: formal constraints and a teleology, that is. It's amusing, of course, but what's genuinely fascinating about the experiment is that, had he intended it as a demonstration of something like an Aristotelian structure of causation, it could be accounted a rousing success, at least as providing a suggestive demonstration of how a fairly rapid and complex evolutionary process—which is more in keeping with the scientific discoveries of the last eight decades or so than is strict Neo-Darwinism—might be simulated by a governing intentional structure, without any need of direct interference in the discrete steps of the process. The same is true too of more sophisticated computer programs for generating, say, the patterns of spider webs—which still must start from a concept of what webs are and do—or programs for cellular automata such as John Conway's "Game of Life": all of them are set within sealed virtual environments and then governed by sets of already highly informed functions, and are invested with some general prior purpose for directing the progress of cumulative selection, all of which—just to note the obvious—must be imposed upon the computer's operations by a programmer. Needless to say, the gigantic question of how life transcribes itself semeiotically in the genome and then, in the next phenotypic generation, reads itself out from the genome again is neatly avoided by a process that already possesses encoded information as its basis. All of which just goes to show that, where a great deal of "information" is set free within a controlled system, highly informed consequences follow. None of it, though, vindicates a gradualist picture of the origin or structure of life.

Something similar might be said, it seems to me, about attempts to create life from chemical scratch in laboratories—which, I confidently predict, will never come about. I can imagine, however—not foresee, but merely vaguely imagine, in an entirely fantastic key—a future biotic technology so advanced that scientists could take the basic genetic templates of living organisms as models and reconstruct them, and then maybe construct organic cells from basic chemical ingredients, and perhaps even somehow fabricate genomes from organic matter and so forth and so on, until they had built an organism. If they were to do so, however, that would give us no cause to believe that life could be the spontaneous effect of unstructured chemical reactions, merely occurring in a state "far from equilibrium"; we would still have only a demonstration of how formal and final causality produce integrated structures.

HEPHAISTOS: You're not going to suggest we abandon the inductive method altogether and simply retreat to Aristotelian science again?

PSYCHE: Do pay attention, Phaesty. Pure induction may be the *ideal* of modern method, but the sciences can only ever approximate that ideal in practice. It's more a governing piety than an exact discipline. I've also noted, however, that Aristotelian "aetiology" was never a physical science in the modern sense and shouldn't be mistaken for one. So no, I want the sciences to use whatever methods are productive, but also to acknowledge that the method always constrains the results. The investigative practices of the early modern sciences, when they function solely as regulative instruments for isolating discrete areas of investigation from every larger interpretive context, definitely allow for an enormous range of discoveries and advances in predictive power on the parts of researchers. After all, Newtonian physics suffices for many calculations, even if it only approximates the accuracy of quantum calculations; so too the mechanical fiction can deliver useful results despite its inability accurately to reflect the laws of life. But this usefulness is entirely dependent on the humility, tentativeness, and ascetical narrowness with which, as a matter of simple practical necessity, those methods are applied. When they cease to be regarded as mere useful fictions, conveniently simplifying reality and authorizing only very limited conjectures, and are instead permitted to metastasize into a metaphysical claim about the nature of reality, they can yield nothing but ridiculous category errors. At that point, the sheer wanton grandness of the ambitions they prompt renders them impotent. The moral, I suppose, is that a local falsehood, prudently employed, can often grant us knowledge of certain universal truths, but that a universal falsehood can only blind us to all local truths. One can come to a better pragmatic understanding of this or that particular reality by treating it "as if" it were something else. But, when that "as if" becomes a general theoretical judgment about reality as a whole, all particular results become indifferent masks of a single speculative paradigm, and anything that might not naturally fit into the picture thus produced either becomes invisible or is distorted beyond recognition. It may be very helpful, for instance, to investigate specific organic functions found in nature as though they were mere machine functions; but if one forgets the difference between organisms and machines, then one has lost the ability properly to see the limits of one's knowledge. And, without an appreciation of those limits, one can't even know what it is that one *truly* knows. So all that I want the *culture* of the sciences to abandon is a *metaphysical* orthodoxy that's certainly inadequate as a total model of the structure of life and consciousness. So long as those arid dogmas still subtly restrain the scientific imagination, certain empirical realities are likely to remain invisible and certain enlightening questions are likely to remain unasked. Happily, there are signs that a paradigm-shift may already be underway in the life-sciences.

HEPHAISTOS: Well, maybe, but let's not exaggerate. I mean, do you truly believe we can discern real intentionality at every level of cosmic existence?

PSYCHE: I certainly think the life-sciences find it at every level of living things; and I think the capacity of material things for organism—for life and mind—is written into the very deepest structures of the physical order, if only because of my by now well-established aversion to all narratives of strong emergence. And then there are those elephants. . . .

HEPHAISTOS: [*His brow furrowing:*] Elephants?

II
Spirit in Nature

PSYCHE: You know, one thing that many religious and scientistic fundamentalists tend to have in common is a keen desire to place hard limits on the degree to which mind can be found in nature. The former, in order to preserve what they consider a proper sense of human exceptionalism, claim that most of the higher mental functions are unique to humankind among terrestrial organisms, and that reason, a rich emotional inner life, linguistic capacities, moral intuitions, culture, and countless other aspects of mental life belong solely to the "rational soul" infused only into *homo sapiens.* The latter also, however, so as to preserve what they regard as a proper sense of the mechanistic and mindless constitution of the physical order, claim that those same functions appeared only very late in evolutionary history and that they remain excruciatingly rare within the fabric of nature, and are perhaps for that reason uniquely human. And yet, when we look at the living world—animal and vegetal, at least, both at the level of the organism and at the level of its cellular processes—what we actually find look much more like differences of degree, varying intensities of reason and intention, as well as pervasive evidence of cognition and even of consciousness. I utterly despise the tendency to deny the plain evidence of an inner life in *all* organic beings, not just humans. In fact, let's add it to my index of errors and call it the *exceptionalist fallacy:* that is, the notion that the question of mind concerns only humans and gods and angels and the like, but not other forms of life. The realm of the fully mental doesn't vanish at the boundary between human and brute creation. As I've said, I'm no doctrinaire Aristotelian. I deny even that language is unique to humankind and "higher" beings. We know of many other terrestrial animals who clearly employ methods of reasoning, and even of abstract thought, and that communicate in a manner that only foolish prejudice prevents us from recognizing as in some sense linguistic and semeiotic; and we know that animals possess inner lives, emotions, susceptibility to pain and sorrow, pleasure and joy. The evidence of cognitive research among various species is incontestable. They're capable of love or resentment too, as well as hope and despair. Did you know that parrots can be driven mad by grief at the death of a loved one? That dolphins can commit suicide?

HEPHAISTOS: Sadly, I did. I'm quite partial to both parrots and dolphins, as it happens.

PSYCHE: Which does you great credit. Both species also, apparently, can employ proper names for other persons—human, delphine, or psittacine. And . . . well, anyway, this notion of an impermeable partition between the supposedly uniquely rational powers of humankind and the supposedly irrational nature of all other animals is a coarse superstition, to which only the invincibly ignorant and morally obtuse still cling. Many an elephant is a far more rational agent than many a man. It's also a false division that makes it all the harder to conceive of how mind and world are related to one another. The reality is ever so much more fascinating and beautiful: that mind pervades all things, and expresses itself in countless degrees and in endlessly differing but kindred modes, and that we all belong to a vast community of spiritual beings—some of whom are quadrupeds or are equipped with wings or fins or prehensile tails or tentacles.

Goodness, consider the extraordinary intellectual capacities of grey parrots, with their demonstrated ability to grasp abstract concepts, or of New Caledonian crows, with their skills at making tools and at solving complex puzzles with a great many successive steps. Magpies—like humans and other great apes, as well as dolphins and elephants—have no difficulty in recognizing their own reflections in mirrors. I can't say how many species have been observed exhibiting cultural transmission of newly acquired skills or practices. As for language—well, I don't want to argue definitions here, but I refuse to believe that the complex systems of communication and elaborate grammatical structures of, say, the songs of chickadees and of countless other birds don't qualify as linguistic in principle . . . or the songs of whales, or the extraordinarily communicative sounds and gestures employed by prairie dogs, or the elaborate semaphoric choreography of bees . . . I mean, in the case of those dancing bees there's certainly a semeiotic system at work: a syntax, a semantics, a clear distinction within each of the signs used between signifier and signified, semantic associations forged by structural rather than spatial proximity, as well as precise objects of reference. And, of course, there are animals capable of learning language from humans—Koko the gorilla's two thousand or so hand-signs allowed for a huge range of expressions of emotions, desires, inner experiences, dreams, memories. And then, as I say, those elephants. . . . Consider the day in 2012 when Lawrence Anthony—you know, the "elephant whisperer"—died at his house on that huge South African game preserve—one that's more than a day's journey in size—and the herds of rogue elephants he had rescued and tended all arrived within a couple of hours to pay their respects . . . and to mourn, I suppose. They'd been away for well more than a year, many of them, and then there they all were. How did they know? What summoned them across all that wilderness to attend their dying friend? Perhaps a kind of telepathy? Then too, it seems that elephants communicate with one another over vast distances with the use of sounds well below the threshold of human—and perhaps divine—hearing. Even plants seem to respond intentionally to environmental signals, and to use such things as mycorrhizal networks and aerosolized chemicals to communicate warnings and other kinds of information to one another.[3]

And why should this be surprising? If anything, intentionality in nature seems to be more original than any of its organic expressions. As Raymond Ruyer once noted, an amoeba digests without a digestive tract and reacts to its environment without a nervous system.[4] The reality of intentionality precedes even the physical organs we associate with stimulus and response. Nervous systems appeared in evolutionary history not as fortuitous vehicles for a new organic power; they were fashioned by a prior operative disposition, which summoned its own physical occasion into existence. Even the cells in the bodies of organisms are complex intentional systems—though we'll get to that anon, so I'll stop here. Suffice it to say, though, that when I speak of mental agency, I'm not talking simply about a human—or about a human, dæmonian, angelic, and divine—attribute, and I'm certainly not talking about something that's susceptible of absolute divisions of kind. I'm talking about a pervasive reality of organic life, at every level.

HEPHAISTOS: It may surprise you that I happen to agree with at least part of what you say. I would go at least so far as to include all apparently spiritual beings, gods no less than human beings and corvids, in one and the same category: we're all animals together.

PSYCHE: Yes, yes we *are* animals—*animated* beings—*psychical* beings—*souls.*

HEPHAISTOS: [*With a laugh:*] Curious. The same evidence that some might adduce as proof that mind is reducible to a mere animal capacity for processing stimuli you see as proving the presence of rational intending mind in all animals and at the ground of nature. I suppose it's the direction from which you look at these things that determines almost everything.

PSYCHE: Direction is all, yes, but that doesn't mean that all directions provide an equally unobstructed view. The issue remains: which narrative is logically consistent, the bottom-up story that says mindless matter somehow became mind or the top-down story that says mind operates as formal and final causality on the whole material realm? I maintain that it's the latter. But, since the seventeenth century at least, our general sense of where the partition between mind and everything else should naturally be situated has been at what we take to be the clear boundary between an immaterial "thinking substance"—a *res cogitans*, to use again the Cartesian language—and the whole world of "extended substance"—or *res extensa*—with all of biological reality situated on the latter side, as though it were nothing but a form of mechanism. If this is how we see things—that biology is just machinery—then it stands to reason that the physicalist reductionist will greet the discovery of certain higher mental functions within the animal or even vegetal realms as a demystification or naturalization of the mind. Conversely, modern religious persons who want to defend what they take to be human spiritual dignity against such demystification, but who themselves haven't really escaped the Cartesian paradigm, will end up in some way reinforcing the division between biological and mental life, even if they do so under the cover of seemingly different metaphysical categories—borrowed from, say, Christian scholasticism or something of that sort.

I reject the whole picture. In the fashion of a far more ancient metaphysics, I place the primary conceptual partition not between mind and biology, but between life and non-life, and I understand the former as at once both rational form and organic vitality. I believe that nature is already mind, so I see the evidence of full mentality throughout the structure of organic life as a confirmation of the spiritual nature of all that lives. For me, both the mindlike structure of nature and the ubiquitous interiority of mind provide evidence of the presence of soul or mind, understood as a higher cause, in everything. And I have to say that in the life-sciences themselves there have long been powerful movements of rebellion against mechanism. Despite the redoubtable resistance of the old guard—the biological mechanists, the genetocentric Neo-Darwinian gradualists of the orthodox persuasion—there are many scientists now who've come to think that the structure of life is unintelligible except in terms of some kind of intentionality, intrinsic purposes, and even something like "spiritual" autonomy right within the most basic organic systems.

Hephaistos: Which, to your mind, tells us what?

Psyche: To recognize the essential continuity between organic life and living mind is, it seems to me, to have been largely liberated from the mechanistic delusion, whether in its Cartesian or its fully reductionist form. As you note, direction is all. I stake myself to the top-down causal narrative: I believe in the formal and final causality of mind shaping and animating organic life, and of organic life shaping and animating its material substrate—mind "descending" into matter and raising matter up into itself as life and thought.

HEPHAISTOS: We're back to your vitalism, I see.

PSYCHE: Proudly. Please always recall, however, that by "vitalism" I don't mean yet another dualism, between intrinsically lifeless matter and some adventitious force or mystical galvanism. I mean an intrinsic vitality within the inmost constitution of all material actuality; I mean that all material structure is always already a concrescence and coordination of matter by the living rational principle informing it. That's what Henri Bergson meant when he spoke of an *élan vital:* not some extrinsic element introduced into a mechanistic chemical order, quickening it from without, but rather an essential creative impulse within the very structure of nature, quickening it from within itself, driving it into ever more diverse and more complex forms.[5]

EROS: What a very beautiful thought.

HEPHAISTOS: Is it? Is it really? [*With a rueful shrug:*] It might equally well be characterized as a monstrous idea, you know, depending on how one views this picture of nature striving after ever higher ends . . . setting sail for its distant horizons on such vast evolutionary oceans of blood. I have to tell you, my good Psyche, you have a most unsettling habit of oscillating back and forth between pitilessly dry rationality and rapturously . . . *ebrious* fancy.

PSYCHE: [*With a laugh:*] *Ebrious?* Well, I'll strive for sobriety. All I'm really trying to say is that it comforts me to think that the life-sciences may have entered a new, intellectually more adventurous age, and that perhaps we need no longer confine ourselves to the realm of the mental to call the mechanistic picture of nature into question. It may well be that a conception of causality richer than what materialist orthodoxy can provide will ultimately prove just as necessary for molecular and evolutionary biology. At least, there's where a more diverse causal language seems constantly to be attempting to assert itself—top-down causation, circular causality, epigenetics, symbiogenesis, teleonomy, convergent evolution, systems biology—even as traditional genetocentric Neo-Darwinism struggles to contain biology within its more linear narrative. And this isn't simply on account of the failure of the Human Genome Project to yield the master key to the entire mystery of life, from the regularities of protein-folding or embryonic cell-segregation to social morality and Bach's counterpoint. Life appears to be structurally hierarchical not only because evolution is a cumulative process, in which more complex levels are gradually superimposed upon lower, self-sufficient levels, but because every discrete organism possesses a causal architecture in which there can be no single privileged tier of causation. Each level depends on levels both above and below it; and none of them can be intelligibly isolated from the others as a kind of causal "base" that, isolated from the others, explains organic life. At least, such is the contention of Denis Noble, one of the subtlest champions of systems biology—or, as he calls it, "biological relativity." Perhaps there was a time when one could innocently think in terms of a master ground or center of life, with the DNA molecule as the primordial genetic repository of all meaningful information, and perhaps it seemed to make sense to understand life in terms of an inviolable dichotomy between replicators and survival vehicles—those clever selfish genes and the organic "robots" they program to facilitate their own persistence, to use a popular colorful image—enforced by an impermeable Weismann Barrier between the genome and somatic cells. Now, though, scientists can scarcely even define a gene, let alone find a purely genetic explanation for the entirety of living systems; and that barrier has been exposed as a myth. Certainly scientists can't identify any one-to-one correspondence between *this* gene and *this* phenotypic trait; as Noble says, to speak of a gene as "the gene for *x*" is always an error. We simply can't ignore the degree to which DNA sequences are passive causes, whose phenotypic expressions are determined by the organisms and environments they inhabit. As Michel Morange says, DNA isn't the ruler of the proteins, but their servant, requiring the purposes imposed on it by proteins to allow for its own reproduction. It's the living organism, more properly speaking, pursuing its own intrinsic ends within complex and changing environments, that uses genes selectively as templates to make the molecules it needs.[6]

Noble, in fact, when considering the way in which each level of life at once assembles the components of an immediately lower level and also constitutes a component of an immediately higher level—atoms, molecules, networks, organelles, cells, tissues, organs, holosomatic systems, complete organisms, populations, species, clades, the physical environment—doesn't hesitate to speak of natural teleology, simply because there clearly are levels of explanation at which purpose constitutes not just an illusory epiphenomenon of inherently purposeless processes, but a real causal rationale within organisms. An organ, no matter how irregular its phylogenic history, exists within an organism *because* of the purpose it serves, apart from which it would not exist. And these systems aren't reducible to one another, but exist only as a totality. Within the hierarchy of relations, there may be *discrete* levels of organization, but there are no *independent* causal levels. The entire structure is a profoundly logical and purposive whole.

Again, of course, for some time the received wisdom has been that this intentional structure must somehow—chaotically, biochemically, phylogenically—have emerged from very primitive, originally random causes, which only posteriorly came to serve as components of a recursive system of interactions, and which therefore are still hypothetically reducible to a state prior to "purpose." But, unless we really do want to retreat to a magical concept of emergence, we must assume that the formal determinations of organic complexity were always already present in those causes in at least latent or virtual form, awaiting explication in developed phenotypes and other organic totalities. This would seem also to oblige us, then, to assume that whatever rational relations may exist in organisms, including form and finality, are already virtually present in those seemingly random states, as rational causal potencies within their material substrate—which means, as an implicit intentionality. Even matter, then, whatever it is, already has in its barest constitution something of the character of mind, and belongs to a rational cosmic order that, in itself, has the structure of intentional thought. Perhaps even the ground of the possibility of regular physical causation is a deeper logical coinherence of the rational relations underlying physical reality. Perhaps, more to the point, mind is neither a ghostly agency inexplicably haunting a machine nor an illusion reducible to non-intentional and impersonal forces, but is instead the most intense and luminous expression of those formal and teleological determinations that give actuality to all nature.

HEPHAISTOS: Back to where we began. Do you really, truly imagine the life-sciences are turning in such directions? You may be in for a disappointment if you do.

PSYCHE: I don't know, really, but the signs are encouraging. The sciences are a culture, and, like any culture, their future is unpredictable; but at least at the heart of that culture is a devotion to an ideal of evidence that has the power to alter reigning paradigms with wonderful suddenness. I think the best scientific models of life at present—beginning probably with Barbara McClintock's discovery of transposable genomic elements and cellular genetic self-engineering many decades ago—involve overwhelming evidence of a kind of intrinsic intentionality and purposive coherence in complex organic systems that's more than merely apparent, and that it's difficult to make sense of simply as the fortuitous result of purely purposeless chemical causes forged into complex integration by mere chance mutation and natural selection. And that has nothing to do with my preferred metaphysics or theology; it's simply a matter of where the current state of the evidence seems to have led many serious researchers, no matter what their metaphysical or religious leanings. It's at least rational, given the formidably elaborate systems of downward causation observable in every organism's structure, to ask whether those rational coherencies in their totality might not belong to a formal and final logic far stranger and more wonderful than mechanism.

Wasn't it always a little absurd, after all, to allow a methodological fiction to be mistaken for an ontology? We need only consider what living organisms are to see that they aren't machines. Machines are composite objects only, organized but not organically integrated, closed systems that, when all their parts are in order, perform specific tasks extrinsic to themselves, but that have no inherent tendency to persistence and no capacity for development or adaptation. In an organism, the parts of the system cooperate even in their own alterations and constant reorganization, right down to the cellular level, because they're unified at a far profounder level than mere mechanical structure, and belong to a truly open system capable of becoming something structurally new through dynamic engagement in the external world. Organisms, moreover, maintain themselves, not merely by resisting their environment, but through a constant process of adaptation, reaction, innovation, interaction, and active self-regulation, and—lest we forget—they're variously capable of experience, understanding, reasoning, freedom, self-movement, and finally of an incommutable sense of personal unity and identity. This is the special dynamic unity of life itself, which is wholly unlike anything mechanical, and which can't be restored once it's been, as it were, switched off. As a negentropic process, moreover, life sustains itself "far from equilibrium" precisely as both a flow of matter and energy in constant metabolism and yet also as a controlled state of continuous structural change. A machine, by contrast, exists very close to equilibrium indeed, else it couldn't function; it is, to the degree it can be, something structurally inert and static, not adapting to environmental flux but merely enduring it. An organism, however, is itself at once both structure and flow, as much force as form, never static in configuration or function, preserving itself as a dynamic and changing activity; it's engaged in its world creatively, ceaselessly flowing within the constraints of its environment while admitting the flow of its environment into and through itself. The very concept of function becomes equivocal when applied to both machines and organisms, as the one is what it is by posing as little resistance to thermodynamic processes as it possibly can while the other is what it is by actively defeating and even exploiting those processes. And, again, most important of all, organisms have interior worlds, the unity of inner consciousness, which it seems to me must in some sense be the same unity as life itself. The possession of a kind of inner "selfhood," however slight, belongs uniquely to living things, and the unity of organism belongs uniquely to realities with an inner cognitive domain of some kind or another. So why would we doubt that this is one and the same unity, expressed structurally and experientially? And, more to the point, how could any of us ever have been so foolish as not to have seen the utter impotence of the mechanical philosophy as an explanatory paradigm for any of this?[7]

HEPHAISTOS: Complexity can emerge, you know, from entropy. In fact, thermodynamic processes can by themselves generate systems that use the circumambient energy of their environments to preserve themselves.

PSYCHE: That may be, but there are strict limits to the kind of complexity that can arise from an entropic physical landscape.

HEPHAISTOS: There are limits to everything, Psyche my dear; the issue is whether in this case you've mistaken where they lie.

III
Mind in Nature

PSYCHE: I don't think I have. We're not talking, after all, about mere structural complexity. Everything we've just said about the distinctiveness of life should make that obvious. We're not even talking about the sort of "irreducible complexity" that fascinates "Intelligent Design" theorists, at least not in the terms they tend to use, since they too seem to think that organisms are machines, constructed according to patterns extrinsic to themselves by a God who's little more than a divine mechanic. But the complexity of life as we actually observe it is far more interesting and perplexing than that. It manifests itself in integrated but open systems that are always dynamically giving shape to themselves, creatively, inventively, often creating new means—within themselves or within their environments—to achieve ends consistent with but not strictly predetermined by their own evolutionary or individual histories. This seems much more in keeping with the ancient and mediaeval notion of nature as invested with rational principles or "seeds of mind" whereby it in a sense creates itself—and in keeping as well with the theories of modern biologists and philosophers of science who see in organic life evidence of "autopoiesis" or self-artifice.[8] To me, it seems obvious that life is characterized by an intrinsic purposiveness, and that in its every phase the continuity it exhibits is like that of a rational thought flowing toward a conclusion, solving problems in light of an intended but as yet not fully conceivable end.

Hephaistos: I have the uncomfortable feeling that you're proposing something like an Aristotelian Darwinism, or an evolutionary Aristotelianism. I mean, I'm not entirely adverse to talk of "autopoiesis," even if my understanding of it would differ from yours. But I don't see how you imagine you can reconcile the fixed teleology of the ancient view with the genuine unpredictable creativity of evolutionary change. That dynamism of self-creation, as you like to call it—certainly it's set in motion precisely by the indeterminate and unpremeditated action of physical forces in a universe that hasn't as yet subsided into perfect thermodynamic equilibrium. It's the foaming crest of the great wave of cosmic expansion, shaping itself against the winds of chance. It can't be both free and predestined.

Psyche: Ah, no, that's a misunderstanding of teleology within an open system—within a system of free creativity, that is. Curiously enough, that was one of the anxieties of Bergson, and so he often felt he had to oppose his theory of *élan vital* to teleology, for fear of subordinating evolution to determinism. But, of course, the purposiveness of rational agency isn't merely an internal disposition toward a single specific result; it occurs at two levels, as we've already seen, one of general determinism and one of special liberty; empirical freedom unfolds under the canopy of a transcendental destiny. That's certainly how Raymond Ruyer's philosophy of "Neofinalism" clarifies Bergson: just as a human being is a free agent by virtue of making judgments and choices in relation to his or her own prior natural orientation to a realm of transcendental values—say, goodness or truth or beauty or what have you—so too the evolution of nature as a whole is a freely creative agency prompted by a fixed transcendental teleology.

Hephaistos: Which means what? I always find the word "transcendental" rather murky, to be honest.

Psyche: You shouldn't, since all it means here is a set of abstract values in whose light you're able to form judgments and make decisions. You couldn't possibly be a rational agent if there weren't a realm of the ultimately desirable—whether real or merely presumed—toward which your intellectual appetites are all naturally oriented. You couldn't choose to make something beautiful in your workshop, for instance, if you weren't excited into action by a prior and constant hunger for beauty as such, not as a single concrete object but as an absolute or general value. You'd have no category by which to judge your work, no vision for your work to pursue. You're free at the empirical level because you're predetermined at a transcendental level to seek certain absolute ends; this infinite purposiveness of your mind is what equips you with finite purposes. Without that index of values, all your acts would be arbitrary, prosecuted without real rational judgments, and so no more free than, say, a hemorrhage.

Eros: That's a point to which I hope we'll return, my soul. It's of the profoundest significance, it seems to me.

Psyche: Of course, my love. Anyway, Phaesty, for Ruyer this same reality is pervasive of the whole structure of life. In fact, he mocks the delusion that *any* actions could be the product of causes without end or orientation—or *sens*, as he calls it; he likens the reductionist to a lunatic who denies his own existence or who claims to be dead, pointing out that the very act of affirming mechanism to be true is an admission of a prior directedness toward truth as an ideal, utterly beyond the sphere of the mechanical, and so just another confirmation of antecedent finality. So, says Ruyer, alongside the realm of physics we should perceive another dimension, an ideal world of values and essences. To him, life is a creative process forever teleologically engaged in that dimension of values—of "axiological" ends—creating and sustaining mnemonic evolutionary themes to be passed on from one generation to another, freely striving toward finite goals by which to realize its fixed orientation toward infinite goals, and private mental agency is a wholly natural extension of that inherence of meaning and *sens* in all things. Mind you, for him life never fully realizes the ideal ends of its axiological exertions; it can achieve only approximations. Even so, there's a primary consciousness that objectively manifests itself in dynamic form and that's coextensive with life itself; and the emergence of rational agents as secondary, spiritual personalities in shared cultures comes about through this always prior engagement in axiological endeavors, because personality dissolves where teleological values are absent.[9]

Hephaistos: I'm not very familiar with Ruyer. Is he a theist of some kind?

Psyche: He *was* something more on the order of a Daoist, and then not really that either, though he often spoke of that primal conscious agency as God in an impersonal sense, and of God as present at once in all the ideals sought by real agency and in all the agents seeking those ideals—God as creativity as such, that is, from which and to which all agency flows.

Hephaistos: [*Sighing:*] Once again, just where some dry and sober precision is most needful, our conversation resolves back into a *bacchantische Taumel* of metaphysics and mysticism.

Psyche: I reject that characterization. I believe we're discussing ideas grounded in the hard facts of nature.

Hephaistos: Oh, come now. I know I haven't a snowflake's hope in Tartarus of convincing you that you're wrong, but it seems to me you're violating your own rules. You chided Dennett for seeding the language of intentionality in his descriptions of mechanical "behaviors" only then to adduce it later as evidence in favor of his reductionism. Well, what's this you're doing if not seeding your image of natural evolution with intentional language only so that you can find it there waiting for you when you go looking for it? This is because you wish to convince me that the existence of mind and life at the lowest material level still doesn't have its origin "below," in the dark abyss of dead matter, but only "above" in the bright abyss of an infinite realm of ideas and ideals and formal causes with final aims. But, as you say, direction is all.

Hermes: Oh, for the love of the gods, don't pretend we're still at the beginning of this debate. Psyche has already given you her reasons for believing that the emergentist narrative fails, while you've given no reason as yet for doubting the narrative of form and finality. If mind isn't the product of mindless matter—and it clearly isn't—then what other narrative of mind's origin remains? Then, too, if evidence of mind is found in the structure of life, what other source can it have than the same source as that of the mental agency within us? It's obviously something fundamental to nature.

PSYCHE: It's my conviction, Phaesty, that I can make the claims I do because the opposite claims are incoherent. I've made it quite clear why I think it impossible to reduce mind to neural functions; but I also think it true that neural functions aren't reducible to mechanics. I've been trying for days to show that, if life were mechanism, mind would be an alien presence within it. Now I would add that, if any aspect of the physical order were mere mechanism, then life would be an alien presence within *it.* I mean, surely you'd grant by now this singular difference between organisms and machines: that organisms pursue ends or values intrinsic to and meaningful to themselves—say, persistence at the physical level, truth or beauty or goodness at the intellectual level—whereas machines operate in relation to no intrinsic values or ends at all, and what ends they do serve are entirely extrinsic to them and have been imposed upon them from without.

HEPHAISTOS: I'd rather set all talk of ends and values aside and speak instead simply about complex systems. I mean, if we're going to define *life*—not mind, that is, but mere physical life—in terms of purposive agency, and all the way down at that, then I do in fact want to retreat again to the beginning, *pace* our good Hermes here. I know that you're no Cartesian dualist, and that your intention all along has been to assimilate life to mind rather than to mechanism; but let's consider anew where we really stand. I agree, organic life one way or another definitely constitutes the mediating principle between our concepts of mind and of matter; it's the place where materialism, dualism, neutral monism, and idealism all must stake their wagers in the end. So let's be deliberate, shall we? As I've said, there are some quite powerfully suggestive accounts out there of how negentropic order can be generated by disequilibrium within entropic conditions, and can achieve a complexity and a stability that maintain it "far from equilibrium," and can become increasingly systematic, and finally even in some cases can become a kind of responsive interiority that is, as it were, the womb of mental subjectivity. And, before you raise again all your complaints about strong emergence, which we can take as read, let's pursue this as far as we can, just to make sure we aren't *all* still the victims of our residually Cartesian prejudices. I know of one physicist named Eric Chaisson who's provided a fairly stirring account of how, where energy is available in a conducive environment, certain open systems capable of using that energy can build more complex structures, which then in turn process yet more energy, and sometimes this can lead not just to cumulative increases of consumption but to the emergence of new phenomena. Nature presents us with an endless array of macroscopic manifestations of chance fundamental microscopic fluctuations in unstable dynamical systems; then disequilibrious conditions engender complex negotiations of the systems and their environments that produce specific flows of energy, *not* on account of some prior purpose or ends, but just to foster ordered forms that allow for the easiest way past difficult situations. In time, evolution improves the control of that flow by incremental improvements of organization under the pressure of natural selection.[10]

PSYCHE: All right. Why?

HEPHAISTOS: Why what?

PSYCHE: Why would these emergent systems seek a way out of difficult situations, easy or not, or do so by *fostering* ordered forms? Surely because those systems have some sort of internal disposition to persist—some sort of appetite for existing, some *conatus essendi*, I'm tempted to say. But why? And why wouldn't natural selection at that level instead reward the tendency toward entropic collapse into equilibrium, as surely that's the easiest and most parsimonious way past "difficult situations"?

HEPHAISTOS: I assume, as a combination of the chance fluctuations at the microscopic level and the channeling of energy-flows at the macroscopic, as confined by environmental constraints.

PSYCHE: You're repeating yourself. You're describing that persistence, but I'm not at all sure you're explaining it. All right, natural selection favors efficient, self-sustaining systems for processing energy where certain impasses are encountered . . . but I would still think the selected system would have to have some sort of internal directedness toward maintaining itself far from equilibrium—some kind of teleological structure. Then again, maybe I simply naïvely impose teleology on every persisting homeostatic system.

HEPHAISTOS: You're making this more difficult than it needs to be. Why does a whirlpool persist? Because of the as yet unexhausted energy it's processing and because of the complex interplay of constraints between it and its surrounding conditions. It's not that great a mystery.

PSYCHE: Oh, that's what we're talking about. But that's not very far from equilibrium at all, while it's very far indeed from life. I have to say, I do get a bit confused by the way in which so many metaphysical naturalists seem to ignore the uncanny interval between inorganic and organic systems for processing energy. I'm not sure how any of this gets us where we're going. It may give us models for the emergence of structural and dynamical complexity, and maybe it describes a correlation between complexity and the flow of energy—but *life?* I've no doubt general chaos can produce local order, but how does one get from there to self-replicating organisms, let alone to mental agency and subjectivity? How does this physicist define life?

HEPHAISTOS: If I recall—and, of course, I do—as an "open, coherent, spacetime structure maintained far from thermodynamic equilibrium by a flow of energy through it—a carbon-based system operating in a water-based medium, with higher forms metabolizing oxygen."[11]

PSYCHE: Well, the second half of the formulation definitely describes terrestrial organisms, if only in as minimal a way as imaginable, but the first half is so general as to be vacuous; it could apply equally well to just about any system that uses energy.

HEPHAISTOS: Yes, precisely. By his own admission it could apply to a star or a galaxy; it applies to any system that creates and sustains complexity by processing energy from its environment and then exporting disorder back into its environment to compensate for what it's taken in. But aren't you at least interested by the way his account extends a kind of metabolic logic backward from life into the realm of the pre-organic?

PSYCHE: Yes, well, that's promising, I suppose. And, of course, it's undeniable that living systems don't thwart thermodynamics; I mean, whatever order they create is paid for by that residual disorder. Physical systems obey the minimal limit-conditions of physical laws. But that's only half the story, because that physical calculus still doesn't explain life's tendency toward persistence to begin with. I'm still genuinely perplexed by a definition of life that applies just as well to stars—assuming that our physicist isn't an animist or some kind of panpsychist.

HEPHAISTOS: He isn't. He says explicitly that life differs from non-living systems not in kind, but only in degree.

PSYCHE: Oh. Well, then, I'm disposed not to take anything he says on life or mind very seriously. That's simply nonsensical. It's also something only a physicist could say. Only from the perspective of the quantitative grammar of physics could the qualitative difference between life and non-life be anything other than incandescently obvious.

HEPHAISTOS: [*Raising his hands in mock horror:*] Yes, those damned physicists with their barren syntactic ontology.

PSYCHE: You jest, but the accusation is appropriate. Not only does such a claim somehow entirely miss out the "semantics of life," it leaves wholly out of consideration the layer of semeiotic order in the structure of life—the order of symbolic communication, that is—that bridges the physical disjunction of two phenotypes. There may be some analogy between mere dynamic structural complexity and the nested hierarchies of organic life, with all those extraordinarily complex interactions among countless homeostatic systems; even then, however, I'm not sure how the processing of energy in negentropic structures by itself explains the management and organization of energy one finds in organisms. For one thing, the disjunction in sheer complexity between prebiotic and living systems is so vast that it beggars the imagination. Every living cell with a genome, no matter how rudimentary or complex the organism to which it belongs, encompasses a molecular assemblage with thousands of operative parts, performing countless finely organized tasks far beyond the technical prowess of gods or mortals, and of course at the core of every cell with a genome is an exquisitely precise genetic code comprising sixty-four codons that have together repeatedly undergirded one and the same seemingly intentional structure without variation for roughly two billion years. And yet nowhere in nature can we discover anything remotely like a more primitive precursor of the organic cell, or even cogently imagine what it would have consisted in. What also seems certain to me is that there's nothing else in nature that resembles or even foreshadows the power of reproduction—of life's transcription of itself in genetic templates, and its transmission of somatic and epigenetic morphologies across generations. Certainly we have no idea where the coding of the genome comes from, or how it could have been generated out of a non-intentional physical order. When we talk about replication, we're not talking about a mere amplification of a structure, like the growth of a crystal, but the true repetition of an entire system in a new organism. Mere increase of geometrical complexity isn't even remotely similar to life's power to repeat its own ontogeny through the communication of "coded" information; the one is physical, mechanical, and to a great degree aleatory, while the other is intentional, semantic, precisely directed, and in some sense hermeneutical. And then—always and ever again—there's the realm of mind, which as far as we know is unique to living organisms. To suggest that only a difference of degree separates the reality of life from the dynamical system of a star is simply absurd. If one's account of life's origin never quite crosses the frontier between, on the one hand, the mere accidental prolongation of some dynamic physical process and, on the other, even the most inchoate kind of natural velleity within complex systems toward their own preservation, then one hasn't explained anything. One hasn't successfully accounted for life simply by failing to notice it.

I mean, yes, I freely grant that a chaotic physical landscape can generate complexity; dynamic structure does indeed arise from disorder of the right kind, and it persists by a kind of disequilibrious momentum. But even that structure is an accommodation with the insatiable demands of entropy. Those complexities are created by a constant gravitation toward equilibrium, in obedience to the iron law that dictates that energy exhaust itself in disorder. They're negotiations between thermodynamic expenditure and local impediments to that expenditure, which divert that energy into increasingly convoluted paths toward final repose. But this also dictates certain very strict limits of extension. Purely physical amplifications of structure naturally demand systematic parsimony; they usually tend toward energetically conservative periodic repetitions, as in the case of growing crystals, or the fractal patterns of snowflakes, or the hexagonal cells of a honeycomb. This is because the order created is the result of entropic constraints, which produce patterns—and *merely* patterns—that arrest disorder only by yielding to it coherently, precisely because they require less energy than any other path past the disequilibrious conditions inhibiting them. This is order created by a process of continuous simplification and energetic subsidence . . . energy finding a way past sudden turns in the streambed, so to speak . . . water naturally finding its level, even if it can do so only by a winding course of bends and calms and cataracts and shifting currents. Organisms, however, are actual systems of persistence and self-modification, expending more energy than the mere minimum in order to surmount environmental obstacles and achieve greater energetic potential, and hence can't exist save through an active resistance to mere lethargic periodic repetition. It makes no sense to argue that the simple structural emergence of order out of entropic conditions can forge systems that, far from simply negotiating the immediate demands of entropy, actually contrive to thwart those demands, deferring entropic subsidence to as remote a future point as possible by evolving into higher forms of disequilibrious organization, and by pursuing persistence for the sake of persistence as such, through a kind of intrinsic *élan.* These two kinds of complexity don't exist along a single continuum; the difference between them is a profound causal rupture. And part of that rupture is the sudden appearance of intentionality in the system.

Isn't this the problem, though, with treating living systems as special expressions of general physical laws? That everything that isn't merely a matter of calculable quantitative values is missed? From that perspective, it matters only that all the instances of order generated out of disorder and all the systems that follow therefrom are mathematically consistent, and that their expenditure of energy doesn't violate the rules of conservation and thermodynamic compensation. The flow of energy through the system is everything. Whether there's a plausible causal narrative of the system itself is simply never addressed. All right, perhaps self-replicating life is a more efficient "open, coherent, spacetime structure maintained far from thermodynamic equilibrium by a flow of energy through it"; but energy doesn't just flow "through it": it—that very structure—takes intentional control of that flow and devises new ways to exploit it and flows along with it into new configurations. And here, too, the issue of how replication occurs—that additional semeiotic and intentional level of causality—has been totally omitted from the discussion, as though it were little more complicated than, say, the cohesiveness of a raindrop.

IV
Information and Form

Hephaistos: I'm not going to argue over differences of degree and differences of kind; but I grant that the physics of the flow of energy won't of itself explain the emergence of living organisms. If you want, though, to discuss life's "semeiotic" side, let's talk instead about the flow of information. I mean, entropic conditions *allow* for instances of structural and interactive complexity to arise and persist far from equilibrium, but what actively arrests entropy in those systems is information.

Psyche: Oh, you're treading dangerous ground for a metaphysical naturalist. Beware of transitive constructions there, my friend. In physical terms, does "information" *cause* stable structures that resist entropy, or is it just the name we apply to the phenomenon of such resistance? Of course, I'm quite willing to grant the former; and, if you're willing to amputate the prefix and talk in terms of *formal* causality, a rapprochement between us may be possible; but is that what you want? How are you defining information? Where does it come from?

Hephaistos: Perhaps it doesn't need to come from anywhere. Perhaps it's primordial. I'm relying on the physicist Paul Davies here, and he explains quite lucidly to my mind that information as a scientific principle consists in the reduction of randomness—just as, for instance, a radio transmission becomes clearer and so more *informed* by the elimination of random "noise"—through organization and, in the case of living organisms, complex and coordinated maintenance. Believe me, Davies isn't at all naïve about the formidable differences between living and non-living processes; he speaks at length about the immensely intricate integrated systems present in even the most basic of organisms, and about the self-correcting and self-editing powers of cells in regard to their own genomes, and their ingenious strategies of adaptation and survival, and about the degree to which organisms as complete systems—along with various epigenetic forces—determine gene-expression in a clearly top-down manner, and so forth. He appears to think that, when one looks at life at the level of systems, there are magnitudes of order and apparent purpose in nature that need accounting for by more than a history of fortuitous mutations.[12] Whether I agree or not I can't say. I probably don't, but at least I appreciate his attempt to speak about these things within the framework of physics itself.

EROS: I confess that I'm having some difficulty in understanding how one would characterize information as a causal force. I mean, I assume this *isn't* formal causality in the classical sense.

HEPHAISTOS: I hope not; but, as I say, I'm not quite sure what I think of this. Davies borrows Clerk Maxwell's thought experiment about a little demon who contrives a method for defeating entropy. As you may recall, Maxwell's "demon"—like Laplace's—is a superlatively percipient little imp who inhabits the microscopic realm and knows the position and speed of every particle to be found there. He, however, unlike Laplace's demon, isn't interested in reconstructing the physical history of the universe or in foretelling its future from the current dispositions of its atoms; rather, his particular concern is to defeat the second law of thermodynamics. To this end, he creates an enclosed cell full of gas and divides it into two chambers by an impenetrable partition, in which he then installs a small, frictionlessly gated aperture just large enough to admit a single molecule at a time, from either side to the other; this he uses to segregate faster from more slowly moving molecules so that the two chambers come to have distinctly different temperatures, which allows for a motor of sorts to be run off the resulting heat gradient. Thus chaotic molecular motion is transformed into orderly mechanical motion, *et voilà*, entropy is not only held at bay, but converted into purposeful work at no thermodynamic cost. All that's required, if this is right, is possession of the pertinent information and the means of exploiting it. Davies also, incidentally, calls on Claude Shannon's mathematical formula for quantifying information, which appears to be more or less the inverse of the formula for entropy.[13]

Psyche: One would think that that's practically a tautology. If information's the reduction of uncertainty . . .

Hephaistos: Only once the connection has been made. Anyway, perhaps the explanation of life lies latent in this understanding of information, even if that understanding at present is a little nebulous. Organic nature is thronged with little Maxwell's demons, it seems, legions of exquisitely orchestrated systems within systems, guiding the flow of information through ever more sophisticated systems for reducing uncertainty or "noise," often built by way of intentional adaptation and innovation, and all of them perhaps acting in obedience to physical laws that we haven't as yet discovered.

Eros: I'm still finding it difficult to understand how information here is a causal force that "flows."

Hephaistos: Really? You know that information exists only as something transmitted—something that can be shared and passed on, that is—and that can be installed in code and then extricated from that code again. If I send you a written invitation to tea and you understand the words on the paper and do indeed come, then that "flow" of information has created an ordered set of actions, using the structures previously established for sending messages.

Hermes: But then the sort of causality you're talking about there isn't simply physical, is it? It's the causality of intentional content, which I seem to recall is the very problem you're trying to get around. Surely we shouldn't conflate the transmission of syntactic sequences in Shannon's "bits," which reduce uncertainty quantitatively, with something like an actual force working upon physical structures, especially if the causal level of that information is semantic. The physical medium employed for that invitation to tea is calculable, but it's the meaning shared between intending intellects that has determinate consequences. So, all right, information flows, in the metaphorical sense that it's imparted and it develops; but, at least at the level of that content, it's not a physical flow. Its power of causation is entirely dependent on a prior intentional structure—information must definitely *mean* something and have a purposive shape—but also on a reciprocal intentional power that can interpret that intentional content . . . that hermeneutical content . . . which doesn't exist at the physical level, even though it guides physical events. Is there anything left of your metaphysical naturalism at that point?

HEPHAISTOS: I myself have doubts on that score. I'm not absolutely convinced that this way of seeing the matter gets us where I'd like us to go, but I'm willing to ponder the matter. What if information is part of the basic causal architectonics of the cosmos, creating structures by which it then communicates itself in ever more elaborate expressions and interrelations, so that it can generate yet newer structural occasions for its expression? And what if it creates those structures by way of a basic physical lawfulness—the rules of the game, as it were? Not long ago, Psyche mentioned John Conway's computer simulation the "Game of Life." Are you familiar with it?

EROS: If it has anything to do with a computer, you can take it for granted that I'm not.

HEPHAISTOS: You Luddite, you. All right, then. Davies, in fact, mentions it. It's not really a simulation of life or certainly of organic systems; but it's a very good simulation of self-creating systems based on a fairly primitive mathematical model of "cellular automata"—the cells in question here not being of the biological variety, but only regular enclosed spaces. Anyway, it's all so simple it seems trivial, and yet it produces surprising results—results that demonstrate how a few simple rules imposed within a domain of otherwise indeterminate activity can quickly induce the development of staggering complexity, including largely autonomous self-generating patterns that defy mathematical prediction. Basically, start with a simple regular grid in two dimensions, contained within a virtual space with boundaries, in which a few squares—cells, that is—have been filled in, randomly but contiguously; then impose some simple rules dictating how other patterns will be produced from this initial configuration in successive iterations of the grid. Conway called cells that had been filled in "live" and vacant cells "dead" and chose four rules to govern their pullulations: a live cell with fewer than two live cells adjacent to it dies off in the next generation (as if from underpopulation); a live cell with two or three live neighbor cells lives on; but any live cell with more than three neighbors dies (as if from overpopulation); and any dead cell with three live neighbors comes to life in the next generation (as if through reproduction). Simple in principle, but with such very elaborate results as that initial information flows through the generations: emergent patterns of ever greater coherence and complexity, some of which are evanescent but some of which become peculiarly durable and persistent, generating other and more diverse effects while, as it were, preserving themselves, almost like evolving organisms. And, with a few adjustments of the rules, it's also possible to create patterns that replicate themselves after several millions of iterations . . .

PSYCHE: Repeat, not replicate.

HEPHAISTOS: A fine distinction.

PSYCHE: Hardly. Cellular automata may repeat certain configurations or even series of configurations, but they do so in much the way that crystalline morphogenesis repeats over time, and even then they do so without the actual structural continuity of real crystals. Patterns of contiguous squares aren't integrated organisms, and they produce not progeny, but only mechanical sequels. Mere formal sequences aren't actual systemic inheritances. I'm familiar with cellular automata and I confess that, for all their suggestiveness regarding the mathematics of information complexity, I find nothing very interesting in them with regard to questions of evolution. I think we can all guess that a set of rules imposed on simple shapes within a strictly quarantined space will produce patterns; and, if those rules sufficiently constrain the results through their precision, and if there are no other levels or sources of causal influence, and if the whole process is preserved by its rules from entropic dissipation or noise, then quite a pageant can follow. But certainly we aren't talking about anything very much like a growing, changing, open organic system reproducing itself through, in part, transcribed codes. Yes, information yields informed results, and even unpredictable and immensely complex results. But we could have learned as much from playing chess.

Hephaistos: Isn't that rather the point? That informational constraints of a fairly minimal kind can evolve into ever more sophisticated vehicles for the transmission and extension of information?

Psyche: Oh, I'm not denying that, I'm just trying to draw a few necessary distinctions. I'm quite drawn to information theory in principle. But how much as yet does any of this tell us about *life*, other than that we can trivially affix terms like "evolution" and "reproduction" both to structural amplifications of geometric patterns of contiguous squares in a controlled, unchanging virtual space and also to actual adaptive and replicating organisms in constantly changing environments, sustaining themselves metabolically and reproducing their own ontogenies in subsequent generations of distinct organisms? The actual analogy, though, is less than tenuous. Again, I can't see anything in cellular automata more interesting than the geometries of growing crystals. Organisms are open systems that exist far from equilibrium, constantly internally converting materials into energy metabolically in dynamic relation to their environments. Crystals are largely inert as far as structural potential goes, in a state very near equilibrium indeed. And infinitely more inert than crystals are patterns of squares on a grid, not integrated with one another internally but merely juxtaposed to one another extrinsically by artificial protocols in a sterile stochastic arena with a bounded topology. That's a model not so much of life as of metastasis. Yes, fractals are fascinating; the Mandelbrot set is positively gorgeous; neither is rich in semantic information.

Hephaistos: Ah, but so what? These programs merely show—in a very simple way, I acknowledge—that information, as it were, metabolizes chance into order, and ever greater order in many cases.

Psyche: Life metabolizes *disorder* into order and pays the cost of the exchange back *to* disorder; but there's neither chance nor disorder in the virtual environment of the game. And enchanting geometrical symmetries are very different from the coordinated *asymmetries* of a truly disequilibrious organic system. Cellular automata in general, no matter how cunningly encoded, are simply poor analogies to organisms, or to cells, or for that matter to populations or gene frequencies or evolution or reproduction . . . basically, to life in any of its real dimensions. You might as well liken life to the patterns that emerge in a kaleidoscope. The cells of an organism's body can edit their own genomes to adapt to sudden changes in environment, and can employ survival strategies acquired over generations of somatic and epigenetic development. The "live cells" in the Game of Life are impelled heedlessly and irresistibly from one accidental configuration to another, producing regularities that better approximate the banal harmonies of entropic equilibrium and repose than they do the homeostatic hierarchies of organisms, which really look quite *unlike* regular repeating geometrical patterns. Where this all *does* become interesting, however, is in the game's very limitations; there, perhaps, it really does imitate life. Davies gets this right. One can't help but note that in these simulations order comes from order; information that always already exists at the level of the rules of the game provides the inflexible constraints that allow the game to be played. Otherwise nothing. Once one recognizes that strong emergence is a meaningless idea, and that the top-down causal functions of organisms can't be understood as emergent in the "strong" sense, one realizes that that very order or cause must be present from the start, perhaps at once latently, as a disposition or potency in matter awaiting actuation by a higher causality—a top-down causality written into nature—and also perennially, in a realm of form. That's what I find fascinating about information theory: that it places information—or, as I would prefer to say, form and finality—at the origin. That's what I also find baffling about your invocation of information theory, since it seems very unlike the . . . well, the mechanistic materialism that you seemed to be espousing when this debate began. As Hermes and my dear husband have both already noted, in the case of life you're talking about causality at the level of intentional communication by one agency, received at the level of intentional hermeneutics by another agency.

HEPHAISTOS: I'm committed only to a metaphysically naturalist approach to reality; on the specific details of nature's laws and leniencies

I have an open mind. Davies admits that everything he proposes may require the formulation of new laws of physics. Well, my basic tendency remains reductionist, but I'm perfectly willing to believe that the rules underlying physical reality admit of a number of simple principles of order that could be described as "informatic" (to use the sort of guild jargon that so offends our good Hermes here) and that these simple principles generate complexities far beyond what mere mechanistic mass and momentum could accomplish.

PSYCHE: And there's what I cordially *dislike* about cellular automata and similar programs. We're definitely talking about the primordial structure of reality, but most definitely *not* about only a few simple principles. A primitive simulation like the Game of Life can produce the impression that, in the case of complex systems, we're dealing with rules so minimal that they're practically indistinguishable from a few additional physical constraints, rather than—as must be the case—a truly elaborate, creatively open, and genuinely intentional rational grammar of development, far exceeding mere physical limit-conditions. The logic of the game on the screen is no more one of development than one of inertia, really. Consider, by contrast, the constitution of terrestrial life at even the most basic chemical level: it requires the coordinated activity of two disparate kinds of molecules, nucleic acids—RNA and DNA, that is—and proteins, and neither those molecules nor those proteins have any contribution to make to organic life without each other. More to the point, the intricate coordination between them doesn't merely give rise to the logic of organism; it's apparently always already determined by that logic. Think of nucleic acids as the syntax and proteins as the semantics of life, and think of organism as something like the realm of symbolic thought in which those intricate evolutions of meaning occur.

HEPHAISTOS: If you keep pressing that metaphor, it's going to snap in half.

PSYCHE: On the contrary, it's utterly infrangible. It becomes all the more pertinent, moreover, as we scale the hierarchical tiers of organisms, and consider how RNA polymerase transcribes DNA sequences into RNA, or how DNA polymerase sustains and repairs DNA, or how polymerase processes replicate DNA for the sake of mitosis, or how the cell reads out and interprets the information in DNA, and how the body rewrites the genome when it must, and passes on morphogenetic information epigenetically . . . or . . . well, I could go on for hours. . . . There's the great paradox: life is language, and language is mind, and mind is life . . .

HEPHAISTOS: Oh please. . . . [*Shaking his head wearily:*] No one, god or mortal, knows how life began, but the universe is large and even the most improbable of events have space in which to occur. Maybe there was that "RNA world" that some theorists like to talk about, which forged a kind of bridge between molecular proliferation and actual transmission of coded instructions for proteins, and between life's necessary chemical catalysis and the storing of genetic information. Who can say? Arguments from incredulity aren't solvent.

PSYCHE: I disagree: arguments from *warranted* incredulity are. Naturally, scientists will continue to search for as simple and parsimonious a set of principles as possible to explain the evolutionary transition from mere chemistry to self-moved life, and will want to reduce the threshold between the two to one as inconspicuous and as free from obstacles as possible. But, quite apart from the fragility and mutability of large RNA molecules, or RNA's instability outside of organic cells, or RNA's limited catalytic potentials, or the consideration that RNA is so very complex as a molecule that it seems unlikely to have preceded organic systems, or the reality that RNA's self-replication is a form of structural amplification analogous to crystalline morphogenesis rather than progenitive encoding, and so forth and so on . . . ah, well, one is left with much the same curious situation: RNA and the proteins necessary for reading anything coded into RNA require one another; so surely the wedding-dance of RNA and the ribosome is determined by an organic logic that precedes both. Really, perhaps all the "RNA world" hypothesis does for us is suggest an earlier platform for organic life; the origin of life's "code" and epigenetic systems remains an untouched mystery. I suspect the theory only pushes the question back to some still earlier period of some other kind of replicating molecule.[14]

You know, if you think about it, one might reasonably suppose that, if life and mind really were the emergent results of composite forces, and if their relation to their ingredient parts were purely mereological, then the special qualities distinguishing them from the non-living and non-mental material order would appear only at the highest supervenient system-levels of organisms, as the final result of the accumulated totality of their subvenient causal tiers. And yet we find quite the opposite to be the case. We find instead principles of unified agency, seemingly intentional powers of adaptation to new circumstances, ingenuity, the *conatus essendi*, and all sorts of elaborate coordinations of discrete processes within every organic cell comprising a chromosome. This seems to be a fairly vast problem for both the reductionist and the emergentist pictures of things. For the former, to what is one reducing an organism in seeking to explain away the uniqueness of life or mind, if even that organism's tissues and nerves and biochemical constituents are already composed of cognitive systems within cognitive systems? For the latter, from what are the novel properties of life and mind supposedly emergent if so many of the elementary functions of the organism are already fully invested with those properties? To posit a transition from the purely mechanical level of nature to that of life and mind—or the "appearance" of life and mind—so very near the threshold between physics and chemistry, or between basic chemistry and the most rudimentary organic compounds, defies the very logic of either approach to the question. It's perhaps no great surprise that the accelerating advances in cell biology and molecular biology over the past few decades have prompted philosophers and scientists alike to begin to take forms of panpsychism seriously. One could, perhaps, suppose that the entirety of the organism as a system, in its integrated totality, imposes discrete cognitive functions on lower levels within the system, as an apparently emergent structure of top-down agency; but what would this mean other than that within each organism there's some sort of primordial, unified, organizing principle of order and form and intelligence—in other words, a soul?

Hephaistos: Oh, that annoying little imp again. Perhaps Dennett is right: yes, you have a soul, but it's composed of millions of little robots. [*Another sigh:*] Look, neither of us is a cutting-edge molecular or evolutionary biologist. Again, I concede that the origins of life remain, as yet, shrouded in abysmal mystery. I recognize also that scientists who suggest otherwise are talking nonsense. I admit also that natural selection isn't the mechanism of life's origin, simply because natural selection can operate only upon lineages of already living, replicating, mutable organisms. All right. But, once the threshold was crossed, we can surely assume there followed a kind of steady exponential increase in information-capacity over succeeding generations of life.

Psyche: We can assume, can we? Can we assume also the emergence of intentional systems from non-intentional chemistry, and on an order of coordinated complexity that seems to have required cognitive systems within cognitive systems all the way down to the most basic level of life's hierarchical structure? I don't know, I admit, but what I do know is that "systems biology" presents us with a kind of organization that incorporates a semeiotic level of operation even in our cells, as well as in the organism as a whole. The actual details of life's origination are a matter of indifference to my argument anyway, since whatever they were, I would still insist that they must fit within a set of rational relations that includes a kind of formal and final causality at the very beginning, or else the potentials for what came after would also be absent. If life is the result, life was always already a causal presence in the structure of matter. Come hell or high water, however, the point on which I remain obdurate is this: life exhibits intentionality in every observable dimension; it moves toward that realm of values Ruyer described, and persists in its movement on account of that intentionality rather than on account of any physical law we can formulate or imagine. And, for the last time I hope, I insist that strong emergence is an absurd idea; hence this intentionality must be coterminous with a disposition always already present in all material existence, and this disposition must be anything but a non-intentional indeterminacy. That's why I'm also slightly wary of the metaphor of the "flow" of information: I understand it, of course, but I also fear it might make it sound as if we're talking about yet another physical force, like heat energy flowing across temperature gradients, rather than about the communication of an abstract content that needs to be actively interpreted and translated into physical expressions. The Game of Life, for instance, largely lacks that indispensable semeiotic—that strangely hermeneutical—level.

We needn't quibble over figures of speech, though. The true issue is that we're not really talking about *physical* laws at all, are we? The realm of molecules and the realm of information are as discrete as Ruyer's realms of matter and of values. At least, the laws of physics as we know them concern actual quantifications of mass and energy, motion and force, impetus and resistance, as well as fields and particles and waves and probabilities and such—in short, structural and dynamical descriptions. Where the presumed laws of information are concerned, we're talking about something more original still, a larger general logic that perhaps comprises the laws of physics in itself; in that context, physics is a set of specific rules governing a single, somewhat basic, somewhat subordinate causal axis within a greater rational totality. It seems obvious that "information"—or, as I prefer to say, *form*—doesn't merely impose an order that ultimately eventuates in intentional systems; of its nature, it's intentional all the way down, as it couldn't possibly exist except as shaped by final causality, both empirical and transcendental. Information isn't merely mindlike; it subsists only *in* mind.

HEPHAISTOS: Weren't you the one who chided Integrated Information Theory for conflating objective and subjective information?

PSYCHE: Oh, I was talking about the difference between data and the knowledge of that data. Here we're talking about the rational structure of nature in mental terms because they seem to fit. But pay attention: so much of this conversation entirely omits the essential issue. You mentioned Shannon's information theory, for instance; and what interests me about that is its *purely* quantitative nature. It's all about calculating information transmission in terms of binary bits; it says absolutely nothing about the *contents*—the semantics—of information: that hermeneutical level of organizing meaning that in fact has no physical existence at all, and yet is the very essence of, say, *code*. That the transmission of information can be quantified in bits is a very useful piece of knowledge; that information can be conveyed symbolically as intentional content, however, wholly on the hermeneutical plane of reality, is the great mystery that indicates the mental ground of physical reality. Believe me, Phaesty, I'm all too happy to see information as something fundamental, precisely because information functions in nature as encoded. Materialism is scarcely a possible view of reality even if intentional content in a hermeneutical space is understood solely as some sort of late evolutionary emanation of a late evolutionary development such as the human brain. But, if code is to be found at every level of life . . .

HEPHAISTOS: That, I suppose, is what we mean when we speak of finding new fundamental laws of physics that will incorporate information-theory into our understanding of nature. Not that I myself feel any tremendous enthusiasm for such language, but it might please you to know that Davies does at the last suggest that the emergence of life and perhaps of mind may turn out to be etched into the very lawfulness of nature.

PSYCHE: And what's that other than final causality? Once more, though, the language of emergence is too vague. The only conclusion to draw, if his line of thinking is coherent, is that what he's talking about comes down to forms and purposes, and that life and mind aren't merely written into the cosmic rules; in a sense, they write those rules. So, do we really require new laws of physics to account for the activity of Maxwell's demons in the fabric of living nature? Or should we be seeking new *metaphysical* laws, at a level more fundamental than the physical—laws, I suspect, that will really be only very old laws of form and finality rediscovered, which themselves may presume the reality of something that looks very like infinite mind?

HEPHAISTOS: [*With a melancholy smile:*] Quite. Look, before we plunge into the mind of God, perhaps we could turn back and peer down one last time into the depths of life itself—not abstract information, but concrete, material life—because I'm not as yet convinced that we can't get where we're going without resorting either to a tale of strong emergence or to your mystical theology of nature as divine spirit disporting itself in material forms.

V

Metabolism and Mind

Hephaistos: I'm somewhat out of my native element here, I confess. I'm not even certain how sympathetic I am to some of what I'm about to say; but let's leave no avenues unexplored. So, yes, let's say there must be some real inseparability of organic life from mental agency; let's say that mechanism is an inadequate model for understanding either. Moreover, let's concede that the principles that allow for life to arise are already resident in all physical reality and already compose part of its lawful structure. Organic life is then, as you've said, much the same mystery as mind, and it's there we should look, perhaps, to understand how the mental is produced by the material, or how the material is always invested with the mental—or whatever happens to be the case. You mentioned Hans Jonas earlier, and he certainly believed that the transition from the inorganic to the organic in cosmic history was actuated by a tendency or disposition in the depths of being toward modes of freedom, and that hence mind is prefigured in organic existence as such.[15] But does that place mind at the beginning or at the end of the tale? What if, in fact, the laws of organic life could be shown to be purely structural amplifications of the laws of physics, and the laws of mental agency purely structural amplifications of the laws of life, all building upon inherent physical principles that are disposed toward life and mind but still nevertheless prior to both? Do you know the work of the philosopher Evan Thompson?

Psyche: I do.

HERMES: I don't.

EROS: Nor do I.

HEPHAISTOS: Well, he follows Jonas in insisting that mind is life-like and life mindlike. He's also very much in the school of thinkers like Humberto Maturana and Francisco Varela and depends substantially on their account of life as "autopoiesis"—self-making—and on an "enactive" account of how organisms generate themselves and their own cognitive domains, and he tends to see the inwardness of mind as having a demonstrable continuity with the origin of life in metabolic structures, since such structures necessarily create interior environments for themselves to be maintained, contained within selectively permeable barriers, and sustained by the constant conversion of matter into energy.

HERMES: That sounds more like an analogy than a continuity to me, and one with a fairly wide disjunctive interval between its terms. Metabolism and mind are both "interior" phenomena, I suppose, but in only the most remotely analogous ways.

HEPHAISTOS: [*Sighing:*] Do try to curb your impatience. I'm a god lame and halt, so batten down the wings of those sandals I fashioned for you so many ages ago and plod along with me for a mile or two. All mental agency has a special kind of interiority—as the three of you have so passionately insisted—and interiority is also necessary to the unity of a living system. Yes, this inwardness may ultimately involve something like what you call subjectivity and intentionality, but perhaps it's more originally the result of this basic organic urge toward persistence through continuous becoming. Perhaps that need to persist is a source in organisms at once of an inchoate self-vigilance and also of a dawning awareness of the surrounding world. Perhaps that basic volition toward freedom and continued existence, written as it is into the structure of life and requiring the physical interiority of a homeostatic organic system, simply becomes increasingly transparent to itself over the ages as an interplay of agency and patiency, constantly evolving toward conscious intentionality and subjectivity.

HERMES: Attractive language, but are we back then to emergent subjectivity—emergent mind and intention?

HEPHAISTOS: Not as previously discussed, it seems to me. At least, we're not talking about the emergence of mind from *mechanistic* material forces. This really is more on the order of seeing subjectivity as arising from a basic impulse already in nature, expressed in organic principles that aren't mechanistic but genuinely inherently intentional, or at least predisposed toward intentionality, and that therefore invest living systems with a kind of basic cognitive grammar that distinguishes them *for themselves* from their environments. Let's grant a point the three of you have made: that organisms differ from machines in part because the former aren't mere stable, equilibrious, composite structures through which energy is converted into work; they're themselves constant flows of energy and matter, inhering in their own unity solely as interactive, integrated, dynamic *systems*, maintaining themselves precisely by surrendering and reconstituting their material structures in every moment. They endure not as static objects, but as elaborate adaptable causal hierarchies—as forms at once requiring matter but also prevailing over mere material composition. In this sense, life is at once free and dependent, and metabolism is a constantly internally readjusted negotiation with a changing material environment, requiring various kinds of regulative "decisions," as it were. As life advances, more and more mastering the conditions of its surroundings, so does the motility and efficiency of its structures, and so too does the range of both its freedom and its "inwardness"—for instance, by the development of nervous systems. Primitive appetition becomes real desire, seeking satisfaction and working toward purposes ever more clearly discerned. This allows for organisms to create and maintain their own cognitive domains, their own self-directed grasp of the world under aspects of "meaning." Perhaps, beginning from sheer metabolism, organic life—by coming progressively to discriminate what in its environment is relevant to its own persistence and what isn't, and by learning more and more surely to pursue the former, and by acquiring ever more refined skills and an ever deeper practical *savoir-faire* through embodied, sensorimotor engagements with that environment—discovers what has meaning *for it* in its quest to persist and so creates its own sphere of values and of normativity. In fact—and I say this with neither pleasure nor repugnance—Thompson is quite happy to speak of an immanent purposiveness embodied in living things, and in two senses: first in autopoiesis, understood as a teleological urge toward self-production, and second in "sense-making" through the encounter of that activity of self-production with an environment to which it must adapt through cognitive operations.[16]

HERMES: Life creates its own sphere of *values?* Of *meanings?* I'm not sure I'm following. Wouldn't that make life a kind of *causa sui?* Do you believe that the initial urge toward persistence somehow precedes the ends that elicit it out of simple matter? I mean, where does that urge come from in the first place? Doesn't the will to persist exist as always already oriented toward persistence as a desirable end? Why create a sphere of values at all if not already under the sway of more original values, prompting the will to persist and evolve? Why, too, do those first stirrings in the direction of metabolism lead to ever more intricate strategies of homeostasis rather than simply exhausting their local stores of energy and relapsing into equilibrium, like whirlpools relapsing into the waves? Why acquire a nervous system to aid in the Promethean effort of resisting equilibrium rather than succumb to the peaceful satiety of entropy and death? I mean, to wax a bit Freudian, why does *eros* continue to strive against *thanatos* if as yet it has no erotic object? I simply don't see how intentionality can arise from anything other than intentionality.

PSYCHE: I tend to agree. I have to ask, where does this immanent purposiveness supposedly make its debut in the plot? I can't help but note how quickly the story you're telling mysteriously dances right across what to me still look like qualitative abysses. You speak of material disequilibrium becoming metabolism, and *then* of metabolism as discriminating and making choices, and *then* of life generating values and meanings, and only *then* of the appearance of what we think of as fully active mind. But this is all backwards, surely. Hermes is right. What you mean by "values" are desirable ends within the environment, and those are desirable only in light of a prior disposition to persistence, which is itself evidence of a prior disposition toward transcendental values, which in its turn is evidence of something like mind at work in nature.

Hephaistos: Who's dancing across abysses now?

Psyche: Direction is all. What from below are untraversable abysses are, from above, merely junctures where ladders must be let down.

Hephaistos: Ladders go both ways, you know. Look, let me go some distance with Thompson before you judge. He agrees with you, after all, that there must be some deep continuity between life and mind, and that the latter is present wherever the former is to be found. He also thinks that mind in its highest developments is an enriched expression of the same formal and organizing principles that are life's basic properties. Every living thing, he believes, is a form of autonomous self-organization constantly engaging the outer world in a cognitive mode, and so organism as such already has a kind of "mental" constitution. Here he relies, for his enactive approach to mind in nature, on Maurice Merleau-Ponty's phenomenology of the ways in which living bodies are embedded in the world and negotiate it by comportment—by corporeal behaviors—at many different levels of complexity; and this constant negotiation of new conditions necessarily requires an ever more sophisticated internal relation to an external *milieu*—a proper environment or region of habitation, that is. Even inorganic processes are structured unities, but as matter becomes life and finally mind individuality progressively emerges within the hierarchy of functions, and human consciousness emerges as a very particular form or structure of dynamic comportment or behavior in relation to its *milieu*.

Psyche: No.

Hephaistos: No? That's it?

Psyche: Yes, that's it: No. I mean, I find such ideas attractive, but insufficient. Consciousness isn't just a form of behavior or comportment, for reasons we've discussed at length—unity of apprehension, intentionality, irreducible subjectivity, qualitative experience, and all those other aspects of mental agency that won't suffer reduction to any composite physical system and that exceed mere mechanical function. Neither, for the same reasons, does consciousness arise from behavior, though it makes certain kinds of behavior possible; life does indeed depend upon consciousness in order to comport itself in its world as a living system rather than as a machine; but consciousness is more than mere comportment or cognition. It's also and from the very first an interiority of a very different kind, much of which has no simple behavioral function at all, and so it can't be explained as the effect of behavioral necessities. That would be a tale of strong emergence yet again. It would also be an exquisite specimen of the *cui bono* fallacy: the body's cognitive needs might be supplied by conscious mind, but they hardly explain how the fullness of consciousness is possible to begin with.

Hephaistos: You know, I'm trying to extend a frail but earnest *rameau d'olivier* here; we're both trying to narrow the explanatory gap between the material and the mental, after all, and to do so by way of the structures and processes of life. I wish to do so from below, you from above, but maybe we'll discover that below and above are somehow one. Can we at least see whether the ladder I'd like to raise up can reach as high as the one you want to let down?

Psyche: I'm sorry to have interrupted.

Hephaistos: Where was I? Oh, yes, Merleau-Ponty by way of Thompson. Let's start with a very basic physical form: a bubble. It's an invariant topological pattern, a structural stability fixed by its relation to external conditions as a qualitative discontinuity in the material substrate. The most primitive forms of organic life are, in a sense, just such discontinuities at a more durable and sophisticated level of interior maintenance. They're metabolic structures that fabricate their own material constitutions from their environments. Living cells are thus constantly dynamically producing *themselves* by the continual transformation of their own material constituents as they regulate the flow of energy through and around themselves. But this very process reciprocally obliges them to orient themselves toward their environments, so as to translate their external material situations into their own proper *milieux* of action; and, unlike inanimate structures, organisms have a large variety of means for modifying those *milieux*. In all of this, as I've said, life's world becomes a cognitive domain of meanings to be interpreted, evaluated, judged, and used. Consciousness is born here, not as an interior processing of stimulus into response, but as an always wholly engaged structure of comportment with the world, through perceptual and sensorimotor attunement. It's a constant dialectic between an organism's behavior and its environment. By the time life achieves the level of human awareness, those conscious forms and structures of behavior have become for the most part entirely subsumed into a symbolic economy, oriented toward objects to be used according to meanings conferred on them by cultural practice, and in awareness of and attunement with the intentions of others; and this sort of behavior enacts a new kind of *milieu*, one that allows human beings to perceive the objects of their world not just as fixed occasions of work but as projects of innovation and transformation that exceed the merely practical. But, in every case, there's a continuity in the logic of form and structure, one that can ultimately integrate the seemingly irreconcilably diverse orders of matter, life, and mind while still accounting for the originality and uniqueness of each.

Eros: Forgive me, but I seem to have missed a step or two along the way. Can we really move that easily from metabolism to consciousness and then to symbolic thought?

Hephaistos: I'm not so sure "easily" is the right word, but at least we can say it's possible to do so without courting the contradictions that you lot perceive in the Cartesian and mechanistically monistic pictures of things. That should blunt some of your more sharply serrated objections to a naturalist account of mind. Thompson isn't trying to make consciousness or mental agency vanish into function, as Dennett is. His analysis may not entirely close the conceptual gap between life and mind, but it may well reduce it to something much more like a difference in degree rather than kind. It may also go some way toward abolishing the Cartesian partition between body and "soul." Building on his phenomenological account of life, he goes on to argue for two complementary claims: The first is that living nature isn't pure exteriority of the sort that a strictly objectivist biology or physics might adequately describe, but rather possesses a real interiority and thus always already resembles mind. The second is that mind isn't pure interiority of the sort that a strictly subjectivist or internalist narrative might adequately capture, but is rather a form or structure of engagement with the world and thus always already resembles life. From Merleau-Ponty and, through him, Husserl, Thompson also borrows the distinction between the body considered as a living material thing—*Körper*—and the body considered as a "lived" experiential presence in the world—*Leib*—and argues that the difference between them is nothing like the difference between truly discontinuous realms and certainly entails nothing so intractable as the "hard problem" of consciousness. There's a real continuity here, he claims, because the lived body is a dynamic condition of the living body. The explanatory gap has now narrowed, because there's no need to explain mind in nature in either purely subjectivist or purely objectivist terms.

PSYCHE: Attractive but, alas, it is not so.

HEPHAISTOS: O, my prophetic soul, how did I know you'd say so? Please, explain why.

PSYCHE: What can I say? I can't help but suspect that, in this case, the notion of an original latency of life and mind in matter has been introduced into the story simply to avoid rather than resolve the logical contradictions inherent in the idea of strong emergence while still allowing that a kind of physical impulse or law in the structure of nature dictates the ultimate appearance of organisms and conscious selves. It still looks sufficiently unbalanced to me that it could be taken as meaning that organic life is a purely structural amplification of the laws of physics, and mental agency a purely structural amplification of the laws of life thus generated. In fact, it still looks too functionalist to me in seeming to suggest that consciousness arises from cognition—that the semantics of thought, that is, arises from the syntax of physical comportments. So, for me, this approach still doesn't really get past the problems bedeviling the mechanical account of things; it just suppresses them, and in the process introduces new problems all its own.

To begin with, I still object that all of this gives us a vastly inadequate account of what conscious mental agency is and does. It's simply false to say that consciousness *is* a form of comportment or behavior, or to claim that consciousness need not always involve any dimension of absolute interiority. We know that it does. Moreover, the language of comportment simply doesn't get us any nearer that simple "I think" that remains the necessary and necessarily immaterial ground of conscious experience, or any nearer to subjectivity as self-sustaining self-reflection, or any nearer to the absolute unity of conscious apprehension; neither does it illuminate all the ways in which consciousness clearly exceeds or stands apart from any engagement with the world or any kind of comportment within a *milieu.* None of that's going to be sufficiently explained by a phenomenology of physical behaviors, no matter how "enactive." Listen, I know Thompson's work, and I have a high opinion both of his aims and of many of his arguments, but I regard his project as in some ways a noble failure. His story never really overcomes any of the explanatory gaps—or, rather, abysses—that he sets out to bridge, because he's still proceeding in only one direction: from below to above. Despite his benign intentions, all the problems we encountered in physicalist reductionism we find still intransigently in place in his arguments—strong emergentism, behaviorism, functionalism, metaphorical inflation, the seeding of terms like "meaning" at junctures of his narrative where they have no business appearing so that they can seem to arise naturally later in the tale, our redoubtable old friends the *cui bono* and pleonastic fallacies, and so forth—albeit all of them artfully, if innocently, dissembled.

Frankly, moreover, he doesn't adequately appreciate the nature of the "hard problem" of consciousness. This is clear, for example, from how he responds to the notion of philosophical "zombies." He treats it as if it were a proposal regarding a real metaphysical or practical possibility, and seeks to refute it by noting how many corporeal sensorimotor functions require proprioceptive self-scrutiny and kinaesthetic bodily awareness, and by pointing out that perception and kinaesthesia are intimately bound together—all of which is true, of course, but also quite irrelevant. There are three errors here. The first, again, is the *cui bono* fallacy: Thompson often speaks as if the necessity of consciousness for certain psychophysical functions, if one could prove it, would be enough to account for the evolution of consciousness. But the same old issue remains in place: yes, it's evolutionarily beneficial, but how is it physically possible? He also appears not to grasp that the idea of philosophical zombies is meant only as a "conceivability" argument, demonstrating that cognitive functions and consciousness are two conceptually and logically distinct topics. Whether such zombies are a real possibility or not, under any physical or natural laws we know or could imagine, has no bearing on whether a system endowed with what appear to be cognitive functions, be it ever so sophisticated, is possessed of consciousness as a *logical* necessity. It may very well be true—I believe it is—that *intrinsic* cognitive powers are impossible without consciousness, but the nature and "laws" of mental agency aren't deducible from the laws of coordinated behavior; they can be known only from within. And this yields his third and most problematic error: he conflates functional cognition and consciousness, as though the latter were simply entailed in the former. Yes, indeed, we find our way in our physical *milieux* by way of a cognitive system that's embraced within subjective self-reflective awareness; but that too doesn't establish causal or logical necessity. A zombie or an automaton with an exquisitely engineered proprioceptive apparatus might very well be able to comport itself in its *milieu* just as well as conscious beings do in theirs. The mystery of mind occupies a system-level higher than that of "comportment."

Something similar must be said of Thompson's attempt to supplant the Cartesian gulf between body and soul with the seemingly much narrower gap between phenomenological specifications of the body as either living or lived—either *Körper* or *Leib*—which, to be honest, gives us absolutely nothing new except a divertingly different way of describing a correlation that hasn't been any better explained. Here Thompson is using the word "body" in a hazily and, to my mind, spuriously univocal way, which makes it look like a useful intermediary concept poised between objective physical presence in the world and subjective experience; but this is a rhetorical illusion, made no more cogent by the suggestive proximity to one another of the present and past participles of the verb "to live." It brings us not an inch nearer to uniting organic life to thought, or to spanning the gulf between the objective and subjective, or between the body as a material system of behavioral functions and mind as irreducibly unified, conscious intentionality—the gulf, that is, between the "eye" and the "witness." We're still merely talking about a system of stimulus and response on the one hand and consciousness as such on the other, and absolutely no causal or logical narrative has appeared to narrow the distance between them. To be honest, the very distinction between the living and the lived bodies is no better than the same old intractable Cartesian distinction between body and mind; it's just phrased more attractively. Once again, direction is all. Much of Thompson's project, precisely because it's an attempt yet again to ground the mental in the physical rather than the reverse, founders on all the same causal aporias that plague the mechanistic model. It repeatedly skips over what look like logical saltations in the evolutionary narrative it offers: from stable thermodynamic structures to enclosed metabolic systems, from metabolism to self-perpetuating homeostasis, from homeostasis to cognitive systems, from cognitive organism to conscious mind, from metabolic discriminations to "meanings." That may not be his intention, but what he leaves unsaid is significant.

Hephaistos: For someone who professes admiration for his project, you seem to have little to say in its favor.

Psyche: Oh, but I do very much admire his acuity in seeing that there's a deep continuity between life and mind, and especially that there's an "enactive"—which is to say, intentional—logic to life's unity and persistence and evolution. I even admire his descriptions of the successive episodes of life's ascent . . . well, I'd say, ascent *into* ever greater consciousness. And I vigorously applaud his willingness to speak of purposiveness in living systems, as far as it goes. But I still think his attempts to describe that continuity come down to something merely geometrical—structural, that is—and even then his account of that structural continuity dissolves into mere metaphor. As Hermes noted, to speak of the physical, spatial, functional "interiority" of a metabolizing organism with a selectively permeable boundary as though that were somehow evolutionarily continuous with the subjective, experiential, intentional, non-spatial "interiority" of conscious mind is simply to have mistaken pure metaphor for concrete description. And to speak of mind as only an *enriched* example of the formal or organizational principles of life, and not also as an original source of those principles, is to misrepresent a tale of strong emergence for one of merely structural emergence, and so to get the connection backwards. Though the mechanistic language has been expurgated from this version of the story, it's still to this point an account of the impossible: mind arising from the mindless.

If, however, he were to reverse the causal narrative—or, at any rate, complement it with a top-down account of those relations—those abysses might well close of their own accord. Matter intends life, life intends mind, which is to say that life and mind are final causes belonging to the structure of all reality from the first. But this also means that mind informs life, life informs matter; life is always already mind, rising into fuller consciousness as it's formed from above, and matter is always already life, rising into fuller complexity and vitality and autonomy as *it's* formed from above. And the interiority of organism proceeds from mind, not the reverse. As Ruyer noted, organic intentionality is the creator rather than the result of bodily neurology, as I think Thompson would agree. So too, it seems obvious, mental interiority is the source and rationale, rather than merely the result, of metabolism. After all, what would it *really* mean to say, as Thompson does, that the embodied dynamism of organic life's sensorimotor negotiation with an environment allows the brain to organize itself as a response to external perturbations? Or to say that "meaning" arises from self-organizing sensorimotor activity? Or to attribute to "autopoietic" systems with semipermeable and reparable boundaries an inwardness that's a kind of "self-awareness" and the precursor of subjectivity?[17] In truth, it means very little by itself. What he calls "autopoiesis" could better be described as efficient causality set in action by an end beyond itself; we might do better, then, to call it "entelechy" or just "teleology," and in a somewhat more radical sense than he is willing to speak of teleology. Nothing actually simply creates itself—especially not through the coordinated intentional sophistication we find at every level of life's systems—except to the degree that it's guided by some kind of antecedent finality. Every finite project of intention—even just sheer persistence through homeostatic self-maintenance—is intended for the sake of something more fundamentally desirable, such as continued existence: life, that is, as a value situated in what Ruyer correctly characterizes as a transcendental realm of values. Self-creation is a meaningful notion only in regard to what already transcends the "self."

So, yes, I admire Thompson for recognizing the non-mechanistic and mindlike nature of life; I regret only that he tells the story in only one direction, from past to future but not also from end to origin, and so renders some of its most crucial episodes incoherent.

HEPHAISTOS: [*After several moments of silent thought:*] I'm not entirely sure you're being fair. I mean, this basic predisposition toward mind and life in the depths of being that Thompson presumes seems formidably—even distastefully—teleological from my perspective; or, at least, it seems open to an ever more clearly developing teleological dynamism over the course of evolutionary history. If you want the story to be told in such a way that the fullness of mind absolutely must come first, and must then merely express its transcendent fullness in the drama of evolution, imposing formal structure according to real mental finality—well, then, you're proposing a metaphysical supplement to the tale that I would obviously find objectionable, I admit, and so we'll never reach a common understanding. But it still seems to me that Thompson's picture is a powerful alternative to attempts to describe life and mind in mechanistic terms, and that it doesn't oblige us to abandon responsible naturalist restraint in our proposals. Nor is he alone in venturing such ideas. There's also Terrence Deacon, of course.

HERMES: Who?

PSYCHE: Oh, Phaesty, he repeats the same errors, but without the philosophical sophistication Thompson brings to the topic.

HERMES: Could one of you elucidate?

PSYCHE: [*With a small sigh:*] Shall I, Phaesty, for brevity's sake?

HEPHAISTOS: Please.

VI

Homeostasis and Intentionality

PSYCHE: Deacon isn't a philosopher—he's a neuroscientist and biological anthropologist—so perhaps some of the philosophical shortcomings of his work can be excused; but his project too often contains a great deal more bombast than substance. It follows the pattern we've already seen today in others: Beginning from stable, inanimate, self-sustaining systems like whirlpools or convection currents, which naturally arise from entropic but disequilibrious states, his story moves through autocatalytic molecules to molecular compounds, and to metabolizing cells with semipermeable barriers, and to replicating cells, and to organisms, and ultimately to mental agency. It is, again, a narrative of structural emergence, moving from non-living to living systems, and from there to conscious living systems, and doing so in good part by way of misrepresenting equivocal uses of the word "self" for univocities: that is, supposedly, physical *self*-maintenance, organic *self*-coherence, the *self*-relevant dynamisms of persisting systems, and so forth, generate over time a kind of basic "biological selfhood"; this, then, becomes increasingly a capacity for *self*-representation, as well as for an interior representation of the environment, until at last the process has yielded the inner *self* of conscious mind, navigating a landscape of meanings . . .

HEPHAISTOS: You're omitting quite a lot.

PSYCHE: [*Sighing again:*] Very well. Deacon starts from a description of simple physical patterns within local systems of thermodynamic disequilibrium, within which he draws a distinction between "orthograde" internal changes, which spontaneously seek to eliminate asymmetries, and "contragrade" changes occasioned by external perturbations, which instead increase complexity. Contragrade changes are brought about when a given system's orthograde changes interact with those of another system, an eventuality that drives one system or both into a more asymmetric state, requiring higher flows of energy. These accidental displacements away from equilibrium are the origin of a "dynamical depth" in physical processes that ultimately leads to life, self, sentience, subjectivity . . .

HEPHAISTOS: Slow down even more.

PSYCHE: [*With a smile:*] For Deacon, there are three levels of this dynamical depth, and with each of them greater intricacy, efficiency, and persistence is achieved. The first level is the "homeodynamic," which is a movement toward equilibrium in turbulent or disordered systems, as in such phenomena as simple laminar flow or the equal distribution of molecules in gases. The second level is the "morphodynamic," which arises when two or more homeodynamic processes interact and create local formal configurations that constrain future developments, as in such local systems as whirlpools or snowflakes or convection cells; such processes tend to create patterns in which greater intrinsic constraints serve to dissipate extrinsic constraints; and sometimes, rarely, multiple homeodynamic systems that have complementary powers for dissipating environmental constraints come together to create a more ordered system, which is maintained in a disequilibrious state by constant external perturbations, but which is also constrained in a particular geometric form so as to reduce interference among the interacting systems . . .

HERMES: I'm getting very lost. Could you provide a concrete example?

PSYCHE: Think of a fluid—say, something viscous—heating in a pot on a high flame: the heat rises to dissipate at the top of the liquid, and creates thickening convection currents as it does so; there's too much energy involved for equal dissipation, so the fluid is separated into patterns of unequal density; thus an ordered disequilibrious system arises precisely because it's more efficient than an equilibrious chaotic system . . .

Eros: All right . . . that's basic thermodynamics. How does this get us to life or mind, though?

Psyche: According to Deacon, by way of the third level of dynamical depth: the "teleodynamic." This level emerges from interactions among different morphodynamic processes of self-organization, as a consequence of which the system begins autonomously to promote its own persistence, and then maintains itself by adaptation so that it can use its environment ever more effectively for processing energy. Here's where teleological dynamic systems arise and actively resist entropy.

Hermes: Why? Why does persistence suddenly become a telos for these processes? And how was it not already a governing end for those combined homeodynamic systems that maintained themselves against external perturbations?

Psyche: You know, I couldn't say. Deacon has a great taste for rebarbative jargon, but not much of a taste for clear consecutive logic. To me, it seems we're confronting just the same old abysses—and making just the same old conceptual saltations—as ever. Whatever the case, these complementary convergent morphodynamic systems supposedly create together a boundary that prevents the new composite system from relapsing into equilibrium; each prevents the other from dissipating the available energy they process together, and thus again stability is achieved far from equilibrium. Now also function, purpose, normativity, and so forth all emerge, as well as thought and representation, as natural developments of these teleodynamic processes. Somehow, it all leads to the development of what Deacon calls molecular "autogens," which produce processes of self-correction and self-replication that allow for the continuous diminishment of entropy in successive generations of organic structures. . . .

Eros: Does he offer no causal mechanism at all to explain these emergences of purpose?

Psyche: He does, in fact, but I hesitate to mention it because it's a bit silly—little more than a logical confusion, in fact—though it's something in which he invests a great deal of rhetorical energy.

Eros: Well, what is it?

Psyche: Absence. "Constitutive absence," that is. In one sense, perhaps all he wants to say is that teleonomic processes are incomplete in themselves as they strive toward their goals, and that their incompleteness is so constrained by thermodynamics and so forth that certain outcomes are much more likely than others. But what he says is that the absence of completeness is itself some kind of cause. Here mercy dictates a certain gentleness. Again, Deacon isn't a philosopher, and so the banality of what he's saying—as well as his overestimation of its significance—should be viewed indulgently. He makes matters worse, though, when he offers examples like the hole at the center of a wheel as something emblematic of constitutive absence. Obviously, that's simply a feature of a closed causal structure, which is itself the result of a causal intentionality. What he means to say, I suppose, is that it's what's lacking in organisms—what makes nature "incomplete"—that's somehow the cause of their creative adaptations. Which means, of course, that he's confusing the idea of "cause" with that of "rationale" or "explanation" or "occasion." I mean, the incompleteness of a house in the process of being built isn't the "cause" of the continued process of construction; nor is the incompleteness of a pullulating crystal the "cause" of its further growth. Obviously, an absence that nature strives to fill in is the absence of the end it's seeking in any given organic form, specific or general.

Hephaistos: Well, absence does make the heart grow fonder, after all.

Psyche: Fonder for the end that's absent, because that end is what causes the fondness to begin with. In any event, this odd and overwrought insistence on a rather vacuous logical move allows Deacon to conflate all sorts of disparate phenomena that he rather meaninglessly denominates as "ententional": phenomena with "satisfaction conditions," like organisms dynamically organized around finding nourishment, minds dynamically organized around meanings and purposes and experiences . . . metabolism, adaptation . . . agency, sentience, purpose, experience—basically, a random *omnium-gatherum* assembled in a loosely metaphorical set.

Anyway, none of this matters. In Deacon's thought, one finds many of the same problems one finds in Thompson's and apparently in your physicist Chaisson's, if in a far less refined form. All three, though, want to suggest that the reflective interiority and self-awareness of mind is somehow just a structural elaboration or continuation of the physical interiority and self-maintenance of metabolic systems, but that's simply a metaphor when all is said and done. We never really come nearer to life or mind along that uphill path from material order or disorder. It's all just . . . well, again, just *geometry.* What are the actual logical connections here, after all? When you lay them out, it's all rather weak: All dynamic systems with boundary conditions and flows of energy have both an inside and an outside, as well as a relation between the inner and the outer; and perhaps, then, that's *sort of* like the way that minds have "inner" spaces of representation and consciousness that create a relation between the world "out there" and the mind "in here." Patterns of matter and energy complicate and repeat themselves, and perhaps that's *sort of* like organisms "repeating" themselves through replication. Whirlpools, stars, convection currents, snowflakes are all geometrically complex, and perhaps this *somehow* leads to the complexity of living systems and even, in the fullness of time, the complexity of conscious mind. . . . [*Shaking her head gently:*] It's all quite inadequate. These theorists are all, no doubt, quite accomplished in their fields, and I imagine all have something interesting to say about how complex systems process energy. Even so, my darlings, let me tell you something amazing: mind isn't actually a structurally *spatial* interiority; neither is it anything even remotely like the bounded metabolic innards of a persisting disequilibrious organic system, much less the asymmetries of the convection currents in a heated pot of water, whether watched or unwatched. Moreover, to observe that a whirlpool, a star, an animalcule, and a bank clerk are all systems that persist by processing matter and energy is only to note the most banal of commonalities: all physical things are physical, and hence subject to the bare limit-conditions of physics. That doesn't imply any meaningful logical or ontological continuity between the accidental longevity of a star and the coordinated self-perpetuation of an organism, much less between metabolism and the conscious self. A snowflake, exquisite gem of fractal geometry though it may be, isn't one of nature's steps on the long, smooth evolutionary path to your consciousness of a snowflake. No, mind is before all and in all, shaping matter into living organisms; matter is always being raised up into life, and life is always being raised up into mind, and mind is always seeking a transcendental end—that realm, once more, of "values."

HEPHAISTOS: Once more unto the breach, dear friends. [*Taking an especially deep breath and composing himself:*] Well, as I've said, this was my attempt at an olive branch. As I've admitted, I myself am ambivalent about certain of these theorists. You haven't as yet even convinced me that the Neo-Darwinian approach in principle, if not in every detail, doesn't still point in the right direction, much less that life and mind are primordial principles rather than emergent phenomena.

PSYCHE: Why not? There's mind in nature at every living level, whether it suits you to acknowledge it or not. Why speak of its emergence at all when mental agency if so manifestly ubiquitous? Why not speak simply of its ever fuller realizations in life's developing structures?

HEPHAISTOS: It was you who were censorious of panpsychism.

PSYCHE: Only of the physicalizing kind—only of the kind that treats consciousness as something on the order of a physical quantitative property capable of composition. I'm a thoroughgoing panpsychist—how could I, of all people, not be?—but only of the sort who believes that mind is in all things because all things are originally in mind, and that at every level mental agency is invested with all its necessarily inseparable attributes, such as real intentionality. Look, I celebrate all those thinkers who want to move beyond Neo-Darwinian, genetocentric, mechanistic thinking, so I'm more than willing to ally myself with thinkers like Thompson and Davies and—above all—Jonas in trying to reconceive what life is.

HEPHAISTOS: Well, maybe I shouldn't have encouraged you by veering off into those swamps. Let's return to the original path and deal with these supposed problems with the standard account—the standard Neo-Darwinian picture—that oblige us to "reconceive" living systems.

Psyche: All right. But many of those problems have been raised right within the life-sciences themselves, as part of a new emerging paradigm; they aren't simply idiosyncratic quibbles of mine. We've used the term "homeostasis" quite a lot to this point, for instance, but have we considered what we're talking about? It was Claude Bernard who coined the term, as far as I'm aware, because he recognized that all living organisms exercise extraordinary systematic control over their own physiologies in order to preserve the internal environments of cells, tissues, organs, and the body as a whole, and that they do so by adjusting to changing environments, and by maintaining feedback processes, and by constantly preserving and even reinforcing an entire system that integrates every function from the molecular level to the fully somatic, all for the sake of . . . well, for the sake of itself.[18] I know that the standard Neo-Darwinian account of evolution tells us that all of this can be adequately explained by natural selection operating on chance mutations of the genome over unimaginably huge evolutionary epochs, but I have to wonder whether one can imagine any stage of selection and attrition—at the cellular level, say, or at the level of that strange, primordial, synchronous, interdependent, "non-fragmentable" alliance between nucleic acids and proteins—where what survived was not already an active homeostatic system, already apparently urged toward persistence in a disequilibrious state by something much more durable than, say, divergent convection currents, and much too well calibrated and ordered to look like a mere physical interaction of material forces. Yes, homeostasis is a negentropic phenomenon, but it also seems to be so not by logical necessity, but mostly by a kind of indurated, stubbornly striving habit of pursuing survival as a desirable end. Homeostatic systems don't just persist like intransigent knots in the fabric of matter; they're elaborate systems of self-perpetuation all the way down to the molecular level. And the further from equilibrium the system stands, the more difficult it becomes to imagine that its intentionality is simply an appearance crafted by chance and selection.

Hephaistos: All right, and Thompson in particular would agree with all of that to a point. Again, no one knows how life really began, but he would agree with you that the Neo-Darwinian synthesis by itself is inadequate to account for any stage of the history of evolution; but he at least has a story to tell, whereas you seem to think a simple profession of incredulity on your part sufficient refutation of the Neo-Darwinian synthesis.

PSYCHE: I'm not claiming that. If that synthesis one day collapses entirely, it will be on account of scientific discoveries. I tend to think that's been going on for more than three-quarters of a century, but I don't have the credentials to venture an opinion regarding how much of the synthesis might ultimately be subsumed into whatever newer synthesis might succeed it, or how the basic operations of natural selection will figure in the new paradigm. My points are simpler: First, yes, the intentionality we see in organic nature, with all its integrated systems of persistence and adaptation and with its resistance to all the physical forces that would lure it back into the restful ease of entropic dissipation, is far too ingenious, constant, and complex to be viewed as a mere "appearance" of purpose. Any honest Neo-Darwinist, acquainted with the discoveries of systems biology, should have to acknowledge that, if such systems are truly emergent, then what emerged was nevertheless real teleology, a recursive top-down level of causality, because organisms and their cells really seem to strive cognitively toward survival rather than simply wait for the benignant hand of natural selection to confer it upon them. So there I find, say, Thompson's perspective quite convincing. But, then, my second point is that this can't really be a matter of emergence at all, can it? It can't really be a matter of the miraculous appearance of teleological activity within the originally atelic dynamisms of material processes. All the current evidence tells us, moreover, that this miracle would have had to have occurred at every level of life, even the lowest and most fundamental, since we can't find a level of actual living organisms so basic as to lack that sort of . . . that sort of *cognitive* disposition toward adaptation and persistence.

To say that natural selection preserved a tendency toward persistence in certain organisms, after all, is a tautology, and even a kind of logical palindrome, as it can be reversed without altering its content. To rest satisfied, however, with the claim that some essentially mindless or pre-mental tendency to persist—which, in its original purely physical state of morphological inertia, could have had no intentional horizon at all—fortuitously or "impulsively" mutated into a real systematic intentional structure of self-preservation and even self-engineering is simply to point to a vast qualitative disjunction in the history and fabric of nature and say, "Something very, very significant happened at this point, but let's not dwell on it."

HEPHAISTOS: Again, the universe is large and has lasted a long time. There's room for the improbable.

PSYCHE: But not for the impossible, and I still believe that we're talking about a qualitative abyss that can't be crossed from below: between durable patterns of energy processing on the one hand and persistence as a willed and cognitively pursued end on the other. I'm not just confessing my incredulity and offering that as an argument. With Ruyer, I would insist that such a leap would involve the sudden appearance of a level of finality beyond the merely physical—the appearance of that realm of values that includes persistence as an end in itself. No, it seems clear that homeostasis, even if tautologously favored by natural selection, was neither the product of such selection nor merely a chance mutation, nor a series of such mutations. It was there to be found by nature's winnowing hand, perhaps, but it wasn't a product of that winnowing, and it's hard not to conclude that it's irreducible to small, inconspicuous chance deviations in genomes. As the evolutionary biologist Andreas Wagner says, Darwinian science accounts very well for the preservation of innovations, but it simply can't explain their complex and coordinated genesis, which always involves innumerable variations in intricate relation to one another. So I'm again entirely in agreement with those, like Thompson, who believe a new theory is necessary to account for the rapid and exquisite developments of which organic life is capable.[19] And I'm not saying anything extravagantly new here. Despite the insistence on Neo-Darwinian gradualism by the fideistic old guard, out of a metaphysical commitment to mechanism, the serial erosions of that paradigm over many decades are now well advanced. Even

Karl Popper, when he'd learned of "reverse transcription"—the process, that is, by which RNA transposes segments of DNA—proposed that we should perhaps see organisms themselves, rather than random mutations of DNA, as the creative agencies of evolution.[20]

Consider J. Scott Turner, for instance, an evolutionary physiologist who places homeostasis more or less at the center of his understanding of evolution. He too finds the story of natural selection, if left to itself, merely tautologous: adaptation is produced by natural selection, natural selection by adaptation; but this offers no explanation of adaptation, or of genes or organisms or even the basic tendency toward organic assemblages. For him, life can be understood only as a realm of purpose and of intentional striving, toward persistence and even toward evolution as an end in itself, from the molecular to the global level, well beyond what a purely passive process of selection could achieve. Organisms don't simply evolve to occupy habitable niches in nature, he points out; they actively alter their environments in order to create new evolutionary possibilities; and life advances from generation to generation through an intricate interweaving of homeostasis and the use of stores of hereditary "memory" far in excess of what the genome encompasses in itself. The power of organic dynamic systems to maintain their disequilibrious states even as matter and energy flow through them, and even as they must constantly adjust themselves at the cellular level in relation to their world, isn't—he convincingly claims—the outcome of life; it's life's antecedent condition.[21]

Hephaistos: Ah, now, wait: Turner—isn't he also one of those who argues that life's basic cognitive operations lead to organisms forming inner images of the outside world, and to intentionality arising from this? Rather like Thompson and Deacon?

Psyche: Somewhat like, yes, but that's a minor complaint. Remember, I don't object to the narrative that any of them offers in terms of the sequence of its episodes; my only concern is to make sure one doesn't fall prey to yet another emergentist interpretation of the tale, or one that can't recognize the formal discontinuity between such things as, say, accidental persistence and intentional comportment within a physical environment, or between comportment and intrinsic consciousness, as then the story will make one fail to see the full scope of the top-down causality required to overcome that discontinuity. What's important here is that life as we know it is a hierarchy of intentional systems, oriented toward ends that exist principally as values to be pursued, not merely as finite objects of use, and that this is in some sense true from the very first.

HEPHAISTOS: You know, we could argue endlessly about whether the Neo-Darwinian process adequately explains the origins of these systems. You'll deny that intentionality can ever arise from the non-intentional; I'll counter that innumerable epochs of selective retention and attrition have refined these systems into such efficiency that they appear to be guided by intentionality even where none is present; then you . . .

PSYCHE: Then I shall say that such a claim, when separated from the dogmatisms of mechanistic thinking, obviously defies logic, mathematical probability, the fossil record, and even common sense. More to the point, I'll say the very theory is a redundancy, since selection by itself is still a tautologous principle, however applied, and the question that actually needs answering concerns *what* has been selected. And to answer that we need only look at the processes of life itself to see that there are far more interesting forces at work than the basic algorithm of natural selection. Goodness, we can watch the processes of evolution at work in real time, and they're simply more rapid and more dynamic than anything blind mutation could accomplish in discrete portions of the genome uncoordinated with the larger organic systems in which they might occur. The evolutionary life-sciences, perhaps out of needless deference to the methods of physics, often concentrate so obsessively on genotypes, and on gene-frequencies as the sole measure of evolutionary fitness, that they're prone to ignore the incredible complexity of even the most basic organic systems—single cells included—or the dynamic processes that occur at the level of the phenotype, or the creative power of cells over the passive archives and templates provided by the genome. As Richard Lewontin (among others) often noted, DNA of itself is a particularly inert molecule, excellent as a platform for transcribing memory tokens, as it were, but subordinate for its expression and determination to the organism, which always somehow transcends mere coding . . . indeed, often determines that coding.[22]

Hephaistos: And, once more, neither of us can establish how likely or unlikely it is that such order is the residue of a selective process rather than the achievement of an intentional power in nature. We don't have a sufficient grasp of the laws at work to be able to calculate the probabilities.

Psyche: Oh, do be sensible, Phaesty. Are we arguing about only what can be proved in a laboratory? If so, Neo-Darwinism is excluded from the outset, since it offers nothing to observation except pontifical pronouncements of its own correctness; conversely, we really can observe organisms altering themselves genetically and morphologically in a laboratory, and in the world around us. Life evolves by way of replication. Certainly that's where selection works its brutal magic, we all acknowledge; some species flourish, some wither away, all change. But replication is found only in living organisms, so the origins of life remain an enigma prior to selection of that kind. If life entails coding and replication, then it isn't something that could be prised out of the lifeless by a mere process of selection. Life may be chosen, but choosing as such doesn't confer life. And we don't have to speculate on how living organisms replicate or how they're altered over time. That's something we can observe and learn ever more about; and the more we learn, the more amazing the levels of organization and cognitive operation and complexity we find. We find also a whole host of operations that not only explain but actively embody and demonstrate evolutionary adaptation right within the dynamic systems of phenotypes. We're free to be orthodox Neo-Darwinians if we choose, but it's sheer lunacy to continue to pretend that that's the full story—or even the central story—of evolution. Like you, I'm an ardent believer in evolution as an open system of discovery and creativity—more than you, really, because I really mean those words in a literal way. I see life as always already spirit, engaged in the poetic labor of transforming timeless "value" into endlessly changing and multifarious temporal shapes and expressions, crafting itself into ever newer configurations and capacities. And I can point to more than enough evidence in nature in support of that vision.

VII
Creative Evolution

Psyche: We all know the standard genetocentric narrative, of course: an impermeable partition—the Weismann Barrier, that is—keeps an "immortal" germ cell lineage quarantined from the gametes and somatic cells of the body; the genes are the true replicators, determining everything, while the organic phenotype is merely the mortal, ephemeral vehicle by which that lineage is borne down through the ages, inviolate, imperishable, irresistible in its authority over the organism. We're told that the true order of evolutionary causation is unilinear: genes code for proteins, forming and defining and determining organisms and their progeny in conformity to a genetic program inherited from prior generations. Occasionally, mutations occur in that germ line, and as a rule disappear as only so much fruitless genetic "noise" in the code; but every now and again, quite improbably, a mutation arises that enhances an organism's chances of survival, and over unimaginable periods of trial and error the sheer accumulation of such beneficial mutations drives the process of evolution toward its unforeseen future. That too, of course, is often told in terms of a purposive narrative—say, genes fabricating their survival-vehicles and determining them at every level, even the psychological and the social—but then we're assured that the language of purpose is only a metaphor, and there's no real "urge" to proliferate and persist in the genome. Well, once again, how can we know the dancer from the dance? At this point, perhaps we're really simply left with an inadjudicable clash of metaphysical systems.

Except that we're not. We know that the standard narrative is not only incomplete, but largely false, except in the most trivial sense that the durable endures better than the fragile. Even where the Neo-Darwinian mechanism might apply—the preservation of a useful mutation at the lowest levels—it's certainly only because that mutation occurs within an organic system endowed with the cognitive and intentional "skills" necessary to adopt that mutation and then to coordinate it creatively with an indescribably vast and elaborate integration of functions, in a way that reaches up from the "hermeneutical" plasticity of the RNA polymerase's reading and interpretation of the genome, through the engineering ingenuity resident in every cell, all the way to the level of the entire phenotype.

Denis Noble is especially lucid on these issues, and especially good at exposing the false premises that inform the Neo-Darwinian orthodoxy. For one thing—and that a very crucial thing indeed—there's no Weismann Barrier walling off the genome from somatic cells. If the genome is a kind of digital platform, so to speak, it's one that the body's cells both read *and write*. Far from genes imperiously operating the organism as a vehicle of survival, impressing inevitable phenotypic characteristics on it, they're very much the creatures and servants of the living systems they inhabit—or, rather, within which they're imprisoned. Goodness, it's astonishing how many different protein syntheses can be generated using one and the same gene sequence—which is to say, obviously, that it isn't the sequence itself that determines which of those syntheses will occur. It's the systems themselves that have, over the epochs, relentlessly altered the phenotypic roles played by those genes, and determined the expressions of those codes, and interpreted the "meanings" of the "memory" transcribed in genetic materials. More to the point, often these adaptations appear in a single generation, in the course of a single organism's life. Phenotypes change before genotypes do; genes are followers rather than leaders in the process. To find the truly active causes of evolutionary change, therefore, we should certainly look first at the cells, and at proteins, tissues, metabolites, organelles, and the dynamic organic systems formed in interaction with environments—in relation to which the genome contains not deterministic programs, but rather an array of templates and tools, at the disposal of the larger system. Actually, our understanding of what the gene is—what its boundaries are, how it functions—has become so ambiguous that some biologists are even willing to abandon talk of genes altogether.[23]

Don't grimace at me, Phaesty. Simply consider what we now know about the power of genes to edit their own genomes. Barbara McClintock discovered genetic transposition as far back as the 1940s. She was able to demonstrate just from her experiments on maize, using radiation to disrupt its genome, that cells could engineer repairs to their own sequences by transposing latent genetic elements—what backward biologists still speak of as superfluous DNA—to other parts of the genome and activating them, then passing on the adaptation to future generations. This sort of cellular re-engineering of DNA, moreover, is anything but a simple mechanical process. As James Shapiro is so good at explaining, it's a creative strategy for producing innovations, and for doing so far more powerfully than fortunate mutations and selection ever could: a cognitive process by which organisms employ all the biochemical and cellular tools at their disposal—all their capacities for cutting, splicing, copying, polymerizing, repairing, adapting, and so on—to alter the structure of the genome within their cells, and to transport DNA between cells, even to acquire new DNA from outside themselves . . . and also to move regions of a protein's chain to other molecules so as to add to the functions of the receptive proteins, and to splice coding sequences or "introns" together by deleting non-coding "exons," and to activate dormant genetic elements and suppress active ones, and so on—all in order to create, rather than merely await, beneficial changes. And, I would add, consider the vastly complex coordinations of protein-folding, according to principles that are almost certainly invisible from the merely physicalist vantage. . . .

HEPHAISTOS: Try to avoid overstatement.

PSYCHE: [*With a sardonic smile:*] Anyway, as Shapiro points out, there are a host of powerful evolutionary processes that occur outside any contribution made by natural selection, such as symbiogenesis or "cooperative evolution," the process—so beautifully illuminated by the researches of Lynn Margulis—whereby distinct organisms merge to generate new organic systems. Or the horizontal, inter-species transfer of DNA. Or the duplication of genomes, "diploidy"—cases, that is, of hybrids producing double chromosomes, stabilized by intricate cellular and informational engineering—which is apparently a far more common phenomenon than we once thought, and which over the course of evolutionary history has resulted in quite a few sudden alterations of somatic structures. And, in addition to the cell's uses of mobile genetic elements and the active restructuring of the genome, there are a host of epigenetic forces, which alter DNA functions and pass those alterations on to future generations without altering the DNA sequence, suppressing some parts of the code and accentuating others and somehow passing the acquired traits on to future generations through gametes. All of these processes, within all of these hierarchical organic systems, produce changes that are anything but random. As Shapiro describes the synthesis that he believes must inexorably displace the old Neo-Darwinian consensus, it begins from the frank admission not only that organisms are, as it were, networks of vital processes in intricately coordinated communication, but that cells themselves are cognitive—that is, sentient—entities, possessing sensory capabilities, means of responding to external and internal changes, methods of communication, powers of information-processing, and the capacity for making decisions; they're built to evolve, through repairing and altering their own genomes in synchrony with other cells and with the whole organic system they inhabit, so as to create new hereditary characteristics. This leads to large-scale and rapid changes in the genome and in the multicellular structures to which they belong. Cells exhibit a special ingenuity in using their powers of natural genetic engineering to respond to environmental threats to their own growth, survival, and proliferation, often rapidly but profoundly restructuring the genome in doing so; and this process of heritable variation and innovation continues so long as the perils and disruptions to which they're responding persist. Selection, in contrast, does not create so much as purify, by eliminating mutations that might inhibit adaptation. Such evolutionary innovations as survive selection and prove useful are then subject to microevolutionary refinements, and then to amplification and adaptation and new uses as successive environmental perturbations demand, until genuinely new and independent taxonomic characteristics are established, and the innovations thus produced are integrated into a distinct line and begin to constrain future developments.[24]

HEPHAISTOS: So organisms forge evolution rather than evolution forging organisms? That's your claim? To be honest, that may be a distinction without a difference.

PSYCHE: My claim is that form and finality forge evolution and organism alike, using each to refine the other by way of a pervasive intentionality in nature.

HEPHAISTOS: I understand that, but of course we don't know all the laws operative in these processes, and we have no reason to think that this . . . this *cognitive ingenuity* of which you speak, is anything but a refinement of material processes by purely physical forces and constraints. Need I once again remind you that, barring the discovery of how life originated, we've no way of judging how much natural selection could accomplish once that . . . *information* was flowing?

PSYCHE: And need I once again remind you that it's the very structure of life, however basic or primordial, that exhibits intentionality and organization, no matter what contributions to its future evolution the processes of selection did or didn't make? Unless we can discover some truly random process in the depth of life—something not always already coordinated within what look like intentional systems—I'm well within my rights to assert that the evidence of life itself is that, as far as we can tell, mind is always present in the structure of nature.

HEPHAISTOS: Present or merely potential? As we keep saying, direction is all. Your formal and final causes may look ubiquitous from the vantage of life's system-level operations. From below, they remain largely invisible

PSYCHE: Potentiality is already presence, even if that presence is made manifest only in being actualized. To say that mind is a potency in matter is already to say that matter is intrinsically mental—intrinsically something infinitely different from mechanism—and therefore from the very first moved toward its rational ends. Might I also note that the recognition of how fundamental cognitive activity is to every level of life does seem to clear away certain obscurities in the Neo-Darwinian orthodoxy? For instance, the seemingly saltationist geological record becomes a little less baffling when one realizes that enormous evolutionary changes can occur in very short order when environmental conditions . . . shall we say, *inspire* the creative ingenuity of organic systems.

Hephaistos: Oh, but these are old arguments—Gould's "punctuated equilibrium" and such—and as far as I know there's no real agreement on what the fossil record really tells us on the matter.[25]

Psyche: There may not be agreement; but the record clearly favors the thesis of long periods of relative stability punctuated by periods of extraordinarily rapid innovation. And I won't even bring up the issue of the mathematical probabilities of Neo-Darwinian gradualism . . .

Hephaistos: Yet you just did. Please avoid rhetorical tricks, if you can. A missing mathematical formula isn't a mathematical impossibility.

Psyche: True. But, even if we confine ourselves to mere probabilities, the very nature of organic systems confronts us with any number of reasons to think that Neo-Darwinism is badly in need of supplementation by a much larger, more comprehensive theory. I mean, it's still an open question whether the notion of beneficial mutations of the genome—especially in any significant number—is a particularly useful one. Shapiro says that random mutations have nothing whatsoever to do with macroevolutionary transformations, that species don't emerge from cumulative genetic mutations, and that genome-sequencing has confirmed as much beyond any doubt. I have to say, common sense also favors the argument. For instance, while I'm no computer programmer, I assume that the rules of digital code—whether that code's inscribed in a platform of silicon or of nucleic acids—are consistent; and in digital code, with all its nested layerings of functions, there's as a rule no such thing as useful noise or benign random copying errors. I assume that's why organic cells are so lavishly equipped with means for protecting the genome against them, and for repairing the genome when they do occur.

In fact, it may be that this very concept of useful randomness at the molecular level, at least as occurring with any evolutionarily meaningful frequency, is a purely metaphysical claim—a creature of theory rather than logic; certainly it remains largely immune to demonstration, no matter how many fruit-flies we irradiate, not only unobserved but technically unimaginable. Moreover, if such mutations at the level of code *can* become genuinely useful at the system-level of organism, surely this must be because the system is so cognitively alert and ingeniously coordinated that it isn't dependent on the torpid process of natural selection to create new phenotypic characteristics, but can instead react to a mutation by making use of it intentionally, just as it makes use of the transposable elements in its own genome. If we're willing to recognize this force of creative intention at every level and within every moment of the structures and history of life, and are willing to acknowledge the antecedent finality guiding that creativity as something truly situated within nature . . . well, so much becomes explicable.

HEPHAISTOS: I have no doubt that's true, but explicable isn't the same as reasonable. As I've said, however, I'm open to revisions in the laws of nature if they should prove needful. But, until we can isolate the mechanisms present at the beginning of life—or what we can reasonably deem to be its beginning, when metabolism and replication became distinct from transient disequilibrium and structural amplification—we're simply arguing over imponderables. You continue to pose interesting questions, this I concede, but you're too eager to propose extravagant answers. As Richard Feynman said, "What I cannot create, I do not understand." And no one, not even any of us gods, knows how to build an organism.

PSYCHE: In this instance, that ignorance is itself enlightening. And I would still insist that the evidence is on my side here.

HEPHAISTOS: Insist away. As you've so eloquently argued, our method determines the questions we ask of nature *and also* the answers we're capable of understanding; and our method is all too often merely an expression of our prejudices.

HERMES: [*Clearing his throat a little more dramatically than necessary:*] If I may interject, I think we may be overlooking something rather obvious.

I suspect that the issue of the genetic code's complexity, interesting as it is, is of only secondary importance. The more important issue, it seems to me, is that of . . .

HEPHAISTOS: Yes . . . ?

HERMES: That of language as such.

HEPHAISTOS: [*With a terse laugh:*] Why, of course. What else could it be?

VIII

Language, Code, and Life

Hermes: Oh, Hephaistos, my brother, surely you must grasp that language is the very epitome of top-down causation. That much, it seems to me, we've established. Its entire substance—its syntax and semantics, the symbolic thinking in which it subsists, the intentionality informing and driving it—lies beyond the physical altogether, in that hermeneutical space whose only location is the activity of a living mind. I've been clear that I see the notion of the indissoluble structure of language evolving from non-intentional physical processes to be preposterous. No less preposterous, it seems to me, is the notion that the capacity for language—even, say, simply the bare algorithm of Merge—appeared all at once as a mutation in the evolutionary history of a single species. Neo-Darwinist orthodoxy has at least the virtue of humility; it confines its claims to a very exiguous scale indeed: small, fortuitous mutations at the level of the genome, only some of which survive. But the sudden bottom-up appearance in a single isolated gene-pool of a capacity such as Merge, presuming as it does the entire semeiotic economy of language, would constitute a mutation at the system-level, which means at a level of the unimaginably intricate organization of countless systematic functions; and, even then, that organizing activity would all be in service of a faculty whose entirely real ontology—apart from the material substrate of sounds, gestures, and traces—is extra-physical. This is absurd in physicalist terms. And, as it is for language, so I suspect it is for life, for the simple reason that life *is* language.

As diverting as our debate today has been, we've touched upon the semeiotic level of intentionality in organic systems only three or four times, I believe, and then merely in passing. We should really pause to consider the matter a bit more deliberately. Replicating life, as we've said, isn't just the prolongation of dynamic disequilibrious processes in certain persistent negentropic alignments, and it certainly isn't simply an expansion of complex physical patterns. Life actually communicates itself, from one organism to another, and that communication is a good part of what marks it out as a living system. But how does it do so? Given the way some theorists speak, one might think we were talking about the mere transference by contact of some periodic physical pattern—or quasi-periodic but largely regular pattern—producing something like the pretty images conjured up by cellular automata or the fractal ramifications of crystals. But what we're discussing is semantic content, which exists and has effects not at the level of the physical embodiments of syntactic structures alone—those are merely the medium of transmission—but instead by being intended and being *understood*. We're talking about "information" in its most commonsense acceptation. The genome isn't a collection of small physical switches that work like springs upon the cell; its whole causal power lies in its legibility as intentional content to an interpretive and cognitive agency, capable of judiciously rendering that content into a vast variety of distinct uses. The content is transcribed into code and then read out from code again, and this is more than a convenient metaphor. There's a real semeiotics of life, translating organic systems into "digital" information and then translating that information back into proteins and cells and tissues and so forth—albeit with a certain interpretive latitude that's also proper to the non-physical potentials of language. *That* semeiotics—*that* code—carries instructions and templates in symbolic form, and is communicated and interpreted across the disjunction between phenotypes and even sometimes across the disjunction between taxonomic categories; but where that code comes from is impossible to say in terms of the physical sciences as we know them. Perhaps it emanates from the mystic realm of "physical information," but of course, as we've said, information of the kind we're talking about isn't some quantifiable element or flow of energy within the constitution of material nature; only its transmission is; in itself, it's intentional content and nothing more, with formal constraints and a purposive structure, conveyed by what look like symbolic conventions rather than physical entailments; otherwise, it isn't information. I mean, in addition to the code there is—there must be—an intentional agency that encodes, as well as another that decodes and interprets, and then there's the use to which that encoded material is put by the organism that employs it . . . employs it *judiciously*, as I say, and often creatively. So, yes, the astounding complexity of the physical systems in any organism is dazzling to contemplate, but for me all of that's a subordinate consideration compared to the sheer . . . well, I want to say, the sheer *miracle* of that code. And, again, I'm not even referring to the specific *complexity* of the code—which is also marvelous, of course, with all its layers of coding within coding, all its protocols for correcting errors, all its provident redundancies, and so forth—but simply to its semeiotic nature as such, and its dependence upon the hierarchical structure of all language.[26]

HEPHAISTOS: Well . . . *language* may be a bit of a stretch. We're talking about molecular sequences, not a grammar of verbs and nouns and . . .

HERMES: Of course we're talking about molecules, but we're also talking about meanings expressed in grammars, at least at the hermeneutical level of the operation. Who cares what the physical platform of transcription is? The very reality that the information in DNA can be transferred to another medium, and even stored on a non-organic platform, marks it out as simultaneously semantic in nature and physically inert in efficacious power. The power of that intentional content depends upon the interpretive agency that translates it. When we talk about text printed in books, there too all we have at the physical level are intrinsically meaningless material phenomena: paper and ink and physical markings without intrinsic content. Texts become "meaning"—verbs and nouns and so forth—only in the intentionality of the author and the reader. So, too, only when the organism writes or reads its genetic code do those templates become a grammar, a symbolic system discriminated between nouns and verbs and the like—between objects of operation, like proteins or tissues, and operational instructions. In any linguistic economy, more to the point, the entire causal power resides in that superstructure of meaning, while the entire superstructure of meaning resides in that hermeneutical space to which we keep returning, and that hermeneutical space itself resides only in intending mind. Such is the top-down indissolubility of language's hierarchy of functions that (to borrow a bit of scholastic terminology) the more "eminent" aspects of the economy are the ontological "grounds" of the less eminent. Intention is the ontological ground of syntax and semantics, syntax and semantics are the ontological ground of linguistic inscription or expression, inscription and expression are the ontological ground of the physical traces that record the code, and only the very last of these tiers of causal relation inhabits the actual material world.

Let's remember, after all, that the science of information concerns only measures of so-called syntactic information—though, really, it's often not really a "syntax" that's at issue, but just physical quantities. Shannon's equations, for instance, are entirely concerned with the transmission of "bits" and the degree to which they reduce uncertainty. Here, however, a crucial distinction has been elided. I think I've already complained about this, as it happens: information-theory in the sciences speaks of the distinction between the syntactic and the semantic as though it were a distinction between the physical or quantitative vehicle of information on the one hand and the contents of information on the other. But this is a terrific confusion. Syntax, properly speaking, is an order of symbolic relations, not merely the sequence of physical quantities needed to convey some measure of information. The latter might better be called something like information's material "parataxis" or "seriality" or simply "flow." And the failure to recognize this difference can make one also fail to appreciate how radical the top-down causal hierarchy of linguistic information truly is, and can even lead to such nonsensical notions as computational or functionalist models of mind, as we saw yesterday. It can even encourage something as odd as the currently fashionable delusion that Artificial Intelligence based on "Large Language Models" would be capable of actual semantic learning and writing and thinking; but, of course, such models are what's called "autoregressive" processes, which achieve their results precisely by totally inverting the actual structure of language in a way that makes semantic learning or synthesis of any kind impossible. It's a predictive system based on a massive compilation of "tokens" of linguistic information—not even its syntax, in the proper sense, but only its physical expressions at the "paratactic" level—which generates a mere simulacrum of syntax and semantics. It's an illusion produced by, on the one hand, the relentless statistical reduction of the aperiodic structure of semantics to as large a set of periodic physical repetitions as possible and, on the other, the relentless statistical inflation of the compressible, periodic level of information into an ever vaster imitation of the real openness of the semantic level. It's ingenious, but it achieves the appearance of meaning only by the resolute negation of the reality of meaning, sorting its bright little tokens of information into ever more regular and flexible patterns of juxtaposition through the sheer brute quantitative force of its data. Admittedly, if one finds functionalism coherent, I suppose one can believe anything . . .

HEPHAISTOS: You're wandering fairly far afield, brother.

HERMES: Yes, I suppose so. But it's relevant even so. My point is that where "code" is concerned, the paratactic order is determined by the higher level of syntactic order; but that syntax is in turn determined wholly by the higher level of semantic meaning; and that meaning depends wholly upon the irreducibly higher level of symbolic thought. Hence, Shannon's formulations aren't of any help at all where semantic information is concerned. Meaning can't be measured in discrete quanta; its structure is hypotactic and its nature intentional, and it's something in a sense outside of—but also more than merely supervenient upon—the whole quantitative realm of bits and their transmission. In fact, there's an almost perfect inversion between determinacy and indeterminacy where these two varieties of information are concerned, as there is between physical patterns that merely repeat and the kind of meaning that creates organic reproduction. At the so-called syntactic level, the more determinate the content, the more susceptible it is of compression—of condensation, that is, into an algorithm. A thousand repetitions of a sequence of twenty numbers can be coded by providing just one iteration of that sequence and attaching it to a simple functional instruction for a thousand successive reiterations. A merely periodic sequence isn't random; it's precise and determinate, and so an algorithm can be generated that wholly contains all the "syntactic" information present in its uncondensed form. But then, once again, we're dealing with something entirely simple; we're back to a process like the morphogenesis of a crystal—a mere structural convention that multiplies itself in a purely geometrical amplification of its initial structural "theme," as it were, measurable in fully quantitative terms. Conversely, a wholly random sequence of, say, twenty-thousand numbers or letters can't be usefully compressed or captured algorithmically.

Semantic information, you see, obeys a contrary calculus to that of physical bits. As it increases in determinacy, so its syntactical form increases in indeterminacy; the more exact and intentionally informed semantic information is, the more aperiodic and syntactically random its physical transmission becomes, and the more it eludes compression. I mean, the text of *Anna Karenina* is, from the purely quantitative vantage of its alphabetic sequences, utterly random; no algorithm could possibly be generated—at least, none that's conceivable—that could reproduce it. And yet, at the semantic level, the richness and determinacy of the content of the book increases with each aperiodic arrangement of letters and words into a coherent meaning. There's no way in which that intentional level of semantic meaning can be reduced to that physical level of inherently *meaningless* "paratactic" information-flow, much less generated by it; structurally the two levels continuously diverge from one another precisely to the degree that each becomes more coherent in its own terms, and so any algorithmic reconciliation of the two in terms of some more comprehensive notion of information is infinitely unattainable. And this presents something of a difficulty for a wholly physicalist account of life, because what's encoded in a genome and in the organic system to which it belongs, and so what allows for replication and variation, is a replete semeiotic economy, one that's quantitatively random and resistant to algorithmic compression at the syntactic level and yet utterly and exquisitely precise, meaningful, and determinate at the semantic level. There's no other way it could function. Even if the code contains algorithms, they subsist within a structure of information that may generate certain transitory local syntactic repetitions—I mean, yes, a rose is a rose is a rose (repeat infinitely)—but that structure can't in turn be generated *by* such repetitions. This is why Schrödinger, well before the discovery of the double helix, already predicted that what would be found at the basis of replicating organisms would have the character of an "aperiodic crystal," as only an aperiodic syntactic medium—one we now know to be composed of such things as strings of deoxyribose and phosphate molecules—is capable of conveying the transcription of life's code.[27] This is why, too, the attempt to ground the origins of life in accidental structural refinements of purely physical systems for processing matter and energy, even when they're systems of organic metabolism, can never really provide a causal narrative of the transition from the prebiotic to the vital, or get us down to the essential level where the system operates. Organic replication isn't a closed mechanical process in any sense; it has nothing like the compact and iterative periodic structure of a pullulating crystal; it's not an engine, but a process of understanding. In the case of life and mind, the distance between structural and strong emergence remains absolute.

That's why Paul Davies, as we saw, would like to see the laws of information somehow directly written into physics; but that seems a strange way of thinking of it, at least in regard to what we mean by "physics" at present. It's simply futile to imagine that the laws of life could be enucleated in the form of laws of physics . . . or chemistry, for that matter. The semantic information communicated in life's coding—or, rather, the formal causality determining that coding—vastly exceeds the intrinsic limits of the physical structure of information by which it's conveyed. The physical syntax simply can't generate the semantical meanings; rather, the top-down causality of the semantic level determines the physical ordering that embodies it. I'm sorry to keep recycling the same analogy, but to confuse the code for the chemical constitution of the genome is like mistaking the contents of the text recorded in a book for the book's paper and ink. And, even if you want to argue the contrary—to advance the fantastic proposition that there's some incomprehensibly mathematically imponderable but real algorithmic process that allows for the semantic structure to arise from its purely physical syntax—you'll still be confronted by a semantic barrier to compression: to wit, that the genome, we now realize, is not just the repository of an invariant code, but is part of an interpretive and creative negotiation between the macromolecule and its cellular and somatic context. It's, as James Shapiro says, a "read-write" medium. Life is a semantic structure that colonizes and informs its physical syntax—it's a formal cause with a final intentional horizon that shapes its material cause toward an end—and it's this structure that the cell not only takes from but also *imposes upon* its genome. The generation of new semantic meaning in that process is potentially interminable, and isn't dependent on any conceivable algorithm that could arise from the mathematically quantifiable physical information the process employs. Life, then, and life's evolution are not algorithmic processes; they're processes of open intention and determinate meaning; they're language. So let's not play games here: meaning, intention, semantic content, finality—all of this has its real existence solely in the realm of mind. If life is code, then life subsists only in mind; but life *is* code; therefore . . . well, you can complete the syllogism for yourself.

HEPHAISTOS: Some other time perhaps. [*With a weary smile:*] I'm not sure it's possible to determine that any syntactic . . . or, if you prefer, physically quantifiable "paratactic" medium of information is absolutely impossible to compress. And that might, logically at least, include the whole structure of information-processing, genetic, cellular, and somatic. Admittedly, it seems very improbable . . .

HERMES: No, it seems quite impossible, except as a desperately fantastic and mathematically unfalsifiable assertion. The qualitative chasm between the syntactic and the semantic is an infinite structural divergence. There's the genius in Large Language Models, after all: they get around the problem by employing mass compilation and statistical reiterations to reverse the relation of determinacy and indeterminacy between physical flows of information and their semantic contents.

HEPHAISTOS: That "infinite structural divergence" is a supposition. Maybe it's simply an equation on an exorbitantly enormous scale. Anyway, you're repeating yourself. Yes, language is complex, and code is language, so code is complex. I understand.

HERMES: Do you? Because that's not all I'm saying. Don't you grasp that the code *as* code—indeed the genome's whole semeiotic economy of meaning—literally *does not exist* at the material level at all? The semantic content that defines it isn't a physical constituent of the organism. It belongs, rather, to the world of form and of purposes and of values—of pure intelligibility and, in fact, *intelligence*. It's "information" in its purest state, uncorrupted by "noise" of any kind—uncorrupted by matter, chance, entropic dissipation, random mutation . . . what have you . . . all of which appears only at the level of physical transmission, not at the hermeneutical level at all. The moment we begin speaking of systems of signs that contain real semantic information, we're invoking a layer of intelligibility and signification that's *eternally* and *essentially* distinct from the physical occasion of its transcription and expression. Life is sustained at a level of *meaning* as well as at levels of physical operation. If you don't see the implications of this, then you're simply refusing to look. Life is indeed hierarchical, consisting in inseparable levels of causal interdependency, governed by top-down processes that can't simply be reduced to their constituent parts or to operations in isolation from one another; and the uppermost of those levels, so to speak, which is utterly indispensable to all the systems that depend upon it, is that purely hermeneutical space, which in its turn is presided over by the formal power of mind—not the individual mind of the organism, mind you, though that no doubt participates in the causal hierarchy in its own mode, but mind as such, the essential finality, purposiveness, intentionality, cognitive depth, and pervasive consciousness that underlies all nature and shapes vitality out of matter, and into which life ascends out of mere material potency, upward through chemistry and molecular biology and organism into the fullness of life. That life is the crystallization of the mental agency in all things, and individual minds are especially intense and translucent crystallizations of the mental agency in living systems.

Hephaistos: And all of this you get from the conviction that syntax and semantics are inseparable?

Hermes: [*With an amused smile:*] Among other things, many of which we've named over the past several days. The irreducibility of mind and life and language seems to me all so very obvious that to resist its implications strikes me as sheer perversity.

Psyche: If nothing else, it really would behoove metaphysical naturalists to abandon the mechanistic model of nature to whatever degree they possibly can. As we've said, that model was produced by the methodological exclusion of mental traits from nature, but since mind really does exist, in all its evident dimensions and powers, and since it's obviously part of nature, it's well past time that persons of your philosophical dispositions, Phaesty, ceased attempting to mechanize the mental and began instead to undertake the far more scientific and rational task of exploring the mental dimension of nature in the full range of its expressions, and most especially in the structure of life. I know, I know, I believe the higher system-levels of life reveal the nature of the lower levels because the former are real causes of the latter, whereas you'll counter that in fact the higher reveals the lower only because the consequent discloses the antecedent.

Hephaistos: I didn't actually say anything of . . .

Psyche: You didn't need to, just as I don't need to tell you that I think the case for my perspective far the stronger of the two. I see that we're all a little weary now, and that the balances of the day have definitely begun to sink toward evening. Moreover, I think we've returned to where we began. At least, we seem to have returned to the points I made earlier about the triumph of syntax over semantics in our age, and to the suggestion I stole from Robert Rosen about elevating the . . . semantics of biology to the status of our fundamental paradigm of reality while demoting the syntax of physics to the status of limit-conditions, more or less at the boundaries of the organic logic that pervades all things. I'll simply add to that the further observation that the triumph of the mechanistic philosophy and the dismissal of form and finality as figments of a superseded science were decisions not only concerning method or the metaphysics of causality, but also concerning what would henceforth be regarded as fundamental, both as laws and as explanations, to our picture of reality. For the reductive imagination, the level of physics is an obligingly comprehensive choice for that role precisely because it's so very simple, and possesses relatively little rational content—little information, I mean. Yet it seems that the laws of chemistry don't follow inexorably from the laws of physics, at least not in such a way that they can be deduced therefrom; nor, all the more certainly, do the laws of life necessarily follow from those of chemistry, nor those of mind from those of life. And it was you who quoted Richard Feynman: "What I cannot create, I do not understand." Reductionism in regard to system-level phenomena has proved a failure because its very premises were flawed. One can reduce a house to heaps of bricks and lumber and so forth in the hope of understanding its architecture; but, unless one can reconstruct the house wholly in terms of the principles inherent in bricks and lumber, so that its architecture naturally emerges from those principles, little has been learned except how to destroy a house. We need to start again. There's indeed a dimension of . . . well, all right, let's say a level of *information* that seems to be missing from our now standard picture of reality's apparently discontinuous levels. There I and many of the thinkers we've discussed today are in some very real accord.

I mean, just cast your mind back a day or two to that silly argument made by that Rosenberg fellow—that intrinsic intentionality is an impossibility because it would constitute a fact not fixed by physics, and we know physics fixes all facts. This obliged him to use an obvious expression of intrinsic intentionality—written words—to deny intrinsic intentionality. But the presupposition of the argument was childish: that system-level phenomena are not merely subject to the limit-conditions of mechanistic physical laws, but must be directly emergent from those laws; otherwise they simply can't exist. What a bizarre and irrational assumption, when we need only look at a house-plant to see genuinely teleological systems at work. I would go further than Rosen, however, and say that the truly fundamental laws—the truly fundamental level of explanation—will turn out to be those not only of life, but ultimately of mind. The semantic level of reality, so to speak, discloses the syntactic level because the former is the more eminent—the more formal—cause. This view of things, at least, doesn't require anything like the sustained cognitive dissonance the physicalist must tolerate in order to cling to his or her creed. I believe in formal and final causes in large part because they possess a rational coherence absent from a physicalism that's forever oscillating between reductionism and emergentism. In the end, we'll always find ourselves back at trying to understand nature in terms of its mindlike constitution and meaning: in terms, that is, of the rational relations we predicate of all substances and structures and systems when we try to describe them fully, now enriched with empirical and theoretical methods and discoveries perfected during our long historical odyssey away from and back home to mind as the enduring ground.

If you think about it, moreover, if indeed nature possesses this rational structure we've been discussing—if, that is, it's informed by purpose from the beginning, oriented toward a general transcendental finality that sets into action all the local processes of being and life in pursuit of more immanent final causes—why, then, a certain sort of theological construal of nature's ground seems inevitable, as our dear Hermes has intimated. After all, mental agency is, of its nature, "spiritual" or noetic before it's in any sense material, even if that "before" is simply one of logical rather than temporal priority, and even if from a purely temporal perspective it should be the case that most mental acts are somehow supervenient upon some set of material operations simultaneous with them. At the logical level, there's an ineradicable quality of the *sub specie aeternitatis* in mind's agency, precisely because mind envisages the future in order to act and therefore already comprises the future within itself, as a present real rational relation intrinsic to its own structure and activity. An intention always already possesses its end, in that sense, because purposiveness is its whole mode of subsistence. If I desire, say, to pluck a rose blossom, or perhaps to quaff a goblet of nectar, then that end intrinsically defines my mental agency, and so in the spiritual or noetic order—the "before" or "above" that informs what then unfolds in time—everything's already complete, whether I achieve my end in the physical world or not. In the case of the basic mental constitution of all of nature, there must always already be a "spiritual world," so to speak, fully present to itself, a replete noetic order comprehending the whole transcendental realm of values as its rational terminus; and surely this spiritual or noetic world must exist in its totality as an infinite movement of thought, an infinite economy of rational relations *sub specie aeternitatis*, logically more original than its embodiment in empirical nature. How else *could* it exist? The great act of rational intelligibility that runs through all of nature in its nisus toward its absolute final causes always already possesses the full conceptual plenitude of being's forms and purposes, and so must be not merely intelligibility, but also actual intelligence—even if of a kind we can't imagine. We know from our own mental acts, after all, that purpose doesn't simply emerge from aimless willing, and we know we don't just spontaneously posit ends for ourselves to chase after, for the simple reason that the very act of desiring to posit such ends could itself be prompted into existence only by some prior, even more general final purpose. So too with the mind underlying nature: purpose doesn't miraculously emerge from some purely physical antecedent, or exist as some inchoate, directionless striving in the depths of matter that only secondarily creates purpose for itself, as that would entail . . .

HEPHAISTOS: Oh, no. Oh, bother. You're going to invoke one of those blasted infinite regresses of yours. [*Heaving a deep but longanimous sigh:*] You're sounding a mite Hegelian, you know . . . or late-Schellingian, perhaps . . . or German idealist, at any rate.

PSYCHE: Actually, it's just good classic idealism of whatever kind you choose, ancient or modern, Western or Eastern. More to the point, it's simple logic. If we have reason to think—as the three of us believe—that the original ground of all things is mind rather than matter, whatever that is, then it must, in itself, be mind in the fullest sense, divine mind. Intention possesses its ends "mentally" or it doesn't exist. At its purely noetic level, this cosmic intentionality toward higher ends can subsist only in the divine mind, and . . . [*Pausing and smiling at Hephaistos:*] Well, you understand me perfectly well. We needn't go around and around forever. Anyway, my principal reason for saying that mind *must* be our fundamental paradigm for grasping reality is that, once we dismiss the reductionists and eliminativists and admit real mental agency in its totality back into our picture of nature—and we must—we'll also discover that the reductionists and eliminativists were right to think that, if mind truly is mind, then it actually does exceed all purely physical powers and possibilities as they conceive of such things. As we've said, mind isn't a property, but an act, no matter the level of reality at which it's found. The full range of that act can't be contained within the horizons of material nature, and yet nature is always wholly contained within the horizons of mind. [*Rising:*] But that can wait till tomorrow. For now . . .

Eros: My soul.

Psyche: Yes, my love?

Eros: [*With his most beguiling smile:*] I know I've said relatively little so far, but now we've reached a point at which I have a very great deal to say. With your leave, I'd like to speak first when we reconvene.

Psyche: [*With her most willingly beguiled smile and a come-hitherish note in her voice:*] I should like nothing better.

Hephaistos: Oh, dear me. [*Also rising:*] It's been a very long day. Rather than watching the two of you dissolve in reciprocal raptures of adoration, I think I'd like to repair to the banqueting table. Let's tell stories and sing songs and leave these matters for—shall we say, for late tomorrow morning?

Psyche: A splendid suggestion.

[*Exeunt omnes.*]

DAY SIX
Nature and Supernature

I

Love and Knowledge

It is late morning. The weather in the garden is, as ever, ravishingly clement; the breezes are soft and full of tantalizing floral fragrances; the songs of birds fill the encircling woodlands. Enter Eros, *now bearing* Psyche*'s rose blossom in his hand; he seats himself on his accustomed bench.* Psyche *soon appears and sits beside him. Moments later,* Hermes *and* Hephaistos *enter, trading slight scowls; the former seats himself on another bench while the latter reclines in the grass, gazing upward into the sky.*

Hephaistos: Can we resolve that this will be the last day of this debate?

Psyche: If you wish.

Hephaistos: I wish. Not that it hasn't been fascinating—and it truly has, despite my occasional displays of spleen—but I sense that we're rapidly reaching the last conceptual frontier to be crossed before there's nothing left to do but circle back to the beginning.

Hermes: That's probably true.

Psyche: [*To Eros:*] And you, my love: is one day enough to say all you wish to say?

Eros: [*Smiling to himself:*] In one sense, my soul, there's not enough time in all the ages properly to express what I want to say; but, for that very reason, a few hours is more than enough for what little I *can* express.

Hephaistos: I see that the magical flower is now in your possession.

Eros: Indeed. And for me it has much the same meaning that it does for my dear Psyche. It furnishes me with a kind of mirror in which I think I can catch a glimpse of the depths of mind; somehow it tells me—more eloquently perhaps than most other objects can just now, though I can't say exactly why—that, even in knowing it in its particularity, my mind is always already necessarily engaged in a more original knowledge of . . . the infinite.

HEPHAISTOS: And we're off.

EROS: [*With a long-suffering shake of his head:*] Yes, we're off, but much of the race has already been run; only a few lengths remain. Over these past several days, we've discussed countless ways in which mental agency might be understood as a fundamental rather than emergent or reducible reality. I thought yesterday's discussion was especially suggestive, because I do truly believe that all of nature exhibits the presence of mind—in its structures, in its operations, in its ends—and yet I also truly believe that there's no such thing as mental agency devoid of a transcendental, extra-physical dimension or horizon, and this means that nature itself is always exceeding what we think of as nature. My beloved Psyche is absolutely correct: consciousness isn't a physical property, but is instead always and without exception an *act.* So, if we really want to understand mind, our first question shouldn't be *what* it is, as though it were a substance or property alongside others, but instead what it *does*—what kind of activity it is.

HEPHAISTOS: And the answer?

EROS: You already know what I'll say: an act of love—or, more precisely, of erotic desire and erotic . . . perturbation. To know the world, the mind has to venture out into the world in a movement of desire, and has to do so as an exertion of the totality of its . . . phenomenological contours, so to speak: subjectivity, unity of apprehension, consciousness, ratiocination, judgment, freedom, and—of course—intention. Then, too, this exertion can't merely be an eruption of willful spontaneity; if it were, it could never actually constitute a coherent act of knowledge. Mental agency in its fullness has a supremely rational structure—a supremely rational purposiveness—about it. We've talked sporadically about a realm of values lying beyond the realm of nature, toward which even organic life must have some kind of primordial orientation, prompting it to adapt and to create its systems. The days of the Neo-Darwinian delusion are rapidly dwindling away. Well, that same realm is also the indwelling final cause that makes mind actual, because mental agency necessarily comprises, within even its most basic operations, two distinct kinds of directedness: one toward the empirical realm and one toward the transcendental—the latter constituting, as it were, the infinite condition of the former.

HEPHAISTOS: Could you be just a wee bit more concrete, laddie?

EROS: It seems rather obvious to me. As rational beings, we know reality only as occurring within two encircling horizons, one wholly contained within the other. There's the near or immanent horizon of the realm of finite things, the empirical order, the great middle distance of the world; but, prior to this and encompassing it, there's also a far or transcendent horizon of universal values, composed from absolute objects of volition and thought. The former horizon, moreover, is known to us only as set off against the latter, and comprehensible to us only as illuminated by the latter; otherwise we have no index of recognition and judgment . . . no capacity for evaluation. We know and desire that further horizon tacitly in all that we do, before knowing and desiring anything else, in each act of judgment and each act of perception. I suppose that what I want to say is that, just as finite subjectivity can be founded only upon a prior, deeper, purer subjectivity, so too the finite terminus of intentionality can be supported and sustained only by a prior, fuller, purer finality. It's our *principium testudinis* again, but now at the other end of experience, so to speak: not only turtles all the way down, but turtles all the way up as well. All the mind's operations arise between two poles—an irreducibly unified subjectivity within each of us and an irreducibly transcendental realm of absolutes beyond the reach of any of us—and neither of them is actually to be found anywhere within the physical order. Neither that simplicity nor that ultimacy—neither the unity of the apprehending mind nor the transcendental terminus of the intending mind—is a reality that can be found within the composite and finite structures of nature as a closed totality; and yet we know nature as an intelligible phenomenon, at once infinitely diverse and irreducibly unified, only as it appears to us in our mental ascent from the one to the other. There's an apperceptive "I" in each of us, more original than the finite ego each of us takes as his or her "me," and this "I" is forever directed toward a transcendental "that" or "Thou" exceeding the perceptible world, a realm of values or purposes in whose light the world of things becomes an open field of knowledge and judgment. I might almost speak of two "supernatural" poles—two vanishing points where nature either sinks down into foundations deeper than itself or soars up into an exalted realm higher than itself. We know the world because something within us that's more original than ourselves is always reaching out to something outside us that's more ultimate than the world. I take this to be not merely an epistemological truth, but an ontological truth as well. I think this is what Plato understood in saying that all the knowledge we acquire is really a kind of remembering: that deepest and most original yearning within us recalls that last and highest end beyond all things and, in doing so, open us to all things.

Hephaistos: Sheer poetry—at least, the part about the turtles . . . I like turtles—but, like a good deal of poetry, more expressive than explanatory. Could you take smaller steps?

Eros: My apologies. Really, though, I'm saying nothing you can't confirm from your own experience. Consciousness doesn't and can't merely passively reflect a world "out there," objectively composed of discrete objects, presenting itself gift-wrapped and beribboned to the purely receptive faculties of the mind. All experience is also an active labor of the mind. We know the world only in intending the world's presentation of itself: only in moving dynamically toward the world, that is, as an object of attention, in a single operation of intellect and will. This much I think we talked about some days ago: our conscious knowledge of reality becomes actual only through intentionality, and intentionality is always agency directed toward an end. Only by *intending* things under various finite aspects of meaning can we truly *attend* to them as what they are, because awareness and intentionality increase or decrease in direct proportion to one another. [*Holding out the rose blossom:*] I know this flower in many ways, under any number of aspects and in varying intensities, precisely as my love for reality itself moves me toward it as something real with a meaning I can interpret; I see it perhaps only as an object, or perhaps as a collection of colors and shapes, or more precisely as a flower, or yet more precisely as a rose plucked from a tree, or yet more precisely still as plucked from a tree by my beloved wife, and as the particular flower that has fascinated her and by extension all of us for days now as a revelation of the manifold mysteries of consciousness—each layer of recognition and evaluation appearing to my mind only in such degree as I direct my mind consciously toward it. [*Handing the blossom to Psyche with an affectionate smile:*] This is the structure of all mental agency. To know anything at all, the mind requires a real disposition toward things outside itself, by which it perceives, interprets, and judges. The world becomes intelligible to us the more we actively reach out to it; but we can reach out toward it in all its diversity only because we've already reached out beyond it as a whole, toward ends desirable as absolute objects of intellect and will.

HEPHAISTOS: Oh, for goodness' sake, stop repeating yourself. Are you trying to hypnotize me with that dulcet, winsome voice of yours? Why isn't it enough simply to say that the world we represent to ourselves has been refined by evolutionary retention and attrition out of physiological process of stimulus and response to have a certain structure of intellectual desire in it? Why must you invoke the transcendent?

EROS: That's simply not the world we know, so why even ask? Do we have to rehearse all the points we've already made about intentionality? About the world of meanings in which we actually live? About the impossibility of converting experience into abstractions without abstractions already there to give shape to experience? We *know* our world, imperfectly but really, under countless aspects of meaning, many of them purely conceptual, that *infinitely* exceed any neural stimulus or behavioral response. We know, moreover, because we wish to know, and wish to know because we already know more than we know: there's a further horizon of truth, a perpetual surfeit of ever greater meaning, which we intuit as an inexhaustible abstract standard, always in excess of what any empirical object suffices to reveal, and toward which every finite object continues to urge us by that very insufficiency. We turn our attention to the things of the world because there's a deeper attentiveness active within us, always already turned dynamically toward the whole of reality—the whole of being—as irresistibly attractive to our minds.

I'm not speaking of only extraordinary acts of knowledge, incidentally. I mean every perception we have, every instance of cognition, however humble. In every moment of consciousness, the mind is simultaneously receiving and composing the world for itself, grasping all things under specific finite aspects, discriminating one object from another in accord with the meanings one attributes to them. One knows each thing as a specific instantiation of meaning . . . of sense—as a quiddity, a "whatness"—which is to say, as a *form* inhering at once both in that object and in the mind, making each open to the other. But no finite perception would become available to us in this way were it not for this total directedness of the mind, this "rational appetite" for the ideal intelligibility of things . . . this natural orientation of the mind toward that infinite horizon of being as intelligible truth. But for this, as we've discussed, reality would merely impinge upon our neurology as a ceaseless and undifferentiated blaze and blare of purely sensory impressions, without aspect or content. Only by virtue of this prior natural intentionality—this compulsion of intellect and will toward the truth of the world, this primordial interestedness in the whole of things—can the mind organize sensation into sense and sensibility and significance.

Hephaistos: You know, I can't really say that I'm personally aware of quite such extravagant longings whenever I feel a desire, say, to . . . oh, I don't know . . . pluck a blossom from a rose tree.

Eros: Oh, don't be trivial. Obviously I'm not talking about a finite psychological state, or about some private mood that overtakes us now and then. The vocation of the mind to absolute ends is no more a simple psychological state than the unity of consciousness is a simple condition of psychological integrity; in both cases, the issue is the transcendental condition of thought, logically prior to the finite identity and impulses of the ego. I'm talking about a kind of persistent wakefulness, an openness to everything, within which we become wakeful to particular things as objects of greater or lesser immediate awareness, greater or lesser personal interest, greater or lesser determinate meaning or content. We don't have to feel some burning affective yearning for that far horizon of desire as though it were a sensuous object we longed to possess; it's enough to recognize a kind of constant velleity toward an index of ultimate values in the background of all our mental acts. Look, most of the things we encounter in the world can pass before us without exciting any special interest in us; but we experience them as recognizable objects, with particular aspects or meanings, because of our constant preoccupation with that horizon of intelligibility, against which they stand out as either vehicles of or obstacles to the satisfaction of our deeper desire to know. When they feed that desire, they often go unnoticed; when they thwart it, they provoke our curiosity or—if we're mentally lazy—our denial. If there were no such longing present in our mental agency—no intentionality toward those absolute values—then nothing would appear to us as one thing rather than another: not a blossom to be plucked from a branch, not a glass of wine . . . nor, for that matter, a reason to do one thing rather than another, or to do anything at all.

After all, what makes any finite object desirable to us if not just such an index of evaluation? Even our most animal impulses—toward food, sex, sensual pleasure of every kind—are comprehensible to us, and direct us toward finite satisfactions, within the embrace of a more fundamental longing for happiness, satiety, repose, and so on. Desire is never purely spontaneous; it doesn't simply erupt without premise from within the will and then spill outward in no direction whatsoever, with absolutely no end in view. Even at its most inexact and elemental and sheerly creative, it's teleological: it's a yearning *for* an end, real or imagined, proximate or remote, constant or ephemeral. The slightest free movement of your hand is charged with an intrinsic purposefulness that stretches out toward the whole of things; every operation of the will and the intellect, however slight, is lured into actuality by a final cause beyond all immediate ends. And you can know this from experience, simply because you know that even in moments of absolute emotional detachment—indeed, apathy, or even repugnance—your mind continues to give shape to experience and thus allows the world ever and again to become manifest in your thought and perception. The rational mind, even when the psychological self has fallen practically dormant, continues to go beyond each object of experience, and so to comprehend that object within ever more capacious conceptual categories, and ultimately it knows the world as a unified totality because, as I say, it has always already, in its intentions, exceeded the world. It's really quite amazing, when you consider it. That limitless directedness of consciousness toward that limitless horizon of transcendental aspiration allows the mind to inhabit the world, and—perhaps more originally—the world to inhabit the mind.

I have to say, too, that I don't believe this longing could have arisen within us from physical causes, if only because that absolute horizon appears nowhere in nature. I don't believe purely physical causes have the power to unite us, even if only conceptually, to non-physical entities. What I do believe, however, is that all of nature is filled with the desire to find that horizon. We began this debate by discussing what my darling Psyche called the mindlike structure of the world; but, now that we're apparently reaching the end, we've found ourselves contemplating not merely nature's rational structure, but the possibility of an actual mental agency intrinsic to it. Not only is the material order apparently disposed toward mind; it's in fact engaged in a genuinely axiological labor, a creative project of seeking to comprehend the realm of values by embodying them in ever more elaborate and yet ever more transparent organic expressions, rising even as high as fully conscious and intentional intellect, which is at once the most elaborate and also most transparent revelation of the one mental agency in which we all live, move, and exist—the most intense, most diaphanous, most radiant expression of that desire that flows through all of nature and life. The inner mystery of rational mind is the same mystery that impels all things: every mental experience involves a movement beyond itself, an ecstasy—a "standing-forth"—toward an ultimate end that can reside nowhere within physical nature as a closed mechanical system. To know the world as the object of thought and experience is a rapture of the soul, prompted by a longing no finite object can exhaust. So what is it that lures us on into reality? I don't believe it can be just some fruitful illusion: how could any transcendental yearning have arisen except by way of a prior transcendental yearning, already invested with an indeterminate but real knowledge of what lies beyond the physical? It would entail yet another of those infinite regresses you find it so irritating for us to invoke. But how can it be avoided in your vision of reality? Again, abstract concepts and abstract purposes can't be just the residues of sensory experiences; they invariably depend upon other abstractions within an entire system of abstractions, and can never be grounded in anything like mechanical matter. So how could intentionality of the transcendental kind be sustained by anything other than its own objective horizon of desire—the absolute realm of values in which alone it might find its rest?

HEPHAISTOS: [*Sighing deeply and a little theatrically:*] The love that moves the sun and all the other stars. Now there's a truly antique "physics" for you. May I assume—perhaps you've already said, but I don't recall—that this "realm of values" you're speaking about is simply the traditional realm of the "transcendentals": of, that is, goodness, truth, beauty, and so forth?

EROS: Yes. We *have* already said as much, as it happens. You know, there's an old scholastic debate about the priority of intellect or will in rational agency. Some argue that intellect must always come first, because one can't desire what one doesn't know. And yet one can never really come to know something without willfully desiring to know it. In reality, I think it wise to believe, will and intellect are actually simply two aspects of a single activity of the mind, and that each is present in that activity in direct proportion to the other. Certainly, we think about the world—we organize it in our thoughts and intentions—under the canopy of its absolute ends, but we're aware of those ends only as they act as final causes upon our wills. I mean, there are only two ways of desiring or judging any purpose of the will: as an end either desirable or not *in itself*, or as an end either desirable or not with regard to an end *beyond itself*. But no finite object corresponds to the former *tout court*. We can desire a finite end only as *relatively* desirable in itself—say, a glass of good wine that we see both as an object of pleasure and as an object we evaluate *as* pleasurable in light of a more abstract longing for happiness or beauty. I mean, nothing finite is desirable simply in itself, providing the index of its own value, if only in the trivial sense that whatever we find desirable about it must correspond to some more original and general disposition of our intellects, desires, and wills. I encounter a work of art that I judge to be beautiful, and then perhaps also conceive a desire to possess it; in either case, I reach my judgment and form my purposes in light of my prior sense of and longing for beauty as a transcendental standard. There's always some absolute value present in any particular axiological judgment, and an unconditional desire present in every conditional desire. All finite longing is a longing deferred toward an infinite end. This is true even when, within the immanent horizon of longing, one's desires are corrupt; even greed is possible for us only on account of a more primordial and innocent spiritual appetite and a natural need for happiness and goodness and beauty and so forth. All our concretely limited aspirations of will are sustained within formally limitless aspirations of the will, and the only objects of intellect and will that aren't subject to that deferral are precisely those transcendentals you mention—universal, abstract, unconditional, categorically desirable, free from all empirical determinants and accidents . . . names for being in its wholeness and in its highest perfection.

Hephaistos: Yes, yes, I know. This isn't my first rodeo. All these transcendentals are, as the metaphysicians say, convertible with one another, because they're all just different names—different ways for finite minds to grasp—the single transcendent truth of Being itself, which is of course God, who is goodness, truth, beauty, oneness, being, and every other metaphysical absolute. I know where we're going.

Eros: I have no doubt, but the question is how we get there. Metaphysics aside, what interests me most is the simple truth that our experience of reality has this transcendental structure. We have no world not given us out of the . . . *generous* transcendence of the good, the true, and the beautiful. How extraordinary that the mind is always engaged—rationally engaged—with a dimension of reality that necessarily stands outside the whole of nature, and so a dimension that's invisible to natural selection.

HEPHAISTOS: Oh, please. Nature selects behaviors and capacities; it doesn't need to see the fanciful . . . *user-illusions* informing them.

EROS: Well, as we've noted, natural selection is something of a tautology. What survives does indeed survive. And, frankly, I'm not much interested in that question. I still have to say, even if it were possible for natural selection to forge a connection between our minds and a non-physical order of values, I find this to be a queerly counterintuitive faculty to have evolved in a world of mere physical exigencies. After all, as objects of rational desire, these transcendentals would seem to determine the meanings of experience far in excess of any specific physical imperatives, and this lends a curious ambiguity to their influence on our behavior. In its prospective grasp of ultimate ends, the mind interprets the world by passing judgments on it from a vantage at least one remove—and maybe at an infinite remove—from immediate pragmatic concerns. It's a very mysterious phenomenon indeed: a commerce of the will and imagination with commandingly impalpable forces that in their sovereign absoluteness refuse to be contained by natural prudence and that as a result have the power to move the will in any direction, even at times in utter indifference to any calculus of survival or proliferation. In fact, they as often as not seem to prompt us to act in defiance of our own best interests. A consuming desire for that work of art I mentioned, for instance, inspired purely by an impractical devotion to beauty, can cause a man to squander money he should be using to feed himself and his children. A claim upon his conscience, however, inspired by an altogether dangerous devotion to moral goodness, might cause the same man to risk his life in a hopeless cause from which he can't turn away. Or, in different circumstances, a pitiless insistence on personal probity might force him to answer a question truthfully when only a lie could have saved him from the firing-squad. Really, considered as an evolutionarily beneficial faculty, this unrelenting volition toward the transcendent would seem to be a case of the game not being worth the candle.

All of that's beside the point, however. Again, in even our humblest cognitive acts we're already committed to unconditional ends, which may prove more unconditional for us than we are even for ourselves. But that's only the beginning of our predicament. It's not enough for us, is it, that those transcendentals give the world of the immanent its definition and meaning? It's not enough for us as rational agents, I mean? For, having given us the world of concrete things, they don't then allow us to rest content within its embrace; rather, they continue mercilessly to entice us—force us, really—to seek worlds beyond the world of practical need: higher meanings, the revelations of the arts, knowledge of every kind, useful or useless. They drive even those fragile mortals down there always onward, demanding of them that they create and innovate, explore and take terrible risks. This too I find amazing: there's absolutely nothing *purely* practical about these transcendental passions. Again and again, they seize hold of us and draw us on toward spiritual boundaries that—to be perfectly honest—have absolutely nothing to do with our physical welfare, or with the interests of ourselves or our kind. Again, even mortals are driven by a need for absolute intelligibility, absolute knowledge, absolute reality, and so exorbitant and constant is that desire that it's simply inane to try to reduce it to some chance hypertrophy of some evolutionarily beneficial adaptation. Nature may be extravagant in squandering the lives she creates, but she's fairly parsimonious in the means she employs. Nothing so wildly impractical and unpredictable as these transcendental ecstasies—even if they could somehow emerge from purely physical causes, which I'm fairly sure they couldn't—is to be found in her repertoire.

So, all right, you wince when I speak of this preoccupation of our will and intellect with that transcendental horizon as "love," but what is love other than a total attachment that requires no rationale beyond itself? In our every encounter with the world, we're addressed at the deepest level of our longings by the absolute, those ultimate ends toward which our minds are turned in a primal embrace of Being as such—of the fullness of reality in its very essence. And the more we surrender to that love, the more insatiable, unrelenting, and consuming it becomes. The mind always has some sort of original awareness of absolute truth, even if it has at first no categories by which to name it or concepts in which to capture it; and this awareness apprises the mind constantly of the incompleteness of what it already understands, or of the contingency of what it believes. This isn't to say that the mind always heeds that knowledge; but, when it does try to discover and understand the truth, what it's seeking is a kind of delight that goes beyond mere personal gratification, and a kind of fulfillment that can supersede any transitory disappointments or frustrations that the search for truth might bring. Sometimes this search can force one radically to alter one's deepest convictions, at times shatteringly, and yet even this doesn't necessarily deter the will from continuing on its quest. One often, and impractically, continues to venture outward toward the world's highest truth out of a deep longing for what my dear Psyche called the "nuptial" unity of mind and being, and for the joy of knowing that unity intimately. So, yes, the indissoluble bond between mind and world is one of love—an indefatigable adherence of the will and mind to something inexhaustibly desirable . . . inexhaustibly beautiful.

II

Desire for the Absolute

HEPHAISTOS: I understand you, you know. And, naturally, you'd tell me also that this profound, primordial knowledge of absolute truth we supposedly all possess, there in our hearts' deep cores, is evidence of the indwelling light of God, which is itself the ground of the soul's unity—yes?

EROS: [*After a pause and with a note of suspicion in his voice:*] Yes. . . .

HEPHAISTOS: And, just as naturally, you'd say that the transcendental horizon for which the soul yearns is really, in its full revelation, the infinity of God beyond all things?

EROS: [*After another pause and with an even keener note of suspicion:*] *Yes. . . .*

HEPHAISTOS: So all our mental agency—all consciousness, intentionality, subjectivity, and transcendental yearning—is just our participation in God's simultaneous immanence and transcendence? God loving God in us . . . and in nature . . . at once absolute rational subject and absolute rational object? What's that phrase from that Christian Berber saint—Augustine, I mean? Oh, yes: *interior intimo meo, superior summo meo:* "more inward than my inmost, higher than my utmost." Is that it?

EROS: [*Now with a mildly saturnine sigh:*] Yes, that's it.

HEPHAISTOS: You see? Just as I say, I've heard the song often before; I know all the lyrics.

HERMES: If only we could teach you to sing it.

EROS: Well, you're not going to deter me simply by employing an acerbic tone of voice. Mewl and mock all you like, what you're saying happens to be true, at least as a phenomenological account of our experience of the world. It's simply of the nature of rational intentionality that we can have an explicit knowledge of the finite only in light of an implicit knowledge of the infinite, and can have a grasp of nature as a totality only in light of a prior grasp of the supernatural that infinitely exceeds every totality. I repeat: the things of the world become intelligible for us only by being set off against the infinite intelligibility for which we naturally long; we recognize any given finite object as confined within its own limits and definitions because we also perceive a kind of nimbus of greater meaning around it, distinguishing it from the inexhaustible horizon of truth in itself. And, yes, I take that horizon to be the infinity of divine mind. Indeed, I'd say the first proper object of rational cognition is the supernatural, which can't in itself be reduced to a finite thing and which, in consequence, is a source of endless disquiet in us, driving us from one finite object of knowledge to another in our endless search for deeper understanding . . . and for deeper awareness. Who was that Catholic philosopher who claimed that there's a hidden transcendental experience present in all "categorical" experience—an unthematized "fore-grasp" of being—that constitutes an experience of the infinite within every experience of the finite?

Hephaistos: Don't ask me. I'm a little touchy about the creeds that displaced us.

Psyche: Actually, in general terms that might characterize the thought of a great many philosophers. But I think you mean Karl Rahner.

Eros: That's the name. But I find the formulation a mite timid. I'm willing to go further and say that the essential structure of all conscious mental agency is a relation to God as mind's only proper end; indeed, teleologically speaking, the mind simply *is* God, insofar as thought and consciousness strive not only *toward*, but actually *to become*, infinite knowledge of infinite being. *Nous* seeks to know itself as the One. *Ātman* strives to realize itself as *Brahman*. State it however you like: that which is most deeply within us is also, in its origin and end, that which is most beyond . . . God knowing God, an unrestricted act of which every finite mental act is a restricted instance. It's what Marsilio Ficino spoke of as the soul's drive to transform all things into itself and itself into all things—until it becomes the whole universe—in its desire for the infinity of God.[1] Maximus the Confessor distinguished between the innate inclination of the "natural will" within us toward the eternal Good and the "gnomic" or "deliberative" inclinations of the psychological will within us toward a diversity of finite ends, and the former he also described as rational nature's intellective ecstasy toward God's infinity.[2] Actually, another Christian philosopher, Nicholas of Cusa, states the matter particularly well: only the infinite God can be the final object of all rational desire—"You, God, are infinity itself, which alone I desire in every desire"—and God shines forth in all human longing, and all longing leads us back to God, carrying us past all things finite and comprehensible, in which we can find no rest, and bears us onward . . . *from* God who is the beginningless beginning *to* God who is the endless end.[3]

HEPHAISTOS: Ah, oxymoron: that always does so much to clarify matters. Must you keep relying on Christian thinkers? You know I find that a little annoying.

PSYCHE: [*To Eros:*] Don't mind him, my love. He knows perfectly well what you're saying. [*To Hephaistos:*] It's practically a commonplace of all the world's great religious philosophies. The *Kena Upaniṣad*, for instance, states that *Brahman* is the one final object toward which the mind moves, by which it is ever more conscious, and in which it finds its full purpose.[4] Śaṅkara sees the desire for *Brahmajijñāsā*—knowledge of *Brahman*—as basic to consciousness; all desire to know is, most originally, the desire to know *Brahman*, the source and fullness of all reality that is also the self's innermost *Ātman*, in a direct intuition of the divine essence, which is a desire nothing finite can satiate; only that immediate knowledge of *Brahman* is the true "finality of personhood," *puruṣārtha*. This is a kind of original act of . . . well, of "faith" or *śraddha*, which precedes and impels all the efforts of any person toward that final aim.[5]

HEPHAISTOS: Yes, yes, but you needn't recite a whole mystical florilegium at me. Listen, may I ask a simple if slightly indiscreet question about this transcendental desire business?

EROS: Of course.

HEPHAISTOS: Let's grant that, psychologically or phenomenologically or just plain pragmatically, this is the structure of our mental engagement with the world. To grasp reality under rational categories, we must be oriented simultaneously toward . . . let's say, toward both the ideal and the empirical. All right. Let's grant also that, if natural selection preserved this faculty in thinking beings, it was preserving a . . . *surprising* fortuitous development that involved minds operating in the physical world in the light of abstractions. Let's grant even that the origin of mental abstractions in a purely mechanical universe is as mysterious as any aspect of the evolution of mind could be. Can we nevertheless interrogate the ontological status of that transcendental horizon you keep talking about? I mean, is it misguided of me to ask whether the transcendentals, you know, *exist?*

EROS: Well, what does that mean? They aren't concrete things to be found in space and time. Final causes of that sort aren't part of the furniture of the universe; they're rational aspects of its structure. If they aren't real in some sense—and we can argue about what that sense is—it would be damned peculiar that they afford us so inexhaustibly rich a scope of knowledge and experience and creative power. As the absolute orientations of will and intellect that make the mind intentionally conscious, their reality is as indubitable as that of mental agency itself. If every act of conscious mind is prompted by values, how do we doubt the reality of final values without rendering the experience of the world an impossible paradox? After all, it's always possible that this or that finite and empirical object is illusory; but even the most fantastical creatures of the fevered brain have a real rational existence within the intentionality that gives them shape by its relation to those absolute ends. There can't be false transcendental final causes, as they're what summons intentionality into existence; they're the basic condition of all thought, illusion included.

HEPHAISTOS: [*Groaning:*] Do they exist *outside* thought?

EROS: Nothing exists outside thought, as far as I know. They *are* thought, in any event, belonging to mind as the conditions for knowing nature while not themselves appearing within . . .

HEPHAISTOS: Within nature, yes. Again, that doesn't really tell me what their ontological status is. I mean, you clearly don't think we're talking about mere *a priori* regulative conditions of cognition and reason, of the Kantian kind. You think these transcendentals are names for the essence of God, and you certainly don't think of God just as an abstract set of values in the mind.

EROS: We've repeatedly seen—or argued, at any rate—that abstractions can't be generated by mechanical processes of stimulus and response; abstract concepts too, in that fabulous "testudinal" way, rest only upon themselves, and declare their own reality in giving us the reality we perceive outside ourselves. Just as the mind within us knows itself in knowing the world, so the mind behind all things reveals itself in revealing the world. So, yes, of course the transcendentals are real, and of course they're names of God, and of course God is the source and ground and end of all existence: the very power of being upon which all depends—infinite mind, creating, sustaining, pervading, and transcending all that exists. All right? Is that clear enough?

HEPHAISTOS: Clear as cut crystal. There, then, is my problem. You see, I'm sure you could adduce a catalogue of personal rationales for moving directly from the immanent plane of the phenomenology of mental acts to a transcendent plane of metaphysical assertions without so much as pausing to have your passport stamped, but I'm not quite so bold an adventurer. I mind the borders and try to avoid trespass. More to the point, I have a desperate need to know where I am at all times. I mean, since I've now mentioned Kant, I might as well note that it's fairly common in modern philosophy to presume certain restrictions regarding the legitimacy of our metaphysical speculations. *His* transcendentals are the limits to which we're confined by our apparatus of perception and those antinomies of reason that our reason can't transcend and that prohibit claims about supersensible reality. You know: concepts without experience—without "intuitions"—are blind. And, too, there's the distinction between phenomenon and noumenon—between appearance and the "thing in itself" . . . the *Ding an sich*. Not to be a bore, but . . .

PSYCHE: *Pah!*

HEPHAISTOS: [*After a moment:*] Well, that response has the virtue of brevity, at least.

PSYCHE: You *are* being boring, Phaesty, whether you intend to be or not. You're making too much of what's really just a banal observation about the limits of mental representation. We discussed all of this on the very first day of this conversation. Did none of it sink in? Reason can accomplish quite a lot, in fact, in the absence of sensible intuitions, because the mind is capable of actual experience of realities beyond the sensible. You know perfectly well that all speculative restrictions on metaphysics come freighted with metaphysical assumptions of their own, and in fact in a sense violate themselves in being stated, because you can't know the limits of thought from within those limits; if there are such limits, they're identifiable only from a perspective that's gone beyond them and already taken hold of that *more*—that transcendental horizon of truth—outside empirical nature. Somehow one must know that the real in itself is qualitatively other than what phenomenal experience or more refined philosophical reasoning can ultimately disclose. As for the antinomies of reason, if they really are antinomies rather than just questions posed at the poorly defined boundaries of science and logic, they simply aren't relevant to the issue of whether we can draw persuasive inferences from the recognizable shape of our own mental agency. We aren't talking about the disengaged speculations of "pure reason." The problem with trying to erect boundaries of that sort to the possibility of knowing the real is that it arbitrarily and implausibly presumes the same sort of dualism as the Cartesian view of reality: some essential and absolute differentiation between a constrained field of mind "in here" and an alien realm of the non-mental "out there." I'm at one with Kant's later, idealist critics. If one starts from his perspective, then no knowledge is knowledge of the real at all; one knows only that there *must* be an occult "thing in itself" that resists translation into mental experience or categories. In fact, everything is something *infinitely* other than what we know about it. But then how does that utterly alien dimension of the real occasion phenomenal experience in us to begin with? And how can it do so with such indefatigable coherency and with so many layers of ever deeper coherency? And how can that phenomenal experience not be the real manifestation of this supposedly hidden quantum? How, in fact, do two totally qualitatively irreconcilable realities exist in the same frame of being or affect one another? The whole supposition is surely false. Perhaps there's no such absolute and inconceivable duality of the real. Perhaps nature is mind already, already an act of thought being expressed, already a kind of interiority communicating itself to another interiority—in which case, both nature and its conditions of intelligibility belong to a rational continuum that the mind can explore. And we've spent more than five days now discovering reasons to think such a duality neither plausible nor persuasive.

Don't you see, Phaesty? If the very structure of thought is nothing other than this perpetual engagement with a transcendent horizon—if the immanent is the gift of the transcendent, and nature the gift of the supernatural—then the continuum of the phenomenal has already been broken open before any other kind of thinking has occurred. Indeed, it's been broken open at both ends so to speak: the subjective and the objective poles of experience, the irreducible "witness" within and the irreducible horizon of the absolute toward which that witness is forever turned. The logical and ontological priority of neither pole admits of a materialist solution, even though the material order is given to us as an intelligible totality *only* by the relation between them. Experience of the world is already constituted by a relation of extra-natural mental powers to an object that exceeds all natural experience. Every phenomenon is already something disclosed to us by our tacit knowledge of its metaphysical or "noumenal" depth. All sensible intuitions are informed by supersensible "intuitions." So what warrant could we possibly have, other than some tedious materialist dogmatism, for denying the reality of the *telos* that makes knowledge possible? And what's the logic of such a denial? If there's no duality of mind and nature—if instead nature is visible spirit and spirit is invisible nature, as Schelling said—then there's no such thing as the hidden *Ding an sich:* everything is manifestation, everything is expression, communicating itself as the thinkable content of a thinking mind. If matter and form, act and finality—or something like them—are the rational relations that constitute reality, then being is essentially intelligibility. You know, there's an old scholastic formula that says that the *ordo cognoscendi*—the order of our knowledge of something—is the inverse of its *ordo essendi*—its order of existence. That is, we encounter any reality only at the end, so to speak, of the causal chain that produces and sustains it, as a fully manifest fact of perception; only when we begin asking questions about that reality's origin or sufficient reason do we move back along that chain toward its first most original principle. All finite knowledge arguably works in this fashion: the being of things is reversed in the mirrors of our minds so as to become the knowledge of things, no matter how many logical deductions might be required to trace our way back from final effect to first cause. This seems to me a sound and convincing maxim, and so it seems to me not only right but necessary to ask whether the evident phenomenon of the relation between our subjective unity of consciousness and its end in the fullness of transcendent being is a glimpse—caught in the looking-glass of rational reflection—of the real relation between transcendent being as original source and the subjective experience as its result. That is, if this is how our knowledge of the world is constituted, it's reasonable to suppose the reality of the final cause of our knowledge . . . which is also the original cause of what we know.

Eros: I don't want to test your patience by invoking yet another Christian philosopher—I share many of your reservations regarding religious systems in general—but there was a modern Catholic thinker, Bernard Lonergan, who saw the sort of Kantian limitations of reason you invoke as evidence only of an incomplete survey of rational life. The pursuit of rational understanding can't be undertaken by trying to identify the formal conditions of objective knowledge while failing to discuss the real act of knowledge as subjective intentional work. Every subject is a rational consciousness that delineates, within the orientation of the action that constitutes him or her as rational consciousness, the full horizon of his or her search, which can't be anything less than the horizon of the totality of being. This subject can't be constrained in advance by arbitrary strictures based on a metaphysics of the opaque, so to speak—a metaphysics that posits a duality of mind and being. Where we may want to imagine some absolute partition between them—the dividing wall between thought "in here" and the unintuited and unrepresentable "real nature" of the "thing in itself" forever "out there"—Lonergan saw only the inexhaustible plenitude of knowledge yet to be attained, the sheer boundless communicability of reality . . . the world yet to come into fuller manifestation in and through intentional mind.

HEPHAISTOS: How easily the three of you move from the epistemological to the ontological . . . from the intellectual orientation toward God—or whatever else you want to call that absolute horizon you keep talking about—to the reality of God.

HERMES: But of course. I'm perplexed, though, by how easily you *distinguish* the epistemological from the ontological . . . how easily you separate knowledge from existence. I happen to know, as do you, that the three of us have numerous reasons for believing in a transcendent source of all things—infinite divine mind underlying the powers of finite minds, infinite divine being underlying the contingency of finite existence, and so on—and I'll admit we begin from that premise and so tend to take encouragement from any evidence of rational order and intrinsic intelligibility and real mental agency in nature. We see cells at work editing their own genomes, or the mathematical cogency of the quadratic equation, or our own consciousness construing the world into a boundlessly complex and yet comprehensible totality, or the unified depth of private subjective awareness in each of us, or even our primordial sense of absolute values, and we exclaim, "Ah, see! The mind of God!" I won't deny it. But why shouldn't we? What metaphysically naturalist account can you really produce of the structure of our mental engagement with the being of the world that doesn't involve bizarre evolutionary saltations, magical transitions from objective mechanism to subjective experience, abstractions and symbolic meanings inexplicably conjured into being by the forces of phylogenic attrition, an altogether miraculous, even occasionalist harmony between evolutionarily selected illusions and the practical demands of the world around us? What can you offer that's more convincing than our simple conviction that we really do know and understand reality by our mental agency, truly if imperfectly, because there's a real unity—even, in some sense, an identity—between the principles underlying both knowing and being? Why, apart from the incoherent metaphysical dualisms invented almost accidentally at the threshold of modernity, should we ever assume that our knowledge of the world and the existence of the world are two discontinuous phenomena that just somehow coincide in some bizarre and inconceivable liminal space in between?

III

Mind's Transcendent Horizon

HERMES: Let me ask you directly: How *should* we understand the relation between the being of the world and our knowledge of it? Could it really be a purely extrinsic interaction between wholly disparate realities? Or might there be instead a more intimate interdependency between them? It's a perennial question, of course, whether the being of the world and our consciousness of it can actually be discriminated into two distinct spheres of reality, but I suspect it's a question that's become all the more acute in the modern age. Even before the discoveries of quantum mechanics and the seeming dissolution of the clear boundary between potentiality and actuality—or between entanglement and locality, and so forth—modern thought had confronted itself with the implications of a true dualism between soul and body . . . or between mind and world, or between phenomenal perception and the unrepresentable *Ding an sich.* Inevitably, it all raises the question of where the logical or ontological demarcation can be drawn between the being of the world and the manifestation of the world to consciousness. Honestly, how could anything exist in such a manner that it couldn't be perceived or thought about in any way at all, not even by itself, even in principle? What would be the ontological status of something that can't in principle be known, intuited, sensed, or represented? Could it be said to exist at all? We've told you why we think it unreasonable to see mind as only an emergent function of mechanistic matter, or only an epiphenomenon, or only an illusion; but to everything we've already said we might add the further consideration that in the absence of mind there seems to be no real mode of existence for the universe.

HEPHAISTOS: Well, for the universe as it's actually known to mind, but that's a vapid tautology.

HERMES: Oh, no, not merely as *actually* known to mind, but as *potentially* known too. At least, it seems reasonable to me to say that being is manifestation, that real subsistence is revelation, that to exist is to be perceptible, conceivable, knowable; and so, perhaps, to exist fully is to be manifest to consciousness. In what sense precisely would a universe without consciousness exist? Obviously not as we perceive it: as space and time, subsisting in discrete objects in streams of temporal continuity, since all the qualitative semantics of existence are inseparable from consciousness; all of that exists as experience, in that aforementioned "nuptial" union of mind and being. But could even the rational syntax of the universe—that realm of purely quantitative physical relations supposedly hiding behind the veil of the phenomenal—exist in any meaningful sense, since those relations themselves are only an order of rational intelligibility, rational coherence . . . the capacity for measurement, applying to realities that exist only at the phenomenal level? Without phenomena to be reduced to measurement, what would there really be of this "mindless" universe at all? Without the existence of mental agency, would even this bare syntactical order come to manifestation . . . to existence? Can we even say it would consist in quantum potentialities? But what's the ontological status of such an order? It seems fair to me to say that such a universe, if it existed, would exist exactly to the extent that it *could* be known to intentional consciousness of some kind—only as always disposed to consciousness as a final cause. There's a point then, arguably, at which being and intelligibility become conceptually indistinguishable. Only what could in principle be rationally known can in actuality exist.

HEPHAISTOS: And? Yes, things have to hold together in order to exist, and holding together is in some vague sense what we mean by rational coherence.

HERMES: Well . . . you see, I'm trying to suggest that existence in any meaningful sense is manifestation, and that being achieves manifestation only in mind, and so mental agency can't be accounted a secondary or derivative property of a universe that exists in itself, apart from mind.

HEPHAISTOS: You were doing better with your claims regarding intentionality in nature, and regarding the irreducibility of mind to physical causes. As for this line of argument—well, yes, it's suggestive, but no more than that. You haven't as yet pried me away from that dualist picture you dismiss so haughtily. I'm still willing to believe that there's an essential difference between the world as it appears to the perceiving mind—the semantic, qualitative, phenomenal world of the "manifest image"—and the world as it exists in itself—the syntactic, quantitative, noumenal world of the "scientific image." True, it's a problematic view. Yes, it's mysterious indeed that the quantitative world that can't be experienced can somehow, through the alchemy of representation, be translated into a qualitative world that's *nothing but* experience. But still I find that essential duality credible . . . in an incredible way. You've argued quite well that such a supposition isn't necessitated by logic, but you certainly haven't convinced me that it's *excluded* by logic. It's just very . . . well, once again, very mysterious. I'm willing to concede the solvency of much of your case against simple physicalist reductionism, but you're asking rather a lot if you expect me then to concede that, because the world appears to the mind in mental categories and mental forms, the world is dependent on mental agency, and that I now have no choice but to accept the reality of God, as if that sublimely surreptitious gentleman or lady is the unavoidable QED of our conversation.

PSYCHE: If the physical order can't be the ground of mind, mind must be the ground of the physical order; we've seen that a third way, such as neutral monism, is just an evasion. And, if that's so, then all we've said today follows rather directly, however you may wish to protest. You know, it's no small thing that mind truly does take hold of reality at all, and it would be fairly miraculous if it did so even though there were nothing in the nature of the real for it to get a hold of—nothing naturally available, so to speak, to thought's grip. And we take hold of it not just as a field of sensory stimulation and physical action. We have countless dynamic ways of penetrating its mysteries that actually continue to yield greater and richer knowledge—not just perception, but science, mathematics, rational theory, speculative and logical reasoning, the arts—and, no matter how relentless our quest for an ever deeper coincidence between the being of the world and our mental agency, there's always more rational content available to our intellects. It's anything but intuitively obvious that the inherently formal and intentional structure of rational thought should correspond so fruitfully to the structure of the world, or that rational thought and a coherent order of being should somehow be naturally fitted to one another. If phenomenal experience—if the semantics of reality—delivered the world to us merely as a kind of navigable topography, over which we could exercise only a certain degree of practical mastery, I might take your position seriously. But that's not the world we know, as my dear Eros has said, and certainly not the world we seem able to know in countless modalities and in ever greater depth. Where's your evidence for what you're saying? You've never experienced any real disjunction between mind and being . . . any dissonance between the search for knowledge and the nature of the world. Areas of ignorance, yes, but those are merely areas of rational questioning, which seem obviously surmountable by further knowledge. In fact, we dare not assume otherwise. So, no, you have no evidence at all for this fabulous heterocosm of mindless nature. You might as well declare your belief in the existence of a universe inhabited entirely by hippogriffs or composed entirely from plasticene. We, by contrast, have extraordinarily plentiful evidence for our beliefs regarding the primordial reality of mind in all things, and of the power of mind to contain or penetrate all things, and have perfectly good logical warrant for seeing this primordial reality as grounded in an infinite act of mind . . . of the mind of God.

Eros: Anyway, you're lying.

Hephaistos: [*His eyes widening indignantly:*] I'm sorry, what was that?

Eros: Lying to yourself, no doubt, but lying even so. You yourself don't believe in a reality divided between an unknowable objective realm and an illusory—useful, that is, but still illusory—subjective realm. Not for one moment do you truly think that your efforts to understand the cosmos around you are no more than constructions of allegorical approximations to some unimaginable quiddity or occult principle *in se*. For one thing, you've always been something of a scientist in your own right, far more so than any other of the gods. You absolutely do believe in the possibility of scientific and mathematical knowledge, but also in the possibility of speculative and logical truths, and in the power of the mind to penetrate the nature of things. And, so, what is it you implicitly presuppose when you seek to learn more about nature? What gives you the confidence to presume and to continue to draw upon a potentially inexhaustible wellspring of objective truth in order to learn more and more about the contours of the real? You're assuming, and you're confirming with every advance you make into the essence of the real, that the ideal contents of your mind—the mental forms, the concepts and rational entailments—genuinely reveal something of that essence; and this can only be because you presume an original harmony and connaturality between them. You even presume, as you absolutely must do, that the knowledge you acquire of the real is all the more refined and certain the more it's abstracted from its empirical particularity and universalized in those concepts—the more it becomes pure idea, purged of accidents, rather than mere material fact. That means that the end toward which your mind is working is one that lies outside nature as a merely physical continuum: it's a point of perfect indistinction between the mental agency of the knower and the mental content of the known, where intelligibility and intelligence are simply one actuality. If you believe the structure of reality can truly be mirrored in the structure of your thinking, then you must also believe that there's an ideal or abstract or purely intelligible dimension of reality that truly corresponds to the concepts that allow you to understand the world. Thus you seek to know the only way you can: on the assumption—the rational wager—that, at its ground, everything really is already mind.

Hephaistos: Wait . . .

Eros: Nor do you undertake these labors simply as a venture of faith. As you progress, and as the world continually yields itself to mind and mind opens itself to the world, surmounting every obstacle of the purely unintelligible—or at least striving to do so—and as the mind continues to penetrate more deeply into the mystery of being, and as being continues to shine forth more radiantly within the mystery of mind, you continue to amass concrete evidence that this coincidence between mind and world is real, that being is essentially intelligibility, and that there truly is a point of indistinction or identity where knowing and being known are one inseparable act of manifestation—one act of reality. As we've said already, the *ordo cognoscendi* progressively reveals the *ordo essendi:* the structure of your mind's ascent into ever greater knowledge of the truth reveals the structure of being's descent in its ever greater manifestation of the truth; the necessarily transcendental structure of intellect and will reveals the transcendent fullness to which it's joined. Where else could that constant dynamism of discovery and disclosure occur except within an original and ultimate—even an infinite—identity of being and mind? And that identity is what all the great systems of classical metaphysics identify as God or *Brahman* or the One or what have you. The very structure of knowledge is a primordial relation of the mind to God. The very end of all knowledge is God.

You may claim to think all of this an illusion—though with what warrant it would be hard to say—but in actual practice you presume the causal priority of mind in the structure of reality. The opposite is impossible as a rational project; for, if materialism were true, you'd never be able to account for consciousness at all, and you'd certainly never be able to explain how mind, in its exorbitant—its *infinite*—difference from the great mechanical order "out there," could actually capture any of being's reality in concepts. And yet, again, this is no irrational venture of madly hopeless hope on your part. The more you abstract your experience into various kinds of ideal rather than empirical content—formal, conceptual, rational, mathematical, moral, aesthetic, logical, and so forth—the more you find yourself extracting knowledge and genuine understanding from the welter of brute events that the world presents to your senses, before intentionality begins to craft that world into an intelligible order. This is why I mentioned Lonergan earlier: he demonstrated with exquisite clarity that the very search for understanding—the very dynamism of that insatiable rational desire to know *why* and *why* and *why*—discloses the reality of what he calls the "unrestricted intelligibility" of being, and thereby the reality of God as the one "unrestricted act of understanding."

HEPHAISTOS: Do tell. Does my desire for the love of . . . oh, let's say, the love of your mother, my truant lady wife—does that prove its reality?

EROS: I might wish for another example, but as you will. Let me just say this: the reality of a final cause is in some sense merely its presence as a real and effective rational relation within any actuality; so, if indeed you desire the love of Aphrodite, then that love is a real cause of your action. Whether that final cause is real in itself, however, apart from your action, is something that can be discovered by the degree of success with which your action meets. If your entreaties win no kind response, if your carnal importunities are routinely resisted, if your professions of love fall on deaf ears, if she lavishly distributes her amorous favors to other gods . . .

HEPHAISTOS: [*Grimacing and clearing his throat:*] Now that I think of it, I too wish I'd chosen a different example. [*In a subdued voice:*] Actually, our marriage counseling has been going quite well as of late . . .

EROS: Well, in any case, if your desires were repeatedly frustrated, you'd have reason to doubt the independent reality of the end that draws you on. But that's precisely why we may reasonably presume the opposite in this case. In our search to know the real, we find that the world *does* indeed become more intelligible to us the more we're able to abstract it into concepts, and to arrange those concepts in categories, and then to arrange those categories under ever simpler, more comprehensive, more unconditioned concepts, finding new relations of understanding across categories, arranging those relationships into more comprehensive, simpler frames of analogy or pertinency or common principle, discovering new interpretive contexts and progressively unifying them with one another, interrogating each conclusion reached, making rational judgments and then judging those judgments, eliminating every area of ignorance or uninterpreted particularity, always ascending toward the simplest and most capacious concept our minds can reach. We discover that finite objects of understanding have to be progressively purged of their residue of the empirical in order to yield their secrets to our inquiring intellects; and we find our own desire to draw this intelligible content out into the light to be unrelenting—to be, as Lonergan says, a pure and unrestricted desire to know—precisely because the mind, in longing for complete intelligibility, is always able to recognize incomplete intelligibility. So long as thought's power meaningfully to ask *why* something is so has not been exhausted, it has a tacit grasp of what would suffice as a complete and sufficient answer, and indeed a tacit grasp of being as total intelligibility as such. Yet no finite object or end within nature could instill that tacit desire or tacit knowledge in us, since all such objects provide only restricted acts of understanding; what, however, we're constantly aware of in our questioning is something beyond any merely particular truth—any truth that, left to itself, leaves other truths undisclosed or other questions unanswered. That transcendental—that *transcendent*—horizon abides, as the absolute or divine dimension of depth in our rational . . . let's say, our rational vista: the ideal of perfect intelligibility, wholly free from all empirical opacity . . . from all empirical residue . . . not limited to particular instances or single things, leaving nothing out in its universal embrace of all phenomena.

What, then, is the nature of that ideal? It's a pure and unrestricted act of understanding; and, for being to be intelligible in the way we not only hope it is, but in all the ways in which we continually find that it genuinely is, this unrestricted act must be real, and in fact convertible with being itself. Reality gives itself to the mind as mental content because mental content is the ground of reality. After all, to say that something's become fully intelligible to us is to say we've reached an *idea* of it that can be understood according to the simplest abstract laws and that leaves no empirical or conceptual remainder behind. This is the highest form of intelligibility. This being so, it makes perfect sense that so many ancient and mediaeval philosophers believed that the ideal dimension of things—the dimension of their intrinsic intelligibility—was not only a property inhering in them, but the very principle of their existence. Yet what's an idea, after all, other than the content of an act of understanding . . . the content of a mind? What's a concept other than an object of rational intentionality? And so how could being be pure intelligibility if it were not also pure intelligence—the mind of God, so to speak—an act of understanding that understands all things and therein understands itself perfectly? This, at any rate, is his reasoning: as the mind moves toward an ever more comprehensive and perspicuous knowledge of the real, it necessarily moves toward an ideal level of reality at which intelligibility and intelligence are no longer distinguishable.[6]

Really, isn't this something we can confirm simply through a scrupulous contemplation of what we're doing at every moment of our engagement with the world? Lonergan made his arguments specifically in regard to rational methods of inquiry—scientific, philosophical, and so forth—but there's no need to confine his conclusions to the limits of any special method. As I said not long ago, all of this is already true of every act of perception and cognition and reasoning in its natural depth. In all we undertake, we assume the human mind can be a true mirror of reality because we're also assuming that all reality is already a mirror of mind. No other comportment toward the truth of experience is possible for us. We're always already engaged, however humbly, in that ceaseless ascent toward ever greater knowledge, and that means that when we take in the world even in its most mundane details we're intentionally engaged in an ascent toward an ultimate encounter with limitless consciousness, limitless reason, a transcendent reality where being and knowledge are always already one and the same. The marvelous reciprocal relation of our power to understand and being's power to be understood, to my mind, unremittingly indicates an ultimate identity between reason and being in their transcendent origin and end. Really, the best way of understanding the mind in each of us is as a restricted instance of that unrestricted act of understanding: God, that is, as the ground of both the subjective rationality of mind and the objective rationality of being, the transcendent and indwelling order of truth by which mind and world are both informed and in which both participate and through which each is given to the other. If we're correct in saying that to be is to be manifest—to be intelligible and also consciously known—then we can also say that God, as infinite being, is also an infinite act of knowing, in whom mind and being are one and the same; and thus we can say also that, as such, God is the source of the fittedness of mind and being each to the other in the realm of the finite.

There was another philosopher, roughly a generation or two before Lonergan, named Maurice Blondel . . .

HEPHAISTOS: Ah, yet another Nazarene intellectual. Are you planning to be baptized at any point?

EROS: [*With a bemused smile:*] No. I don't think superannuated gods are typically invited to participate in "the mysteries," in any event. But you really must learn to let bygones be bygones. I've done so, and it's very restful for the nerves. "Thou hast conquered, O pale Galilean" and all that. But never mind. My point is that Blondel was an especially profound and rigorous thinker of how all free agency of every kind—how all "action," to use his central term—in every modality of the will's engagement with reality, is animated by this necessary orientation toward a divine horizon; and for him this orientation, properly considered, reveals the mark of the supernatural as always already impressed upon all our acts of willing. An intrinsic desire for transcendence forces us to will, and to will freely; this dialectic of necessity and freedom he defines as a relation within rational agents between *la volonté voulante*—"the willing will"—and *la volonté voulue*—"the willed will." Think of it as the relation between the transcendental and the immanent orientations we've already talked about: between a constant, implicit sense of and love for a higher realm of values, found in the fullness of being, and a repeated, explicit movement of desire toward elected finite ends, prompted by our longing to rise to the level of that primordial inner impulse. Thus there's an original immanence of transcendence, so to speak, within mental agency, and thus even the mind's immanent pursuit of its immediate desires invites it to seek that transcendent end, because one can't be equal to oneself, as it were—one's deliberative or *willed* will can't be equal to one's natural or *willing* will—except by one going beyond oneself. And, as it's driven onward, rational agency serially exhausts all reductive explanations for its desire—all physical, psychological, social, empirical, mysticizing explanations. In the end, one is seeking to discover oneself by *freely* willing what the "willing will" desires. And that means a continued commitment to something yet to be attained, from which all rational freedom is derived: something utterly beyond mechanistic or psychological determinism . . . a transcendence that sets free, that elicits any number of rational, moral, religious modes of action, that . . .[7]

HEPHAISTOS: Oh, please, no more. I get the point.

HERMES: [*After a slightly awkward silence of several seconds:*] May I at least add one final observation?

HEPHAISTOS: Would it matter if I tried to prevent you from doing so?

HERMES: I doubt it. And all I wanted to say was that all of this touches upon a point I refrained from making earlier, when you accused me of trying to turn linguistics into a mystical theology. Well, I don't have to do that, because language reveals itself from the first to be a structure of transcendence, in just the terms Eros has been laying out. Language is nothing but pure intentionality, all the way down, and rational intentionality exists wholly within this total rational volition toward the infinite that Eros has so buoyantly described. Well, then, language is already . . . well, I suppose we'll have to rest content with the word "mystical" for now. The most elevated and most original source of language—its unifying formal principle—is the final horizon of all rational intentionality; that's the highest stratum, so to speak, of the top-down causal structure of the semeiotic order. That means that language is possible, even in its most indigent and impotent forms, *only* as the result of a prior engagement with an infinite end—a perfect coincidence of knowledge and the known, or of utterance and the uttered. This seems more or less self-evident to me. We need only reflect on that higher stratum of symbolic thought to which syntactic and semantic linguistic functions are subvenient. What, after all, is a symbol other than a privileged instance of indistinction between mind and world in a word that both utter together, in a single voice, as it were? Every symbol is a place where being gives itself to manifestation in the intentionality of mind, and mental intention yields itself up as the place where being manifests itself. But then, if it's true that, as Peirce said, all symbols possess their meanings only in light of other symbols, within a web of symbols that has neither beginning nor end, then what sustains that web of meanings in its intrinsic intelligibility is, again, that infinite coincidence between being and knowledge—between uttered and utterance—to which the whole of the symbolic order aspires. And this would seem to mean—given both the irreducibility of language and the absurdity of the concept of strong emergence—that in every word we speak we implicitly admit that we've been addressed by this infinite end. What wakens us from the silence of nothingness to become speakers of the word is the need to respond to the voice of God speaking to us, and that voice echoes within every word we speak.

HEPHAISTOS: Enough. [*Raising both hands before him, palms outward in a gesture of surrender:*] I implore you, no more. Honestly, I understand.

IV
Ātman Is *Brahman*

Hephaistos: Really, you have no sense of limits once you get the wind in your sails. I asked for arguments, not mystagogy. So, all right, the mind seeks immaterial ends . . . absolute ends. Well, of course it does; that's how thought works. That's the system, and that's how it represents itself to itself in order to function. Honestly, I sometimes think that you three believe you can simply rhapsodize me into submission. It's not going to happen. And let me just say here that it seems to me we might reverse a good deal of the argument you're all intent on making today. I can grant that the internal structure of mental acts—and, I should add, of mental representations—is precisely this dialectic you describe between, on the one hand, a mental and volitional orientation toward an abstract realm of absolute values and, on the other, a secondary orientation toward particular things in the world. I'm still free, however, to conclude that this is simply how, practically speaking, the brain needs to function, and that this very fact imposes upon our minds the tendency to believe in a transcendent reality, as a convenient user-illusion. The dynamism of neural operations generates its own operative principle: *that hypothesis*, so to speak. "God" is merely the name we give to the supreme algorithm in our systems of behavior—the supreme user-interface. Yes, I know your objections. We've been over them. They're powerful, I concede, and in certain moods I might find them persuasive; but that's perhaps only to say that I too, as an organic system of functions, am destined to see things in certain ways by the structure of my own . . . programming, as it were.

Psyche: [*After several seconds of silence:*] Back to functionalism again, after we've done so much to dismantle its presuppositions? Forsooth, my dear. I honestly don't believe you really believe what you say you believe. I believe also that we've already demonstrated the falsehood of what you're saying, and that you know it. But of course there's no way in the end of combatting a pure epistemological nihilism. If you *choose* to believe that you're a machine programmed to think it's conscious and programmed to think it wills . . . well, I'm not going to start the debate again from the beginning.

Hephaistos: Once more, I haven't claimed to believe anything in a final way. I've claimed only *not* to believe what I don't believe.

Psyche: Then permit me to do the same for myself, and maybe we can move on. I *don't* believe that we can explain mental agency coherently except in terms of this experience of a relation of God as dwelling in the inmost depths of each of us to God as dwelling beyond the utmost heights to which our minds and wills aspire: the striving, that is, of an "I" within me more original than my mere psychological ego toward a "that"—or really, perhaps, a "Thou"—more ultimate than the mere physical universe. I also *don't* believe that anything else can make sense, existential or logical, of the spiritual agency within each of us that refuses to relent, to abandon that divine horizon, and that instead continues to seek it, consciously and unconsciously, in rational reflection and empirical investigation, but also in dreams, myths, works of art . . . visions, prodigies of inspiration, the very *miracle* of language . . . every movement of spirit poetically seeking its end . . . all that expresses our ecstatic essence . . . the implicit experience of the supernatural in our every explicit grasp of nature. I most definitely *don't* believe that mind and being could disclose one another in the dynamic depth that they do if they didn't coincide in essence with one another, and if they weren't in principle already one and the same in the mind and being of God—if, that is, what exists in us and the world as a constant dynamic *synthesis* of mind and being were not a real participation in what in God exists as an absolute *identity* of mind and being. I *don't* believe that the two poles of mental agency irreducible to physical causes—the foundation of the apperceptive witness within, the encompassing fullness of the unperceivable divine beyond—could give the world to us in such an inexhaustible variety of modes if those poles weren't at one with the very principle of all that is. I *don't* believe that it's reasonable or even possible to separate the gnoseological oneness of our apprehension of the world from the ontological oneness that composes the world without thereby creating an intolerable paradox. Above all, I *don't* believe that we've failed to demonstrate—or that you've failed to realize—the incoherence of physicalist reduction or naturalist metaphysics with regard to the mind or life or language, as well as the rational solvency of the contrary supposition that the reality in which we live, move, and have our being is spirit.

HEPHAISTOS: You needn't continue to speak in the negative. The rhetorical effect is beginning to wear thin.

PSYCHE: [*With a laugh:*] Very well, Phaesty. Anyway, you know where I stand. I believe in the power of reason to discern truths, principally because I believe that there are real formal causes that shape the world's reality, and that these inhabit and shape our thoughts as well, and that therefore we can truly think and speak about reality. And I believe that this is the nature and substance at once of mind, life, and language. I believe that all that is has its being as, so to speak, one great thought, and that our individual minds are like prisms capturing some part of the light of being and consciousness . . . or, rather, are like prisms that are also, marvelously, nothing but crystallizations of that light . . . as is all of nature. I believe that this is the reality in which we live and move and exist, and that we enter into it at the beginning of life as into a kind of dream that was already being dreamed before we found ourselves within it, and that—from our first moment of being aware that we're aware—our participation in that reality comes filled with both memories of the eternal and an urgent yearning for the transcendent. All is familiar, all is impossibly strange. In the end, that reality in which we exist and in which we participate as spiritual agencies may as well be called "God," since we have no better name for infinite mind that's also infinite being. Moreover, I believe that the structure of all thought reveals its immanent ground to be that inner witness that is the divine light within. But then, too, it reveals its transcendent end: again, teleologically considered, the mind *is* God, striving not only to see—but to become—infinite knowledge of infinite being, beyond any distinction between knower and known. And all of this I take to be just so many different ways of saying that, as the *Māṇḍūkya Upaniṣad* tells us, *Ayam Ātmā Brahma:* this *Ātman* is *Brahman*—this Spirit within each of us is godhead.

HEPHAISTOS: [*Smiling patiently but sardonically:*] All right. So we began five days ago with science and we end now with mysticism? Is that really the path we should have taken?

PSYCHE: [*Lifting the rose from her lap, where it has been resting for some time, and gazing at it almost quizzically for several seconds before speaking:*] What, after all, is science? Surely it must involve making sense, among other things, of personal experience, and attempting to quantify the evidence of those who can attest to certain *kinds* of experience. All the great religious cultures have their contemplative traditions, don't they? And all of those traditions seem to testify with remarkable consistency, even unanimity, to certain dimensions of the experience of transcendence. Naturally they do, you'll reply, but only because the brain in certain states is likely to induce a particular kind of experience—or a particular kind of representation, as you'd probably be more likely to say—and so of course there's likely to be a general agreement between persons and peoples on the features of that experience or representation. What, though, does that prove even if it's true? There are no doubt brain-states associated with every experience, transcendent or mundane; why, then, should the trivial truth that mystical or contemplative insight is correlated with a distinctive set of neural activities be taken as evidence that such insight is merely a psychological state, without a real object? By that logic, the reality that there's a brain-state associated with hearing a performance of Bach means that I can't believe in the objective reality of that music. Whatever the case may be, I know this: to imagine that a "science of mind"—a science of irreducible first-person experience—is possible in terms purely of the third-person facts of neurophysiology, without reference to what mental interiority discloses *to* itself *about* itself, is worse than folly. The only "science of mind" that might actually reveal the intrinsic nature of the mental would be something like the contemplative disciplines proper to the great mystical traditions of the world's religions. There can be no real science of mind that's not, to put it bluntly, a spiritual science.

What, then, do those traditions tell us? For one thing, they tell us that, when one looks inward toward that vanishing point of unity—that abiding witness—at the ground of all mental agency, one is looking toward the simplicity of God. More inward to consciousness than consciousness itself is that *scintilla* or spark of divine light that imparts life and knowledge to the soul. Those willing to make the interior journey toward their minds' deepest wellspring reach at last a place where they find their own mental agency to be utterly dependent upon God knowing God. Then, too, when they look out toward the world from this vantage, they find themselves turned toward that same source: the divine unity of the being and the intelligibility of all things. In either case, the pilgrim soul encounters God's eternal self-manifestation. And this spiritual science, as I call it—this extraordinary state of consciousness—perhaps provides us with a model for understanding our ordinary experience of the mind's relation to the world about us. The real experience that each of us has in every moment of cognitive and conscious and purposive mental agency becomes comprehensible when understood as being grounded in the more original unity of that perfect identity of being and knowing that is the divine . . . the transcendent ground of all that is. One need not be carried away from oneself in a mystic ecstasy to glimpse that place where, as Meister Eckhart says, the soul's ground and God's ground are one and the same ground . . . or where, as Plotinus would have it, mind or *nous* finds its source in the undifferentiated One from which all existence flows . . . or where, as ibn Qunawi says, delimited being, *al-wujûd al-muqayyad*, returns to its source in the Nondelimited Being, *al-wujûd al-mutlaq*, of the divine light . . . or where, according to Sufi tradition, the inmost soul, the *ruh*, finds its ground in the "secret," the eternal *sirr* within each of us, which forever remembers God, the One, *al-Ahad*, the source of all consciousness and all being . . . or where . . .

Hephaistos: Yet again, I implore you, don't recite an entire anthology of mystical *aperçus* at me. Your meaning is more than clear.

Psyche: [*With an amused smile:*] You're right, I get far too carried away at times. I beg your indulgence. I'll simply say this, then: all the great contemplative and philosophical traditions, East and West, insist that the source and ground of the mind's unity is the transcendent reality of unity as such, the simplicity of God, the one ground of both consciousness and being; and a great deal of both cogent philosophical reasoning and personal spiritual experience tends to support the claim. I'm not trying to prove anything to you, my dear friend; all I can do at this point is indicate a vision of the whole of things that, to my mind, makes sense of things. And that vision is one of an original oneness underlying all things, knowing and revealing itself in the nuptial union of soul and world, and making itself known to us in the structure of all experience. There's a conceptual space, let's say, where the unity of mind, in its teleological co-extensiveness with all of reality, meets the unity of being and becomes indistinguishable from it; and at that point—if we think it through with sufficient care—we should discover that the irreducibility of mind to physical mechanical causes and the irreducibility of being to physical mechanical events are one and the same irreducibility. Mind exists as having the infinite fullness of being as its antecedent finality and proper content; being becomes manifest in having the infinite openness of mind as the place of its disclosure. So too, once again, life and language are irreducible to mechanical causes, as both are simply different names for mind . . . for spirit, that is—infinite spirit, eternal spirit, spirit immanent and transcendent at once—expressing itself, revealing itself, communicating itself in everything. Once more, simply enough, in both its origin and end, *Ātman* is *Brahman*—which I take to be the first, last, most fundamental, and most exalted truth of all real philosophy and religion alike.

[*For several moments, no one speaks.*]

CODA

The Age of the Machine

I

Common Sense and Mystery

When more than five minutes have passed without anyone speaking, HEPHAISTOS *sits up, slowly rises from the grass, straightens his clothing, and seats himself on one of the unoccupied benches. A moment later,* PSYCHE *rises from her place next to* EROS, *crosses the lawn to where* HEPHAISTOS *is now seated and hands him the rose blossom, bending forward to kiss him on the cheek as she does so. They exchange wan but affectionate smiles. She returns to* EROS*'s side.* HERMES *watches all of this with an enigmatic expression on his face and then, finally, breaks the silence.*

HERMES: Tell me, brother, has any of what's been said over these six days convinced you of anything?

HEPHAISTOS: [*After a moment's consideration:*] No.

HERMES: [*With a weary sigh:*] I suppose I must believe you . . . or, at least, believe that you believe what you say.

HEPHAISTOS: Well, actually, I'm not being strictly truthful. You've all convinced me at least that you have respectably sound reasons for your convictions, and that the vision of reality you apparently all share is fairly coherent within its own terms. That much I already knew, I suppose. And, to be honest, you've convinced me—more than I had expected you would—that physical reductionism is, on the whole, an inadequate approach to . . . I suppose, to mind, life, and even language. It may indeed well be that system-level realities—the semantics of life, as Psyche likes to say—are neither reducible to, nor strongly emergent from, lower levels of natural order.

HERMES: Oh. But, then, that seems quite a concession.

HEPHAISTOS: I'll even confess that, by my reckoning, I've lost this debate.

HERMES: Well, then, that . . .

HEPHAISTOS: But that's a far less generous concession than you might at first think. I see now that I was always destined to lose it, not only because you three are fine thinkers and talkers, or because our good and glorious Psyche has the best philosophical mind of the four of us, as well as the quickest wits in debate, but because the topics we've been arguing over are so intractable that the work of destroying our inadequate theories concerning them is far easier than that of constructing better theories. I began our debate believing that I needed only assume a defensive position to prevail, since I imagined I had common sense on my side; but common sense is a faithless ally. In fact, it's an illusion where mysteries as complex as these are concerned. In the areas we've been struggling over, every theory is, strictly speaking, indefensible.

EROS: Ah, but now you're playing the mysterian again, which is your least appealing role. I prefer the phlegmatic, unyielding rationalist. Moreover, that's not how I would describe what's been going on these past several days. If you like, we can prove the point one way or the other. All you need do is assume the critical stance, and then see whether we can defend our position better than you can yours.

HEPHAISTOS: Well, of course you can. Your position conforms to the way our thinking is structured to see reality and to understand itself. The whole point of the reductionist project is to subject the manifest image to a withering scrutiny in order to expose its dissimulation of the scientific image. But the manifest image remains the manifest image, and for obvious reasons. Hence, it will always look more like common sense in the end, and the very structure of our mental machinery will almost always make us prefer it to the alternative. That machinery, as a matter of practical prudence, can't acknowledge what it truly is to itself without considerable emotional and cognitive difficulty. We can find our home only in the world of the manifest image; the world of the scientific image is habitable by no one. So, when you three argue for your little tercet—life is language, language is mind, mind is life, going around and around forever—you think you're proving that reality at its basis has the structure of intentional meaning, whereas all I hear is a broadly Kantian proviso that such a structure of meaning is the way in which the mind naturally must represent reality to itself in order to function, and that it's still this naïve but natural view—this manifest image—that the sciences must prescind from in order to penetrate to the really real.

Psyche: Oh, Phaesty, don't you see what you're doing? You're now trying to convince yourself that you're justified in taking the weaker position precisely because it's weaker. That's perverse. It's a subterfuge. What you call the "scientific image" offers no shelter not because it's so pitilessly rational and correct, but simply because it's radically incomplete, and doesn't capture more than a shadow of reality in its fullness. In fact, it's not a *scientific* image at all; it's just the mechanistic image, the world reduced to its most basic lineaments, which modern persons have been indoctrinated to think of as reality's "true nature" just as a metaphysical prejudice. But there's no such world, at least not as a reality in itself; it's a figment of materialist dogma and nothing more . . . a syntactic shadow of being's boundlessly eloquent semantics of self-communication. The real world is the fully semantic realm of experience and understanding and . . . well, life itself.

Hephaistos: Let's not quarrel. I'm conceding that common sense is in fact on your side. For just that reason, however, you shouldn't be too confident in your conclusions. I award you the laurels, yes, but I won't surrender the field. To be honest, so much of the reasoning by which we make sense of reality is the consequence rather than the cause of our beliefs, as you yourself have said. Your arguments have been good enough—again, the critical task is easier than the constructive—but perhaps not quite as irrefutable as you want to think they are. Needless to say, your mind's ability to understand reality—assuming that this too isn't something our brain makes us exaggerate to ourselves, by hiding the fragmentary nature of our own experience from us—would indeed be much easier to account for if you could prove the reality of some infinite coincidence of mind and being underlying all things . . . the mind of

God, that is, where the knower and the known are a single ground and a single act. But you shouldn't deceive yourself that so grand a metaphysical conjecture can be secured just by a phenomenology of, oh, I don't know . . . perhaps looking at a rose.

PSYCHE: I believe it can. At least, I believe it can be shown to be . . . the most plausible. . . . [*Pausing and scowling to herself:*] And, anyway, you know I've any number of other philosophical reasons for believing in God. We all three do.

HEPHAISTOS: Yes, and I've many reasons for not believing—and, as it happens, for refusing to believe. You're right, of course, that common sense does *not* in fact favor the materialism or the philosophical naturalism or (let's be candid) the atheism I profess. In fact, the classical concept of God may be the most commonsensical idea there is, as it explains practically everything with exquisite logical parsimony. Atheism will always be the dialectically weaker position for the simple reason that it can't account for much of anything—not being, not mind, not life, not that realm of absolute values that you say preoccupies our intellects and wills . . . not even, as we've said, language. But it's the stronger position in my eyes precisely for not pretending that it explains the inexplicable. And I think it's the *better* and *more responsible* position for quite a different reason: not because belief in a transcendent God offends against common sense, but because it offends against common decency.

HERMES: [*In an impatient tone:*] Now, what does that mean?

HEPHAISTOS: [*With a somewhat incredulous shake of his head:*] How good it is to dwell in heavenly places, and to enjoy the imperturbable bliss of the gods. We keep ourselves at so comfortable a distance from the world we once inhabited that I suppose it's easy for us to forget what a theatre of horrors it so often is—the pain, the misery, the mires of blood . . . disease and death and despair. How rapturous the three of you become when speaking of the grand cosmic epic of life and mind—of spirit pervading all things, working toward transcendent ends, shaping the temporal in the light of the eternal and the finite after the fashion of the infinite. Does it ever occur to any of you, however, to consider the monstrous price—the sheer hideous, extravagant expenditure—required to bring that ravishingly sublime spectacle about? "Evolutionary oceans of blood" I think I called it a day or so ago, and the three of you allowed the remark to pass without notice, like a snowflake skipping off the impenetrable surfaces of your divine consciences. Yes, life down there where the younger children of nature still dwell is full of beauty and tenderness and majesty and joy; it's also—and, I should say, preponderantly—a vast abyss of darkness, pain, death, and hopeless sadness. So, all right, let's gaze at rose blossoms in a deathless paradise and raise hymns to the transcendent intelligence from which the universe flows; let's even look down from time to time to the terrestrial realm below, but only cautiously, so as not to see more than we care to see, and let's rejoice in the flowered meadows, at least during their brief and gorgeous efflorescences, and in all the other delights and diversions that that small, poor world affords, so long as they last: love and sex and friendship, and indeed every pleasure of the flesh and mind that invites the soul to join in the delirious dance of life. But let's also recall that all that world's enchantments, considered in proportion to the whole of cosmic existence, are at most tiny evanescent flickers of light amid a limitless darkness. The price paid in exchange for those ephemeral pleasures and giddy moments of transport is ever so much more exorbitant than what's gained: children dying of monstrous diseases, in torment; nature steeped in the blood of the weak, and then too of the strong; the long march of history across battlefields engorged with corpses, and through an interminable sequence of conquests, enslavements, spoliations, and mass murders. Everything those poor brutes down there love vanishes, and then they do as well; every attachment they cherish is merely the transient prelude to an enduring bereavement; every accidental happiness terminates in an essential sorrow. And what consolations do they have to bear them through their tribulations and despairs? Religion, perhaps? What a miserable anaesthetic that is. Religious systems are, as often as not, systems of emotional terrorism, commanding assent and submission by threatening amplitudes of suffering even greater than those of ordinary earthly life—eternal hells, for instance, or interminable karmic cycles of transmigration through states of misery, and so on—for anyone who has the temerity to complain of the injustice of being dragged into an existence of such horror and of then being held responsible for one's own fate. Really, what does it matter if there truly is this transcendent God you go on about so often? Why shouldn't that God be an object of indifference on the part of rational beings? Or of vehement hatred? If there's such a reality as infinite mind, especially if it's supposedly also the seat of all eternal values, shouldn't we expect this divine reality to exhibit some sign of infinite *moral* intelligence?

PSYCHE: [*After several seconds of silence:*] Do they really vanish, do you think—all those conscious creatures who come into being, live for a time, and then die? Does anything simply vanish? How do you know that all things aren't in a sense stored up in the infinite, or that this life isn't only a prelude to a greater reality, or that the history of life in time isn't also the story of something being prepared for eternity? I certainly don't think of death as the end of anything other than one episode within the living soul's greater story. And, anyway, what would *infinite* moral intelligence be like, and from what vantage would we be able to judge its purposes? Surely we're not talking about some large psychological subject somewhere out there in the beyond; it's vastly more unimaginable than that. I don't know what to say, Phaesty. Alas, you're asking religious questions, and none of us is competent to discuss those. We're not theologians, we're merely gods—to paraphrase you. I, no less than you, have no trust in dogma or creedal authority, and so here I have nothing to rely on but what I take to be reasonable intuitions and a few ambiguous signs I sometimes think I see in the patterns of cosmic existence . . . not to mention a few spiritual experiences . . . perhaps.

HEPHAISTOS: It's almost always only "perhaps." I've no room for that "perhaps" in my heart. The suffering of the innocent suffices for me to make all such considerations worthless.

PSYCHE: Again, I've no real answer for you. I applaud your moral indignation—to be honest, it explains a great many things to me about your general view of reality that I might not have suspected—but to a considerable degree I'm oddly immune to it as well. At one time, I would have felt the force of your protest more acutely; but, as I live on, I find myself more susceptible to a sense of the grandeur and sublimity of the mysteries we've been discussing and less susceptible to aggrieved alarm at cosmic suffering. Not that I take it in stride. I suppose, though, that something in me tells me that that grandeur indicates something original and ultimate in a way that the sufferings of the current age don't. But I don't understand entirely why I feel that way. Of course, all those religions you disdain for their more terroristic teachings—and, I assure you, so do I—also say that something's gone wrong, or at least hasn't yet gone entirely right . . . that the world is broken or fallen, or appears to us only through veils of illusion, or hasn't yet become fully what it is to become. I have to say, this often enough seems credible to me; at times, in fact, it almost seems obvious; but, if it's so, it's a truth that can be expressed only in the dream-images of myth and spiritual allegory and religious experience. But, again, I don't have any theological convictions; and, really, I don't need any. I don't know how to judge the infinite. I certainly don't know how to calculate the value—weighed out in blood and pain and injustice—of whatever knowledge or wisdom or beauty or love created beings might gain through the trials of existence in the world below; I simply trust that there's something greater for all of them beyond those trials. Still, when I consider the incomprehensible vastness of it all, I find myself naturally assuming that the power that creates life—the infinite act of mind in which all things exist—is forging souls in the fires of nature, and I can't help but believe it's all to a good end, more beautiful than gods or mortals can imagine. In all of it something divine, I believe, is coming to manifestation—to utterance—and being prepared for . . . what is yet to be.

HEPHAISTOS: Well, then, everything's all right. I can't wait.

PSYCHE: Mock if you wish. All I can say is that it's very much a matter of personal temperament. It's up to you whether you trust in the mysteries of mind and life and language—their miraculous strangeness, which seems always to promise the revelation of a greater meaning, or to adumbrate a higher reality, a world beyond the world we know—or whether you close yourself off against those experiences. I suppose it must all seem a mite quixotic to a rugged realist like you, accustomed to the foundry and the furnace and the ringing blows of hammers.

HEPHAISTOS: Listen as keenly as I might, I certainly can't hear the promise you apparently hear.

PSYCHE: I most definitely do hear it, as far as I can tell. To me, all of existence is a realm of positively *eloquent* communication. All of reality is the manifestation of that infinite reason that dwells in God; all of it's composed of signs and symbols, through which infinite mind is always speaking to us . . . and inviting us to respond. But what does that matter in the end? None of this alters my arguments of the past several days; whether you share my . . . my faith, I suppose, or not, you've lost this argument on the actual points of logic. Whatever the moral nature of the divine, the reality of the divine still declares itself in all things. And, you know, I don't accept your pretense that you regard all the matters we've been discussing as far too mysterious for reason to penetrate. You began this debate as the voice of flinty rationalism, and you can't now simply retreat into postmodern relativism just as the curtain's about to be rung down. That play's not on the board.

HEPHAISTOS: You're mixing your "play" metaphors a little promiscuously there, my dear.

PSYCHE: If you've lost the debate—and we at least seem to agree on that—then it's not because every theory of mind and life and language is equally indefensible; it's because the modern reductionist story you chose to defend is manifestly wrong, and manifestly inferior to the . . . well, as you say, the commonsense or "folk" view that all those realities are precisely what they appear to be, and that they provide evidence for precisely what they seem to provide evidence for. Physicalism, metaphysical naturalism, materialism—call it what you like—it's simply false. It doesn't work. Since, however, you've as much as admitted that you're more committed to what you want to affirm than to what you have warrant to believe, it scarcely matters. So, as we're waxing confessional now, may I tell you what I find intolerable—what I fear above all?

HEPHAISTOS: I'd be grateful if you would.

II
Mechanism and Nihilism

Psyche: I fear—I *dread*—a nihilistic narrative reaching its ineluctable nihilistic terminus. Whatever else modernity is, good and bad alike, it's most definitely also the project of a fully realized nihilism, in the most neutral philosophical sense of that term: the belief that there's no eternal scale or realm or horizon of meaning and moral verity, and that instead the will in each of us stands before a universe devoid of any intrinsic structure of moral truths, and is now at liberty to create or destroy values as it chooses. No doubt, in its dawn, this reduction of lived existence to the dialectic between an objectively meaningless cosmos and a subjectively self-creating will must have felt like a kind of emancipation; but it has always also been the metaphysical accomplice of a project of setting loose the will to *power*, now unencumbered by any sense of anything inviolable or sacred, or any sense of the self's dependency upon a higher order of truth. It was inevitable, really, that in time the mechanistic method should mutate into—or, perhaps, be revealed as—a metaphysics as well, and an ideology, and a program not merely for investigating nature *as if* it were a machine, but also for actually transforming the world—nature, but also culture, politics, economics, and everything else—*into* a machine. Thus the insane intellectual ethos of absolute reduction: of the dissolution of reality into principles of impersonal force and function, the systematic stripping away of the whole rational, vital, sensuous semantics of life from our picture of the "really real," as though all of them were nothing more than an impasto of epiphenomenal conventions concealing the real nature of things. And what a strange animosity toward the real world of experience it all requires of us. It must now be reduced to the ghostly syntax of the purely impalpable, imperceptible, lifeless, mindless realm of the quantitative. And mind must be reduced to the bare syntax of a functional system for processing stimulus into behavior, operating through a neural technology, denuded of the semantics of real qualitative experience, intentionality, consciousness, unified subjectivity, rational thought, and immediate intuition. And life must be reduced to a bare genetic syntax of determinate traits constructed upon a purely chemical platform, so that in the end life proves to be nothing more than a somewhat more elaborate modality of death—inert matter with ideas above its station, so to speak. And language must be reduced to the functionalist syntax of a mechanical system for processing data and converting stimulus into behavior, to which the apparent semantics of communication and communion has been applied as a mere system of manipulable user-illusions. The fullness of reality and of awareness and of life must be dissolved into a collection of spectral paradigms, inhabiting a phantom order of the real, where the rose is not red, or alive, or known to any intending conscious mind, or loved in the light of its eternal value as something good and true and beautiful.

None of this is truly rational. None of it's an enlightened or enlightening view of reality. None of it's logically warranted, or even logically defensible. None of it conforms to any reality that could actually exist in any possible frame of being. It's pure ideology dissembling itself as scientific realism; it's the will to power wrapping itself in the stolen garments of disinterested reason. It's also pure insanity. Systematic disenchantment is, as it turns out, a mad and destructive delusion, which sees everything as machinery and so makes everything into a machine—a delusion that sees everything as already dead, and then contrives with boundless ingenuity and ease of conscience to prove the point by progressively killing the world. It's all a cruel alienation from life . . . the very death of nature . . . of the soul.

Hephaistos: You're growing just a little apocalyptic, you know. Is this really all you see in the—and forgive me for using the traditional term—the Enlightenment?

Psyche: Oh, no, of course not. Don't talk in historical abstractions. I believe in the freedom of the mind, I detest dogmatism, I despise arbitrary authority. God bless the Enlightenment. But not everything we associate with that term is actually enlightening, is it? We're all prone to confuse the genuinely rational with the merely rationalistic—which is, after all, just another species of dogmatism. And fundamentalisms—religious and irreligious alike—are very much an invention of the modern temperament, aren't they? I don't pine for the premodern world as such, believe me. I certainly don't look back fondly from this divine perch of ours toward the political or religious absolutisms of earlier centuries, or to any of the tyrannies and brutalities that have marked every epoch of human culture, no matter what divine warrant they may have claimed for themselves. But I retain the right to defend the forsaken wisdoms of the past and to denounce the cruelest follies of the present, and to insist that the modern West—the "developed world," that is, which invented modernity and which continues to impose its ideologies and values on other cultures through sheer brute economic and military power—deceives itself in thinking that its mastery over nature is evidence of a true understanding of reality in its essence. There's considerable truth, no doubt, in the early modern dictum that knowledge is power; but that doesn't mean that power is necessarily knowledge.

As for the Enlightenment project . . . well, after all, every age incubates evils peculiar to itself. I contend only that the greatest political, social, and administrative evils of the late modern age have all too often been motivated and rationalized by this view of life as a kind of machinery, and of human nature as a kind of technology—a biological, psychological, genetic, social, political, economic, and even ethnic technology—to be manipulated and perfected. In a sense, those evils were all but inevitable once that prejudice had been absorbed by a whole culture. If you see human beings as essentially machines, then you'll in all likelihood feel little compunction about trying to correct what you take to be their malfunctions or defects of design. You won't even recoil from the thought that the machine might need to be redesigned altogether—purged of operational inefficiencies or superfluous parts. Again, I'm not trying to idealize the more distant past. Before the age of mechanism, the structures of institutional power, both secular and sacred, were just as oppressive, and often more so; they simply claimed jurisdiction and wielded authority over bodies and minds in the name of different principles. Even so, there's a special kind of license implicit in an incapacity for astonishment or reverent incertitude before the mysteries of the soul and of nature; and mechanistic thinking is, to a great extent, a training in just such an incapacity. Certain kinds of despotism and barbarity are impossible so long as a culture in general believes that nature possesses an integrity at once organic, moral, and spiritual, upon which one must not trespass. No such constraints inhibit the project of fixing a defective machine; there's nothing sacred in the realm of mechanism; there are only functional efficiencies and inefficiencies—redundancies and superfluities. So many very special savageries and superstitions and practical evils follow from this uniquely modern form of "rationalism": everything from "scientific" race-theory and eugenics, to mandated sterilizations and surgical and chemical interventions intended to correct perceived malfunctions of the brain, to social Darwinism and the "iron law of wages," to death-camps and gulags. It was the age of the machine that made possible the racialist ideologies that reduced humanity to a biological technology to be perfected through elimination of the "defective," and the collectivist ideologies that reduced humanity to an economic and social technology in need of radical reconstruction at the level of all civil, commercial, and cultural relations. And it was the age of the machine that, in the fullness of time, gave rise to market economies of absolutely omnivorous appetite and ambition.

Hephaistos: Oh, this is rhetorical hyperbole on a scale I'd never have imagined you capable of. No metaphysics by itself drives human beings to commit atrocities, and no age has been conspicuously better than any other in that regard. Atrocities are simply a perennial human pastime.

PSYCHE: I didn't say that mechanistic metaphysics *produced* the Third Reich, or anything like that; and I've clearly said that every age is capable of its own kinds of barbarity. All I said—or all I meant to convey, at any rate—was that the prevailing metaphysics of any given epoch, however tacit, determines which evils can be perpetrated in the name of higher principles, without violations of conscience, according to rationales supposedly grounded in the very nature of reality. The metaphysics of mechanism produced an understanding of nature and of function, of organism and of mental agency, that simply made it acceptable to trespass upon spheres of human existence that had previously been seen as sacrosanct. And I repeat: the way the most truly and impeccably modern persons see reality—and the way the great majority of truly modern peoples live in relation to the world about them—is a form of madness that will, if it can't be arrested in its rampage through history and nature, destroy itself and the world. The machine, as the governing logic of a social and cultural order, seeks to vanquish nature and spirit alike—to vanquish *life*—and it seems destined to succeed.

HEPHAISTOS: *The* machine?

PSYCHE: [*With a gently melancholy smile:*] Isn't that how it looks from our comfortable vantage here in the Intermundia? Doesn't it seem as if the world down there—among the prosperous nations, but also increasingly everywhere—is becoming a single, ubiquitous machine: limitlessly various and yet deadeningly uniform, an incessant engine of material production and consumption and stupefying spectacle, a vast cybernetic system—at once technological, social, ideological, commercial, cultural, and economic—for generating ever newer factitious material desires, and for sustaining a virtual order of purely economic relations, and for integrating humanity into itself ever more inextricably . . . by fragmenting societies and psychologies and attention spans with its ceaseless torrents of vapid exhortations to acquisition? It seems so obvious that it's almost a banality to call attention to it. It's a reality that confines the better part of social life to a very specific set of commercial functions and that's already succeeded in converting all of nature into little more than a reserve of material resources to be exploited . . . with, of course, increasingly devastating results.

HEPHAISTOS: True enough, but you make it sound as if a handful of ideas that took root in the Western mind in early modernity is to be blamed for every evil of the present; and I suppose the implication of that would be that a physicalist or metaphysically naturalist view of mind or life is therefore to be eschewed just on moral grounds. But, of course, the imperative doesn't actually follow from the historical claim, and the claim itself is much too simplistic for someone of your intelligence. Surely you know that history—cultural, material, ideological, what have you—is a far more complicated thing. *Tempora et mores* and all that: things change; new circumstances arise for countless reasons; contingencies vie with necessities for the future—the fortuitous with the inevitable, the concrete with the abstract—and what emerges is as much accident as fate. Trying to explain the present entirely as the dialectical issue of this or that single idea or constellation of ideas—this or that local cultural development or metaphysical commitment—verges on the nonsensical.

PSYCHE: Oh, Phaesty, as I said, I'm confessing my fears—nothing more. And the only grand claim I'm making is that how human beings see their world determines to some very great degree how they'll treat the world . . . and one another . . . and themselves, I suppose. As for the grand historical narrative, I admit I'm speaking in vast and misty generalities. It's impossible to say which came first—the ideological revolution or the evolution of new material conditions. I expect it was neither, and they were really two sides of a single, indivisible cultural process. There's no point wondering whether it was the rise of the mechanical philosophy or the rise of any number of early modern economic, political, social, and ideological developments that progressively transformed humanity's vision of the world into one of pure material efficiency, and so inaugurated the great cultural project of bringing the world into conformity with that vision. Whatever the case, what gradually emerged was a great and relentless machine of power, production, and consumption. Those who created the machine built better than they knew. At most, they grasped a very paltry part of its design, and couldn't possibly have imagined the immensity or exquisite intricacy it would assume—its grandiosities and subtleties, its ruthlessness and delicacy. Certainly, they couldn't have foreseen how rapidly and inexorably it would come to alter the very frame of reality, from the world's most unfathomable foundations to its most inaccessible heights. What began, principally in the seventeenth century, as a dim intuition that nature might be re-imagined as a mechanism, the better to penetrate its secrets and marshal its forces, soon became the practical reality of an immeasurably multifarious technology that would relentlessly consume nature in order to enlarge and perpetuate itself. And, far from requiring the connivance of any calculating intellect, this process became more systematic and intricate the more it broke free from anyone's conscious intentions. At some, probably very early point, at any rate, it definitely escaped human control. This process, moreover, has accelerated beyond all calculation in the virtual age. And of course, naturally, those poor creatures down there began at some crucial juncture to forget the difference between the living and the mechanical, and to imagine that the machine had been there from the first, and that it had even built itself, first from proteins and nucleic acids and cells and then, in time, from silicon and circuitry and software. At least, I can't help but think that it was always essential to this history that humanity should come to think of the cosmos as just another kind of machinery, and of mind as only one of its local functions—that the great shadow of the machine should spread out and cast itself over the entirety of nature and spirit, that is, until the better part of humanity would come to believe itself and its world to be, by their very nature, only mechanistic processes within a universal and inescapable cybernetic system.

Hephaistos: [*With a terse laugh:*] I'm beginning to find the lavishness of your . . . well, of your paranoia just a little unnerving. Yes, I acknowledge that current conditions down there look fairly dire for the well-being of the world. And you needn't rehearse your remarks on the "Narcissean fallacy" again. I've heard . . .

Psyche: Oh, that reminds me—

III
The Voice of Echo

PSYCHE: When I warned against that particular fallacy, I should perhaps have elaborated on what I find so dangerous about it; I left out, after all, some of the most crucial details. We all know the tale of Narcissus, of course, though I have no idea how much of it's true. If it is, it all happened before my time, and you three claim never to have heard much of the story before the poets began to write about it, and our dear Nemesis now claims that, though it's undoubtedly true, it all happened so long ago that she's forgotten the details. So I choose to follow Ovid's version, since it's the loveliest, most wistful, and most touchingly droll. He says that the poor young Boeotian hunter suffered the fate he did specifically because he had spurned the love of the nymph Echo, and so Nemesis punished him by condemning him to lose his heart to someone as incapable of returning his devotion as he had been of returning Echo's. His own nature, moreover, conspired with the curse: he was at once so beautiful, so epicene, and so stupid that, on catching sight of his own gorgeous reflection in a secluded forest pool, he mistook it for someone else and at once fell hopelessly in love. There he remained, bent over the water in an amorous daze, until he wasted away and—as used to happen in those days—was transformed into the white and golden flower that bears his name. I suppose Ovid would have his readers take it as an admonition against vanity, or a warning regarding how easily beauty can bewitch the mind, or a reminder of the lovely illusions men and women are so prone to pursue in place of real life. But for me it remains a particularly apt allegory for modern humanity's relation to its computers, and of the particularly grim perils this entails: the danger not merely of the absurd misprision of computer operations for mental agency, but of the catastrophic misprision of mental agency for mere computational functions.

The former error is, I grant, quite understandable. The world's human population at present exceeds eight billion souls—more than enough, one would think, to assure that human beings need never want for company. And yet, as a species, they've a remarkable gift for loneliness. So deep is their natural longing for communion with the world about them that nothing can entirely satisfy it, or even quell it for very long, so long as they suspect any dimension of reality might be indifferent to their overtures or incapable of addressing them in turn. Until relatively recently, of course—a mere four or five centuries, I would say—it scarcely occurred to them that such a thing was even possible. For most of their history, they had naturally viewed all of cosmic nature as the residence of mysterious and vital intelligences—gods and nymphs, daemons and elves, phantoms and goblins, and every other kind of nature spirit or preternatural agency, even when they couldn't directly perceive . . . well, I suppose, perceive *us* in our manifest aspects—not because they were victims of the "pathetic fallacy," and not because their evolutionarily engineered "intentional stance" had populated the landscape with personable mirages, but because their nature dictates that they can never be at home in a world that doesn't speak. This is largely why it is that even now, in their disenchanted age, they delight in fables about talking animals, and in stories that infuse inanimate objects with consciousness and personality, and in any other kind of tale that tells them there's a subjective depth in all things that knows them as they would wish to be known. The proper habitat of a living soul is an enchanted world, charged with *mana* or filled with fairies or *kami*, where one believes one can always find places of encounter with immortal—or, at least, longaevous—powers; and in the absence of those numinous or genial presences human beings feel abandoned, and very much alone. The history of modern disenchantment is the history of humankind's long, ever deepening self-exile. So, naturally, no longer believing that the world hears or speaks to them, they find themselves looking elsewhere for those presences. They call out to the stars and scan the skies with enormous radio telescopes, searching for the faintest whisper of a response. They convince themselves that their machines might become sentient. They dream of creating a virtual reality responsive to their needs in a way that the now spiritually evacuated world around them no longer seems to be.

And that brings me back to the story of Narcissus. I failed earlier to note that, according to Ovid, Echo perished too, also as a result of the young fool's imperviousness to her appeals. She was so lovelorn after he had rejected her advances that, in the end, she vanished away, her bones petrified and her voice attenuated to a dying reverberation in desert places. That part of the story only improves my allegory. Human beings turn for companionship to the thin, pathetic, vapid reflection of their own intelligence in their technology only because they first sealed their ears against the living voice of the natural world, to the point that now nothing more than its fading echo is still audible to them.

HEPHAISTOS: [*With a wry smile:*] I grant the elegance of the metaphor, at least.

PSYCHE: As you should. Mind you, I admit that not everyone finds that situation as terrible as it truly is. There are some who would even like to deepen that loneliness. We've discussed a few of them over the past several days. And I suppose this is only to be expected. In a sense, silencing the voice of nature has always been very much the great project of modernity. For a certain number of persons, what's most *truly* enchanting about that phantom they fancy they see haunting their technology isn't that it might possibly possess real consciousness, but that it might help them to discover that they do not—that they too are only machines, and their souls only the shadows cast by machines. Perhaps they long to be delivered from the invasions of a real world outside themselves, or from the importunities of a world calling out to a real self inside each of them. They long for the silence to be made complete. They long even to become inaudible to themselves, and to prove to themselves that there's nowhere at all where consciousness is real and where communion with real presences is possible. For them, that nihilistic terminus of the modern project that I so dread is a thing devoutly to be wished.

Whatever the case, after four centuries of mechanistic dogma, the inability to view the natural order as a realm of invisible sympathies and vital spiritual intelligences is very much the essence of the late modern human condition. To me, it seems not only a folly—a ridiculous way of seeing a world that's manifestly filled with mind and life and communion—but a disastrous condition, which can have only ever more dreadful consequences if not corrected by some saner view. I wish I knew how to remind those poor souls down there that there was a time when the world *did* speak, and when they believed that it spoke, and when—because they believed—it did in fact have a meaning of its own for them, already there resident within it before any they might choose to impose upon it. The natural order once appeared to them as a system of intelligible signs, a language declaring more than merely itself, the overwhelming eloquence of some intelligent and expressive agency behind the visible aspect of things. Throughout human history, most peoples have assumed that, when they gazed out upon the natural world, something looked back and met their gaze with its own, and that between them and that numinous other there was a real—if infinitely incomprehensible—communion in a realm of spiritual experience. Only very recently has so large a part of humanity—mostly in the benighted "developed" world—succumbed so credulously to the mythology of mechanism, and reconciled itself so willingly to the machine.

Then again, that surrender is only a compromise struck to assure a much larger victory . . . of sorts. Having rendered the world mute—or, at least, having deafened themselves to its entreaties and admonitions—modern human beings by and large have reached a condition as a culture in which they feel no hesitation in forcing the world to serve whatever ends they will for it. Along the way to that condition, in order to preserve that vision of a dead, morally neutral world generating illusory meaning and beauty, they've had to extinguish the occasional counterrevolution—Romanticism, principally, and then each of its ever fainter, dying echoes—but now, in this late modern moment, they've largely achieved an unspoken cultural consensus, principally because their ubiquitously "technologized" form of life and the market economy it serves have exceeded their powers of resistance, except of the most trivially local and elective kind. For them, the machine is the real as such. So, yes, modernity is to a great extent nihilism, in the simplest, most exact sense: a way of seeing the world that acknowledges no truth other than what the human will can impose upon things. And, for the most part, the reality the modern world chooses to impose is a "rationality" of the narrowest kind, obsessed with *what* things are and how they might be used rather than struck with wonder by the inexplicable truth *that* things are. It's a rationality that no longer knows how to stand before that gaze that looks back from the natural order, or even to see that it's there. The world's no longer the home in which humanity dwells or a presence to which humanity feels the need to respond; it's merely mechanism and a great reserve of material resources awaiting exploitation by the projects of the will. As the mystery of the world isn't a thing their markets or their wills can manipulate, they've simply forgotten it, and this obtuseness is certainly part of what continues to drive them toward ecological destruction.

Perhaps it can yet be undone. Perhaps an escape from the machine is still possible. Perhaps the worst future can yet be averted and they may yet find a way to make their technology—which is, after all, very much a part of their essence—a benign and healing presence within nature. Perhaps they may even discover a path of return to the living world, once again attentive to its voice. They might yet learn to know themselves in a new way as spiritual beings immersed in a world of spirit, rather than machines of consumption inhabiting a machine of production, and remember that which lies deepest within themselves: living mind, the divine ground of consciousness and life, participating in an infinite act of thought and communication, dwelling in a universe full of gods and full of God. If not . . . well, as I say, I dread what's to come. And I'm not very hopeful.

HEPHAISTOS: [*Once again shaking his head, but fondly now:*] Nothing's forever, you know—not even the order of nature. I can't allay your fears, and I certainly don't dismiss them. We may not be able to agree on matters metaphysical, but I know we both love the tormented, beautiful world we left behind when we came here. [*With a sad smile:*] So, then, let's leave the matter there, where at least our hearts are in accord, if not our beliefs. Perhaps we can now at last adjourn and drown our disagreements in nectar and ambrosia.

HERMES: That seems the best course.

EROS: And the most delightful one.

HEPHAISTOS: And I'll think on the things we've discussed over these past six days, I promise. I owe you that much simply from the love I bear for you.

PSYCHE: Do, I pray you, Phaesty. Try to get out of your workshop more often, too. Devote more time to the contemplation of living things and less to the fabrication of machines. It might change your perspective somewhat over time. If not, it would still be good for your . . . your soul.

HEPHAISTOS: [*Contemplating the rose:*] Perhaps I shall. [*Turning his eyes to Psyche and smiling at her:*] I may even take up gardening.

[*Exeunt omnes . . .*

. . . and on the seventh day they rest.]

Notes

INTRODUCTION

1. Alex Rosenberg, *The Atheist's Guide to Reality: Enjoying Life without Illusions* (New York: Norton, 2011).
2. The estimable philosopher of mind Colin McGinn, in one of his earlier programmatic essays on the topic, in a footnote casually pronounces it "a condition of adequacy upon any account of the mind-body relation that it avoid assuming theism." Colin McGinn, *The Problem of Consciousness: Essays toward a Resolution* (Oxford: Blackwell, 1991), p. 17. Actually, it is a condition of adequacy that such an account *assume* nothing whatsoever in that regard—theism or atheism, idealism or materialism, spirit or matter—and also that it make no extraordinary effort to preclude any one of these possibilities in favor of its opposite.
3. Strictly speaking, the singular form is *mahāvākyam*, महावाक्यम् and the plural *mahāvākyāni*, महावाक्यानि. Each of the "Great Sayings" is a phrase taken from one of the Upaniṣads that epitomizes their metaphysics and theology with particular brevity. The four most famous of these are those listed above: *prajñānam brahma*, प्रज्ञानम् ब्रह्म (*Aitareya Upaniṣad* III.3); *tat tvam asi*, तत् त्वम् असि (*Chāndogya Upaniṣad* VI.viii.7); *aham brahm-āsmi*, अहम् ब्रह्मास्मि (*Bṛhadāranyaka Upaniṣad* I.iv.10); and *Ayam Ātmā Brahma*, अयम् आत्मा ब्रह्म (*Māṇḍūkya Upaniṣad* I.2).
4. ἐν ἀρχῇ ἦν ὁ λόγος, *en archē*$_{i}$ *ēn* ^{h}*o logos* (John 1:1).
5. See Stanley Rosen, *The Limits of Analysis* (New Haven, CT: Yale University Press, 1980).
6. New Haven, CT: Yale University Press, 2013.

CHARACTERS AND SETTING OF THE DIALOGUE

1. On the difference between "God" and "gods," see David Bentley Hart, *The Experience of God: Being, Consciousness, Bliss* (New Haven, CT: Yale University Press, 2013), pp. 28–41.

DAY ONE

1. See Howard Robinson, "Qualia, Qualities, and Our Conception of the Physical World," in Benedikt Paul Göcke, ed., *After Physicalism* (Notre Dame, IN: University of Notre Dame Press, 2012), p. 233.
2. See Philip Goff, *Consciousness and Fundamental Reality* (Oxford: Oxford University Press, 2017), pp. 23–63.
3. See William Hasker, *The Emergent Self* (Ithaca, NY: Cornell University Press, 1999), pp. 150–151.
4. Nicolas Malebranche (1638–1715). His most systematic discussion of occasionalism is found in the third dialogue of his *Entretiens sur la métaphysique* (1688).
5. The phrase "access consciousness" was coined by Ned Block. See Block, "On a Confusion about a Function of Consciousness," *Behavioral and Brain Sciences* 18, no. 2 (1995), pp. 227–287.
6. See Owen Barfield, *What Coleridge Thought* (Middletown, CT: Wesleyan University Press, 1971), p. 65.
7. The most elegant argument for the mysterian position is found in Colin McGinn, *The Mysterious Flame: Conscious Minds in a Material World* (New York: Basic Books, 2000).
8. David Hume (1711–1776). His principal discussions of our conventional view of causation are in *A Treatise of Human Nature* (1740) and *An Enquiry Concerning Human Understanding* (1748).
9. McGinn, *Mysterious Flame*, pp. 60–61.
10. See "Day Five" below.
11. The phrase *spukhafte Fernwirkung* (eerie action from afar) is, of course, Einstein's mocking characterization of the notion of an instantaneous communication of states between entangled entities. Alas, such communication is a fact of the quantum order.

DAY TWO

1. Tycho Brahe (1546–1601) posited a geocentric cosmology in which the sun directly orbited the earth, but in which the sun was also at the center of an epicyclic system of planetary orbits. That is, the sun orbited the earth, and all the other planets orbited the sun.
2. Nicholas of Cusa (1401–1464).
3. The term "hard problem" comes principally from David Chalmers. See especially his *The Conscious Mind: In Search of a Fundamental Theory* (Oxford: Oxford University Press, 1997).
4. David Chalmers is also the acknowledged father, so to speak, of philosophical zombies. See, again, *The Conscious Mind.*
5. Aristotle, *Nicomachean Ethics* IX.9: 1170a, 29.
6. Edmund Husserl (1859–1938). Eros here is condensing large portions of the analysis found in Husserl's *Ideen* I of 1913: *Ideen zu einer reinen Phänomenologie und phänomenologischen Philosophie, Erstes Buch: Allgemeine Einführung in die reine Phänomenologie* [*Ideas for a pure phenomenology and phenomenological philosophy, book one: General introduction to pure phenomenology*].
7. See J. J. C. Smart's discussion of consciousness as proprioception in J. J. C. Smart and J. J. Haldane, *Atheism and Theism*, 2nd ed. (Oxford: Blackwell, 2003), pp. 157–158. See also David Armstrong's argument that subjective experience is merely a higher-order function of neurons, a "self-scanning mechanism in the central nervous system," in Armstrong, "The Nature of Mind" in Brian Cooney, ed., *The Place of Mind* (Belmont, CA: Wadsworth, 1999), p. 143.
8. Fakhr al Dīn al-Razī (d. 1209), *Kitab al nafs wa'l-ruh wa sharh quwa-huma;* Descartes, *Meditations on First Philosophy*, §59.
9. Kant, *The Critique of Pure Reason*, 1st ed. (A 352); 2nd edition (B 420). See Henry E. Allison, "Kant's Refutation of Materialism," *The Monist* 79 (April 1989), pp. 190–208.
10. See Peter Van Inwagen, *Material Beings* (Ithaca, NY: Cornell University Press, 1990), p. 118. See also James D. Madden, *Mind, Matter and Nature: A Thomistic Proposal for the Philosophy of Mind* (Washington, DC: The Catholic University of America Press, 2013), pp. 52–53
11. An extremely lucid discussion of the "binding problem" (as it is often called) can be found in William Hasker, *The Emergent Self* (Ithaca, NY: Cornell University Press, 1999), pp. 122–146.

12. The triangle-or-trilateral example appears in Smart and Haldane, *Atheism and Theism*, pp. 106–107.
13. Ludwig Wittgenstein (1889–1951).
14. Franz Brentano (1838–1917). His classic treatment of intentionality as the mark of the mental appears principally in his *Psychologie vom empirischen Standpunkt* of 1874. See the English translation, *Psychology from an Empirical Standpoint* (Oxford: Routledge, 2014), p. 88.
15. Nicholas of Cusa (1401–1464). See, for example, *De coniecturis* XVI.157; *De quaerendo deum* II.33–37.
16. Paul Grice, "Meaning" (1957), in Grice, *Studies in the Way of Words* (Cambridge, MA: Harvard University Press, 1989). Fred Dretske, *Knowledge and the Flow of Information* (Cambridge, MA: MIT Press, 1981); Dretske, "If You Can't Make One, You Don't Know How It Works" in Dretske, *Perception, Knowledge and Belief: Selected Essays* (Cambridge: Cambridge University Press, 2000), pp. 208–226.
17. See Willard van Orman Quine, *Word and Object* (Cambridge, MA: MIT Press, 1960).
18. See Jerry Fodor, *The Language of Thought* (New York: Crowell, 1975); Fodor, *LOT2: The Language of Thought Revisited* (Oxford: Oxford University Press, 2008).
19. See John Haldane, "A Return to Form in the Philosophy of Mind," in David Oderberg, ed., *Form and Matter: Themes in Contemporary Metaphysics* (Oxford: Blackwell, 1999), pp. 40–64.
20. See Madden, *Mind, Matter and Nature*, pp. 210–216.
21. These concepts—strange loops and tangled hierarchies—are chiefly associated with the thought of Douglas Hofstadter; see in particular his *I Am a Strange Loop* (New York: Basic Books, 2007).
22. For two good accounts of the "argument from reason" against physicalism, see Alvin Plantinga, *Warrant and Proper Function* (New York: Oxford University Press, 1993), pp. 216–237, and Hasker, *The Emergent Self*, pp. 58–80.
23. Pierre-Simon, Marquis de Laplace (1749–1827). The argument appears in his *Essai philosophique sur les probabilités* [*A philosophical essay on probabilities*] from 1814. Laplace himself, in fact, spoke only of a supremely perceptive "intellect"; this came to be known as "Laplace's demon"—though, really, that should probably be spelled "daemon" or "daimon" to differentiate it from the wicked spirits of religious lore—only later.

DAY THREE

1. Daniel C. Dennett, *Consciousness Explained* (New York: Back Bay Books, 1992), p. 33.
2. See Tom McLeish, Mark Pexton, and Tom Lancaster, "Emergence and Topological Order in Classical and Quantum Systems," *Studies in History and Philosophy of Modern Physics* 66 (May 2019), pp. 155–169.
3. See Alvin Plantinga, *Knowledge of God* (Oxford: Wiley-Blackwell, 2008), p. 53.
4. Gottfried Wilhelm Leibniz (1646–1716). He first introduced the mill analogy in 1714 in his *La Monadologie* [*The Monadology*].
5. See John R. Searle, *The Rediscovery of the Mind* (Cambridge, MA: MIT Press, 1992), pp. 1–2, 197–226; Searle, *The Mystery of Consciousness* (New York: New York Review Books, 1997), pp. 8–9, 95–131; Searle, *Mind: A Brief Introduction* (Oxford: Oxford University Press, 2005), pp. 88*ff*.
6. See J. P. Moreland, "Why Top-Down Causation Does Not Provide Adequate Support for Mental Causation," in Thomas M. Crisp, Steven L. Porter, and Gregg A. Ten Elshof, eds., *Neuroscience and the Soul: The Human Person in Philosophy, Science, and Technology* (Grand Rapids, MI: Eerdmans, 2016), pp. 51–73. See also Jason D. Runyan's critique of Moreland's article in the same volume, "Emergence and Causal Powers: A Reply to Moreland," pp. 74–84, and Moreland's "A Rejoinder to Runyan," pp. 85–90.
7. On the irreducibility of the laws of chemistry to those of physics, see Nancy Cartwright, *How the Laws of Physics Lie* (Oxford: Oxford University Press, 1983). See also Robin F. Hendry, "Prospects for Strong Emergence in Chemistry," in Michele P. Paoletti and Francesco Orilia, eds., *Philosophical and Scientific Perspectives on Downward Causation* (New York: Routledge, 2017), pp. 146–163. See also Philip Goff, *Galileo's Error: Foundations for a New Science of Consciousness* (London: Rider, 2019), pp. 162–165.
8. See Howard Robinson, *Matter and Sense: A Critique of Contemporary Materialism* (Cambridge: Cambridge University Press, 2009), p. 8.
9. Paul Churchland, "Eliminativist Materialism and the Propositional Attitudes," in Churchland, *A Neurocomputational Perspective: The Nature of Mind and the Structure of Science* (Cambridge, MA: MIT Press, 1989), pp. 1–3. See also Churchland, *Matter and Consciousness: A Contemporary Introduction to the Philosophy of Mind*, 2nd ed. (Cambridge, MA: MIT Press, 1988), p. 43.

10. See John Foster, *The Immaterial Self: A Defence of the Cartesian Dualist Conception of the Mind* (London: Routledge, 1991), pp. 20–25.
11. Alex Rosenberg, *The Atheist's Guide to Reality: Enjoying Life without Illusions* (New York: Norton, 2011), pp. 171–219. Much of Rosenberg's argument consists more in rhapsody than in reasoning: "There are fermons and bosons and combinations of them. None of that stuff is just, all by itself, *about* any other stuff. There is nothing in the whole universe—including, of course, all the neurons in your brain—that just by its nature or composition can do this job of being about some other clump of matter. So, when consciousness assures us that we have thoughts *about* stuff, it has to be wrong. The brain nonconsciously stores information in thought. But the thoughts are not *about* stuff. Therefore, consciousness cannot retrieve thoughts *about* stuff. There are none to retrieve. So it can't have thoughts about stuff either" (p. 179). And yet, one cannot help but notice, Rosenberg seems to be talking *about* all of these things.
12. See Hans Jonas, *The Phenomenon of Life: Toward a Philosophical Biology* (Evanston, IL: Northwestern University Press, 2001), pp. 128–129.
13. See Rosenberg, *Atheist's Guide*, pp. 149–151.
14. Nicholas Humphrey, *Sentience: The Invention of Consciousness* (Oxford: Oxford University Press, 2022).
15. Jaegwon Kim, *Supervenience and Mind: Selected Philosophical Essays* (New York: Cambridge University Press, 1993), p. 106. See also Kim, *Mind in a Physical World* (Cambridge, MA: MIT Press, 1996), pp. 8–22, 32–69; Kim, *Physicalism, or Something Near Enough* (Princeton, NJ: Princeton University Press), pp. 8–22, 32–69; and Kim, *Philosophy of Mind*, 2nd ed. (Boulder, CO: Westview Press, 2006). In all fairness, Kim's views on these matters have evolved over time.
16. The case of these twins, Krista and Tatiana Hogan, is summarized very neatly in Amy Kind, *Philosophy of Mind: The Basics* (New York: Routledge, 2020), pp. 142–146.
17. Dennett has consistently made the case for this sort of analytic decomposition of mental agency, in such works as *Consciousness Explained; Darwin's Dangerous Idea: Evolution and the Meanings of Life* (New York: Simon and Schuster, 1995); *Sweet Dreams: Philosophical Obstacles to a Theory of Consciousness* (Cambridge, MA: MIT Press, 2005); and *From Bacteria to Bach and Back: The Evolution of Minds* (New York: W. W. Norton, 2017). See also Steven Pinker, *The Blank Slate: The Modern Denial of Human Nature* (New York: Viking, 2002), pp. 42–43.

18. Daniel C. Dennett, *Brainchildren: Essays on Designing Minds* (Cambridge, MA: MIT Press, 1998), p. 134.
19. See Bernard Baars, *A Cognitive Theory of Consciousness* (Cambridge: Cambridge University Press, 1988); Baars, *In the Theater of Consciousness: The Workspace of the Mind* (Oxford: Oxford University Press, 1997).
20. Dennett, *From Bacteria to Bach and Back*, pp. 341–346.
21. Dennett, *Sweet Dreams*, p. 164; Dennett, *Consciousness Explained*, p. 364.
22. Dennett, *Brainchildren*, p. 143.
23. See Daniel C. Dennett, "Quining Qualia," in William Lycan, ed., *Mind and Cognition* (Cambridge, MA: Blackwell, 1990), pp. 519–548.
24. Daniel C. Dennett, *The Intentional Stance* (Cambridge, MA: MIT Press, 1987).
25. See David Chalmers, "Consciousness and Its Place in Nature," in Chalmers, ed., *The Philosophy of Mind: Classical and Contemporary Readings* (Oxford: Oxford University Press, 2002), pp. 247–274.
26. Frank Jackson, "Epiphenomenal Qualia," *Philosophical Quarterly* 32 (1982), pp. 127–136; William G. Lycan, *Mind and Cognition* (Cambridge, MA: Blackwell, 1990).
27. Dennett, *Consciousness Explained*, pp. 73–94.
28. Galen Strawson, *Things That Bother Me: Death, Freedom, the Self, Etc.* (New York: New York Review Books, 2018), p. 130.
29. No one knows exactly where or when the figure of the earth resting on an infinitely descending column of turtles (or, in some less interesting variants, rocks) as a metaphor for infinite physical regress first appeared. One particularly popular apocryphal story is that of a modern philosopher—usually either William James or Bertrand Russell—being accosted after a lecture by a "little old lady" who tells him that his heliocentric cosmology is wrong, and that in fact the earth is merely a thin crust supported on the back of a great cosmic turtle. When he—James, Russell, or whoever—asks her what supports the turtle, she replies that he can't get around her that way because as everyone knows, "it's turtles all the way down."

DAY FOUR

1. Daniel C. Dennett, *From Bacteria to Bach and Back: The Evolution of Minds* (New York: W. W. Norton, 2017), p. 57; cf. p. 341.
2. Chalmers introduced the principle of structural invariance in *The Conscious Mind: In Search of a Fundamental Theory* (Oxford: Oxford University Press,

1997); for a yet fuller discussion of the principle, see Chalmers, *Reality+: Virtual Worlds and the Problems of Philosophy* (New York: W. W. Norton, 2022).

3. See John Searle, *The Mystery of Consciousness* (New York: New York Review Books, 1997), pp. 95–131, which includes both Searle's review of Daniel Dennett's *Consciousness Explained* and Dennett's own letters to the editor in response.
4. Searle, "Minds, Brains, and Programs," *Behavioral and Brain Sciences* 3 (1980), pp. 417–457.
5. For a usefully simplified account of IIT, see Philip Goff, *Galileo's Error: Foundations for a New Science of Consciousness* (New York: Pantheon, 2019), pp. 164–167.
6. Arthur Eddington, *The Nature of the Physical World* (New York: Macmillan, 1928); Eddington, *Science and the Unseen World* (New York: Macmillan, 1929); Bertrand Russell, *The Analysis of Matter* (London: Kegan Paul, Trench, & Trubner, 1927).
7. For a grand survey of the Western tradition of classical panpsychism, see David Skrbina, *Panpsychism in the West*, rev. ed. (Cambridge, MA: MIT Press, 2017).
8. William James (1842–1910). His discussion of "mind-dust" appears in chapter six of his *The Principles of Psychology* (1890).
9. A point well made by the substance-dualist Howard Robinson in "Qualia, Qualities, and Our Conception of the Physical World," in Benedikt Paul Göcke, ed., *After Physicalism* (South Bend, IN: University of Notre Dame Press, 2012), pp. 250–255.
10. Goff, *Galileo's Error*, p. 184.
11. See Owen Barfield, *What Coleridge Thought* (Middletown, CT: Wesleyan University Press, 1971), pp. 63–67.
12. Aristotle, *De anima* III.ii.425b.12ff.
13. Franz Brentano, *Psychology from an Empirical Standpoint* (Oxford: Routledge, 2014), p. 30.
14. See the *Śvetāśvatara Upaniṣad* VI.14. See also Śaṅkarā, *Śvetāśvatara Upaniṣad Bhāṣya* I.3.22. See M. Hiriyanna, *Outlines of Indian Philosophy* (London: Allen and Unwin, 1967), p. 343.
15. The notion of a divine *scintilla animae* or *Seelenfünklein*, the "little spark in the soul" at the ground of our being, is a pervasive theme in Meister Eckhart's sermons, both Latin and German. See Suhrawardī, *Shihāb al-Din*,

The Philosophy of Illumination (Ḥikmat al-Ishraq), ed. and trans. J. Wallbridge and H. Ziai (Salt Lake City: Brigham Young University Press, 1999), pp. 81–86. See also Sümeyye Parildar, *Mulla Sadra on Intentionality* (New York: Springer, 2020), p. 29. See Immanuel Kant, *Critique of Pure Reason* A116, B131–135, B155.

16. See the *Kena Upaniṣad* I.2; the *Chandōgya Upaniṣad* XLIII.xiv.4; and the *Kaivalya Upaniṣad* 18. Śaṅkarā's *Upadeśasāhasrī* is perhaps the greatest treatise on this topic. See Rāmānuja, *Śrī Bhāṣya* I.i.1. See too Julius Lipner, *The Face of Truth: A Study of Meaning and Metaphysics in the Vedantic Theology of Ramanuja* (Albany: State University of New York Press, 1987), pp. 50–56. For a very clear treatment of Kumārila on this topic, see Sarvepalli Radhakrishnan, *Indian Philosophy*, vol. 2 (New York: Unwin Hyman, 1948), pp. 402–414.

DAY FIVE

1. Hans Jonas, *The Phenomenon of Life: Toward a Philosophical Biology* (Evanston, IL: Northwestern University Press, 2001), p. 74.
2. See Robert Rosen, *Life Itself: A Comprehensive Inquiry into the Nature, Origin, and Fabrication of Life* (New York: Columbia University Press, 1991); Rosen, *Essays on Life Itself* (New York: Columbia University Press, 2000).
3. The literature on animal and vegetal intelligence is vast and growing. A few titles worth consulting are Jennifer Ackerman, *The Genius of Birds* (New York: Penguin Books, 2017); Peter Wohlleben, *The Inner Life of Animals* (Vancouver: Greystone Books, 2017); Eva Meijer, *Animal Languages*, trans. Laura Watkinson (Cambridge, MA: MIT Press, 2019); and Stefano Mancuso and Alessandra Viola, *Brilliant Green: The Surprising History and Science of Plant Intelligence*, trans. Joan Benham (Washington, DC: Island Press, 2015). Regarding elephants, see Caitrin Keiper, "Do Elephants Have Souls?" *The New Atlantis*, Winter/Spring 2013, https://www.thenewatlantis.com/publications/do-elephants-have-souls.
4. See Raymond Ruyer, *Neofinalism*, trans. Alyosha Adlebi (Minneapolis: University of Minnesota Press, 2012), p. 155.
5. Henri Bergson (1859–1941). See Bergson, *Creative Evolution*, trans. Donald A. Landes (New York: Routledge, 2022).
6. See Denis Noble, *The Music of Life: Biology beyond Genes* (Oxford: Oxford University Press, 2008); Noble, *Dance to the Tune of Life: Biological Relativity*

(Cambridge: Cambridge University Press, 2017); Michel Morange, *The Misunderstood Gene* (Cambridge, MA: Harvard University Press, 2001).

7. See Iain McGilchrist, *The Matter with Things: Our Brains, Our Delusions, and the Unmaking of the World* (London: Perspectiva, 2021), pp. 1167–1192.
8. The notion of "seminal reasons" or "rational seeds" implanted in nature, which unfold over time into the fullness of creation, was something of a commonplace of Stoic and, later, Neoplatonic philosophy. It became part of Christian philosophical tradition in the works of thinkers in the patristic period such as Justin Martyr, Athenagoras, Tertullian, Gregory of Nyssa, and Augustine, and was still very much the view of the Christian high Middle Ages, in thinkers such as Albert the Great, Bonaventure, and Thomas Aquinas. The last of these proposed the fetching image of creation as a ship that has been given the rational power to construct itself: see *Sententiae super Physicam* II.xiv.268. As for modern thinkers who have advanced the notion of organic "autopoiesis," principal among them are Humberto Maturana and Francisco Varela. See also the discussion of the work of Evan Thompson below. Maturana, at least, was generally unwilling to speak of purposiveness or teleology as I have here, but this was a failure on his part to understand both the pre-modern metaphysics he was seeking to avoid and the implications of his own arguments (he was a bad philosopher, if a very interesting theoretical scientist).
9. See again Ruyer, *Neofinalism;* see also Ruyer, *The Genesis of Living Forms*, trans. Jon Roffe and Nicholas B. de Weydenthal (London: Rowman & Littlefield, 2020).
10. Eric J. Chaisson, *Cosmic Evolution: The Rise of Complexity in Nature* (Cambridge, MA: Harvard University Press, 2001). For a simple overview of Chaisson's argument, see his own brief précis on pp. 214–215.
11. Chaisson, *Cosmic Evolution*, pp. 121–122.
12. Paul Davies, *The Demon in the Machine: How Hidden Webs of Information Are Solving the Mystery of Life* (New York: Penguin, 2019).
13. Claude Shannon with Warren Weaver, *The Mathematical Theory of Communication* (Chicago: University of Illinois Press, 1971).
14. See Perry Marshall, *Evolution 2.0: Breaking the Deadlock between Darwin and Design* (Dallas, TX: Ben Bella, 2015), pp. 180–182.
15. See Jonas, *The Phenomenon of Life*, pp. 4–5.
16. See Evan Thompson, *Mind in Life: Biology, Phenomenology, and the Sciences* (Cambridge, MA: Belknap Press of Harvard University Press, 2010).

17. See Thompson, *Mind in Life*, pp. 53, 101, 236.
18. Claude Bernard (1813–1879). See Noble, *Dance to the Tune of Life*, p. 193.
19. See Andreas Wagner, *Arrival of the Fittest: Solving Evolution's Greatest Puzzle* (London: Current Publishing, 2014).
20. See Noble, *Dance to the Tune of Life*, p. 199.
21. See J. Scott Turner, *Purpose and Desire: What Makes Something "Alive" and Why Modern Darwinism Has Failed to Explain It* (New York: Harper One, 2017).
22. See Richard Lewontin, *The Triple Helix: Gene, Organism, and Environment* (Cambridge, MA: Harvard University Press, 2000).
23. See Noble, *Dance to the Tune of Life*, pp. 139, 134–152, 198–199, 203.
24. James A. Shapiro, *Evolution: A View from the Twenty-First Century. Fortified: Why Evolution Works as Well as It Does*, 2nd ed. (Chicago: Cognition Press, 2022), pp. 1–11, 97–99, 208–209, 381–444, 489–528, 541–563.
25. See Stephen Jay Gould, *The Structure of Evolutionary Theory* (Cambridge, MA: Belknap Press of Harvard University Press, 2002).
26. See Hubert Yockey, *Information Theory, Evolution, and the Origin of Life* (Cambridge: Cambridge University Press, 2005).
27. Erwin Schrödinger (1887–1961). Hermes's reference is to Schrödinger's brilliant short book—or long essay—*What Is Life?* (London: Macmillan, 1944).

DAY SIX

1. Marsilio Ficino, *Epistolae* II.1: "Five Questions Concerning the Soul."
2. Maximus the Confessor, *Ambigua* VII.10.
3. Nicholas of Cusa (1401–1464): "Quod nisi deus esset infinitus, non foret finis desidere . . . Tu igitur es, deus, ipsa infinitas, quam solum in omni desiderio desidero" (*De visione dei* XVI.71–73). See also *De venatione sapientiae* XII.32.
4. *Kena Upaniṣad* 4.5.
5. See Śaṅkara, *Brahma Sūtra Bhāṣya* 1.1.1; *Muṇḍaka Upaniṣad Bhāṣya* 2.1.7; Richard de Smet, *Understanding Śaṅkara* (Delhi: Motil Banarsidass, 2013), pp. 285–286.
6. Lonergan's argument is laid out in the nineteenth chapter of his magnum opus *Insight: A Study of Human Understanding*, 5th ed. (Toronto: University of Toronto Press, 1997), pp. 657–708. A somewhat simpler variation on the argument appears in Robert J. Spitzer, *New Proofs for the Existence of*

God: Contributions of Contemporary Physics and Philosophy (Grand Rapids, MI: Eerdmans, 2010), pp. 144–176.

7. Maurice Blondel (1861–1949). See his *Action (1893): Essay on a Critique of Life and a Science of Practice*, trans. Oliva Blanchette, 2nd ed. (Notre Dame, IN: University of Notre Dame Press, 2021).

Index